The Literature of Ancient Greece

By

GILBERT MURRAY

Phoenix Books

THE UNIVERSITY OF CHICAGO PRESS

THE UNIVERSITY OF CHICAGO PRESS, CHICAGO 37
Cambridge University Press, London, N.W. 1, England
The University of Toronto Press, Toronto 5, Canada

PREFACE

THIS book, originally published in 1897, has maintained itself as a popular history of Greek literature for more than half a century. A new preface was added in 1902, giving accounts of the recently discovered papyri of Herondas and Bacchylides. But since that time there have been very large and varied additions to our knowledge of Greek literature; the papyri have given us some long wished for plays of Menander, Satyr plays of Aeschylus and Sophocles to put beside Euripides' *Cyclops*, new tragedies by Sophocles and Euripides, all in an incomplete condition, as well as many small fragments of Sappho and Alcaeus. And besides these new texts, there has of course in these fifty years been such a great advance in knowledge and, I trust, in my own understanding of ancient literature that here and there I have thought it only fair to the reader to note some change of opinion. I have tried, however, not to forget that the book is a "short history" and does not profess to give a complete picture of its vast subject.

It was this consideration that made me in the first edition refrain from any discussion of Aristotle's philosophy as a very large and not exactly a literary subject. I ought perhaps to have said more about the newly discovered (1891) *Constitution of Athens*, as a unique example of Aristotle's "exoteric" style. It avoids hiatus

iii

in the Isocratean manner, a rule which presumably implies that the text in question is meant to be read aloud, though the rule is also observed in Books vii and viii of the *Politics*. The book is of course an immense addition to our historical knowledge of Athens, especially in the times before Cleisthenes and the revolutionary years after 411.

A similar problem on a lesser scale is presented by the *Hellenica Oxyrhynchia*, first published in 1907 (Pap. Ox. 842). This is a large fragment, amounting to twenty-five pages of the Oxford text, apparently forming a continuation of Thucydides and, like him, telling the story year by year. It is quite independent of Xenophon. It must have been written after the Peace of Antalcidas in 387 and before the collapse of Phocis in 346. It touches somewhat briefly on the years between 411 and the Battle of Cnidus, but after that becomes exact and detailed. It was evidently much used by Diodorus, but has been considered by most historians to be too detailed to belong to his usual source, the *Universal History* of Ephorus. The original editors, Grenfell and Hunt, published it as *Hellenica Oxyrhynchia cum Theopompi et Cratippi Fragmentis*. Failing Ephorus, one naturally thinks first of the famous Theopompus, whose fragments number three hundred and fifty-six and whose *Hellenica* covered the period in question. The dates would suit, but the discrepancy in style from that Cynic historian's *Philippica* and *Hellenica* is immense. Cratippus is a little-known author, represented by only four fragments but mentioned once by Plutarch as the typical or chief historian of this particular period. The whole question has been greatly discussed by historians but remains quite unsolved.

Three important authors, however, hitherto almost unrepresented in our tradition, deserve special mention. First, Bacchylides. Just too late for the first edition of this book came the British Museum Papyrus 733 containing twenty lyrics, Epinikoi, Paeans and Dithyrambs, by Bacchylides, six of them practically intact. One, headed *Theseus*, consists of questions addressed to Aigeus, King of Athens, and his answers, in the form of a meliambic dialogue between two choirs. *"What is it that troubles our land, O King? Is it a foreign foe? Or a band of robbers?"* *"It is one man, but marvellous in might; he has slain the robber-king Sinis and Kerkyon and Procrustes, and makes all evil-doers tremble."* *"Has he great forces?"* *"No, only two men, but even so. . . ."* He is, we may be sure, no enemy, but the King's own son, Theseus. The old verdict of Longinus on Bacchylides seems to be true. He is "not to be compared with Pindar for genius," but is nevertheless a good poet, whose thoughts are "smooth and beautifully expressed." He was a nephew of Simonides and, while his dialect and metre are Doric and his ways of thought those of Pindar, instead of Pindar's obscure splendour he writes with an easy lucidity which suggests the influence of the Ionian Simonides. His finest work perhaps is Ode V, a poem of 200 lines, on the meeting of Heracles with Meleager in Hades and Meleager's story of his own death by the burning brand. The description of the eagle's flight—*"The peaks of the great earth hold him not, nor the steep waves of the unwearying sea"*—suggests

Pindar; so does the vivid mention of the *"Ghosts of un-happy men, driving like leaves that a keen wind tosses up the headlands of Ida amid the grazing sheep."* We can get some idea of the average Athenian's image of a lyric poet from the poet in Aristophanes' *Birds*, with his ceaseless harping on "clouds" and "wings" and "snow" and "sunlight," and his strange compound adjectives. That poet, freed from the atmosphere of caricature that enwraps him, would be rather like our new-found Bacchylides. Our knowledge of other lyric poets too has been considerably increased by the papyri. Of Archilochus there are many tiny and unintelligible fragments and one (Pap. Ox. 2310) which gives some thirty continuous iambic trimeters and seems to come from a conversation between a woman and a warrior who has "safely crossed the sea" from Crete.

Of Alcaeus (see p. 91) there are 400 new fragments, and of Sappho 200, most of them unfortunately too small to have any literary value. We can see that both poets used a great variety of metres, and make out a good deal more of Alcaeus' political insurgency against Myrsilus and later against Pittacus, and perhaps a little more about Sappho's brother and daughter, and the exile of both the poets. Many of Sappho's poems were epithalamiums, and one poem at least has a characteristic beauty of description: *"Where cool water ripples through the apple-branches, and the place is all shadowy with roses, and from the quivering leaves comes dropping sleep."* Characteristic also is fr. 16: "Some say a host of horse, others of foot, others of ships, is the most beautiful thing on this dark earth; but I say it is whatever thing one loves" (see Page, *Sappho and Alcaeus*, Oxford, 1955).

The great papyrus of Menander, first published in 1907, contains some 700 lines of οἱ Ἐπιτρέποντες, *The Arbitration*, about 400 each of ἡ Περικειρομένη, *The Rape of the Locks*, and ἡ Σαμία, *The Woman from Samos*, with shorter pieces from a few other plays. In beauty of style, in ingenuity of plot and character-drawing, these plays come fully up to expectation, but have provided two great surprises. We knew of course that the Great Dionysia was the festival of *Dio-Nysos*, "Zeus-Poung," that is, the New Life of the Spring (see below, pp. xvii–xviii). This Being is regularly represented in myth as a babe found outcast amid the fields and flocks but is eventually "recognised" as a Son of God. It is a great surprise to find that every known play of Menander contains this lost or exposed baby of an unmarried mother, at first outcast but eventually "recognised" and established in his true rank. It is the regular Dionysiac myth transferred from the realm of gods and kings to that of the normal citizen. The other surprise is that Menander's heroines are by no means the rather disreputable heroines of Plautus and Terence but most of them apparently war-victims. In the wars of Alexander's successors, towns were constantly being taken, with the slave-traders waiting behind the lines to buy their human wares cheap. We hear of many plays like *The Woman from Samos* bearing the names of towns recently taken in war, such as Olynthos, Perinthos, Andros. Such women, if they escaped slavery, were stateless, or at best foreigners without rights. They could not be lawfully married. They might well be "regarded as wives," like the *Woman from Samos* and the heroine of the *Rape of the Locks*, but, if suspected of any offence, were liable to be suddenly cast out helpless on a troubled world.

Menander's plots are far more intricate and ingenious than anything we are accustomed to in the fifth century. One fragmentary papyrus for example (Pap. Ox. 1235), gives us part of the plot of *The Priestess*. A man's wife had left him long ago, taking her child, and is now a Priestess. The father wants to know what she has done with their son, but the Priestess is unapproachable. However, she specialises in exorcisms, so the father's confidential slave contrives to have a mysterious fit on the temple steps and is promptly taken in for treatment. He thus finds out that the boy is being reared by certain neighbours and tells the father, who at once goes to claim his son. But it so happens that these neighbours have also a son of their own, and by mistake the excited old gentleman lights on him and claims to be his father. The boy decides that the old man is obviously mad and tells his foster-brother, who, consequently, when his father, now better informed, approaches him in the same way, humours him as a lunatic. I omit some minor complexities, but one can see from this account as well as from the fragments of the *Arbitration* or *Rape of the Locks* what a great variety of plot was possible in the New Comedy while always preserving, at least in an unemphatic background, the scheme of the New Year ritual.

Of a "New Tragedy," corresponding to the New

Comedy in the fourth century and later, very few fragments are preserved. But we can see two changes in style. The metre of tragedy became looser and looser up to the last plays of Euripides, but a long fragment of Critias coming a little later is extremely strict. After him the short fragments of Moschion, Sosiphanes, Sositheus, Charês, show no trisyllabic feet at all. Also there was a tendency to take as subjects not the regular heroic legends but more modern historical incidents, like Moschion's *Themistocles* and *Pheraioi* (treating the murder of Jason of Pherae by his wife), or merely pastoral themes like Sositheus' *Daphnis*. The interesting fragment of a tragedy in extremely strict metre, on the theme of Herodotus' story of Gyges, pretty certainly belongs to this school, and it seems likely that the *Rhesus*, with its comparatively strict metre and its postclassical ingenuities of plot, has also a place there. Hermann and others, chiefly on grounds of language, have thought it "Alexandrian."

Akin to comedy was the Mime, or imaginary conversation, for which Epicharmus and Sophron in early days were famous, and which perhaps first suggested to Plato the dialogue form for his writings. We have now the mimes of Herodas, seven complete and several in a fragmentary state. His name was known before, but his work quite unknown, and his date a matter of guesswork varying from the sixth century to the third. But he mentions the "*Theoi Adelphoi*," i.e., Ptolemy Philadelphus and Arsinoê, who were deified in their lifetime, about 268 B.C., and he speaks of the sculptor Apelles as recently dead, which suits the same time. His mimes are written in scazons, a deliberately ugly metre, and depict, with little exaggeration, scenes of daily life on its more vulgar side. The first mime shows a young married woman, Mêtrichê, visited by her old but unvenerable nurse, who descants on the prolonged absence of Mêtrichê's husband in Egypt and the great desire of a certain handsome athlete to offer her consolation. The hostess gently snubs her and changes the subject. In the other mimes a person with hands far from clean pleads a case at law; a mother takes her boy to a schoolmaster to be whipped; two women go round the temple of Asclepius in Cos, admiring the works of art and giving offerings. It reminds one of Theocritus' *Adoniazusae* but seems dull in comparison. Probably the humour of these imaginary conversations depends chiefly on minute topical details which are soon forgotten.

A very different and more interesting figure is Kerkidas, casually mentioned on p. 88, who has now appeared in a very broken condition in Pap. Ox. 1082. His date is fixed in the third century by references in the poems to Zeno and his pupil Sphaerus, and this identifies him as the "Law-Giver," or constitutional reformer, of Megalopolis, who supported Arâtus against Cleomenes and was at the same time a Cynic philosopher. The book is signed Κερκίδου κυνὸς μελίαμβοι. He wrote sermons like the regular Cynic *diatribae*, but in meliambic verse, not prose. One passage comments on the unjust distribution of wealth, proving the utter blindness or indifference of Zeus and the other gods. "Why attend to such unreal beings? Let us leave them to the astrology-mongers, and pay our worship to *Paian* and *Metadôs*; for she with *Nemesis* is a true god upon the earth." Thus not *Aidôs* and *Nemesis*, as in Hesiod and the general tradition, are the two true goddesses who remain when all others are gone, but the new goddess *Metadôs*, "Sharing with Others," and *Nemesis*, "Resentment of Injustice." *Paian*, "The Healer," follows upon their action. Good doctrine for a lawgiver and statesman who felt the injustices of society but saw the harm of revolution. No wonder, either, that the Christian, Gregory of Nyssa, calls him ὁ φίλτατος. The only other passage of any length is on love, quoting Euripides, and praising the love that is like a peaceful breeze, not a destructive storm. Kerkidas and many other newly discovered writers are treated in *New Chapters of Greek Literature* by Powell and Barber (3 vols., 1921–33).

To pass from newly discovered authors to second thoughts upon old questions, we must begin with Homer. The general account here given of the history of the Homeric text is confirmed by later evidence. Out of the hundreds of papyrus fragments of Homer that have been unearthed in Egypt, about twenty are earlier than 150 B.C., the time of Aristarchus, and nearly all of these have texts differing considerably from our vulgate, which seems to have become established about that time. It is worth remembering, however, that both Zenodotus and the "extremely cautious" Aristarchus suspected that the received text already contained large "spurious" additions. As to the actual date of our received text several passages in the *Odyssey* concur in explaining that the reunion of Odysseus and Penelope took place not merely on the twentieth year, but exactly at dawn (v. 93) on the day which was last of the nineteenth and first of the twentieth year, ἔνη καὶ νέα (τ 307, ξ 162); that is, exactly at the completion of the "Great Eniautos" of the astronomer Meton; and Meton was a contemporary of Aristophanes.

The general position stated on pp. 14 ff. is well explained in the Scholia to Pindar (Nem. 2. i): "At a time when the poetry of Homer was not yet brought into one body, but dispersed, variable and divided in parts, the rhapsodes did something equivalent to 'joining' or 'stitching' when they brought it into a unity." This seems to be true; the unity was imposed on scattered traditional material. At the Panathenaea it was recited by a series of rhapsodes, each "taking up" the story wherever it was "thrown down" for him. This implies a continuous story but almost excludes a fixed text (cf. p. 13). The same scholion possibly gives us the name of the poet specially responsible for this unification, when he says that Kynaithos of Chios "was the first person to perform Homer's poems at Syracuse about the 69th Olympiad." The Syracusans must have known traditional Homeric recitations long before 504 B.C.; it seems quite likely that what they now heard for the first time was Homer as recited at the Panathenaea, i.e., the *Iliad* and *Odyssey*. Kynaithos, or at least οἱ περὶ Κύναιθον, had been employed by Pisistratus, and apparently on the fall of Pisistratus in 510 took his great achievement to Sicily with him.

In the Homeric language, many of the so-called "Aeolisms" are merely remnants of that very old Greek which has left identical forms, such as πτόλις and

Ϝάναξ, in Arcadia and Cyprus, but of that whole subject we shall know more after further study of the Greek documents in Minoan script recently deciphered by Ventris and Chadwick, not to speak of the floods of new but uncertain light now being shed on early Greek and Anatolian history by the records of the great Hittite empire. Hittite influence certainly reached the coasts of Asia Minor, and some of the names in Greek myth seem to be those of real historical persons in the Boghaz-kewi tablets. But the mixture of history and pure myth is mostly inextricable. No one would recognise Oenomaus' unfortunate charioteer, Myrsilus, as being by rights a great Hittite king of that name. Agamemnon, the "Lord of Ships," seems like a leader of those "Peoples of the Sea" who attacked Anatolia and even Egypt between 1300 and 1150 B.C. and were called "Akhaiusha," "Danauna," and other suggestive names; but the King of Mycenae seems a different figure. The story of Helen, again, which some critics have thought historical, proves to be simply the ritual of a Spartan Marriage Goddess. The marriage ceremony in Sparta involved the carrying off of the bride, and Helen's chief function is to be carried off. In the tradition she is not only carried off to Mt. Parnon by a robber, but also to Troy or Sidon by Alexander-Paris, to Egypt by Hermes, to Deceleia by Theseus or else by the Apharetidae. But obviously her temple must not be left empty, so, like another Marriage Goddess, Hera, she has to be recovered and reinstalled, or else, in the variant made famous by Stesichorus, it was in reality only an *idôlon* of the goddess that the ravisher took, not the true Helen.

As to Goethe's dictum (p. 22) about the end of the *Iliad*, surely I was wrong in approving it. No end can be so fine as the scene where the two great enemies, Achilles and Priam, weep together over the griefs they have wrought upon one another, and the body of the noble enemy is granted full honours by his conqueror. The last two books, together with the parting of Hector and Andromache in Z, lift the *Iliad* clear above the level of a mere story of triumph and conquest and put it in the region of high Hellenic tragedy, which sees beyond the glory of battle into deeper and more human truth (cf. my *Rise of the Greek Epic* [4th edition, 1924]).

In reviewing my earlier statements regarding the historians (ch. vi and viii), I should note that the very extensive *Fragmenta Historicorum* are now accessible in Jacoby's monumental work.

A phrase used by the ancient critics about Herodotus and Thucydides is striking: they are both ὁμηρικώτατοι, "most Homeric." That means, I think, that among the early writers of logoi, they alone have made great continuous artistic wholes in prose as Homer did in poetry. Hecataeus, for instance, produced a collection of facts that could be added to, and was added to, as late as the fourth century. Hellanicus too was not a unity. Many of the others merely wrote down the local records of particular places. Herodotus and Thucydides, like Homer, were pan-Hellenic. Both books, of course, were meant, like Homer, for reading aloud to an audience, but both were also meant to be κτήματα ἐς ἀεί, "permanent possessions." Thucydides rather over-stresses the difference between them (p. 187).

Thucydides' moral standard in politics is best illustrated by the Melian Dialogue in Book V, in which the war-corrupted Athenians are represented as deaf to all appeals to justice and religion, and proclaim the doctrine of pure Hubris. This is just like the picture given by Plato and others of the unscrupulous demagogues of the time; and in Thucydides, as in all Greek thought, Hubris inevitably leads to Ate. "*The Athenians killed all prisoners of military age and made slaves of the women and children. . . . And the same winter they formed the desire to conquer Sicily, being ignorant, most of them, of the size of the island.*" And so they went to their ruin.

The splendid guesses of the early pre-Socratic philosophers (ch. vii) still retained much of the inspired seer or prophet. They spoke in hexameters, like Parmenides, or in striking oracular phrases, meant to be memorised, like Heraclitus. Some of them claimed, and even exercised, a sort of superhuman authority, like Empedocles and Pythagoras. Their methods were not what we call scientific. Indeed, the physician Hippocrates often remarks that, whereas medical doctors proceed by observing facts and then making experiments and drawing conclusions, the philosophers always start with some unfounded assumption "about the origin of the world or heat or cold or anything they may fancy." In the Attic period, philosophers, like other writers, were increasingly required to be clear and intelligible. Socrates also complained that they talked about things "above our heads or under the earth" which we cannot know, whereas he was interested in human conduct and things we can know and act upon. Aristotle, as a philosopher, learnt much from being the son of a doctor. One would like to know exactly why he considered Anaxagoras to be like *"one sober man in a crowd of chatterers"*; partly perhaps because he introduced *Nous*, Mind, as an active principle, ordering the material world, partly because of his actual scientific outlook. On the whole subject see Cornford, *Principium Sapientiae* (1955).

As to Socrates (pp. 170–77), it is difficult to judge the truth of the innumerable anecdotes about the "scurra Atticus," as Cicero calls him. Allowance must be made for exaggeration, for jokes, for Socrates' own irony in claiming to be ignorant and uneducated. The reported statement of Spintharus about his stormy youth, in which, however, he *"never did anything wrong"* (ἄδικον), is likely enough but merits no special credence.

Pythagoras, whom I passed over much too lightly in the original text, is, like Socrates, one of those great men who left no writings behind them but through memories and reports have exercised an immense and lasting influence. The destruction of Sybaris by the militant philosophers of Croton was soon followed by the sacking of Croton itself and the utter destruction of the Pythagorean School. All that remained were reports of what αὐτὸς ἔφα (*ipse dixit*), memories of the sage's real discoveries, such as the "Pythagorean Theorem" about the square of the hypotenuse, and still more important, that of the relation of the musical note to the exact length of a vibrating chord. This seemed to reveal Number or Proportion as the fundamental reality or cause underlying all phenomena. The idea was applied not only to geometry, where we still speak of "squaring" or "cubing" a number, but to ethics, where the square or the number four is ideally identified with justice, and indeed seemed to offer a solution to many philosophic disputes about the One and the Many, Appearance and Reality. Pythagoras had travelled much in the East. Herodotus speaks of various mystical ideas as being "Pythagorean and Egyptian," among them metempsychosis; and perhaps in general that κακοτεχνίη with which Heraclitus reproaches him included some oriental superstitions. His horror of eating the flesh of animals came partly from the doctrine of metempsychosis, though it was shared by many Greek thinkers up to the time of Plutarch. But the touch of superstition together with the absence of any definite written tradition gave Pythagoreanism, like Orphism and Neo-Platonism, a great appeal to many minds in certain later periods of Greek religion.

On no subject has there been a greater advance in our understanding of Greek literature than on the Drama (ch. ix–xii, pp. 204 ff.), especially owing to the work of Sir James Frazer and Jane Harrison. The very centre of ancient religion was anxiety about the food for next year, and the answer to this anxiety was Dionysus, "Zeus-Young," born of the union of Sky and Earth to replace the outworn Zeus of the Old Year. He is the personification of the secret inexhaustible life shown by the new birth of plant and beast in the spring; by the evergreen, alive when all else is dead; also no doubt by the strange, inexplicable supervitality produced by wine. The Spring God regularly appears as a mysterious baby, outcast in the fields and woods or among the flocks, but is later "recognised" as the son of a God and a mortal Princess, who comes to save the world and establish his new kingdom. When the new corn reaches the stage of harvest it has to be cut down and suffer a *sparagmos*, being torn into separate grains; this involves a death and mourning ceremony which, Herodotus tells us (II. 41, 62, 144), is exactly like that for Osiris, though, as he carefully explains, the name of Dionysus must never be mentioned in connection with death. That would be ἄρρητον. Hence in those many tragedies where the main plot consists of a contest, a death (often a *sparagmos*) narrated by a messenger, and a lamentation, it is never Dionysus who dies but always some one else, a surrogate, the god's enemy, or some one in the god's dress or the like. This is probably the reason why the drama of the god's death is called *Tragoedia*, a goat song; the goat was the god's own sacred animal and a most suitable surrogate.

It has been tentatively suggested that the death was normally followed by a resurrection or new birth, and that this is the explanation of the Divine Being who so often comes at the end of a tragedy bringing comfort or guidance, or even of the Satyr play which normally follows the tragic trilogy. We now know of several Satyr plays besides the *Cyclops* of Euripides. The papyri have given us the *Ichneutae*, "Trackers," of

Sophocles, a fragment 300 lines long. Apollo, searching for his lost cattle, hires Silenus and his sons, the Satyrs, to find them. The tracks are confused, as the cattle have been walked backwards, but presently the Satyrs are frightened by strange music coming from underground. They are warned off by the nymph Cyllene, who explains that she is guarding a new-born child of Zeus in a cave, and that the music is made by a dead tortoise. The truth comes out that the precocious Baby, Hermes, has both stolen the cattle and invented the lyre.

Aeschylus was particularly admired for his Satyr plays, and a good many fragments of them have turned up. The longest are from the *Dictyulci*, "Net-haulers," where a chorus of Satyrs at Serîphos, led by Dictys, the brother of the King, haul up from the sea the chest containing Danaë and her babe Perseus. There is mutual astonishment between the Satyrs and the travellers in the chest; and eventually Danaë marries Dictys. Another is from the *Theôroi* or *Isthmiastai*, in which the Satyrs attend the Isthmian Games and hang up portraits of their own heads on the temple of Poseidon and are then rebuked by Silenus for not attending to their proper business, the dance. The general atmosphere of all the Satyr plays is much the same: the Choir of young wild things, as naughty as possible but harmless and full of music; their grey-bearded Father, just as foolish as they in spite of his air of wisdom and authority; and thirdly, some real legendary hero, but always one with something κωμικὸν about him, the baby thief Hermes, the reveller Heracles, the liar Sisyphus or the wily

Odysseus. There is a certain charm in all the nonsense, a sense of the wild woods and music and absurdity.

As to the individual dramatists, see further my *Aeschylus, the Inventor of Tragedy* and *Euripides and His Age*, which give a much more mature criticism of these writers than appears in ch. x and xii. In Aeschylus' *Seven against Thebes*, the most interesting point is the sudden transformation of Eteocles from the cool and confident soldier of the first six hundred lines to the hag-ridden figure of despair who, as soon as he hears the name of the seventh champion, feels the curse closing fatally upon him yet still whispering the "hope of one good moment before death," the hope of killing his brother. This Eteocles is perhaps the first clearly studied individual character in dramatic literature. In the *Supplices* the horror felt by the Danaids for their pursuers is not quite accounted for by the idea of incest; the marriage of cousins was regular both in Greece and Egypt. There is of course the primitive horror of the white virgin pursued by a black wooer and also the entire aversion from a *gamos* without love, a point emphasized in the final play of the trilogy. The chapter on Sophocles (XI) also is in need of much correction. His treatment of the gods, who seem to be both dreaded and revered as a cause of human welfare and disaster and yet are not by human standards necessarily just or good, has been a subject of much discussion. In the self-criticism of Sophocles the phrase πικρὸν καὶ κατάτεχνον is hard to translate. Perhaps "austere and professional" would be better, that is, not amateurish but strictly according to *technê*. Where the ancients thought him so markedly superior to Aeschylus was in his plots. He knew the art of the theatre. His plays were never mere tragic situations; they had plots with real tragic development.

In my earlier treatment of all the tragedians I made far too much use of the idea of "orthodoxy." There was no requirement of orthodoxy in antiquity. There was fear of "impiety," that is, of breaking some sacred taboo, which might rouse the wrath of some god; great fear of silent prayer or prayer to an unknown foreign god, which might really be a magical charm for evil; also, no doubt, a suspicion that a complete denial of all gods might imply a denial of all piety and justice.

The old account of Aristophanes on pp. 280 ff. needs much correction; see my *Aristophanes, a Study* (1933). Athens and Sparta in their great days had been close partners against the Persian. The policy of Nicias and the more cultured Athenians, with which Aristophanes passionately agreed, was to restore peace and if possible renew the old partnership. Cleon, "the most violent of the citizens" leading the extreme nationalist demos, was for conquest at all costs. The city was overcrowded, impoverished, sometimes starving, but Cleon contrived— by doubling the tribute of the Allies, by further use of "money-collecting ships," by unscrupulous confiscations of property, and by leaving the men on active service unpaid (armed men can always feed themselves)—to get together enough money to feed the ecclesia and the jury courts and by means of their votes to keep in power. Aristophanes with unfailing courage protested against this policy and fought steadily in every play for peace. His last desperate appeal in the *Lysistrata* to the women of Athens and Sparta to unite in overthrowing the Old

Men left in the cities and then refusing their bodies to
any man till peace was made, reads in many ways almost
like a tragedy, and the final chorus of the Athenian and
Spartan women together is a hymn of united Hellas.

He certainly admired the old Athens more than the
new. His first play, the *Daitaleis*, shows us two brothers,
one of whom is of the younger sort, contemptuous of his
parents and quite ignorant of Homeric language but
well up in all the jargon of the law courts. The other
knows his Homer and his duty, but is helpless about
the latest legal technical terms. It is interesting to compare the comedian's easy and intimate ridicule of Socrates and Euripides in the *Clouds* and *Frogs* with his real
hatred of the all-powerful Cleon and the συκοφάνται
or blackmailers and flatterers who "come hissing out of
his hair" like the serpents of the Gorgon. The *Clouds* is
said to have been too high-brow for the taste of the
audience (*Clouds*, 518–525) and the *Frogs* shows a wonderful familiarity with the works of Aeschylus and
Euripides, and indeed with all poetry from Homer onward, so there is nothing surprising in Aristophanes'
presence as a guest at the Platonic *Symposium*. More
curious is Socrates' plea in the *Apology* that the misrepresentations of the comedians have done him griev-
ous harm in Athens. But no doubt a criticism that was
innocent in 425 B.C. might have dangerous effects after
411 and 404.

About the Alexandrians (ch. xviii), much new material is to be found in the three volumes of Powell and
Barber's *New Chapters of Greek Literature*, and for Callimachus there is now the immensely learned edition by

Pfeiffer (Oxford, 1955). The lament for Bion cannot be
by Moschus, the dates do not allow it. It must be left
anonymous, and on the whole Moschus' best work is his
little Epyllion on Europa. There is no poem quite like
it until the *Hero and Leander* of Musaeus, many centuries later.

The metrical rules of Nonnus are curious in detail. He
sometimes counts the particle δέ as an accented syllable.
It is also odd that at the end of the first half of the verse,
while he regularly has a proparoxytone, like κλινόμενος,
he admits a paroxytone before a long syllable, like
κεκλιμένην (never κεκλιμένος), which suggests that the
long syllable was really felt as two short. His practice
is clearly the beginning of a movement towards accen-
tual metric, but the full "politic verse" is not found
before the eighth century. There are no fourth century
instances.

Of the Romances the papyri have given us a good deal
more information (see also Rattenbury in *New Chapters*,
vol. 3). One completely new romance about *Ninos* and
his extremely ideal wife, who bears no great resemblance
to the historical Semiramis, was discovered and published in 1893, but has since disappeared. Charito's romance, *Chairias and Chariclea*, which was commonly
counted among the latest of its class and sometimes
even attributed to the sixth century A.D., has appeared
in papyri of the second century and has some claims to
be considerably earlier. It must also have been unusually popular, to judge from the frequency with which it
reappears on papyri of various dates. It is more adventurous and less sentimental than the average.

As to date, *Ninos* was probably written in the first

century B.C. Most of the other romances appear between the first and the fourth centuries A.D., but one may suspect that most stories of this sort were told to audiences long before they were written down. Listening to stories is a favourite occupation of illiterate or semi-literate peoples all the world over, and we hear in the tragedians of myths and other tales that were told "to maidens at the loom." The faithfulness, chastity, and somewhat excessive modesty of the heroines in most of our romances seem to make them peculiarly suitable for such an audience. They are called *Erotic*, but on the whole seem more concerned with adventures and wonders, accounts of strange lands and marvellous animals from the hippopotamus to the phoenix. In the later stages, however, in writers like Longus and Achilles Tatius, romantic love forms clearly the main interest. Why this type of romance ceased after the fourth century is puzzling; they probably resumed an oral, underground currency till they re-emerged in Byzantine times and took on a new life in the middle ages and after. The normal human heart will always respond to the words "Once upon a time."

GILBERT MURRAY.

BOAR'S HILL, *April* 1956.

PREFACE

To read and re-read the scanty remains now left to us
of the Literature of Ancient Greece, is a pleasant and
not a laborious task; nor is that task greatly increased
by the inclusion of the 'Scholia' or ancient commentaries. But modern scholarship has been prolific in
the making of books; and as regards this department
of my subject, I must frankly accept the verdict passed
by a German critic upon a historian of vastly wider
erudition than mine, and confess that I 'stand helpless before the mass of my material.' To be more
precise, I believe that in the domain of Epic, Lyric,
and Tragic Poetry, I am fairly familiar with the researches of recent years; and I have endeavoured to
read the more celebrated books on Prose and Comic
Poetry. Periodical literature is notoriously hard to
control; but I hope that comparatively few articles of
importance in the last twenty volumes of the *Hermes*,
the *Rheinisches Museum*, the *Philologus*, and the English Classical Journals, have escaped my consideration.
More than this I have but rarely attempted.

If under these circumstances I have nevertheless
sat down to write a History of Greek Literature, and
have even ventured to address myself to scholars as
well as to the general public, my reason is that, after

all, such knowledge of Greek literature as I possess
has been of enormous value and interest to me; that
for the last ten years at least, hardly a day has passed
on which Greek poetry has not occupied a large part
of my thoughts, hardly one deep or valuable emotion
has come into my life which has not been either
caused, or interpreted, or bettered by Greek poetry.
This is doubtless part of the ordinary narrowing of
the specialist, the one-sided sensitiveness in which he
finds at once his sacrifice and his reward; but it is
usually, perhaps, the thing that justifies a man in
writing.

I have felt it difficult in a brief and comparatively
popular treatise to maintain a fair proportion between
the scientific and æsthetic sides of my subject. Our
ultimate literary judgments upon an ancient writer
generally depend, and must depend, upon a large mass
of philological and antiquarian argument. In treating
Homer, for instance, it is impossible to avoid the
Homeric Question; and doubtless many will judge,
in that particular case, that the Question has almost
ousted the Poet from this book. As a rule, however,
I have tried to conceal all the laboratory work,
except for purposes of illustration, and to base my
exposition or criticism on the results of it. This
explains why I have so rarely referred to other
scholars, especially those whose works are best known
in this country. I doubt, for instance, if the names
of Jebb, Leaf, and Monro occur at all in the following
pages. The same is true of such writers as Usener,
Gomperz, Susemihl, and Blass, to whom I owe much;

and even of W. Christ, from whose *Geschichte der Griechischen Litteratur* I have taken a great deal of my chronology and general framework. But there are two teachers of whose influence I am especially conscious : first, Mr. T. C. Snow, of St. John's College, Oxford, too close a friend of my own for me to say more of him; and secondly, Professor Ulrich von Wilamowitz-Moellendorff, of Göttingen, whose historical insight and singular gift of imaginative sympathy with ancient Greece seem to me to have changed the face of many departments of Hellenic study within the last fifteen years.

My general method, however, has been somewhat personal, and independent of particular authorities. I have tried — at first unconsciously, afterwards of set purpose—to realise, as well as I could, what sort of men the various Greek authors were, what they liked and disliked, how they earned their living and spent their time. Of course it is only in the Attic period, and perhaps in the exceptional case of Pindar, that such a result can be even distantly approached, unless history is to degenerate into fiction. But the attempt is helpful even where it leads to no definite result. It saves the student from the error of conceiving 'the Greeks' as all much alike—a gallery of homogeneous figures, with the same ideals, the same standards, the same limitations. In reality it is their variety that makes them so living to us—the vast range of their interests, the suggestiveness and diversity of their achievements, together with the vivid personal energy that made the achievements possible. It was not by 'classic repose' nor yet by 'worship of the human body,' it was not even by the mere possession of high intellectual and æsthetic gifts, that they rose so irresistibly from mere barbarism to the height of their unique civilisation : it was by infinite labour and unrest, by daring and by suffering, by loyal devotion to the things they felt to be great ; above all, by hard and serious thinking.

Their outer political history, indeed, like that of all other nations, is filled with war and diplomacy, with cruelty and deceit. It is the inner history, the history of thought and feeling and character, that is so grand. They had some difficulties to contend with which are now almost out of our path. They had practically no experience, but were doing everything for the first time ; they were utterly weak in material resources, and their emotions, their *desires and fears and rages,* were probably wilder and fiercer than ours. Yet they produced the Athens of Pericles and of Plato.

The conception which we moderns form of these men certainly varies in the various generations. The 'serene and classical' Greek of Winckelmann and Goethe did good service to the world in his day, though we now feel him to be mainly a phantom. He has been succeeded, especially in the works of painters and poets, by an æsthetic and fleshly Greek in fine raiment, an abstract Pagan who lives to be contrasted with an equally abstract early Christian or Puritan, and to be glorified or mishandled according to the sentiments of his critic. He is a phantom too, as unreal as those marble palaces in which he habitually takes his ease. He would pass, perhaps, as a 'Græculus' of the Decadence ; but the speeches *Against Timarchus* and *Against Leocrates* show

what an Athenian jury would have thought of him.
There is more flesh and blood in the Greek of the
anthropologist, the foster-brother of Kaffirs and Hairy
Ainos. He is at least human and simple and emotional,
and free from irrelevant trappings.   His fault, of course,
is that he is not the man we want, but only the raw
material out of which that man was formed : a Hellene
without the beauty, without the spiritual life, without
the Hellenism. Many other abstract Greeks are about
us, no one perhaps greatly better than another ; yet
each has served to correct and complement his predecessor ; and in the long-run there can be little doubt
that our conceptions have become more adequate.
We need not take Dr. Johnson's wild verdict about the
'savages' addressed by Demosthenes, as the basis of
our comparison : we may take the *Voyage d'Anacharsis*
of the Abbé Bartelemi. That is a work of genius in
its way, careful, imaginative, and keen-sighted ; but it
was published in 1788. Make allowance for the per-
sonality of the writers, and how much nearer we get
to the spirit of Greece in a casual study by Mr. Andrew
Lang or M. Anatole France !

A desire to make the most of my allotted space, and
also to obtain some approach to unity of view, has led
me to limit the scope of this book in several ways.
Recognising that Athens is the only part of Greece of
which we have much real knowledge, I have accepted
her as the inevitable interpreter of the rest, and have,
to a certain extent, tried to focus my reader's attention
upon the Attic period, from Æschylus to Plato. I have

reduced my treatment of Philosophy to the narrowest dimensions, and, with much reluctance, have determined to omit altogether Hippocrates and the men of science. Finally, I have stopped the history proper at the death of Demosthenes, and appended only a rapid and perhaps arbitrary sketch of the later literature down to the fall of Paganism, omitting entirely, for instance, even such interesting books as Theophrastus's *Characters*, and the *Treatise on the Sublime.*

In the spelling of proper names I have made no great effort to attain perfect consistency. I have in general adopted the ordinary English or Latin modifications, except that I have tried to guide pronunciation by leaving *k* unchanged where *c* would be soft, and by marking long syllables with a circumflex. Thus Kimon is not changed to Cimon, and Demâdes is distinguished from Æschines. I have not, however, thought it necessary to call him Dêmâdes, or to alter the aspect of a common word by writing Dêmêtêr, Thûkÿdidês. In references to ancient authors, my figures always apply to the most easily accessible edition ; my reading, of course, is that which I think most likely to be right in each case. All the authors quoted are published in cheap texts by Teubner or Tauchnitz or the English Universities, except in a few cases, which are noted as they occur. Aristotle, Plato, and the Orators are quoted by the pages of the standard editions ; in the *Constitution of Athens*, which, of course, was not contained in the great Berlin Aristotle, I follow Kenyon's *editio princeps.*

Philologists may be surprised at the occasional acceptance in my translations of ancient and erroneous etymologies.   If, in a particular passage, I translate ἠλίβατος 'sun-trodden,' it is not that I think it to be a 'contracted form,' of ἠλιόβατος, but that I believe Euripides to have thought so.

An asterisk * after the title of a work signifies that the work is lost or only extant in fragments. Fragmentary writers are quoted, unless otherwise stated, from the following collections : *Fragmenta Historicorum Græcorum,* by Karl Müller ; *Philosophorum,* by Mullach ; *Tragicorum,* by Nauck ; *Comicorum,* by Kock ; *Epicorum,* by Kinkel ; *Poetæ Lyrici Græci,* by Bergk. These collections are denoted by their initial letters, F. H. G., F. P. G., and so on. C. I. A. is the *Corpus Inscriptionum Atticarum,* C. I. G. the *Corpus Inscriptionum Græcarum.* In a few cases I have used abbreviations for a proper name, as W. M. for Wilamowitz-Moellendorff, but not, I think, in any context where they are likely to be misunderstood.

Among the friends who have helped me with criticisms and suggestions, I must especially express my indebtedness to Mr. GEORGE MACDONALD, lecturer in Greek in this University, for much careful advice and correction of detail throughout the book.

GILBERT MURRAY.

GLASGOW, *February* 1897.

CONTENTS

THE

LITERATURE OF ANCIENT GREECE

I

HOMER

INTRODUCTORY

IN attempting to understand the scope and development of Greek literature, our greatest difficulty comes from the fragmentary and one-sided nature of our tradition. There has perhaps never been any society in history so near to the highest side of our own as the Athens of Euripides and Plato. The spiritual vividness and religious freedom of these men, the genuineness of their culture and humanity, the reasoned daring of their social and political ideals, appeal to us almost more intimately than does our own eighteenth century. But between us and them there has passed age upon age of men who saw differently, who sought in the books that they read other things than truth and imaginative beauty, or who did not care to read books at all. Of the literature produced by the Greeks in the fifth century B.C., we possess about a twentieth part ; of that produced in the seventh, sixth, fourth, and third, not nearly so large a proportion. All that has reached us. has passed a severe

A

and far from discriminating ordeal.   It has secured
its life by never going out of fashion for long at a
time ; by appealing steadily to the book-trade throughout a number of successive epochs of taste—fourth-century Greece, pre-Christian Alexandria, Augustan Rome,
the great Hellenic revival of the Antonines, the narrower
Attic revival of the later sophists.

After the death of Julian and Libanius, one is tempted
to think that nobody was really interested in literature
any more; but certain books had long been convention-
ally established in the schools as 'classics,' and these
continued to be read, in ever-dwindling numbers, till
the fall of Constantinople and the Renaissance.   The
eccentricities of the tradition would form material for
a large volume.   As in Latin it has zealously preserved
Vergil and Avianus the fabulist, so in Greek it has multiplied the MSS. of Homer and of Apollonius the Kitian
On Sprains. As in Latin it practically lost Lucretius save
for the accident of a single MS., and entirely lost Calvus,
so in Greek it came near to losing Æschylus, and preserved the most beautiful of the Homeric hymns only
by inadvertence.   In general, it cared for nothing that
was not either useful in daily life, like treatises on
mechanics and medicine, or else suitable for reading in
schools.   Such writers as Sappho, Epicharmus, Democritus, Menander, Chrysippus, have left only a few dis-
jointed fragments to show us what precious books were
allowed to die through the mere nervelessness of Byzantium.   But Rome and Alexandria in their vigour had
already done some intentional sifting.   They liked order
and style ; they did not care to copy out the more tumultuous writers.   The mystics and ascetics, the more uncompromising philosophers, the ardent democrats and the

enthusiasts generally, have been for the most part suppressed. We must remember that they existed, and try from the remains to understand them.

THE LEGENDARY POETS

But the first great gaps in the tradition are of a different nature. An immense amount of literature was never ' preserved ' at all. It is generally true that in any creative age the living literature is neglected. It is being produced every day ; and why should any one trouble himself to have it copied on good material and put in a safe place ? It is only that which can no longer be had for the asking that rouses men's anxiety lest it cease altogether. This is what happened among the Greeks in tragedy, in lyric poetry, in oratory, and in the first great movement of history. The greater part of each genus was already extinct by the time people bethought them of preserving it. Especially was it the case in the earliest form of composition known to our record, the hexameter epos.

The epos, as we know it, falls into three main divisions according to author and subject-matter. It is a vehicle for the heroic saga, written by 'Homêros' ; for useful information in general, especially catalogues and genealogies, written by 'Hêsiodos' ; and thirdly, for religious revelation, issuing originally from the mouths of such figures as 'Orpheus,' 'Musæus,' and the 'Bakides.' This last has disappeared, leaving but scanty traces, and the poems of 'Homer and Hesiod' constitute our earliest literary monuments.

All verse embodiments of the saga are necessarily less old than the saga itself. And more than that, it is clear that our *Iliad*, *Odyssey*, *Erga*, and *Theogony* are not the first, "nor the second, nor yet the twelfth," of such embodiments. These ostensibly primitive poems show a length and complexity of composition which can only be the result of many generations of artistic effort. They speak a language out of all relation to common speech, full of forgotten meanings and echoes of past states of society ; a poet's language, demonstrably built up and conditioned at every turn by the needs of the hexameter metre. There must therefore have been hexameter poems before our *Iliad*. Further, the hexameter itself is a high and complex development many stages removed from the simple metres in which the sagas seem once to have had shape in Greece as well as in India, Germany, and Scandinavia. But if we need proof of the comparative lateness of our earliest records, we can find it in 'Homer' himself, when he refers to the wealth of poetry that was in the world before him, and the general feeling that by his day most great themes have been outworn.[1]

The personalities of the supposed authors of the various epics or styles of epos are utterly beyond our reach. There is for the most part something fantastic or mythical in them. Orpheus, for instance, as a saga-figure, is of Greek creation ; as a name, he is one of the 'Ribhus,' or heroic artificers, of the Vedas, the first men who were made immortal. Another early bard, 'Linos,' is the very perfection of shadowiness. The Greek settler or exile on Semitic coasts who listened to the strange oriental dirges and caught the often-recurring wail '*Ai-lenû*' ('Woe to us'), took the words as Greek, *ai*

---

[1] Esp. θ, 74 ; μ, 70 ; α, 351. The books of the *Iliad* are denoted by the capital letters of the Greek alphabet, those of the *Odyssey* by the small letters.

Λίνου ('Woe for Linos'), and made his imaginary Linos
into an unhappy poet or a murdered prince. Homer's
ancestors, when they are not gods and rivers, tend to
bear names like 'Memory-son' and 'Sweet-deviser'; his
minor connections—the figures among whom the lesser
epics were apt to be divided—have names which are
sometimes transparent, sometimes utterly obscure, but
which generally agree in not being Greek names of any
normal type. The name of his son-in-law, 'Creophŷlus,'
suggests a comic reference to the 'Fleshpot-tribe' of
bards with their 'perquisites.' A poet who is much
quoted for the saga-subjects painted on the 'Leschê'
or 'Conversation Hall' at Delphi, is called variously
'Leschês,' 'Lescheôs,' and 'Leschaios'; another who
sang of sea-faring, has a name 'Arctînos,' derived, as no
other Greek name is, from the Pole-star. The author
of the *Telegoneia*,* which ended the Odysseus-saga in a
burst of happy marriages (see p. 48), is suitably named
'Eugamon' or 'Eugammon.'[1]

As for 'Homêros' himself, the word means 'hostage':
it cannot be a full Greek name, though it might be
an abbreviated 'pet name,' *e.g.* for 'Homêrodochos'
('hostage-taker'), if there were any Greek names at
all compounded from this word. As it is, the fact we
must start from is the existence of 'Homêridæ,' both
as minstrels in general and as a clan. 'Homêros' must
by all analogy be a primeval ancestor, invented to give
them a family unity, as 'Dôros,' 'Iôn,' and 'Hellên'
were invented; as even the League of the 'Amphic-
tyones' or 'Dwellers-round [Thermopylæ]' had to
provide themselves with a common ancestor called
'Amphictyôn' or 'Dweller-round.' That explains

[1] Crusius, *Philol.* liv.

'Homêros,' but still leaves 'Homêridæ' unexplained.
It may be what it professes to be, a patronymic
('Homer-sons'). It is easy to imagine a state of
society in which the Sons of the Hostages, not trusted
to fight, would be used as bards. But it may equally
well be some compound (ὁμῆ, ἀρ—) meaning 'fitters
together,' with the termination modified into patronymic
form when the minstrels began to be a guild and to feel
the need of a common ancestor.

It is true that we have many traditional 'lives' of
the prehistoric poets, and an account of a 'contest'
between Homer and Hesiod, our version being copied
from one composed about 400 B.C. by the sophist Alkidamas, who, in his turn, was adapting some already
existing romance. And in the poems themselves we
have what purport to be personal reminiscences.
Hesiod mentions his own name in the preface to the
Theogony. In the *Erga* (l. 633 ff.), he tells how his father
emigrated from Kymê to Ascra. The Homeric *Hymn
to Apollo* ends in an appeal from the poet to the
maidens who form his audience, to remember him, and
"*when any stranger asks who is the sweetest of singers and
who delights them most, to answer with one voice: 'Tis a
blind man; he dwells in craggy Chios; his songs shall be
the fairest for evermore.*" Unfortunately, these are only
cases of personation. The rhapsode who recited those
verses first did not mean that *he* was a blind Chian,
and *his* songs the fairest for evermore; he only meant that
the poem he recited was the work of that blind Homer
whose songs were as a matter of fact the best. Indeed,
both this passage and the preface to the *Theogony* are
demonstrably later additions, and the reminiscence in the
Erga must stand or fall with them. The real bards of

early Greece were all nameless and impersonal ; and we know definitely the point at which the individual author begins to dare to obtrude himself—the age of the lyrists and the Ionian researchers. These passages are not evidence of what Hesiod and Homer said of themselves ; they are evidence of what the tradition of the sixth century fabled about them.

Can we see the origin of this tradition ? Only dimly. There is certainly some historical truth in it. The lives and references, while varying in all else, approach unanimity in making Homer a native of Ionia. They concentrate themselves on two places, Smyrna and Chios ; in each of these an Æolian population had been overlaid by an Ionian, and in Chios there was a special clan called 'Homêridæ.' We shall see that if by the 'birth of Homer' we mean the growth of the Homeric poems, the tradition here is true. It is true also when it brings Hesiod and his father over from Asiatic Kymê to Bœotia, in the sense that the Hesiodic poetry is essentially the Homeric form brought to bear on native Bœotian material.

Thus Homer is a Chian or Smyrnæan for historical reasons ; but why is he blind ? Partly, perhaps, we have here some vague memory of a primitive time when the able-bodied men were all warriors ; the lame but strong men, smiths and weapon-makers ; and the blind men, good for nothing else, mere singers. More essentially, it is the Saga herself at work. She loved to make her great poets and prophets blind, and then she was haunted by their blindness. Homer was her Demodocus, "*whom the Muse greatly loved, and gave him both good and evil ; she took away his eyes and gave him sweet minstrelsy.*" (θ, 63, 4). It is pure romance—the

romance which creates the noble bust of Homer in
the Naples Museum; the romance which one feels in
Callimachus's wonderful story of the *Bathing of Pallas*,
where it is Teiresias, the prophet, not the poet, who
loses his earthly sight. Other traits in the tradition
have a similar origin — the contempt poured on the
unknown beggar-man at the Marriage Feast till he
rises and sings; the curse of ingloriousness he lays on
the Kymeans who rejected him; the one epic (*Cypria**)
not up to his own standard, with which he dowered his
daughter and made her a great heiress.

THE HOMERIC POEMS

If we try to find what poems were definitely regarded
as the work of Homer at the beginning of our tradition, the answer must be—all that were 'Homeric' or
'heroic'; in other words, all that express in epos the two
main groups of legend, centred round Troy and Thebes
respectively. The earliest mention of Homer is by the
poet Callînus (*ca*. 660 B.C.), who refers to the *Thebais** as
his work; the next is probably by Semonides of Amorgos
(*ca*. 630 B.C.), who cites as the words of 'a man of Chios'
a proverbial phrase which occurs in our *Iliad*, "*As the
passing of leaves is, so is the passing of men.*" It is possible
that he referred to some particular Chian, and that the
verse in our *Iliad* is merely a floating proverb assimilated
by the epos; but the probability is that he is quoting
our passage. Simonides of Keos (556–468 B.C.), a good
century later, speaks of "*Homer and Stesichorus telling
how Meleagros conquered all youths in spear-throwing across
the wild Anauros.*" This is not in our *Iliad* or *Odyssey*,

and we cannot trace the poem in which it comes. Pindar, a little later, mentions Homer several times. He blames him for exalting Odysseus—a reference to the *Odyssey*—but pardons him because he has told "*straightly by rod and plummet the whole prowess of Aias*"; especially, it would seem, his rescue of the body of Achilles, which was described in two lost epics, the *Little Iliad** and the *Æthiopis.** He bids us "*remember Homer's word: A good messenger brings honour to any dealing*"—a word, as it chances, which our Homer never speaks; and he mentions the "*Homēridæ, singers of stitched lays.*"

If Æschylus ever called his plays[1] "slices from the great banquets of Homer," the banquets he referred to must have been far richer than those to which we have admission. In all his ninety plays it is hard to find more than seven which take their subjects from our Homer, including the *Agamemnon* and *Choëphoroi*,[2] and it would need some spleen to make a critic describe these two as 'slices' from the *Odyssey*. What Æschylus meant by 'Homer' was the heroic saga as a whole. It is the same with Sophocles, who is called 'most Homeric,' and is said by Athenæus (p. 277) to "rejoice in the epic cycle and make whole dramas out of it." That is, he treated those epic myths which Athenæus only knew in the prose 'cycles' or handbooks compiled by one Dionysius in the second century B.C., and by Apollodôrus in the first. To Xenophanes (sixth century) 'Homer and Hesiod' mean all the epic tradition, sagas and theogonies alike, just as they do to Herodotus when he says (ii. 53), that they two "made the Greek religion, and distributed to the gods their titles

---

[1] Athenæus, 347 *e.*

[2] The others are the Achilles-trilogy (*Myrmidons,** *Nereides,** *Phryges**), *Penelope,** *Soul-weighing.**

and honours and crafts, and described what they were like." There Herodotus uses the conventional language ; but he has already a standard of criticism which is inconsistent with it. For he conceives Homer definitely as the author of the *Iliad* and *Odyssey*. He doubts if the *Lay of the Afterborn** be his, and is sure (ii. 117) that the *Cypria** cannot be, because it contradicts the *Iliad*. This is the first trace of the tendency that ultimately prevailed. Thucydides explicitly recognises the *Iliad*, the *Hymn to Apollo*, and the *Odyssey* as Homer's. Aristotle gives him nothing but the *Iliad*, the *Odyssey*, and the humorous epic *Margîtes.** Plato's quotations do not go beyond the *Iliad* and the *Odyssey;* and it is these two poems alone which were accepted as Homer's by the great Alexandrian scholar Aristarchus (*ca.* 160 B.C.), and which have remained 'Homeric' ever since.

How was it that these two were originally selected as being 'Homer' in some special degree ? And how was it that, in spite of the essential dissimilarities between them, they continued to hold the field together as his authentic work when so many other epics had been gradually taken from him ? It is the more surprising when we reflect that the differences and inconsistencies between them had already been pointed out in Alexandrian times by the 'Chorizontes' or 'Separators,' Xenon and Hellanîcus.

ILIAD AND ODYSSEY : THE PANATHENAIC
RECITATION

A tradition comes to our aid which has been differently interpreted by various critics — the story of the recension by Pisistratus, tyrant of Athens, in the middle of the sixth century. Late writers speak much of this recension. "*Vox totius antiquitatis*" is the authority Wolf claims for it. It is mentioned in varying terms by Cicero, Pausanias, Ælian, Josephus ; it is referred to as a well-known fact in a late epigram purporting to be written for a statue of "Pisistratus, great in counsel, who collected Homer, formerly sung in fragments." Cicero's account is that Pisistratus "arranged in their present order the books of Homer, previously confused." The Byzantine Tzetzes — the name is only a phonetic way of spelling Cæcius — makes the tradition ludicrous by various mistakes and additions ; his soberest version says that Pisistratus performed this task "by the help of the industry of four famous and learned men—Concylus, Onomacritus of Athens, Zopyrus of Heraclea, and Orpheus of Crotona." Unfortunately, the learned Concylus is also called Epiconcylus, and represents almost certainly the 'Epic Cycle,' ἐπικὸν κύκλον, misread as a proper name! And the whole commission has a fabulous air, and smacks of the age of the Ptolemies rather than the sixth century. Also it is remarkable that in our fairly ample records about the Alexandrian critics, especially Aristarchus, there is no explicit reference to Pisistratus as an editor.

It used to be maintained that this silence of the Alexandrians proved conclusively that the story was not in existence in their time. It has now been traced, in a less developed form, as far back as the fourth century B.C. It was always known that a certain Dieuchidas of Megara had accused Pisistratus of interpolating lines in Homer to the advantage of Athens—a charge evidently implying that the accused had special means of controlling the text.

It was left for Wilamowitz to show that Dieuchidas was a
writer much earlier than the Alexandrians, and to explain
his motive.[1] It is part of that general literary revenge
which Megara took upon fallen Athens in the fourth century. "Athens had not invented comedy ; it was Megara.
Nor tragedy either ; it was Sikyon. Athens had only falsified and interpolated !" Whether Dieuchidas accepted
the Pisistratus recension as a fact generally believed,
or whether he suggested it as an hypothesis, is not clear.
It appears, however, that he could not find any un-Attic
texts to prove his point by. When he wished to suggest
the true reading he had to use his own ingenuity. It
was he who invented a supposed original form for the
interpolated passage in *B*, 671 ; and perhaps he who
imagined the existence of a Spartan edition of Homer
by Lycurgus, an uncontaminated text copied out honestly
by good Dorians !

The theory, then, that Pisistratus had somehow 'interpolated Homer' was current before Alexandrian times.
Why does Aristarchus not mention it ? We cannot
clearly say. It is possible that he took the fact for
granted, as the epigram does. It is certain, at any rate,
that Aristarchus rejected on some ground or other most
of the lines which modern scholars describe as 'Athenian
interpolations' ; and that ground cannot have been a
merely internal one, since he held the peculiar belief that
Homer himself was an Athenian. Lastly, it is a curious
fact that Cicero's statement about the recension by Pisis-
stratus seems to be derived from a member of the
Pergamene school, whose founder, Crates, stood almost
alone in successfully resisting and opposing the authority
of Aristarchus. It is quite possible that the latter tended

[1] *Phil. Unters.* vii. p. 240.

to belittle a method of explanation which was in particular favour with a rival school.

Dieuchidas, then, knows of Pisistratus having done to the poems something which gave an opportunity for interpolation. But most Megarian writers, according to Plutarch (*Solon*, 10), say it was Solon who made the interpolations; and a widespread tradition credits Solon with a special law about the recitation of 'Homer' at the Festival of the Panathenæa. This law, again, is attributed to Hipparchus in the pseudo-Platonic dialogue which bears his name—a work not later than the third century. Lycurgus the orator ascribes it simply to 'our ancestors,' and that is where we must leave it. When a law was once passed at Athens, it tended to become at once the property of Solon, the great 'Nomothetês.' If Pisistratus and Hipparchus dispute this particular law, it is partly because there are rumours of dishonest dealings attached to the story, partly because the tyrants were always associated with the Panathenæa.

But what was the law? It seems clear that the recitation of Homer formed part of the festal observances, and probable that there was a competition. Again, we know that the poems were to be recited in a particular way. But was it ἐξ ὑποβολῆς ('by suggestion') — at any verse given? That is almost incredible. Or was it ἐξ ὑπολήψεως ('one beginning where the last left off')? Or, as Diogenes Laertius airily decides, did the law perhaps say ἐξ ὑποβολῆς, and mean ἐξ ὑπολήψεως?[1]

Our evidence then amounts in the first place to this:

---

[1] One is tempted to add to this early evidence what Herodotus says (vii. 6) of the banishment of Onomacritus by Hipparchus; but he was banished for trafficking in false oracles, an offence of an entirely different sort from interpolating works of literature.

that there was a practice in Athens, dating at latest from
early in the fifth century, by which the Homeric poems
were recited publicly in a prescribed order ; and that the
origin of the practice was ascribed to a definite public
enactment. We find further, that in all non-Athenian
literature down to Pindar, 'Homer' seems to be taken
as the author of a much larger number of poems than
we possess—probably of all the Trojan and Theban epics
—whereas in Attic literature from the fifth century onwards he is especially the author of the *Iliad* and the
Odyssey, the other poems being first treated as of doubtful authorship, afterwards ignored.   When we add that in
the usage of all the authors who speak of this Panathenaic
recitation, 'Homer' means simply, and as a matter of
course, the *Iliad* and the *Odyssey*, the conclusion inevitably suggests itself that it was these two poems alone
which were selected for the recitation, and that it was
the recitation which gave them their unique position of
eminence as the 'true' Homer.

Why were they selected ? One can see something,
but not much. To begin with, a general comparison
of the style of the rejected epics with that of our two
poems suggests that the latter are far more elaborately
'worked up' than their brethren.   They have more unity ;
they are less like mere lays ; they have more dramatic
tension and rhetorical ornament. One poem only can
perhaps be compared with them, the first which is quoted
as 'Homer's' in literature, the *Thebais :* * but the glory
of Thebes was of all subjects the one which could least
be publicly blazoned by Athenians ; Athens would reject
such a thing even more unhesitatingly than Sikyon rejected the 'Homer' which praised Argos.[1]

[1] Hdt. v. 67.

We get thus one cardinal point in the history of the poems ; it remains to trace their development both before and after. To take the later history first, our own traditional explanation of Homer is derived from the Alexandrian scholars of the third and second centuries B.C., Zenodotus of Ephesus (born 325 ?), Aristophanes of Byzantium (born 257 ?), and Aristarchus of Samothrace (born 215) ; especially from this last, the greatest authority on early poetry known to antiquity. Our information about him is mostly derived from an epitome of the works of four later scholars : Didymus *On the Aristarchean Recension ;* Aristonîcus *On the Signs in the Iliad and Odyssey—i.e.* the critical signs used by Aristarchus ; Herodian *On the Prosody and Accentuation of the Iliad,* and Nicanor *On Homeric Punctuation.* The two first named were of the Augustan age ; the epitome was made in the third century A.D. ; the MS. in which it is preserved is the famous *Venetus A* of the tenth century, containing the *Iliad* but not the *Odyssey.*

We can thus tell a good deal about the condition of Homer in the second century B.C., and can hope to establish with few errors a text 'according to Aristarchus,' a text which would approximately satisfy the best literary authority at the best period of Greek criticism. But we must go much further, unless we are to be very unworthy followers of Aristarchus and indifferent to the cause of science in literature. In the first place, if our comments come from Aristarchus, where does our received text come from ? Demonstrably not from him, but from the received text or vulgate of his day, in correction of which he issued his two editions, and on which neither he nor any one else has ultimately been able to exercise a really commanding influence. Not that he made violent changes; on the contrary, he seldom or never 'emended' by mere conjecture, and, though he marked many lines as spurious, he did not omit them. The greatest divergences which we find between Aristarchus and the vulgate are not so great as those between the quartos and the folio of *Hamlet*.

Yet we can see that he had before him a good many recensions which differed both from the vulgate and from one another. He mentions in especial three classes of such MSS.—those of individuals, showing the recension or notes of poets like Antimachus and Rhiânus, or of scholars like Zenodotus; those of cities, coming from Marseilles, Chios, Argos, Sinôpe, and in general from all places except Athens, the city of the vulgate; and, lastly, what he calls the 'vulgar' or 'popular' or 'more careless' texts, among which we may safely reckon 'that of the many verses' (ἡ πολύστιχος).

The quotations from Homer in pre-Alexandrian writers enable us to appreciate both the extent and the limits of this variation. They show us first that even in Athens the vulgate had not established itself firmly before the year 300 B.C. Æschines the orator, a man of much culture, not only asserts that the phrase φήμη δ'ἐς στρατὸν ἦλθε occurs 'several times in the *Iliad*,' whereas in our texts it does not occur at all; but quotes verbally passages from Θ and Ψ with whole lines quite different. And the third-century papyri bear the same testimony, notably the fragment of Λ in the Flinders-Petrie collection published in 1891 by Prof. Mahaffy, and the longer piece from the same book published by M. Nicole in the *Revue de Philologie*, 1894. The former of these, for instance, contains the beginnings or endings of thirty-eight lines of Λ between 502 and 537. It omits one of our lines; contains four strange lines ; and has two others in a different shape from that in our texts : a serious amount of divergence in such a small space. On the other hand, the variations seem to be merely verbal; and the same applies to the rest of the papyrus evidence. There is no variation in matter in any fourth-century text.

The summing up of this evidence gives us the last two stages of the Homeric poems. The canonical statements of fact and the order of the incidents were fixed by a gradual process of which the cardinal point is the institution of the Panathenaic recitations ; the wording of the text line by line was gradually stereotyped by continued processes of school repetition and private reading and literary study, culminating in the minute professional criticism of Zenodotus and his successors at the Alexandrian library.

If we go further back, it is impossible not to be struck by the phenomenon, that while the Homeric quotations in most fourth and fifth century writers, even in Aristotle, for instance, differ considerably from our text, Plato's quotations [1] agree with it almost word for word. One cannot but combine with this the conclusion drawn by Grote in another context, that Demetrius of Phalêrum, when summoned by Ptolemy I. to the foundation of the library at Alexandria, made use of the books bequeathed by Plato to the Academy. [2]

This analysis brings us again to the Panathenaic recitation. We have seen that its effects were to establish the *Iliad* and the *Odyssey* as 'Homer' *par excellence;* to fix a certain order of incidents in them ; and, of course, to make them a public and sacred possession of Athens.

---

[1] Counting *Alcibiades II.* as spurious.
[2] Grote, *Plato*, chap. vi.

Let us try to see further into it.   When was it instituted ?
Was there really a law at all, or only a gradual process
which the tradition, as its habit is, has made into one
definite act ?

As for the date, the establishment of the custom is sure
not to be earlier than the last person to whom it is ascribed; that is, it took place not before, but probably after,
the reign of Hipparchus.   Now, to make the works of the
great Ionian poet an integral part of the most solemn religious celebration of Athens, is a thing which can only have
taken place in a period of active fraternising with Ionia.
That movement begins for Athens with the Ionian revolt ;
before 500 B.C. she had been ashamed of her supposed
kinsmen ; even Cleisthenes had abolished the Ionian tribe
names.   The year 499 opens the great Pan-Ionic period
of Athenian policy, in which Athens accepts the position
of metropolis and protectress of Ionia, absorbs Ionian
culture, and rises to the intellectual hegemony of Greece.
Learning and letters must have fled from Miletus at the
turn of the sixth century B.C., as they fled from Constantinople in the fifteenth A.D., and Athens was their
natural refuge.   We shall see later the various great men
and movements that travelled at this time from Asia to
Athens.   One typical fact is the adoption of the Ionian
alphabet at Athens for private and literary use.

The native Athenian alphabet was an archaic and
awkward thing, possessing neither double consonants nor
adequate vowel-distinctions.   The Ionian was, roughly,
that which we now use.   It was not officially adopted
in Athens till 404—the public documents liked to preserve their archaic majesty—but it was in private use
there during the Persian Wars ;[1] that is, it came over

[1] Kirchhoff, *Alphabet*, Ed. iv. p. 92.

at the time when Athens accepted and asserted her position as the metropolis of Ionia, and adopted the Ionian poetry as a part of her sacred possessions. But a curious difficulty suggests itself. Homer in Ionia was of course already written in Ionic. Our tradition, however, backed by many explicit statements of the Alexandrians and by considerations of textual criticism,[1] expressly insists that the old texts of Homer were in the old Attic alphabet. If Homer came into the Panathenæa at the very same time as the new Ionian alphabet came to Athens, how was it that the people rewrote him from the better script into the worse? The answer is not hard to find; and it is also the answer to another question, which we could not solve before. Copies of Homer were written in official Attic, because the recitation at the Panathenæa was an official ceremony, prescribed by a legal enactment.

There was then a definite law, a symptom of the general Ionising movement of the first quarter of the fifth century. Can we see more closely what it effected?

It prescribed a certain order, and it started a tendency towards an official text. It is clear that adherence to the words of the text was not compulsory, though adherence to the matter was. It seems almost certain that the order so imposed was not a new and arbitrary invention. It must have been already known and approved at Athens; though, of course, it may have been only one of various orders current in the different Homeric centres of Ionia, and was probably not rigid and absolute anywhere. At any rate one thing is clear —this law was among the main events which ulti-

---

[1] See Cauer's answer to Wilamowitz, *Grundfragen der Homerkritik*, p. 69 ff.

mately took the epos for good out of the hands of the rhapsodes.

We know that the epos in Ionia was in the possession of 'Homêridai' or 'rhapsôdoi'; and we have reason to suppose that these were organised in guilds or schools. We know roughly how a rhapsode set to work. He would choose his 'bit' from whatever legend it might be, as the bards do in the *Odyssey*.[1] He would have some lines of introduction—so much Pindar tells us, and the Homeric hymns or preludes show us what he meant — and probably some lines of finish. He would almost inevitably be tempted to introduce bright patches and episodes to make his lay as attractive as others. He would object to a fixed text, and utterly abhor the subordination of parts to whole.

Now, our poems are full of traces of the rhapsode; they are developments from the recited saga, and where they fail in unity or consistency the recited saga is mostly to blame. For instance in *E*, the superhuman exploits of Diomêdes throw Achilles into the shade and upset the plot of the *Iliad*. But what did that matter to a rhapsode who wanted a good declamation, and addressed an audience interested in Diomêdes? The *Doloneia* (*K*), placed where it is, is impossible; it not only makes a night of portentous length; it also rends in two a continuous narrative. In a detached recitation it would be admirable. To take a different case, there is a passage describing a clear night, "*when all the high peaks stand out, and the jutting promontories and glens; and above the sky the infinite heaven breaks open.*" This occurs in *H*, where the Trojan watch-fires are likened to the stars; it occurs also in *Π*, where the Greeks' despair

[1] θ, 73 ff., 500 ff.; α, 326.

is rolled back like a cloud leaving the night clear. Commentators discuss in which place it is genuine. Surely, anywhere and everywhere. Such lovely lines, once heard, were a temptation to any rhapsode, and likely to recur wherever a good chance offered. The same explanation applies to the multiplied similes of *B*, 455 ff. They are not meant to be taken all together ; they are alternatives for the reciter to choose from.

And even where there is no flaw in the composition, the formulæ for connection between the incidents—*" Thus then did they fight," " Thus then did they pray"*—and the openings of new subjects with phrases like *" Thus rose Dawn from her bed,"* and the like, suggest a new rhapsode beginning his lay in the middle of an epic whole, the parts before and after being loosely taken as known to the audience.

Nevertheless, the striking fact about our Homeric poems is not that they show some marks of the rhapsode's treatment, but that they do not show more. They are, as they stand, not suited for the rhapsode. They are too long to recite as wholes, except on some grand and unique occasion like that which the law specially contemplated ; too highly organised to split up easily into detachable lengths. It is not likely that the law reduced them to their present state at one blow. All it insisted on was to have the 'true history' in its proper sequence. If it permitted rhapsodes at all, it had to allow them a certain freedom in their choice of ornament. It did not insist on adherence to a fixed wording.

The whole history of the text in the fourth century illustrates this arrangement, and the fact essentially is, that the poems as we have them, organic and indivisible,

are adapted to the demands of a reading public. There
was no reading public either in Athens or in Ionia by
470. Anaximander wrote his words of wisdom for a
few laborious students to learn by heart; Xenophanes
appealed simply to the ear; it was not till forty years
later that Herodotus turned his recitations into book
form for educated persons to read to themselves, and
Euripidês began to collect a library.

This helps us to some idea of the Ionian epos as it
lived and grew before its transplanting. It was recited,
not read; the incidents of the *Iliad* and the *Odyssey*
were mostly in their present order, and doubtless the
poems roughly of their present compass, though we
may be sure there were *Iliads* without **K**, and *Odysseys*
ending, where Aristarchus ended his, at ψ 296, omitting
the last book and a half. Much more important, the
Iliad did not necessarily stop at the mere funeral of
Hector. We know of a version which ran on from
our last line—"*So dealt they with the burying of Hector;
but there came the Amazon, daughter of Ares, great-
hearted slayer of men*"—and which told of the love of
Achilles for the Amazon princess, and his slaying of
her, and probably also of his well-earned death. The
death of Achilles is, as Goethe felt it to be, the real
end that our *Iliad* implies. When the enchanted steed,
Xanthus, and the dying Hector prophesy it, we feel that
their words must come true or the story lose its meaning.
And if it was any of the finer 'Sons of Homer' who
told of that last death-grapple where it was no longer
Kebrionês nor Patroclus, but Achilles himself, who lay
"*under the blind dust-storm, the mighty limbs flung
mightily, and the riding of war forgotten,*" the world
must owe a grudge to those over-patriotic editors who

could not bear to let the national Epic end with a triumph for the Trojans.

Of course in this Ionic Homer there were no 'Athenian interpolations,' no passages like the praise of Menestheus, the claim to Salamis, the mentions of Theseus, Procris, Phædra, Ariadne, or the account of the Athenians in *N*, under the name of '*long-robed Ionians*,' acting as a regiment of heavy infantry. Above all, the language, though far from pure, was at least very different from our vulgate text ; it was free from Atticisms.

THE EPIC LANGUAGE

We must analyse this language and see the historical processes implied in its growth.

An old and much-scoffed-at division of Greek dialects spoke of Ionic, Æolic, Doric, and 'Epic.' The first three denote, or mean to denote, real national distinctions ; the last is, of course, an artificial name. But the thing it denotes is artificial too—a language that no Ionians, Dorians, or Æolians ever spoke; a 'large utterance,' rhythmic and emotional, like a complicated instrument for the expression of the heroic saga. As has already been remarked, it is a dialect conditioned at every turn by the Epic metre ; its fixed ¡epithets, its formulæ, its turns of sentence-connection, run into hexameters of themselves. Artificial as it is in one sense, it makes the impression of Nature herself speaking. Common and random phrases — the torrents coming "*down from the hills on their head;*" the "*high West wind shouting over a wine-faced sea;*" "*the eastern isle where dwells Eôs the Dawn-child, amid her palaces and her*

dancing-grounds, and the rising places of the Sun"—these
words in Epic Greek seem alive ; they call up not
precisely the look or sound, but the exact emotional
impression of morning and wind and sea. The expressions for human feeling are almost more magical :
the anger of *" what though his hands be as fire, and his
spirit as burning iron"; * or the steadfastness of *"Bear, O
my heart, thou hast borne yet a harder thing."*

There is thus no disparagement to the Epic dialect
in saying that, as it stands, it is no language, but a mixture of linguistically-incongruous forms, late, early, and
primæval.

There are first the Atticisms. Forms like Τυδῆ, ἕως,
νικῶντες, can only have come into the poems on Attic
soil, and scarcely much before the year 500 B.C. At
least, the fragments of Solon's Laws have, on the
whole, a more archaic look. But for the purposes of
history we must distinguish. There are first the remov-
able Atticisms. A number of lines which begin with
ἕως will not scan until we restore the Ionic form ἦος.
That is, they are good Ionic lines, and the Attic form
is only a mistake of the Attic copyist. But there are
also fixed Atticisms—lines which scan as they stand, and
refuse to scan if turned into Ionic ; these are in the
strict sense late lines ; they were composed on Attic soil
after Athens had taken possession of the epos.

Again, there are 'false forms' by the hundred —
attempts at a compromise made by an Athenian reciter
or scribe between a strange Ionic form and his own
natural Attic, when the latter would not suit the metre.
The Ionic for 'seeing' was ὀρέοντες, the Attic ὀρῶντες—
three syllables instead of four ; our texts give the false
ὀρόωντες—*i.e.* they have tortured the Attic form into four

syllables by a quaver on the ω. Similarly σπείους is an attempt to make the Attic σπέους fill the place of the uncontracted σπέεος, and εὐχετάασθαι is an elongated εὐχετᾶσθαι. Spelling, of course, followed pronunciation; the scribe wrote what the reciter chanted.

The historical process which these forms imply, can only have taken place when Athens looked nowhere outside herself for literary information, when there were no Ionic-speaking bards to correct the Attic bookseller. Some of them, indeed, can only have ceased to be absurd when the *Koinê*, the common literary language, had begun to blur the characters of the real dialects and to derive everything from the Attic standard. That is, they would date from late in the fourth century.

But to eliminate the Attic forms takes us a very little way; there is another non-Ionic element in 'Homer's' language which has been always recognised, though variously estimated, from antiquity onwards, and which seems to belong to the group of dialects spoken in Thessaly, Lesbos, and the Æolian coast of Asia including the Troad. Forms like Ἀτρείδαο, Μουσάων, κεν for ἄν, πίσυρες for τέσσαρες, intensives in ἐρι-, adjectives in -εννος, and masses of verbal flexions are proved to be Æolic, as well as many particular words like πολυπάμμονος, Θερσίτης, ἄμυδις.

There is also another earlier set of 'false forms,' neither Æolic nor Ionic, but explicable only as a mixture of the two. κεκληγῶτες is no form; it is an original Æolic κεκλήγοντες twisted as close as metre will allow it to the Ionic κεκληγότες; ἠπύτα κῆρυξ, for 'shouting herald,' is the Æolic ἄπυτα brought as near as metre permits to the Ionic ἠπύτης. Most significant of all is the case of the Digamma or Vau, a W-sound, which disappeared in

Ionic and Attic Greek, both medially (as in our *Norwich*, *Berwick*) and initially (as in *who*, and the Lancashire *'ooman*). It survived, however, in Doric inscriptions, and in such of the Æolic as were not under Ionian influence, till the fifth and sometimes the fourth century. It is called in antiquity the 'Æolic letter.' Now there are 3354 places in the poems which insist on the restoration of this Vau—*i.e.* the lines will not scan without it ; 617 places, on the other hand, where in ancient Æolic it ought to stand, but is metrically inadmissible. That is, through the great mass of the poems the habit and tradition of the Æolic pronunciation is preserved ; in a small part the Ionic asserts itself.

These facts have been the subject of hot controversy ; but the only effective way to minimise their importance is to argue that we have no remains of Æolic of the seventh century, and that the apparent Æolisms may be merely 'old Greek' forms dating from a period before the scattered townships on the coast of Asia massed themselves into groups under the names of Iônes and Aioleis —an historical hypothesis which leads to difficulties.

It is not disputed that the 'Æolic' element is the older. Philology and history testify to it, and weight must be allowed to the curious fact, that to turn the poems into Æolic produces the rhymes and assonances characteristic of primitive poetry in numbers far too large to be the result of accident.[1] And it holds as a general rule that when the Æolic and Ionic forms are metrically indifferent—*i.e.* when the line scans equally well with either—the Ionic is put ; when they are not indifferent, then in the oldest parts of the poems the

---

[1] *E.g.* Ϝρέξομεν ἀθθανάτοισι τοι ὄρρανον εὐρυν ἔχοισι, χόλος δέ μιν ἄγριος ἄγρη (= ᾖρει), and ἀρέπυιαι ἀναρέψαντο.

Æolic stands and the Ionic cannot, in the later parts the Ionic stands and the Æolic cannot. And further, where the two dialects denote the same thing by entirely different words, the Æolic word tends to stand in its native form ; *e.g.* λᾱός, 'people,' keeps its *a*, because the Ionic word was δῆμος. For a 'temple' the Ionic νηός stands everywhere, but that is just because temples are a late development ; the oldest worship was at altars in the open air.[1]

There are many exceptions to these rules. Dr. Fick of Göttingen, who has translated all the 'older parts' of Homer back to a supposed original Æolic, leaving what will not transcribe as either late or spurious, has found himself obliged to be inconsistent in his method ; when Ϝιδέσθαι occurs without a Ϝ he sometimes counts it as evidence of lateness, sometimes alters it into ἱκέσθαι. In the same way a contraction like νικῶντες may represent an Æolic νίκαντες from νίκαμι, or may be a staring Atticism. When we see further that, besides the Ionisms which refuse to move, there are numbers of Æolisms which need never have been kept for any reason of metre, the conclusion is that the Ionising of the poems is not the result of a deliberate act on the part of a particular Ionic bard—Fick gives it boldly to Kynæthus of Chios — but part of that gradual semi-conscious modernising and re-forming to which all saga-poetry is subject. The same process can be traced in the various dialectic versions of the *Nibelungenlied* and the *Chanson de Roland*. A good instance of it occurs in the English ballad of *Sir Degrevant*, where the hero 'Agravain' has not only had a D put before his name, but sometimes rhymes with 'retenaunce' or 'chaunce' and sometimes

---

[1] Cauer, *Grundfragen*, p. 203.

with 'recreaunt' or 'avaunt.' It comes from an Anglo-Norman original, in which the *Sieur d'Agrivauns* formed his accusative *d'Agrivaunt*.[1]

The Subject-Matter of Homer

The evidence of language is incomplete without some consideration of the matter of the poems. What nationality, for instance, would naturally be interested in the subject of the *Iliad?* The scene is in the Troad, on Æolic ground. The hero is Achilles, from Æolic Thessaly. The chief king is Agamemnon, ancestor of the kings of Æolic Kymê. Other heroes come from Northern and Central Greece, from Crete and from Lycia. The Ionians are represented only by Nestor, a hero of the second rank, who is not necessary to the plot.

This evidence goes to discredit the Ionian origin of the main thread of the *Iliad;* but does not the same line of argument, if pursued further, suggest something still more strange—vi*z.*, a Peloponnesian origin? Agamemnon is king of Argos and Mycenæ; Menelaus is king of Sparta; Diomêdes, by some little confusion, of Argos also; Nestor, of Pylos in Messenia. The answer to this difficulty throws a most striking light on the history of the poems. All these heroes have been dragged down to the Peloponnese from homes in Northern Greece.

Diomêdes, first, has no room in Argos; apart from the difficulty with Agamemnon, he is not in the genealogy, and has to inherit through his mother. A slight study of the local worships shows what he is, an idealised Ætolian. He is the founder of cities in Italy; the constant companion of Odysseus, who represents the North-West

---

[1] *Thornton Romances*, Camden Soc., 1844, esp. p. 289.

islands. He is the son of Tydeus, who ate his enemy's head, and the kinsman of Agrios ('Savage') and the 'sons of Agrios' — the mere lion-hero of the ferocious tribes of the North-West.

Agamemnon himself comes from the plain of Thessaly. He is king of Argos ; only in a few late passages, of Mycenæ. Aristarchus long ago pointed out that 'Pelasgian Argos' in Homer means the plain of Thessaly. But 'horse-rearing Argos' must be the same, for Argos of the Peloponnese was without cavalry even in historical times. And a careful treatment of the word 'Argos' shows its gradual expansion in the poems from the plain of Thessaly to Greece in general, and then its second localisation in the Peloponnese. Agamemnon is the rich king of the plain of Thessaly ; that is why he is from the outset connected with Achilles, the poor but valiant chief from the seaward mountains ; that is why he chooses Aulis as the place for assembling his fleet.

Aias in the late tradition is the hero of Salamis ; but in the poems he has really no fixed home. He is the hero of the seven-fold shield, whose father is 'Shield-strap' (Telamon), and his son, 'Broad-buckler' (Eurysakes); if he has connections, we must look for them in the neighbourhood of his brother the Locrian, and his father's brother, Phôkos, whose name suggests Phokis ;— though it is true that some of the legends seem to derive his name from φώκη (seal), and treat him as a seal-hero.[1] So far we get a general conception of an original stage of the story in which the chiefs were all from Northern Greece. Where was the fighting ?

Achilles and Agamemnon must be original ; so must Hector and Ilion ; so, above all, must Alexander-Paris

[1] He was clubbed to death on the sea-shore ; his mother was called '*Psamatheia*,' '*Sea-sand*.'

and Helenê. But need Ilion be in Troia on the site of Hissarlik ? It is worth observing that the scenery of the similes in the oldest parts of the poems is Thessalian, and not Asiatic; that Hector (' Upholder ') is not connected in local legend with the historical Troy—its heroes are Æneas and one Dares;[1] that this Æneas, though afterwards identified with a hero at Hissarlik, seems to be in origin the tribal hero of the Æneânes in South Thessaly, just as Teukros (' Hitter'), the archer, gets in later tradition connected with Ilion, and the Ilion-men become Teukroi ? Of course it is ultimately a myth that we have to deal with. The original battle for Helen was doubtless a strife of light and darkness in the sky, just as the Niblungs were cloud-men and Sigurd a sun-god, before they were brought down to Worms and Burgundy. But it looks as if the Helen-feud had its first earthly localisation, not in Troy, but on the southern frontier of those Thessalian bards who sang of it.

When Dr. Schliemann made his first dazzling discoveries at Mycenæ and Hissarlik, he believed that he had identified the corpse of Agamemnon and recovered the actual cup from which Nestor drank, the pigeons still intact upon the handles. We all smile at this now ; but it remains a difficult task to see the real relation which subsists between the civilisation described in the Homeric poems, and the great castles and walls, the graves and armour and pottery, which have now been unearthed at so many different sites in Greece.

Of the nine successive cities at Hissarlik, the sixth from the bottom corresponds closely with the civilisation of Mycenæ, a civilisation similar in many respects to that implied in the earliest parts of the *Iliad.* The

---

[1] Duncker, *Greece,* chap. xiii.

Homeric house can be illustrated by the castle of Tiryns; the "*cornice of blue kyanos*," a mystery before, is explained by the blue glass-like fragments found at Mycenæ. The exhumed graves and the earliest parts of Homer agree in having weapons of bronze and ornaments of iron; they agree substantially in their armour and their works of art, the inlaid daggers and shields, the lion-hunts and bull-hunts by men in chariots, and in the ostensible ignorance of writing.

On the other hand, the similarity only holds good for the earliest strata of the poems, and not fully even for them. Mycenæ buried her dead; the men of the epos burnt theirs—a practice which probably arose during the Sea Migrations, when the wanderers had no safe soil to lay their friends in. Tiryns actually used stone tools to make its bronze weapons, whereas the earliest epos knows of iron tools; and in general we may accept E. Meyer's account that the bloom of the epos lies in a 'middle age' between the Mycenæan and the classical periods.

Thus the general evidence of the subject-matter conspires with that of the language, to show that the oldest strata have been worked over from an Æolic into an Ionic shape; that the later parts were originally composed in Ionia in what then passed as 'Epic'—that is, in the same dialect as then appeared in the rest of the poems, with an unconsciously stronger tincture of Ionism; further, that the translation was gradual, and that the general development took centuries; and lastly, perhaps, that an all-important epoch in this development was formed by the great Race Migrations which are roughly dated about 1000 B.C. It seems to have been the Migrations that took the legendary war across the sea, when historical Æolians found themselves fighting in the Troad against Hissarlik, and liked to identify their own enemies with those of their ancestors ; the Migrations, which drew down the Northern heroes to the Peloponnese, when a stream of Greeks from the Inachus valley met in Asia a stream from Thessaly. The latter contributed their heroic saga ; the former brought the memory of the gigantic castles and material splendour of Tiryns and Mycenæ.

These Migrations present a phenomenon common enough in history, yet one which in romantic horror baffles a modern imagination : the vague noise of fighting in the North ; the silly human amusement at the troubles of one's old enemies over the border ; the rude awakening ; the flight of man, woman, and child ; the hasty shipbuilding ; the flinging of life and fortune on unknown waters. The boats of that day were at the mercy of any weather. The ordinary villagers can have had little seamanship. They were lost on the waves in thousands. They descended on strange coasts and died by famine or massacre. At the best, a friendly city would take in the wives and children, while the men set off grimly to seek, through unknown and monster-peopled seas, some spot of clear land to rest their feet upon. Aristarchus put Homer at the 'Ionic Migration.' This must be so far true that the Migrations—both Æolic and Ionic—stirred depths of inward experience which found outlet by turning a set of ballads into the great epos, by creating 'Homer.' It was from this adventurous exile that Ionia rose ; and the bloom of Ionia must have been the bloom of the epos.

CRITERIA OF AGE

As to determining the comparative dates of various parts of the poems, we have already noticed several possible clues. Bronze weapons are earlier than iron, open-air altars earlier than temples, leathern armour earlier than metal armour, individual foot-fighting (witness 'swift-footed Achilles') earlier than chariot-fighting, and this again than riding and the employment of columns of infantry. The use of 'Argos' for the plain of Thessaly is earlier than its vague use for Greece, and this than its secondary specialisation in the Peloponnese. But all such clues must be followed with extreme caution. Not only is it always possible for a late poet to use an archaic formula—even Sophocles can use χαλκὸς for a sword—but also the very earliest and most essential episodes have often been worked over and re-embellished down to the latest times. The slaying of Patroclus, for instance, contains some of the latest work in Homer; it was a favourite subject from the very outset, and new bards kept 'improving' upon it.

We find 'Hellas' and 'Achaia' following similar lines of development with Argos. They denote first Achilles's own district in Phthia, the home of those tribes which called their settlement in the Peloponnese 'Achaia,' and that in Italy 'Great Hellas.' But through most of the *Iliad* 'Achaioi' means the Greeks in general, while 'Hellas' is still the special district. In the *Odyssey* we find 'Hellas' in the later universal sense, and in *B* we meet the idea 'Panhellênes.' This is part of the expansion of the poet's geographical range : at first all the actors had really been 'Achaioi' or 'Argeioi'; afterwards the old

C

names 'Achaioi' and 'Argeioi' continued to be used to denote all the actors, though the actual area of the poems had widened far beyond the old limits and was widening still. The last parts of the *Odyssey* are quite familiar with Sicily and Kyrêne, and have some inklings of the interior of Russia, and perhaps of the Vikings of the far North.[1]

Another gradual growth is in the marriage-customs. Originally, as Aristotle noticed, the Greeks simply bought their wives; a good-looking daughter was valuable as being ἀλφεσίβοια, 'kine-winning,' because of the price, the ἕδνα, her suitors gave for her. In classical times the custom was the reverse; instead of receiving money for his daughter, the father had to give a dowry with her: and the late parts of the poems use ἕδνα in the sense of 'dowry.' There are several stages between, and one of the crimes of the suitors in the *Odyssey* is their refusal to pay ἕδνα.

Another criterion of age lies in the treatment of the supernatural. It is not only that the poems contain, as Rohde [2] has shown, traces of the earliest religion, ancestor-worship and propitiation of the dead, mixed with a later 'Ionic' spirit, daring and sceptical, which knows nothing of mysteries, and uses the gods for rhetorical ornament, or even for comic relief. There is also a marked development or degeneration in the use of supernatural machinery. In the earliest stages a divine presence is only introduced where there is a real mystery, where a supernatural explanation is necessary to the primitive mind. If Odysseus, entering the Phæacians' town at dusk, passes on and on safe and unnoticed, it seems as if Athena has

---

[1] The Laestrygones, especially κ, 82–86.
[2] *Psyche*, pp. 35 f.

thrown a cloud over him ; if Achilles, on the very point
of drawing his sword against his king, feels something
within warn and check him, it seems to be a divine hand
and voice.   Later on the gods come in as mere ornaments; they thwart one another; they become ordinary
characters in the poems.   The more divine interference
we get, the later is the work, until at last we reach the posi-
tively-marring masquerades of Athena in the *Odyssey* and
the offensive scenes of the gods fighting in *E* and *T*.   Not
that any original state of the poems can have done without the gods altogether.   The gods were not created in
Asia; they are 'Olympian,' and have their characters
and their formal epithets from the old home of the
Achaioi.

The treatment of individual gods, too, has its significance—though a local, not a chronological one.   Zeus
and Hera meet with little respect.   Iris is like the 'mal-
apert heralds' of Euripides.   Ares is frankly detested for
a bloodthirsty Thracian coward.   Aphrodite, who fights
because of some echo in her of the Phœnician Ashtaroth,
a really formidable warrior, is ridiculed and rebuked for
her fighting.   Only two gods are respectfully handled—
Apollo, who, though an ally of Troy, is a figure genuinely
divine; and Poseidon, who moves in a kind of rolling
splendour.   The reason is not far to seek : they are the
real gods of the Ionian.   The rest are, of course, gods ;
but they are 'other peoples' gods,' and our view of them
depends a good deal on our view of their worshippers.
Athena comes next in honour to the two Ionians ; in the
Odyssey and *K* she outstrips them.   Athens could manage
so much, but not more: she could not make the Ionian
poetry accept her stern goddess in her real grandeur ;
Athena remained in the epos a fighting woman, treache-

rous and bitter, though a good partisan. She will never be forgiven for the last betrayal of Hector.

Great caution must be used in estimating the significance of repetitions and quotations. For instance, the disguised Odysseus begins prophesying his return in τ, 303, with the natural appeal :—

> " *Zeus hear me first, of gods most high and great,*
> *And brave Odysseus' hearth, where I am come.*"

But when he says the same in ξ, 158, not only is the prophecy imprudent when he does not mean to be recognised, but he is also not at his own hearth at all, and a slight surplusage in the first line betrays the imitator : "Zeus, hear me first *of gods* and thy kind board." The passage is at home in τ, and not at home in ξ.

Similarly, what we hear in κ, 136, is natural :—

> " *In the isle there dwelt*
> *Kirkê fair-tress'd, dread goddess full of song.*"

Kirkê was essentially 'dread,' and her 'song' was magic incantation ; but in μ, 448, it runs :—

> " *Calypso in the isle*
> *Dwelleth fair-tress'd, dread goddess full of song.*"

Calypso was not specially 'dread' nor 'full of song,' except in imitation of Kirkê ; and, above all, to 'dwell fair-tress'd,' the verb and adjective thus joined, is not a possible Homeric manner of behaviour, as to 'dwell secure' or to 'lie prostrate' would be.

In the same way the description of Tartarus in *Theogony*, 720—"*As far 'neath earth as is the heaven above*"—is natural and original. Homer's "*As far 'neath hell as heaven is o'er the earth"* (Θ, 16) has the air of an imitation, exaggerating the language it copies.

Yet, as a matter of fact, Calypso (*Celatrix*, 'She who hides') is probably original in the Odysseus-saga, and Kirkê secondary. There were other legends where Kirkê had an independent existence ; and she had turned the Argonauts into bears and tigers before she was impressed to turn Odysseus's companions into pigs. And the *Theogony*, which is here quoted by the *Iliad*, itself quotes almost every part of both *Iliad* and *Odyssey*. The use of this criterion of quotation is affected by two things—first, all the passages in question may go back to an original which is now lost, sometimes to a definite passage in a lost epic, sometimes to a mere stock-in-trade formula ; secondly, the big epics were so long in process of active growth that they all had plenty of time to quote one another. We have mentioned the Odyssean and Hesiodic phrases in the slaying of Patroclus (Π, 380–480). But the most striking instance of all is that the Hades scene in ω, the very latest rag of the *Odyssey*, gives an account of the Suitor-slaying which agrees not with our version, but with the earlier account which our version has supplanted (p. 40).

Besides verbal imitations, we have more general references. For instance, the great catalogues in Homer, that of ships in *B*, of myrmidons in *Π*, of women in λ, are almost without question extracts from a Bœotian or 'Hesiodic' source. Again, much of δ consists of abridged and incomplete stories about the *Nostoi* or *Homecomings* of Agamemnon, Aias the Less, and Menelaus. They seem to imply a reference to some fuller and more detailed original—in all probability to the series of lays called the *Nostoi*, which formed

one of the rejected epics. The story in δ (242 ff.) about
Helen helping Odysseus in Troy, is definitely stated by
Proclus—a suspected witness, it is true—to occur in the
Little Iliad.* The succeeding one (271 ff.), makes Helen
hostile to the Greeks, and cannot come from the same
source. But it also reads like an abridgment. So does the
story of Bellerophon in Z : "*Proitos first sent him to slay
the Chimaira* : *now she was a thing divine and not mortal, in
front a lion, and behind a serpent, and in the middle a wild
goat, breathing furious fire. Yet he slew her, obeying the
signs of the gods.*" What signs, and how ? And what is
the meaning of the strange lines 200 f. ? "*But when he,
too, was hated of all the gods, then verily down the Plain of
Wandering alone he wandered, eating his heart, shunning
the tread of men.*" The original poem, whatever it was,
would have told us ; the *resumé* takes all the details for
granted.

Space does not allow more than a reference to that
criterion of date which has actually been most used in
the 'Higher Criticism'—the analysis of the story. It
might be interesting to note that the wall round the
ships in the *Iliad* is a late motive ; that it is built under
impossible circumstances; that it is sometimes there and
sometimes not, and that it seems to return mysteriously
after Apollo has flattened it into the ditch ; or that
Achilles in Π speaks as if the events of I had not
occurred ; or that Odysseus' adventures in κ and μ, and
perhaps in ι, seem to have been originally composed in
the third person, not the first, while his supposed false
stories in ξ and τ seem actually to represent older
versions of the real Odysseus-legend ; or that the poets
of τ and the following books do not seem to know that
Athena had transformed their hero in ν into a decrepit

old man, and that he had consistently remained so to the end of σ. But in all such criticism the detail is the life. We select one point for illustration — the Suitor-slaying.

In our present version Odysseus begins with the bow, uses up all his arrows, puts down the bow, and arms himself with spear and shield and helmet, which Têlemachus has meanwhile brought (χ, 98). What were those fifty desperate men with their swords doing while he was making the change ? Nearly all critics see here a combination of an old Bow-fight with a later Spear-fight. As to the former, let us start with the Feet-washing in τ. Odysseus is speaking with Penelope ; she is accompanied by Eurycleia and the handmaids. Odysseus dare not reveal himself directly, because he knows that the handmaids are false. He speaks to his wife in hints, tells her that he has seen Odysseus, who is in Thesprotia, and will for certain return before that dying year is out ! He would like to send the hand-maids away, but of course cannot. He bethinks him of his old nurse Eurycleia ; and, when refreshment is offered him, asks that she and none other (τ, 343 seq.) shall wash his feet. She does so, and instantly (τ, 392) recognises him by the scar ! Now, in our version, the man of many devices is taken by surprise at this ; he threatens Eurycleia into silence, and nothing happens. The next thing of importance is that Penelope—she has just learnt on good evidence that Odysseus is alive, and will return immediately—suddenly determines that she cannot put off the suitors any longer, but brings down her husband's bow, and says she will forthwith marry the man who can shoot through twelve axe-heads with it ! Odysseus hears her and is pleased ! May it not be that in the original story there was a reason for Penelope to bring the bow, and for Odysseus to be pleased? It was a plot. He meant Eurycleia to recognise him, to send the maids away, and break the news to Penelope. Then husband and wife together arranged the trial of the bow. This is so far only a conjecture, but it is curiously confirmed by the account of the slaying given by the ghost of Amphimedon in ω. The story he tells is not that of our *Odyssey*: it is the old Bow-slaying, based on a plot between husband and wife (esp. 167).

As to the Spear-fight, there is a passage in π, 281–298, which was condemned by the Alexandrians as inconsistent with the rest of the story. There Odysseus arranges with Têlemachus to have all the weapons in the banquet hall taken away, only two spears, two swords, and two shields to be left for the father and son. This led up to a Suitor-slaying with spears by Odysseus and Têlemachus, which is now incorporated as the second part of our Suitor-slaying. Otto Seeck[1] has tried to trace the Bow-fight and the Spear-fight (which was itself modified again) through all the relevant parts of the *Odyssey*.

It is curious that in points where we can compare the myths of our poems with those expressed elsewhere in literature, and in fifth-century pottery, our poems are often, perhaps generally, the more refined and modern. In the *Great Eoiai*,* the married pair Alkinoüs and Arêtê are undisguisedly brother and sister: our *Odyssey* explains elaborately that they were really only first cousins. When the shipwrecked Odysseus meets Nausicaa, he pulls a bough off a tree—what for? To show that he is a suppliant, obviously: and so a fifth-

---

[1] *Quellen der Odyssee*, 1887.

century vase represents it. But our *Odyssey* makes him use the branch as a veil to conceal his nakedness! And so do the vases of the fourth century. A version of the slaying of Hector followed by Sophocles in his *Niptra** made Achilles drag his enemy alive at his chariot wheels. That is the cruder, crueller version. Our poems cannot suppress the savage insult, but they have got rid of the torture. How and when did this humanising tendency come? We cannot say; but it was deliberately preferred and canonised when the poems were prepared for the sacred Athenian recitation.

This moral growth is one of the marks of the last working over of the poems. It gives us the magnificent studies of Helen and Andromache, not dumb objects of barter and plunder, as they once were, but women ready to take their places in the conception of Æschylus. It gives us the gentle and splendid chivalry of the Lycians, Sarpêdon and Glaucus. It gives us the exquisite character of the swineherd Eumæus; his eager generosity towards the stranger who can tell of Odysseus, all the time that he keeps professing his incredulity; his quaint honesty in feeding himself, his guest, and even Têlemachus, on the young inferior pork, keeping the best, as far as the suitors allow, for his master (ξ, 3, 80; π, 49); and his emotional breach of principle, accompanied with much apology and justification, when the story has entirely won him: "*Bring forth the best of the hogs!*" (ξ, 414). Above all, it seems to have given us the sympathetic development of Hector. The oldest poem hated Hector, and rejoiced in mangling him, though doubtless it feared him as well, and let him have a better right to his name 'Man-slayer' than he has now, when not only Achilles, but Diomêdes, Aias,

Idomeneus, and even Menelaus, have successively been made more than a match for him. In that aspect Hector has lost, but he has gained more. The prevailing sympathy of the later books is with him. The two most explicit moral judgments in the poems are against Achilles for maltreating him.[1] The gods keep his body whole, and rebuke his enemy's savagery. The scenes in Z, the parting with Andromache, the comforting of little Astyanax frightened at his father's plume, the calm acceptance of a battle which must be fatal, and of a cause which must be lost—all these are in the essence of great imagination ; but the absolute masterpiece, one of the greatest feats of skill in imaginative literature, is the flight of Hector in X. It is simple fear, undisguised ; yet you feel that the man who flies is a brave man. The act of staying alone outside the gate is much ; you can just nerve yourself to it. But the sickening dread of Achilles' distant oncoming grows as you wait, till it simply cannot be borne. The man must fly ; no one can blame him ; it is only one more drop in the cup of divine cruelty, which is to leave Hector dead, Troy burned, Astyanax butchered, and Andromache her enemy's slave. If the old poet went with the conqueror, and exulted in Hector's shame, there has come one after him who takes all his facts and turns them the other way ; who feels how far more intense the experience of the conquered always is, and in this case how far more noble.

The wonder is that Achilles is not spoilt for us. Somehow he remains grand to the end, and one is grieved, not alienated, by the atrocities his grief leads him to. The last touch of this particular spirit is where Achilles receives

---

[1] Ψ, 24; X, 395; and Ψ, 176; Υ, 467.

Priam in his tent. Each respects the other, each con-
quers his anguish in studied courtesy ; but the name of
Hector can scarcely be spoken, and the attendants keep
the dead face hidden, lest at the sight of it Priam's rage
should burst its control, "*and Achilles slay him and sin
against God*" (Ω, 585).   It is the true pathos of war :
the thing seen on both sides ; the unfathomable suffering for which no one in particular is to blame.
Homer, because he is an 'early poet,' is sometimes
supposed to be unsubtle, and even superficial.   But is
it not a marvel of sympathetic imagination which makes
us feel with the flying Hector, the cruel Achilles, the
adulterous Helen, without for an instant losing hold of
the ideals of courage, mercifulness, and chastity ?

This power of entering vividly into the feelings of
both parties in a conflict is perhaps the most characteristic gift of the Greek genius ; it is the spirit in which
Homer, Æschylus, Herodotus, Euripides, Thucydides,
find their kinship, and which enabled Athens to create
the drama.

II

LESSER HOMERIC POEMS; HESIOD; ORPHEUS

THE REJECTED EPICS

WHEN amid the floating masses of recited epos two poems were specially isolated and organised into complex unity, there remained a quantity of authorless poetry, originally of equal rank with the exalted two, but now mangled and disinherited. This rejected poetry was not fully organised into distinct wholes. The lays and groups of lays were left for each reciter to modify and to select from. It is an anachronism to map out a series of epics, to cut off *Cypria*,* *Iliad*, *Æthiopis*,* *Little Iliad*,* *Sack of Ilion*,* *Homecomings*,* *Odyssey*, *Têlegoneia*,* as so many separate and continuous poems composed by particular authors. The *Cypria*,* for instance, a great mass of 'Epê' centring in the deeds of Paris and the Cyprian goddess before the war, is attributed to Homer, Creophŷlus, Cyprias, Hêgêsias, and Stasînus; the *Sack** is claimed by Homer, Arctînus, Leschês, and a poet whose name is given as Hegias, Agias, or Augias, and his home as Troizên or Colophon. Some of these names perhaps belonged to real rhapsodes; some are mere inventions. 'Cyprias,' for instance, owes his existence to the happy thought that in the phrase τὰ Κύπρια ἔπη the second word might be the Doric genitive of a proper name, Κυπρίας, and then the question of authorship would be solved.

When the oral poetry was dead, perhaps in the fourth century B.C., scholars began to collect the remnants of it, the series being, in the words of Proclus, "made complete out of the works of divers poets." But this collection of the original ballads was never widely read, and soon ceased to exist. Our knowledge of the rejected epics comes almost entirely from the handbooks of mythology, which collected the legendary history contained in them into groups or 'cycles.' We possess several stone tablets giving the epic history in a series of pictures.[1] The best known is the *Tabula Iliaca*, in the Capitoline Museum, which dates from just before our era, and claims to give 'the arrangement of Homer' according to a certain Theodôrus. One of the tables speaks of the 'Trojan Cycle' and the 'Theban Cycle'; and we hear of a 'Cycle of History'—of all history, it would seem—compiled by Dionysius of Samos[2] in the third or second century B.C. The phrase 'Epic Cycle' then denotes properly a body of epic history collected in a handbook. By an easy misapplication, it is used to denote the ancient poems themselves, which were only known as the sources of the handbooks. Athenæus, for instance, makes the odd mistake of calling Dionysius' 'Cycle of History' a 'Book about the Cycle'—*i.e.* Athenæus took the word 'cycle' to mean the original poems.[3]

Our main ostensible authority is one Proclus, apparently a Byzantine, from whom we derive a summary of the Trojan Cycle, which is given in the Venetian MS. *A* and in the works of the patriarch Photius. If what he said were true, it would be of great importance. But not

---

[1] Jahn-Michaelis, *Bilder-Chroniken.* The *Tab. Il.* is in Baumeister's *Denkmäler.*

[2] See Bethe in *Hermes*, 26.   [3] Ath. 481 *e*, 477 *d*.

only does he start from a false conception of what the poems were—they had probably perished before the days of Pausanias, centuries earlier—he also seems to have reached his results by first taking the contents of some handbook, of which we can only say that it often agrees word for word with that of Apollodôrus, and then, by conjecture or otherwise, inserting " *Here begins the Little Iliad of Leschês of Mitylênê*," or " *Here comes the Æthiopis of Arctînus of Milêtus.*"   It is known from quotations in earlier writers that the individual poems covered much more ground than he allows them.   For instance, the *Little Iliad* * begins in Proclus with the contest of Aias and Odysseus for the arms of Achilles, and stops at the reception of the Wooden Horse.   But a much earlier beginning is suggested by the opening words of the poem itself, which still survive : " *I sing of Ilion and Dardania, land of chivalry, for which the Danaoi, henchmen of Ares, suffered many things ;*" and a later ending is proved by the quotations which are made from it to illustrate the actual sack.   It is the origin, for instance, of Vergil's story about the warrior who means to slay Helen, but is restrained by Venus ; only in the *Little Iliad* it is Helen's beauty unaided that paralyses Menelaus. In general, however, Vergil, like Proclus's authority, prefers the fuller version derived from the special epic on the Sack by 'Arctînus of Milêtus,' while Theodôrus again sets aside both epics and follows the lyrical *Sack* of Stesichorus.

Again, Proclus makes the *Æthiopis* * and the *Sack* * two separate poems with a great gap between them.   His *Æthiopis* * begins immediately at the end of the *Iliad*, gives the exploits of the Amazon Penthesileia and the Æthiop Memnon, and ends with the contest for the

arms of Achilles ; the *Sack** begins after the reception
of the Wooden Horse. The *Æthiopis** has five books,
the *Sack** two; seven in all. But one of the tables treats
them both as a single continuous poem of 9500 lines,
which must mean at the very least ten books. On the
other hand, Proclus makes the *Homecomings*,* which
must have been a series of separate lays almost as elastic
as the *Eoiai** themselves (see p. 60), into a single poem.

As for the date of these poems, they were worked into
final shape much later than our Homer, and then apparently more for their historical matter than for their poetic
value. They quote *Iliad*, *Odyssey*, and *Theogony ;* they
are sometimes brazen in their neglect of the digamma ;
they are often modern and poor in their language. On
the other hand, it is surely perverse to take their mentions
of ancestor-worship, magic, purification, and the like,
as evidence of lateness. These are all practices of date-
less antiquity, left unmentioned by ' Homer,' like many
other subjects, from some conventional repugnance,
whether of race, or class, or tradition. And the actual
matter of the rejected epics is often very old. We
have seen the relation of δ to the *Little Iliad*.* In the
Cypria* Alexander appears in his early glory as conqueror of Sidon ; there is a catalogue of Trojans which
cannot well have been copied from our meagre list in *B*,
and is perhaps the source of it ; there is a story told by
Nestor which looks like the original of part of our Hades-
legend in λ. And as for quotations, the words " *The
purpose of Zeus was fulfilled*" are certainly less natural
where they stand in the opening of the *Iliad* than in
the *Cypria*,* where they refer to the whole design of
relieving Earth of her burden of men by means of the
Trojan War. We have 125 separate quotations from the

*Cypria,** which seems to have stood rather apart and independent in the general epic tradition.

The *Têlegoneia,** too, though in its essence a mere sequel, making Têlegonus, son of Odysseus and Kirkê, sail in search of his father, just as Têlemachus did, is full of genuine saga-stuff. Odysseus is repeated in his son, like Achilles, like Launcelot and Tristram. The sons of the 'Far-wanderer' are 'Far-fighter' and 'Far-born,' and a third, by Calypso, is 'Far-subduer' (Têle-damus). The bowman has a bowman son, and the son wanders because the father did. And the end of the *Têlegoneia** is in the simplest saga-spirit. Têlegonus unknowingly slays his father, who gives him Penelope to wed and protect. He takes all the characters to Kirkê in the magic island ; she purifies him of blood, and makes Têlemachus and Penelope immortal ; finally, the two young men marry their respective step-mothers, Odysseus apparently remaining dead. That is not late or refined work. 'Eugamon' ('Happy-marrier') of Cyrene must have seemed a grotesque figure to the men of the fifth century ; he was at home among those old saga-makers who let Heracles give Deianira to Hyllus, and Œdipus take on the late king's wife as part of the establishment.

The critical questions suggested by the rejected epics are innumerable. To take one instance, how comes it that the *Little Iliad** alone in our tradition is left in so thin a dress of conventional 'Epic' language that the Æolic shows through ? One line actually gives the broad *a* and probably the double consonants of Æolic, νὺξ μὲν ἔην μέσσα, λαμπρὰ δ' ἐπέτελλε σελάνα. Others are merely conventionalised on the surface. Possibly some epics continued to be sung in Lesbos in the native dialect till the era of antiquarian collection in the fourth century B.C. or after ; and perhaps if this poem were ever unearthed from an Egyptian tomb, we should have a specimen of the loose and popular epic not yet elaborated by Ionic genius. Its style in general seems light and callous compared with the stern tragedy of the Milesian *Æthiopis* * and *Sack of Ilion.* *

Among the other rejected epics were poems of what might be called the *World-cycle*. Of these, Proclus uses the *Theogony* * and the *Titan War*,* of which last there exists one really beautiful fragment. The Theban 'Ring,' which was treated by grammarians as an introduction to the Trojan, had an *Œdipodea*,* a *Thebais*,* and a *Lay of the After-born*,* treating of the descendants of the Seven, who destroyed Thebes. The *Driving forth of Amphiaraus*,* the *Taking of Œchalia*,* the *Phocais*,* the *Danais*,* and many more we pass over.

HYMNS OR PRELUDES

It was a custom in epic poetry for the minstrel to 'begin from a god,' generally from Zeus or the Muses.[1] This gave rise to the cultivation of the ' Pro-oimion ' or Prelude as a separate form of art, specimens of which survive in the so-called Homeric ' Hymns,' the word ὕμνος having in early Greek no religious connotation. The shortest of these preludes merely call on the god by his titles, refer briefly to some of his achievements, and finish by a line like, " *Hail to thee, Lord ; and now begin my lay*," or, " *Beginning from thee, I will pass to another song.*" [2] The five longer hymns are, like Pindar's victory songs, illustrations of the degree to which a

---

[1] Pind., *Nem.* 2. *Cf. θ*, 499.   [2] See esp. 31.

D

form of art can grow beyond itself before it is felt to be artistically impossible. The prelude was developed as a thing apart until it ceased to be a prelude.

The collection which we possess contains poems of diverse dates and localities, and the tradition of the text is singularly confused. The first 546 lines, for instance, are given as one hymn 'to Apollo.' But they comprise certainly two hymns : the first (1–178) by an Ionic poet, on the birth of the Ionian God in the floating island of Delos ; the second by a poet of Central Greece, on the slaying of the great Earth-serpent, and the establishment of the Dorian God at Delphi. Further, these two divisions are not single poems, but fall into separate incomplete parts. Athenæus actually calls the whole 'the hymns to Apollo.' The Ionic portion of this hymn is probably the earliest work in the extant collection. It is quoted as Homer's by Thucydides (iii. 104), and Aristophanes (*Birds*, 575), and attributed by Didymus the grammarian to the rhapsode Kynæthus of Chios ; which puts it, in point of antiquity, on a level with the rejected epics. The hymn to Hermes partly dates itself by giving seven strings to the original lyre as invented by that god. It must have been written when the old four-stringed lyre had passed, not only out of use, but out of memory. The beautiful fragment (vii.) on the capture of Dionysus by brigands looks like Attic work of the fifth or fourth century B.C. The Prelude to Pan (xix.) may be Alexandrian ; that to Ares (viii.) suggests the fourth century A.D.

In spite of their bad preservation, our Hymns are delightful reading. That to Aphrodite, relating nothing but the visit of Aphrodite to Anchises shepherding his kine on Mount Ida, expresses perhaps more exquisitely than anything else in Greek literature that frank joy in physical life and beauty which is often supposed to be characteristic of Greece. The long hymn to Demeter, extant in only one MS., which was discovered last century at Moscow 'among pigs and chickens,' is perhaps the most beautiful of all. It is interesting as an early Attic or Eleusinian composition. Parts are perhaps rather fluent and weak, but most of the poem is worthy of the magnificent myth on which it is founded. Take one piece at the opening, where Persephone "*was playing with Okeanos' deep-breasted daughters, and plucking flowers, roses and crocus and pretty pansies, in a soft meadow, and flags and hyacinth, and that great narcissus that Earth sent up for a snare to the rose-face maiden, doing service by God's will to Him of the Many Guests. The bloom of it was wonderful, a marvel for gods undying and mortal men; from the root of it there grew out a hundred heads, and the incensed smell of it made all the wide sky laugh above, and all the earth laugh and the salt swell of the sea. And the girl in wonder reached out both her hands to take the beautiful thing to play with; then yawned the broad-trod ground by the Flat of Nysa, and the deathless steeds brake forth, and the Cronos-born king, He of the Many Names, of the Many Guests; and He swept her away on his golden chariot.*" The dark splendour of Aidôneus, "*Him of the Many Thralls, of the Many Guests,*" is in the highest spirit of the saga.

COMIC POEMS

Of the Comic Poems which passed in antiquity as Homer's, the only extant example is the *Battle of the Frogs and Mice,* rather a good parody of the fighting

epic. The opening is Bœotian ; the general colour of
the poem Attic. An obvious fable—followed strangely
enough by A. Ludwich in his large edition—gives it to
one Pigres, a Carian chief, who fought in the Persian
War. The battle began because a mouse named
Psicharpax, flying from a weasel, came to a pond to
quench his thirst. He was accosted by a frog of royal
race, Physignathos, son of Peleus—(the hero of Mount
Pelion has become 'Mudman,' and his son ' Puff-cheek' !)
—who persuaded him to have a ride on his back and see
his kingdom. Unhappily a ' Hydros '—usually a water-
snake, here perhaps some otter-like animal—lifted its
head above the water, and the frog instinctively dived.
The mouse perished, but not unavenged. A kinsman
saw him from the bank, and from the blood-feud
arose a great war, in which the mice had the best of it.
At last Athena besought Zeus to prevent the annihilation
of the frogs. He tried first thunderbolts and then crabs,
which latter were more than the mice could stand ; they
turned, and the war ended.

There were many comic battle-pieces ; we hear of a
Spider-fight,* a *Crane-fight,** a *Fieldfare-poem.** Some
were in iambics, and consequently foreign to the Homeric style. The most celebrated comic poem was the *Margîtes,** so called after its hero, a roaring blade (μάργος),
high-spirited and incompetent, whose characteristic is
given in the immortal line—

πόλλ' ἠπίστατο ἐργὰ, κακῶς δ' ἠπίστατο πάντα.

" *Many arts he knew, and he knew them all badly ;* " and
again : " *He was not meant by the gods for a digger or a
ploughman, nor generally for anything sensible ; he was
deficient in all manner of wisdom.*" Late writers on metre

say the poem was in a mixture of heroic and iambic verse, a statement which suggests a late metrical refurbishment of a traditional subject. It can scarcely be true of the poem which Aristotle regarded as Homer's. Margîtes must have been more amusing than Hierocles's 'Scholasticus,' the hero of the joke-book from which so many of our 'Joe Millers' are taken. Scholasticus was a mere fool, with nothing but a certain modesty to recommend him.

What is meant by calling these poems Homeric? Only that they date from a time when it was not thought worth while to record the author's name ; and, perhaps, that if you mean to recite a mock epic battle, it slightly improves your joke to introduce it as the work of the immortal Homer.

HESIOD

As the epos of romance and war was personified in 'Homêros,' the bard of princes, so the epos of plain teaching was personified in the peasant poet 'Hêsiodos.' The Hesiodic poems, indeed, contain certain pretended reminiscences, and one of them, the *Erga*, is largely made up of addresses to 'Persês,' assumed to be the poet's erring friend—in one part, his brother. We have seen that the reminiscences are fictions, and presumably Persês is a fiction too. If a real man had treacherously robbed Hesiod of his patrimony by means of bribes to 'man-devouring princes,' Hesiod would scarcely have remained on intimate terms with him. 'Persês' is a lay figure for the didactic epos to preach at, and as such he does his duty. Hesiod wants to praise industry, to condemn the ways of men, and especially of judges : the figure must be an idle dog, ignorant of the world and fond of law. Hesiod wants to praise righteousness : the figure must show a certain light-handedness in its dealings with money. We have then no information of what Hesiod was—only a tradition of what Hesiod was supposed to be. He was born at Kymê, in Æolis ; his father migrated to Bœotia, and settled in Ascra, a charming and fertile village on the slopes of Mount Helicon, which the poet describes as "*bad in winter, insufferable in summer.*" Here he herded flocks on Helicon, till one day the Muses greeted him with the words : "*Boors of the wild fields, by-words of shame, nothing but belly ! We know how to tell many false things true-seeming, but we know how to speak the real truth when we will.*" This made Hesiod a poet. We hear nothing more of him till his death, except that he once went across the channel from Aulis to Chalkis to take part in a competition at the funeral games of Amphidamas, king of Eubœa, and, although much of his advice is about nautical matters, that he did not enjoy the sea. He avoided Southern Greece because of an oracle which foretold that he should die at Nemea ; and so he did, at a little sanctuary near Oineon in Locris, which happened to bear that name. He was murdered and thrown into the sea by the brothers of one Clymenê or Ctimenê, who was supposed to have borne a son to the octogenarian poet ; but the dolphins brought the body to land, and a stately tomb was built for it at Oineon. The son was the great lyrist Stêsichorus !

This is not even pure myth, it is myth worked up by ancient scholars. Yet we can perhaps get some historical meaning out of their figments. The whole evidence of the poems goes to suggest that there was a very old peasant-poetry in Bœotia, the direct descendant in all likelihood of the old Æolian lays of the Achaioi, from which 'Homer' was developed; and that this was at some time enriched and invigorated by the reaction upon it of the full-flown Ionian epic. That is, Ionian poets must have settled in Bœotia and taken up the local poetry. Whether one of those poets was called 'Hêsiodos' is a question of little importance. It does not look like an invented name. At any rate, the Bœotian poetry flourished, and developed a special epic form, based on the Ionian 'Homer,' but with strong local traits.

What of Hesiod's death ? We know that the Hesiodic poetry covered Locris as well as Bœotia ; the catalogues of women are especially Locrian. The Clymenê story is suggested, doubtless, by a wish to provide a romantic and glorious ancestry for Stêsichorus. Does the rest of the story mean that Locris counted Hesiod as her own, and showed his grave ; while Bœotia said he was a Bœotian, and explained the grave by saying that the Locrians had murdered him ? As for the victory at the funeral games of Amphidamas, it is a late insertion, and the unnamed rivals must be meant to include Homer. The story of a contest between Homer and Hesiod, in which the latter won, can be traced back, as we saw (p. 6), to the fifth century at least.

Of Hesiod's poems we have nominally three preserved, but they might as well be called a dozen, so little unity has any one of them—the *Theogony*, the *Works and Days* (*Erga*), and the *Shield of Heracles*.

The *Works and Days* is a poem on '*Erga*,' or *Works* of agriculture, with an appendix on the lucky and unlucky *Days* of the month, and an intertexture of moral sentences addressed to Perses. It is a slow, lowly, simple poem ; a little rough and hard, the utterance of those

Muses who like to tell the truth. There is no swing in the verses ; they seem to come from a tired, bent man at the end of his day's work—a man who loves the country life, but would like it better if he had more food and less toil. There is little sentiment. The outspoken bitterness of the first 'Gnômê' is characteristic : *"Potter is wroth with potter, and carpenter with carpenter ; aye, beggar is envious of beggar, and minstrel of minstrel!"* `So is the next about the judges who rob the poor man : *" Fools, they know not how the half is more than the whole, nor the great joy there is in mallow and asphodel."* Mallow and asphodel were the food and flowers of the poor. The moral sentences increase in depth in the middle of the poem, and show a true and rather amiable idea of duty. *" Hard work is no shame ; the shame is idleness."* *" Help your neighbour, and he will help you. A neighbour matters more than a kinsman."* *" Take fair measure, and give a little over the measure—if you can."* *" Give willingly ; a willing gift is a pleasure."* *" Give is a good girl, and Snatch is a bad girl, a bringer of death!"* *" It is best to marry a wife ; but be very careful, or your neighbours may be merry at your expense. There is no prize like a good wife : nothing that makes you shudder like a bad ; she roasts you without fire, and brings you to a raw old age."* At the end these sentences degenerate into rules of popular superstition—*" not to put the jug on the mixing-bowl when drinking ; that means death!"* *" not to sit on immovable things,"* and so on. One warning, *" not to cross a river without washing your hands and your sins,"* approaches Orphism.

The agricultural parts of the *Erga* are genuine and country-like. They may be regarded as the gist of the poem, the rest being insertions and additions. There is the story how the gods had "hidden away his life from man," till good Promêtheus stole fire and gave it him. Then Zeus, to be even with him, made a shape like a gentle maiden, and every god gave it a separate charm, and Hermes last put in it the heart of a dog and the ways of a thief. And the gods called it Pandôra, and gave it to Epimêtheus, who accepted it on behalf of mankind. There is the story of the four ages : at least there ought to be four—gold, silver, bronze, and iron ; but, under the influence of Homer, the heroes who fought at Troy have to come in somewhere. They are put just after the bronze and before ourselves. We are iron ; and, bad as we are, are likely to get worse. The gods have all left us, except Aidôs and Nemesis —those two lovely ideas which the sophist Protagoras made the basis of social ethics, and which we miserably translate into *Shame* and *Righteous Indignation*. Some day, Hesiod thinks, we shall drive even them away, and all will be lost. Two passages, indeed, do suggest the possibility of a brighter future : all may be well when the Demos at last arises and punishes the sins of the princes (175, 260 ff.). It is interesting to compare the loyalty of the prosperous Ionian epos towards its primitive kings with the bitter insurgency of the Bœotian peasant-song against its oligarchy of nobles.

The *Erga* is delightful in its descriptions of the seasons —a subject that touched Greek feelings down to the days of Longus. Take the month of Lenaion, "*bad days, enough to flay an ox, when the north wind rides down from Thrace, and earth and the plants shut themselves up ; and he falls on the forest and brings down great oaks and pines; and all the wood groans, and the wild beasts shiver and put their tails between their legs. Their hides are thick with fur, but the cold blows through them, and through the bull's hide and the goat's thick hair; but it cannot blow through to the gentle little girl who sits in the cottage with her mother,"* and so on. And how good the summer is, in which foolish people have made it a reproach against Hesiod's poetic sensitiveness that he liked to sit in the shadow of a rock and have a picnic with milk and wine and plenty of goats' flesh.

The *Theogony* is an attempt, of course hopelessly inadequate, to give a connected account of the gods, their origins and relationships. Some of it is more than old ; it is primeval. Several folk-gods occur whose names are found in Sanskrit, and who therefore may be imagined to date from Indo - European times, though they are too homely to occur in the heroic epos : Hestia, Rhea, Orthros, Kerberos. We are dealing with most ancient material in the *Theogony ;* but the language, the present form of the poem, and perhaps the very idea of systematising the gods, are comparatively late. The *Erga* 702 is quoted by Semonides (about 650 B.C.). But it is impossible to date the poems. We have seen (p. 37) that the *Theogony* is quoted by the *Iliad*—whereas the *Theogony* often quotes the *Iliad* and *Odyssey*, and at the end refers to the matter of several of the rejected epics. The text is in a bad condition ; it is often hard to see the connection or the sense. It almost looks as if there were traces of a rhapsode's notes, which could be expanded in recitation. There are remains of real, not merely literary, religion. Erôs (120), Love, is prominent, because he was specially worshipped in Thespiæ, Ascra's nearest big town. Hecatê has a hymn (411–452) so earnest that it can only come from a local cult. A great part of the poem, the mutilation of Ouranos, the cannibalism of Cronos, only ceases to be repulsive when it is studied as a genuine bit of savage religion. To those of the later Greeks who took it more seriously, it was of course intolerable. There is real grandeur in the account of the Titan War, which doubtless would be intelligible if we had the Homeric *Titan War* * before us. And there is a great sea-feeling in the list of Nereids (347 ff.).

The *Theogony* ends (967–1020) with a list of the goddesses who lay in the arms of mortals and bore children like the gods. In the very last lines the poet turns from these—"*Now, sweet Muses, sing the race of mortal women.*" Of course, the Muses did sing of them, but the song is lost. It is referred to in antiquity by various names—'*The Catalogue of Women,*' '*The Poems about Women,*' '*The Lists of Heroic Women*'; particular parts of it are quoted as '*The Eoiai,*' '*The Lists of the Daughters of Leukippos,*' '*of the Daughters of Proitos,*' and so on.

Why were lists of women written ? For two reasons. The Locrians are said to have counted their genealogies by the woman's side ; and if this, as it stands, is an exaggeration, there is good evidence, apart from Nossis and her fellow-poetesses, for the importance of women in Locris. Secondly, most royal houses in Greece were descended from a god. In the days of local quasi-monotheistic religion this was simply managed : the local king came from the local god. But when geographical boundaries were broken down, and the number of known gods consequently increased, these genealogies had to be systematised, and sometimes amended. For instance, certain Thessalian kings were descended from Tyro and the river Enîpeus. This was well enough in their own valley ; but when they came out into the world, they found there families descended from Poseidon, the god of the great sea, perhaps of all waters, and they could not remain content with a mere local river. In *Odyssey* λ we have the second stage of the story : the real ancestor was Poseidon, only he visited Tyro disguised as the river ! The comparatively stable human ancestresses form the safest basis for cataloguing the shifting divine ancestors. There were five books in the Alexandrian edition of the *Catalogues of Women*,* the last two being what is called *Eoiai*.* This quaint title is a half-humorous plural of the expression ἤ οἵη, ' *Or like*,' . . . which was the form of transition to a new heroine, " *Or like her who dwelt in Phthia, with the Charites' own loveliness, by the waters of Pênêus, Cyrene the fair.*" There are one hundred and twenty - four fragments of the *Catalogue** and twenty - six of the ' *Or likes.*' * If they sometimes contradict each other, that is natural enough, and it cannot be held that the Alexandrian five books had all the women there ever were in the Hesiodic lists. When once the formula ' *Or like*' was started, it was as easy to put a new ancestress into the list as it is, say, to invent a new quatrain on the model of Edward Lear's. Furthermore, it was easy to expand a given *Eoiê** into a story, and this is actually the genesis of our third Hesiodic poem, the *Shield of Heracles*, the ancestress being, of course, the hero's mother, Alcmênê.

The *Shield* begins : " *Or like Alcmênê, when she fled her home and fatherland, and came to Thebes ;*" it goes on to the birth of Heracles, who, it proceeds to say, slew Kyknos, and then it tells how he slew Kyknos. In the arming of Heracles before the battle comes a long description of the shield.

There were rejected poems in Hesiod's case as well as in Homer's. The anonymous *Naupactia*,* a series of expanded genealogies, is the best known of them ; but there were Hesiodic elements in some of the Argive and Corinthian collections attributed to 'Eumêlus.' His main rival rejoices in the fictitious name of Kerkôps ('Monkey-face') of Miletus. The *Erga* is Hesiod's *Iliad*, the only work unanimously left to him. The people of Helicon showed Pausanias, or his authority, a leaden tablet of the *Erga* without the introduction, and told him that nothing else was the true Hesiod.[1]

The *Bridal of Keyx*,* about a prince of Trachis, who entertained Heracles, was probably also an expanded *Eoiê* very like the *Shield ;* and the same perhaps holds of the *Aigimios*,* which seems to have narrated in two books the battle of that ancestor of the Dorians against the Lapithæ. The *Descent to Hades** had Theseus for its hero. The *Melampodia** was probably an account of divers celebrated seers. More interesting are the scanty remains of the *Advices of Chiron** to his pupil Achilles. The wise Centaur recommended sacrificing to the gods whenever you come to a house, and thought that education should not begin till the age of seven.

The *Erga* was known in an expanded form, *The Great Erga*.* There were poems on *Astronomy** and on *Augury by Birds*,* on a *Journey round the World*,* and on the *Idæan Dactyli*,* who attended Zeus in Crete. The names help us to realise the great mass of poetry of the Bœotian school that was at one time in existence. As every heroic story tended to take shape in a poem, so did every piece of art or knowledge or

[1] Paus. ix. 31, 4.

ethical belief which stirred the national interest or the emotions of a particular poet.

ORPHEUS—REVELATION AND MYSTICISM

In studying the social and the literary history of Greece, we are met by one striking contrast. The social history shows us the Greeks, as the Athenians thought themselves, ' especially god - fearing,' or, as St. Paul put it, 'too superstitious.' The literature as preserved is entirely secular. Homer and Hesiod mention the gods constantly ; but Homer treats them as elements of romance, Hesiod treats them as facts to be catalogued. Where is the literature of religion, the literature which treated the gods as gods ? It must have existed. The nation which had a shrine at every turn of its mountain paths, a religious ceremony for every act of daily life, spirits in every wood and river and spring, and heroes for every great deed or stirring idea, real or imagined ; which sacrificed the defence of Thermopylæ rather than cut short a festival ; whose most enlightened city at its most sceptical time allowed an army to be paralysed and lost because of an eclipse of the moon, and went crazy because the time - honoured indecencies of a number of statues were removed without authority — that nation is not adequately represented by a purely secular literature. As a matter of fact, we can see that the religious writings were both early and multitudinous.

The Vedic hymns offer an analogy. Hymns like them are implied by the fact that the titles of the Homeric gods, ἑκάεργος Ἀπόλλων, βοῶπις πότνια Ἥρη, ἑκατηβελέταο ἄνακτος, are obviously ancient, and are constructed with a view to dactylic metre. We know that the early oracles spoke in verse. We know that there were sacred hymns in temples, quite distinct from our secular Homeric preludes. We have evidence that the Mysteries at Eleusis depended in part on the singing of sacred music.

The Mysteries are not mentioned by Homer. That does not mean that they are late : it means that they are either too sacred or else too popular. The discoveries of anthropologists now enable us to see that the Eleusinian Mysteries are a form of that primitive religion, scarcely differentiated from 'sympathetic magic,' which has existed in so many diverse races. The Mysteries were a drama. The myth of the Mother of Corn and the Maid, the young corn who comes up from beneath the earth and is the giver of wealth, was represented in action. At the earliest time we hear of, the drama included a vine-god, or perhaps a tree-god in general, Dionysus. This is corn-worship and vegetation-worship : it is not only early, but primitive.

There were other Mysteries, Orphic or Bacchic. The common opinion of antiquity and the present day is that the Bacchic rites were introduced to Greece from abroad — the god of the Thracian brought, in spite of opposition, into Greece. If so, he came very early. But it seems more likely that Dionysus is rather a new-comer than a foreigner : he is like the new year, the spring, the harvest, the vintage. He is each year, in every place, a stranger who comes to the land and is welcomed as a stranger ; at the end of his time he is expelled, exorcised, cut to pieces or driven away. At any rate he is early, and for the real religion of Greece he is of overwhelming importance. A real religion is a people's religion. The great complex conception Dionysus-Bacchus was a common folk's god, or rather had united in himself an indefinite number of similar conceptions which were worshipped by common folk all over Greece. We hear of him mostly through Alexandrian and Roman sources, sceptical through and through, in which he is merely the god of wine. But this is degradation by narrowing. He is a wine-god ; he is a tree-god ; but above all he is one of the personifications of the spirit of ecstasy, the impulse that is above reason, that lifts man beyond himself, gives him power and blessedness, and lets loose the immortal soul from the trammels of the body. The same spirit, in a tamer, saner, and more artistic form, was absorbed in the very different conception of Apollo. This religion doubtless had the most diverse forms. The gods it worshipped varied in names and attributes as they varied in their centres of initiation. But the most important aspects of it seem to have been more or less united in the religious revelations of 'Orpheus.'

Most of the old religious poems belonged to Orpheus or his kinsman Musæus, as the heroic poems to Homer, and the didactic to Hesiod. But we know nothing of them before the great religious revival of the sixth century, associated with the name of Onomacritus. The old separate cults of tribe and family had been disturbed by increasing intercourse. Agglomerated in the Homeric theology, they lost their sanctity ; and they could scarcely survive Hesiod and his catalogues. Hence came, on the one hand, scepticism embodied in the Ionian philosophy, and the explanation of the world by natural science ; on the other hand, a deeper, more passionate belief. It was all very well for Thales to be saved by knowledge; the common man could not look that way. Amid the discouragements of the sixth century, the ebb of colonisation, the internal wars, the fall of Sybaris and of the half-divine Nineveh, came the turning away from this life to the next, the setting of the heart on supernatural bliss above the reach of war and accident.

Hence arose a great wave of religious emotion scarcely represented in our tradition, but affecting every oracle and popular temple from Caria to Italy. The main expression of this movement was Orphism. It appears first as an outburst of personal miracle-working religion in connection with Dionysus-worship. We can make out many of the cardinal tenets. It believed in sin and the sacerdotal purging of sin; in the immortality and divinity of the soul; in eternal reward beyond the grave to the 'pure' and the 'impure'—of course, none but the initiated being ultimately quite pure; and in the incarnation and suffering of Dionysus-Zagreus. Zagreus was the son of Zeus and the Maiden (Korê); he was torn asunder by Titans, who were then blasted by the thunderbolt. Man's body is made of their dead ashes, and his soul of the living blood of Zagreus. Zagreus was born again of Zeus and the mortal woman Semelê; lived as man, yet god; was received into heaven and became the highest, in a sense the only, god. An individual worshipper of Bacchus could develop his divine side till he became himself a 'Bacchos,' his potential divinity realised.

So a worshipper of Kybêbê in Phrygia became Kybêbos; and many Orphic prophets became Orpheus. The fabled Mænad orgies never appear historically in Greece. The connection with wine was explained away

E

by the elect, and was in reality secondary. Dionysus is the god within, the spirit of worship and inexplicable joy : he appears best in communion with pure souls and the wild things of nature on the solitary mountains under the stars.

The Orphic hymns brim over with this joy ; they are full of repetitions and magniloquence, and make for emotion. The first hymn—very late but typical—runs : *" I call Hecatê of the Ways, of the Cross-ways, of the dark-ness, of the Heaven and the Earth and the Sea; saffron-clad goddess of the grave, exulting amid the spirits of the dead, Perseia, lover of loneliness, Queen who holdest the Keys of the World, . . . be present at our pure service with the fulness of joy in thine heart."*

That hymn dates from the fourth century A.D., and so do most of our complete Orphic poems. We only possess them in their last form, when the religion was a dying thing. But it is a remarkable fact, that there is no century from the fourth A.D. to the sixth B.C. which is without some more or less celebrated Orphic teachers. At the height of the classical epoch, for instance, we have evidence of an Orphic spirit in Pindar, Empedocles, Ion of Chios, Cratînus the comedian, Prodicus the philosopher, and probably in Euripides. Plato complains of the "crowd of books by Orpheus and Musæus," and inveighs against their doctrine of ceremonial forgiveness of sins. Besides this 'crowd'—in the case of Musæus it amounted at least to eleven sets of poems and numerous oracles—there were all kinds of less reputable prophets and purifiers. There was a type called ' Bakis '—any one sufficiently ' pure ' was apparently capable of becoming a Bakis — whose oracles were a drug in the Athenian market. Epimenides, the medicine-man from Crete, who purified Athens after Kylon's murder, was the reputed author of *Argonautika*,* *Purifications*,* and *Oracles*.* Though he slept twenty years in a cave, he has more claim to reality than a similar figure, Abâris, who went round the world with—or, as some think, on—a golden arrow given him by Apollo. Abâris passed as pre-Homeric; but his reputed poems were founded on the epic of the historical Aristeas of Proconnêsus about the Arimaspi, which contained revelations acquired in trances about the hyperboreans and the griffins. Aristeas appeared in Sicily at the same time that he died in Proconnêsus.

These were hangers-on of Orphism; the head centre seems to have been Onomacritus. He devoted himself to shaping the religious policy of Pisistratus and Hipparchus, and forging or editing ancient Orphic poems. He is never quoted as an independent author. The tradition dislikes him, and says that he was caught in the act of forging an oracle of Musæus, and banished with disgrace by Hipparchus. However, it has to admit that he was a friend of that prince in his exile,[1] and it cannot deny that he formed one of the chief influences of the sixth century.

Before the sixth century we get no definitely Orphic literature, but we seem to find traces of the influence, or perhaps of the spirit, from which it sprung. The curious hymn to 'Hecatê the Only-born' in the *Theogony* (411 f.) cannot be called definitely Orphic, but it stands by itself in the religion of the Hesiodic poems. The few references to Dionysus in Homer have an 'interpolated' or 'un-Homeric' look, and that which tells of the sin and punishment of Lycurgus implies

[1] Herodt. vii. 6.

the existence of an Orphic missionary tale.[1]   The eternal punishment of the sinners in λ seems Orphic; so possibly does the fact that the hero saw none of the blest.   He could not, because he was not initiated.   The Homeric preludes to Ares, to Athena, and perhaps that to Poseidon, show some traces of the movement.   Among the early epics the *Alcmæônis* * dealt largely with purification, and contained a prayer to 'Zagreus, all-highest of all gods.'   The Corinthian epics of Eumêlus show a similar strain.   Eumêlus was of the clan Bacchiadæ, his *Eurôpia* * was about Dionysus, and he treated the Orphic subjects of Medea and the Titan War.   Several epics, like the *Minyas*,* contained apocalyptic accounts of Hades.   The important fact is that the mystical and 'enthusiastic' explanation of the world was never without its apostles in Greece, though the main current of speculation, as directed by Athens, set steadily contrariwise, in the line of getting bit by bit at the meaning of things through hard thinking.

[1] Z., 132 1.

III

THE DESCENDANTS OF HOMER, HESIOD, ORPHEUS

EPOS

THE end of the traditional epos came with the rise of the idea of literary property. A rhapsode like Kynæthus would manipulate the Homer he recited, without ever wanting to publish the poems as his own. Onomacritus would hand over his laborious theology to Orpheus without intending either dishonesty or self-sacrifice. This community of literary goods lasted longer in the epos than in the song; but Homer, Hesiod, and Orpheus had by the sixth and fifth centuries to make room for living poets who stood on their own feet.

The first epic poet in actual history is generally given as PISANDER of Camîrus, in Rhodes, author of an *Heracleia.** Tradition gives him the hoariest antiquity, but he appears really to be only the Rhodian 'Homer.' The fragments themselves bear the brand of the sixth century, the talk of sin and the cry for purification. Pisander is not mentioned in classical times; he was, perhaps, 'discovered' by the romantic movement of the third century, as the earliest literary authority for the Heracles of the Twelve Labours, the Lion-skin and the Club.[1] Heracles was also the hero of the prophet and

---

[1] W. M. *Herakles*, i. 66 seq (2nd edition).

poet PANYÂSIS of Halicarnassus : the name is Carian, but the man was the uncle of Herodotus, and met his death in a rebellion against Lygdamis, the Carian governor of his native state. He wrote elegies as well as his epic. One Alexandrian critic puts Panyâsis next to Homer among epic poets : generally, he came fourth, after Hesiod and Antimachus. In Quintilian he appears as a mixture of the last two writers—his matter more interesting than Hesiod's, his arrangement better than that of Antimachus. The fragments are un-Homeric, but strong and well written. Accident has preserved us three pieces somewhat in the tone of the contemporary sympotic elegy. One speaker praises drink and the drinker with great spirit ; another answers that the first cup is to the Charites and Hôrai and Dionysus, the second to Aphrodite, the third is to Insolence and Ruin—"*and so you had better go home to your wedded wife.*" Some of the lines haunt a reader's memory :

> " *Demeter bare, and the great Craftsman bare,*
> *Silver Apollo and Poseidon bare,*
> *To serve a year, a mortal master's thrall.*"

CHOIRILUS of Samos was also a friend of Herodotus, and followed him and Æschylus in taking the Persian invasion for his subject, and Athens for his heroine. We hear of him in the suite of the Spartan general Lysander—apparently as a domestic bard—and afterwards at the court of Archelaus of Macedon. His poem is the first 'historical' epic in our sense of the word : an extant fragment complains that all legendary subjects are exhausted. The younger Choirilus who celebrated Alexander and has passed into legend as having been paid a gold philippus a line for very bad

verses—the same anecdote is told of others—may have
been this man's grandson. If he was really the author
of the epitaph on Sardanapallus he was not a bad writer,
though the original prose was finer : " *Sardanapallus, son
of Anakyndaraxes, built Anchialê and Tarsus in one day.
Eat, drink, make merry ; all things else are not worth—
that !* "

A rival of the earlier Choirilus was ANTIMACHUS of
Colophon, author of the *Thebais*,* a learned poet affecting
to despise popularity, and in several respects an Alexandrian born before his time. Naturally, Alexandria admired
him, counted him with Empedocles as master of 'the
austere style,' and ranked him in general next to Homer,
though Quintilian, in quoting the criticism, remarks that
'next' does not always mean 'near.' A vague anecdotic
tradition connects Antimachus and Plato. Plato sent his
disciple Heraclîdes to collect Antimachus's works, or
else stayed in a room which Antimachus's recitation had
emptied of other listeners ; and Antimachus said, " Plato
to me is worth a thousand." There were literary wars
over Antimachus in later times ; and this anecdote is
used by the friends of the learned epos, like Apollonius,
to glorify Antimachus, while Callimachus and Duris took
it as merely proving what they otherwise held, that Plato
was no judge of poetry. The fragments are mostly too
short to be of any literary interest ; the longer pieces are
either merely grammatical or are quoted by Athenæus
for some trivial point about wine-cups. The style strikes
a modern ear as poor and harsh, but the harshness is
studied, as the strange words are. He owed his real
fame more to his elegiac romance *Lydê** than to his
epic.

Lastly, Pausanias tells us : " A person called Phalysios

rebuilt the temple of Asclêpios in Naupaktos. He had a disease of the eyes and was almost blind, when the god sent to him Anytê, the epic poetess, with a sealed tablet." Phalysios recovered, but we know no more of ANYTÊ except that she was a native of Tegea, in Arcadia, and is once called 'the feminine Homer'—by Antipater of Thessalonica, who has handed down to us many of her epigrams, and who may or may not have read her epics.

The descendants of Hesiod are more varied and more obscure. The genealogical epos has two lines of development. The ordinary form went on living in divers parts of Greece. We hear of the Naupaktian Verses, the Samian, the Phocæan; but either they go without an author, or they are given to poets of local legend, the national equivalents of Hesiod—'Carkinus' of Naupaktos, 'Eumêlus' of Corinth, 'Asius'[1] of Samos. On the other hand, the 'Eoiê' type produced the romantic or erotic elegy. This form of poetry in the hands of such masters as Mimnermus, Antimachus, and Hermêsianax, takes the form of lists of bygone lovers, whose children are sometimes given and sometimes not. It is the story of the 'Eoiê' seen from a different point of view. When we hear how the 'great blue wave heaven-high' curled over the head of Tyro and took her to her sea-god, we think not of the royal pedigree, but of the wild romance of the story, the feeling in the heart of Enîpeus or of Tyro.

The didactic poetry of Hesiod developed on one side into the moralising or gnomic epics of Phokylidês, the proverbs of the Seven Wise Men, the elegies of Solon and Theognis; it even passed into the iambics of Sêmonides

---

[1] Our Sillos-like fragment must be by another man, not a Samian.

of Amorgos, Archilochus, Hippônax (see p. 88). On
another side, it gave rise to the poetry of science and
learning. The master himself was credited with an
Astronomy * and a *Tour of the Earth;* * but such subjects
for epos cannot generally be traced to any definite
authors before the fourth century, and were not popular
before the time of Arâtus of Soli (*ca.* 276 B.C.). The first
astronomical poet on record, Cleostratus of Tenedos,
who watched the stars from Mount Ida, is said to belong
to the sixth century. The first medical poem is perhaps
by one Periander, of the fourth. The epics on cookery,
which we hear of in Athenæus, were parodies rather
than dissertations. The arch-gourmand Archestratus of
Gela was a contemporary of Aristotle ; so was Matron.
It was the time of the Middle Comedy, when food
and the cooking of it were recognised as humorous
subjects (see p. 378).

But the main stream of didactic epos in early times
became religious. 'Hesiod' fell under the influence of
'Orpheus.' Even the traditional poems were affected
in this way. Kerkôps, the alleged 'real author' of certain Hesiodic poems, wrote a religious book, and is
called a 'Pythagorean'; which must mean, in this early
time, before Pythagoras was born, an Orphic. Eumêlus
knew things about the under-world that he can only
have learned from Onomacritus. Even the poem of
Aristeas, which might be counted as a secular geographical epos, the forerunner of the various '*Periêgêsês,*'
evidently owed its interest to its miracles and theology.

The Orphic movement worked mostly among the
common people and dropped out of literary record ;
we only catch it where it influences philosophy. It is
the explanation of Pythagoras, the man of learning and

culture, who turns from the world to become high priest of an ascetic brotherhood based on mysticism and purification.

The rise of a distinctly philosophical epos is immediately due to the curious spiritual rebellion of XENOPHANES of Colophon, a disciple of Anaximander, who was driven by the Persian invasion of 546 B.C. to earning his livelihood as a rhapsode. But he knew from Anaximander that what he recited was untrue. "*Homer and Hesiod fastened on the gods all that is a shame and a rebuke to man, thieving and adultery and the cheating one of another.*" He made his master's physical Infinite into God—"*there is one God most high over men and gods;*" "*all of him sees, thinks, and hears; he has no parts; he is not man-like either in body or mind.*" "*Men have made God in their own image; if oxen and lions could paint, they would make gods like oxen and lions.*" He wrote new 'true' poetry of his own—the great doctrinal poem *On Nature,** an epic on the historical *Founding of Colophon,** and 2000 elegiacs on the *Settlement at Elea** of himself and his fellow-exiles. The seventy years which he speaks of as having "*tossed his troubled thoughts up and down Hellas,*" must have contained much hard fighting against organised opposition, of which we have an echo in his *Satires.** He was not a great philosopher nor a great poet; but the fact that in the very stronghold of epic tradition he preached the gospel of free philosophy and said boldly the things that every one was secretly feeling, made him a great power in Greek life and literature. He is almost the only outspoken critic of religion preserved to us from Greek antiquity. The scepticism or indifference of later times was combined with a conventional dislike to free speech on religious matters—

partly as an attack on shadows, partly as mere 'bad taste.'

The example of Xenophanes led his great philosophical disciple to put his abstract speculations into verse form. PARMENIDES' poem *On Nature** was in two books, the first on the way of Truth, the second on the way of Falsehood. There is a mythological setting, and the poet's ride to the daughters of the Sun, who led him through the stone gates of Night and Day to the sanctuary of Wisdom, is quite impressive in its way. But it would all have been better in prose.

EMPEDOCLES of Acragas, on the other hand, is a real poet, perhaps as great as his admirer Lucretius, and working on a finer material. He was an important citizen, a champion of liberty against the tyrants Thêron and Thrasydaios. His history, like that of the kindred spirits, Pythagoras and Apollonius of Tyana, has been overlaid by the miraculous. He stopped the Etesian winds ; he drained an enormous marsh ; he recalled a dead woman to life ; he prophesied the hour that the gods would summon him, and passed away without dying. His enemies said that from sheer vanity he had thrown himself down Mount Etna that he might disappear without a trace and pass for immortal. 'How did any one know, then?' 'He had brass boots and the volcano threw one of them up!' Saner tradition said that he died an exile in the Peloponnese. His character profoundly influenced Greek and Arabian thought, and many works in both languages have passed under his name. His system we speak of later ; but the thaumaturgy is the real life of the poem. Take the words of a banished immortal stained by sin :—

" *There is an utterance of Fate, an ancient decree of the*

gods, everlasting, sealed with broad oaths; when any being stains his hand with sin of heart or swears an oath of deceiving, aye, though he be a Spirit, whose life is for ever, for thrice ten thousand years he wanders away from the Blessed, growing, as the ages pass, through all the shapes of mortal things, passing from one to another of the weary ways of life. The might of the Æther hunts him to the Sea, the Sea vomits him back to the floor of Earth, and Earth flings him to the fires of Helios the unwearied, and he to the whirlwinds of Æther. He is received of one after another, and abhorred of all."

Empedocles remembered previous lives : " *I have been a youth and a maiden and a bush and a bird and a gleaming fish in the sea.*" He hated the slaughter of animals for food : " *Will ye never cease from the horror of bloodshedding ? See ye not that ye devour your brethren, and your hearts reck not of it ?* " But bean-eating was as bad : " *Wretched, thrice-wretched, keep your hands from beans. It is the same to eat beans as to eat your fathers' heads.*" This is no question of over-stimulating food ; beans were under some religious ἄγος or *taboo,* and impure.

ELEGY AND IAMBUS

The use of the word 'lyric' to denote all poetry that is not epic or dramatic, is modern in origin and inaccurate. The word implies that the poetry was sung to a lyre accompaniment, or, by a slight extension of meaning, to some accompaniment. But the epos itself was originally sung. 'Homer' had a lyre, 'Hesiod' either a lyre or a staff. And, on the other hand, the 'lyric' elegy and iambus began very soon to drop their music. All Greek poetry originates in some form of song, in words combined with music ; and the different forms of poetry either gradually cast off their music as they required attention and clearness of thought, or fell more under the sway of music as they aimed at the expression of vague feeling. We can seldom say whether a given set of words were meant for speaking or for singing. Theognis's elegies seem to have been sung at banquets to a flute accompaniment ; Plato, in speaking of Solon, uses sometimes the word ' sing,' sometimes ' recite.' The two chief marks of song as against speech are, what we call the strophe or stanza, and the protracted dwelling of the voice on one syllable. For instance, the pentameter, which is made out of the hexameter by letting one long syllable count for two at the end of each half of the line, is more 'lyric' than the plain hexameter ; and the elegy, with its couplets of hexameters and pentameters, more lyric than the uniformly hexametric epos. The syncopated iambic produces one of the grandest of Æschylean song-metres, while the plain iambic trimeter is the form of poetry nearest to prose.

We hear of traditional tunes in Greece only by desultory and unscientific accounts. The ' Skolia ' or drinking-songs had a very charming traditional tune for which no author is mentioned. Various flute-tunes, such as 'the Many-headed,' 'the Chariot,' are attributed to a certain Olympus, a Phrygian, son of the satyr Marsyas, whose historical credit cannot be saved by calling him 'the younger Olympus.' The lyre-tunes go back mostly to Terpander of Antissa, in Lesbos. Two statements about him have a certain suggestiveness. When Orpheus was torn to pieces—as a Bacchic incarnation had to be—by the Thracian women, his head and lyre floated over the sea to Terpander's island. Terpander is thus the developer of Æolic or native Greek harp-music. But he also learned, we are told, from the Cretan Chrysothemis. Now, Crete was one of the first Dorian settlements. So Terpander is a junction of the native string-music with that of the Dorian invader. All that we know of him, his name '*Charmer-of-men*' included, has the stamp of myth. He gave the lyre seven strings instead of four. Seven tunes are mentioned as his invention ; one particularly, called the 'Terpandrian Nomos,' is characterised by its seven divisions, instead of the simple three, Beginning, Middle, and End. He won four musical prizes at Delphi—at a time before there were any contests ! He is the first musical victor in the Carneia at Sparta. All these contests existed at first without fixed records, and the original victor is generally mythical.

The conclusion is that, as there was heroic legend, so there was song in most cantons of Greece before our earliest records. The local style varied, and music was generally classified on a geographical basis—' the Phrygian style,' 'the Ionian,' 'the Dorian,' 'the hypo-Dorian,' 'the hyper-Phrygian,' 'the Lesbian,' and so on. The division is puzzling to us because it is so crude, and because it implies a concrete knowledge of the particular styles to start with. The disciples of Socrates, who saw every phenomenon with the eye of the moralist, dwell much upon the ethical values of the various divisions : the Dorian has dignity and courage, the Phrygian is wild and exciting, the Lydian effeminate, the Æolian expresses turbulent chivalry. This sounds arbitrary ; and it is interesting to find that while Plato makes the Ionic style 'effeminate and bibulous,' his disciple Heraclîdes says it is 'austere and proud.' The Socratic tradition especially finds a moral meaning in the difference between string and wind instruments. The harp allows you to remain master of yourself, a free and thinking man ; the flute, pipe, or clarionette, or whatever corresponds to the various kinds of 'aulos,' puts you beside yourself, obscures reason, and is more fit for barbarians. As a matter of fact, the 'aulos' was the favourite instrument in Sparta, Bœotia, and Delphi. Too stimulating for the sensitive Athenian, it fairly suited the Dorian palate. It would probably be milk-and-water to us.

The local styles of music had generally corresponding styles of metre. Those of Lesbos and Teos, for instance, remained simple ; their music appeals even to an untrained ear. The ordinary Ionic rhythms need only be once felt to be full of magic, the Dorian are a little harder, while many of the Æolian remain unintelligible except to the most sympathetic students. The definite rules, the accompaniment of rhythmic motion and constant though subordinate music, enabled the Greeks to produce metrical effects which the boldest and most melodious of English poets could never dream of approaching. There is perhaps no department of ancient achievement which distances us so completely as the higher lyric poem. We have developed music separately, and far surpassed the Greeks in that great isolated domain, but at what a gigantic sacrifice !

The origin of the word Elegy is obscure. It may have been originally a dirge metre accompanied, when sung, by the 'aulos.' But we meet it first in war-songs, and it became in course of time the special verse for love.

The oldest known elegist, CALLÎNUS, comes from Ephesus, and writes in a dialect like that used in the Ionic parts of Homer. His wars are partly against the invading Kimmerians (about 650 B.C.), partly against the town of Magnesia. He was about contemporary with the great Archilochus (p. 86) ; but Callînus speaks of Magnesia as still fighting, while Archilochus mentions its fall. TYRTÆUS of Aphidna wrote elegiac war-songs for the Spartans in the Second Messenian War (685–668 B.C.), and speaks as a Dorian noble, a Spartiate. But there was an Aphidna in Attica as well as in Laconia ; and Athenian malice remodelled an old joke into the anecdote that Sparta, hard pressed in the war, had sent to Athens for a leader, and that Athens had sent them a lame schoolmaster, who woke the dull creatures up, and led them to victory. In the same spirit, the Samians used to tell how they lent the men of Priênê a prophetess to help them against the Carians — even a Samian old woman could teach the Prieneans how to fight ! Tyrtæus becomes a semi-comic character in the late non-Spartan tradition—for instance, in the Messenian epic of Rhiânus (third century B.C.) ; but his Doric name, the fact that his songs were sung in Crete as well as in the Peloponnese, and the traditional honours paid to him at Lacedæmonian feasts, suggest that he was a personification of the Doric war-elegy, and that all authorless Doric war-songs became his property — for instance, the somewhat unarchaic lines quoted by the orator Lycurgus. The poems were, of course, originally in Doric; but our fragments have been worked over into Ionic dress,[1] and modernised. The collection, which includes some anapæstic marching-songs, comes from

---

[1] *Cf.* the mixture ἁ φιλοχρηματίη Σπάρταν ὀλεῖ.

Alexandria, and has the special title *Eunomia*, 'Law and Order.'

The greatest poet among the elegists is MIMNERMUS of Colophon. He is chiefly celebrated for his *Nanno*,* a long poem, or a collection of poems, on love or past lovers, called by the name of his mistress, who, like himself, was a flute-player. But his war fragments are richer than those of Tyrtæus or Callînus, and apart from either love or war he has great romantic beauty. For instance, the fragment :—

> " *Surely the Sun has labour all his days,*
> *And never any respite, steeds nor god,*
> *Since Êos first, whose hands are rosy rays,*
> *Ocean forsook, and Heaven's high pathway trod;*
> *At night across the sea that wondrous bed*
> *Shell-hollow, beaten by Hephaistos' hand,*
> *Of wingèd gold and gorgeous, bears his head*
> *Half-waking on the wave, from eve's red strand*
> *To the Ethiop shore, where steeds and chariot are,*
> *Keen-mettled, waiting for the morning star.*"

The influence of Mimnermus increased with time, and the plan of his *Nanno* * remained a formative idea to the great elegiac movement of Alexandria and its Roman imitators. There is music and character in all that he writes, and spirit where it is wanted, as in the account of the taking of Smyrna.

The shadowiness of these non-Attic poets strikes us as soon as we touch the full stream of Attic tradition in SOLON, son of Exekestides (639–559 B.C.). The tradition is still story rather than history, but it is there : his travels, his pretended madness, his dealings with the tyrant Pisistratus. The travels were probably, in reality, ordinary commercial voyages, but they made a fine

F

background for the favourite Greek conception of the Wise Wanderer. We hear, in defiance of chronology, how he met the richest of kings, Crœsus, who showed all his glory and then asked who was the 'most fortunate' man in the world. Solon named him certain obscure persons who had done their duty and were loved by their neighbours and were now safely dead. The words seemed meaningless at the time, but had their due effect afterwards—on Crœsus when Cyrus was in the act of burning him to death ; and on Cyrus when he heard the story and desisted from his cruel pride.

Solon was a soldier and statesman who had written love-poetry in his youth, and now turned his skill in verse to practical purposes, circulating political poems as his successors two centuries later circulated speeches and pamphlets. It is not clear how far this practice was borrowed from the great towns of Ionia, how far it was a growth of the specially Athenian instinct for politics. We possess many considerable fragments, elegiac, iambic, and trochaic, which are of immense interest as historical documents ; while as poetry they have something of the hardness and dulness of the practical man. The most interesting bits are on the war against Megara for the possession of Salamis, and on the 'Seisachtheia' or '*Off-shaking of Burdens*,' as Solon's great legislative revolution was called. As a reforming statesman, Solon was beaten by the extraordinary difficulties of the time ; he lived to see the downfall of the constitution he had framed, and the rise of Pisistratus ; but something in his character kept him alive in the memory of Athens as the type of the great and good lawgiver, who might have been a 'Tyrannos,' but would not for righteousness' sake.

THEOGNIS of Megara, by far the best preserved of the elegists, owes his immortality to his maxims, the brief statements of practical philosophy which the Greeks called 'Gnômai' and the Romans '*Sententiæ.*' Some are merely moral—

> "*Fairest is righteousness, and best is health,*
> *And sweetest is to win the heart's desire.*"

Some are bitter—

> "*Few men can cheat their haters, Kyrnos mine;*
> *Only true love is easy to betray !*"

Many show the exile waiting for his revenge—

> "*Drink while they drink, and, though thine heart be galled,*
> *Let no man living count the wounds of it:*
> *There comes a day for patience, and a day*
> *For deeds and joy, to all men and to thee !*"

Theognis's doctrine is not food for babes. He is a Dorian noble, and a partisan of the bitterest type in a state renowned for its factions. He drinks freely ; he speaks of the Demos as '*the vile*' or as '*my enemies*'; once he prays Zeus to "*give him their black blood to drink.*" That was when the Demos had killed all his friends, and driven him to beggary and exile, and the proud man had to write poems for those who entertained him. We hear, for instance, of an elegy on some Syracusans slain in battle. Our extant remains are entirely personal ebullitions of feeling or monitory addresses, chiefly to his squire Kyrnos. His relations with Kyrnos are typical of the Dorian soldier. He takes to battle with him a boy, his equal in station, to whom he is '*like a father*' (l. 1049). He teaches him all the duties of Dorian chivalry—to fight, to suffer in silence, to stick to a friend, to keep clear of falsehood, and to avoid associating with 'base men.' He is pledged to bring the boy back safe, or die on the field himself; and he is disgraced if the boy does not grow up to be a worthy and noble Dorian. In the rest of his relations with the squire, there is some sentiment which we cannot enter into : there were no women in the Dorian camps. It is the mixed gift of good and evil brought by the Dorian invaders to Greece, which the true Greek sometimes over-admired because it was so foreign to him — self-mastery, courage, grossness, and pride, effective devotion to a narrow class and an uncivilised ideal. Our MSS. of Theognis come from a collection made for educational purposes in the third century B.C., and show that state of interpolation which is characteristic of the schoolbook. Whole passages of Solon, Mimnermus, Tyrtæus, and another elegist Euênus, originally jotted on the margin for purposes of comparison, have now crept into the text. The order of the 'Gnomes' is confused ; and we sometimes have what appear to be two separate versions of the same gnome, an original and an abbreviation. There is a certain blindness of frank pride and chivalry, a depth of hatred and love, and a sense of mystery, which make Theognis worthy of the name of poet.

The gnomic movement receives its special expression in the conception of the Seven Wise Men. They provide the necessary mythical authorship for the widespread proverbs and maxims—the '*Know thyself*,' which was written up on the temple at Delphi ; the '*Nothing too much*,' '*Surety; loss to follow*,' and the like, which were current in people's mouths. The Wise Ones were not always very virtuous. The tyrant Periander occurs in some of the lists, and the quasi-tyrant Pittacus in all: their wisdom was chiefly of a prudential tendency. A pretended edition of their works was compiled by the fourth-century (?) orator, Lobon of Argos. Riddles, as well as gnomes, are a form of wisdom; and several ancient conundrums are attributed to the sage Kleobû-lus, or else to 'Kleobulîna,' the woman being explained as a daughter of the man: it seemed, perhaps, a feminine form of wisdom.

The gnome is made witty by the contemporaries PHOKYLIDES of Miletus and DEMODOCUS of Leros (about 537 B.C.). Their only remains are in the nature of epigrams in elegiac metre. Demodocus claims to be the inventor of a very fruitful jest: "*This, too, is of Demodocus: The Chians are bad; not this man good and that bad, but all bad, except Procles. And even Procles is a Chian!*" There are many Greek and Latin adaptations of that epigram before we get to Porson's condemnation of German scholars: "All save only Hermann; and Hermann's a German!" The form of introduction, "*This, too, is of Phokylides*," or "*of Demodocus*," seems to have served these two poets as the mention of Kyrnos served Theognis. It was a '*seal*' which stamped the author's name on the work. We have under the name of Phokylides a poem in two hundred and thirty-nine hexameters, containing moral precepts, which Bernays has shown to be the work of an Alexandrian Jew. It begins, "*First honour God, and next thy parents*"; it speaks of the resurrection of the body, and agrees with Deuteronomy (xxii. 6) on the taking of birds' nests.

SEMONIDES of Amorgos (*fl.* 625 B.C.) owes the peculiar spelling of his name to grammarians who wished to distinguish him from his more illustrious namesake, Simônides of Keos. His elegies, a history of Samos among them, are lost ; but Stobæus has preserved in his Anthology an iambic poem on women—a counter-satire, apparently, to the waggon-songs in which the village women at certain festivals were licensed to mock their male acquaintances. The good woman in Semonides is like a bee, the attractive and extravagant like a mare, and so on. The pig-woman comes comparatively high in the scale, though she is lazy and fond of food.

There were three iambic poets regarded as 'classical' by the Alexandrian canon—Semonides, Archilochus, and Hippônax. But, except possibly the last-named, no poet wrote iambics exclusively; and the intimate literary connection between, for instance, Theognis, Archilochus, and Hesiod, shows that the metrical division is unimportant. Much of Solon's work might, as far as the subject or the spirit is concerned, have been in elegiacs or iambics indifferently. The iambic metres appear to have been connected with the popular and homely gods Dionysus and Demeter, as the stately dactylic hexameters were with Zeus and Apollo. The iambic is the metre nearest to common speech ; a Greek orator or an English newspaper gives a fair number of iambic verses to a column. Its service to Greek literature was to provide poetry with a verse for dialogue, and for the ever-widening range of subjects to which it gradually condescended. A Euripides, who saw poetry and meaning in every stone of a street, found in the current iambic trimeter a vehicle of expression in some ways more flexible even than prose. When it first appears in literature, it has a satirical colour.

ARCHILOCHUS of Paros (*fl.* 650 B.C.?) eclipsed all earlier

writers of the iambus, and counts in tradition as the first.
He was the 'Homer' of familiar personal poetry.   This
was partly due to a literary war in Alexandria, and partly
to his having no rivals at his side.   Still, even our scanty
fragments justify Quintilian's criticism : " The sentences"
really are " strong, terse, and quivering, full of blood and
muscle; some people feel that if his work is ever inferior
to the very highest, it must be the fault of his subject,
not of his genius."   This has, of course, another side to
it.   Archilochus is one of those masterful men who hate to
feel humble.   He will not see the greatness of things, and
likes subjects to which he can feel himself superior.   Yet,
apart from the satires, which are blunt bludgeon work,
his smallest scraps have a certain fierce enigmatic beauty.
" *Oh, hide the bitter gifts of our lord Poseidon !*" is a cry
to bury his friends' shipwrecked corpses.   " *In my spear
is kneaded bread, in my spear is wine of Ismarus ; and I lie
upon my spear as I drink !*"   That is the defiant boast of
the outlaw turned freebooter.   " *There were seven dead
men trampled under foot, and we were a thousand murderers.*"   What does that mean ?   One can imagine many
things.   The few lines about love form a comment on
Sappho.   The burning, colourless passion that finds its
expression almost entirely in physical language may be
beautiful in a soul like hers; but what a fierce, impossible
thing it is with this embittered soldier of fortune, whose
intense sensitiveness and prodigious intellect seem sometimes only to mark him out as more consciously wicked
than his fellows !   We can make out something of his life.
He had to leave Paros—one can imagine other reasons
besides or before his alleged poverty—and settled on
Thasos, " *a wretched island, bare and rough as a hog's back
in the sea,*" in company with all the worst scoundrels in

Greece. In a battle with the natives of the mainland he threw away his shield and ran, and made very good jokes about the incident afterwards. He was betrothed to Cleobûlê, the daughter of a respectable Parian citizen, Lycambes. Lycambes broke off the engagement; Archilochus raged blindly and indecently at father and daughter for the rest of his life. Late tradition says they hanged themselves. Archilochus could not stay in Paros ; the settlement in Thasos had failed ; so he was thrown on the world, sometimes supporting himself as a mercenary soldier, sometimes doubtless as a pirate, until he was killed in a battle against Naxos. *"I am a servant of the lord god of war, and I know the lovely gift of the Muses."* He could fight and he could make wonderful poetry. It does not appear that any further good can be said of him.

Lower all round than Archilochus is HIPPÔNAX of Ephesus. Tradition makes him a beggar, lame and deformed himself, and inventor of the 'halting iambic' or 'scazon,' a deformed trimeter which upsets all one's expectations by having a spondee or trochee in the last foot. His works were all abusive. He inveighed especially against the artists Bupalos and Athênis, who had caricatured him ; and of course against women— *e.g.*, *"A woman gives a man two days of pleasure: the day he marries her, and the day he carries out her corpse."* Early satire does not imply much wit ; it implies hard hitting, with words instead of sticks and stones. The other satirical writers of classical times, Ananius and Hermippus, Kerkidas and Aischrion, were apparently not much admired in Alexandria.

One form of satire, the Beast Fable, was especially developed in collections of stories which went under

the name of ÆSOP.   He seems to be a mere story-
figure, like Kerkôps or Kreophȳlus, invented to provide an author for the fables.   He was a foreign slave
—Thracian, Phrygian, or Ethiopian—under the same
master as Rhodôpis, the courtesan who ruined Sappho's
brother.   He was suitably deformed ; he was murdered
at Delphi.   Delphi dealt much in the deaths or tombs
of celebrities.   It used the graves of Neoptolemus and
Hesiod to attract the sight-seer ; it extorted monetary
atonement from the slayer of Apollo's inspired servant
Archilochus.   But in Æsop's case a descendant of his
master Iadmon made his murder a ground for claiming
money from the Delphians ; so it is hard to see why
they countenanced the story.   Tradition gave Æsop
interviews with Crœsus and the Wise Men ; Aristophanes makes it a jocular reproach, not to have ' trodden
well ' your Æsop.   He is in any case not a poet, but
the legendary author of a particular type of story, which
any one was at liberty to put into verse, as Socrates
did, or to collect in prose, like Demetrius of Phalêrum.
Our oldest collections of fables are the iambics of
Phædrus and the elegiacs of Avianus in Latin, and the
scazons of Babrius in Greek, all three post-Christian.

IV

THE SONG

THE PERSONAL SONG—SAPPHO, ALCÆUS, ANACREON

THE Song proper, the Greek 'Melos,' falls into two
divisions—the personal song of the poet, and the choric
song of his band of trained dancers. There are remains
of old popular songs with no alleged author, in various
styles: the *Mill Song*—a mere singing to while away
time—"*Grind, Mill, grind; Even Pittacus grinds; Who
is king of the great Mytilene*";—the *Spinning Song* and
the *Wine-Press Song*, and the *Swallow Song*, with
which the Rhodian boys went round begging in early
spring. Rather higher than these were the 'Skolia,'
songs sung at banquets or wine-parties. The form
gave rise to a special Skolion-tune, with the four-line
verse and the syllable-counting which characterises the
Lesbian lyric. The Skolion on Harmodius and Aristogeiton is the most celebrated; but nearly all our remains
are fine work, and the "*Ah, Leipsydrion, false to them
who loved thee*," the song of the exiles who fled from
the tyrant Pisistratus to the rock of that name, is full of
a haunting beauty.

The Lesbian 'Melos' culminates in two great names,
Alcæus and Sappho, at the end of the seventh century.[1]

[1] The dates are uncertain. Athens can scarcely have possessed Sigêum
before the reign of Pisistratus. Beloch, *Griechische Geschichte*, i. 330.

The woman has surpassed the man, if not in poetical achievement, at least in her effect on the imagination of after ages. A whole host of poetesses sprang up in different parts of Greece after her—Corinna and Myrtis in Bœotia, Telesilla in Argos, Praxilla in Sikyon ; while Erinna, writing in the fourth century, still calls herself a 'comrade' of Sappho.

ALCÆUS spent his life in wars, first against Athens for the possession of Sigêum, where, like Archilochus, he left his shield for the enemy to dedicate to Athena ; then against the democratic tyrant Melanchrôs and his successor Myrsilos. At last the Lesbians stopped the civil strife by appointing Pittacus, the 'Wise Man,' dictator, and Alcæus left the island for fifteen years. He served as a soldier of fortune in Egypt and elsewhere : his brother Antimenidas took service with Nebuchadnezzar, and killed a Jewish or Egyptian giant in single combat. Eventually the poet was pardoned and invited home. His works filled ten books in Alexandria ; they were all 'occasional poetry,' hymns, political party-songs (στασιωτικά), drinking-songs, and love-songs. His strength seems to have lain in the political and personal reminiscences, the "hardships of travel, banishment, and war," that Horace speaks of. Sappho and Alcæus are often represented together on vases, and the idea of a romance between them was inevitable. Tradition gives a little address of his in a Sapphic metre, " *Thou violet-crowned, pure, softly-smiling Sappho*," and an answer from Sappho in Alcaics —a delicate mutual compliment. Every line of Alcæus has charm. The stanza called after him is a magnificent metrical invention. His language is spontaneous and musical ; it seems to come straight from a heart as

full as that of Archilochus, but much more generous.
He is a fiery Æolian noble, open-handed, free-drinking,
frank, and passionate ; and though he fought to order in
case of need, he seems never to have written to order.

His younger contemporary SAPPHO — the name is
variously spelt ; there is authority for Psappha, Psaffo,
and even Pspha—born at Ephesus, dwelling at Mitylene,
shared the political fortunes of Alcæus's party. We hear
of a husband, whose name, Kerkylas of Andros, is not
above suspicion ; and of a daughter Kleïs, whose existence
is perhaps erroneously inferred from a poem—"*I have a
fair little child, with a shape like a golden flower, Kleïs, my
darling.*" She seems to have been the leader of a band
of literary women, students and poetesses, held together
by strong ties of intimacy and affection. It is compared
in antiquity[1] to the circle of Socrates. Sappho wrote in
the most varied styles — there are fifty different metres
in our scanty remains of her—but all bear a strong
impress of personal character. By the side of Alcæus,
one feels her to be a woman. Her dialect is more the
native speech of Mitylene, where she lived ; his the more
literary. His interests cover war and drinking and
adventure and politics ; hers are all in personal feeling,
mostly tender and introspective. Her suggestions of
nature — the line, "*I heard the footfall of the flowery
spring*" ; the marvellously musical comparison, "*Like
the one sweet apple very red, up high on the highest bough,
that the apple-gatherers have forgotten ; no, not forgotten,
but could never reach so far*"—are perhaps more definitely
beautiful than the love-poems which have made Sappho's
name immortal. Two of these are preserved by accident ;
the rest of Sappho's poetry was publicly burned in 1073

[1] Maximus Tyrius.

at Rome and at Constantinople, as being too much for the shaky morals of the time. One must not over-estimate the compliments of gallantry which Sappho had in plenty: she was 'the Poetess' as Homer was 'the Poet'; she was 'the Tenth Muse,' 'the Pierian Bee'; the wise Solon wished to "learn a song of Sappho's and then die." Still Sappho was known and admired all over Greece soon after her death; and a dispassionate judgment must see that her love-poetry, if narrow in scope, has unrivalled splendour of expression for the longing that is too intense to have any joy in it, too serious to allow room for metaphor and imaginative ornament. Unfortunately, the dispassionate judgment is scarcely to be had. Later antiquity could not get over its curiosity at the woman who was not a 'Hetaira' and yet published passionate love-poetry. She had to be made a heroine of romance. For instance, she once mentioned the Rock of Leucas. That was enough! It was the rock from which certain saga-heroes had leaped to their death, and she must have done the same, doubtless from unrequited passion! Then came the deference of gallantry, the reckless merriment of the Attic comedy, and the defiling imagination of Rome. It is a little futile to discuss the private character of a woman who lived two thousand five hundred years ago in a society of which we have almost no records. It is clear that Sappho was a 'respectable person' in Lesbos; and there is no good early evidence to show that the Lesbian standard was low. Her extant poems address her women friends with a passionate intensity; but there are dozens of questions to be solved before these poems can be used as evidence: Is a given word-form correct? is Sappho speaking in her own person, or dramatically? what occasion are the

verses written for ? how far is the poem a literary exercise based on the odes written by Alcæus to his squire
Lykos, or by Theognis to Kyrnus ?

No one need defend the character of ANACREON of
Teos ; though, since he lived in good society to the age
of eighty-five, he cannot have been as bad as he wishes
us to believe. His poetry is derived from the Lesbians
and from the Skolia of his countryman Pythermus.
He was driven from Teos by the Persian conquest
of 545 B.C. ; he settled in Abdêra, a Teian colony in
Thrace ; saw some fighting, in which, he carefully explains, he disgraced himself quite as much as Alcæus and
Archilochus ; finally, he attached himself to various royal
persons, Polycrates in Samos, Hipparchus in Athens, and
Echekrates the Aleuad in Thessaly. The Alexandrians
had five books of his elegies, epigrams, iambics, and
songs ; we possess one satirical fragment, and a good
number of wine and love songs, addressed chiefly to his
squire Bathyllus. They were very popular and gave rise
to many imitations at all periods of literature ; we possess
a series of such *Anacreontea*, dating from various times
between the third century B.C. and the Renaissance. These
poems are innocent of fraud : in one, for instance (No. 1),
Anacreon appears to the writer in a dream [1] ; in most of
them the poet merely assumes the mask of Anacreon and
sings his love-songs to 'a younger Bathyllus.' The
dialect, the treatment of Erôs as a frivolous fat boy, the
personifications, the descriptions of works of art, all are
marks of a later age. Yet there can be no doubt of the
extraordinary charm of these poems, true and false alike.
Anacreon stands out among Greek writers for his limpid
ease of rhythm, thought, and expression. A child can

[1] *Cf.* 20 and 59.

understand him, and he ripples into music. But the false poems are even more Anacreontic than Anacreon. Compared with them the real Anacreon has great variety of theme and of metre, and even some of the stateliness and reserved strength of the sixth century. Very likely our whole conception of the man would be higher, were it not for the incessant imitations which have fixed him as a type of the festive and amorous septuagenarian.

These three poets represent the personal lyric of Greece. In Alcæus it embraces all sides of an adventurous and perhaps patriotic life ; in Sappho it expresses with a burning intensity the inner life, the passions that are generally silent ; in Anacreon it spreads out into light snatches of song about simple enjoyments, sensual and imaginative. The personal lyric never reached the artistic grandeur, the religious and philosophic depth of the choric song. It is significant of our difficulty in really appreciating Greek poetry, that we are usually so much more charmed by the style which all antiquity counted as easier and lower.

THE CHOIR-SONG—GENERAL

Besides the personal lyric, there had existed in Greece at a time earlier than our earliest records the practice of celebrating important occasions by the dance and song of a choir. The occasion might of course be public or private ; it was always in early times more or less religious—a victory, a harvest, a holy day, a birth, death, or marriage. At the time that we first know the choir-song it always implies a professional poet, a band of professional performers, and generally a new production

—new dance, new music, new words—for each new occasion. Also, it is international. The great lyric poets are from Lesbos, Italian Locri, Rhegion, Keos, Bœotia; the earliest is actually said to be a Lydian. A poet can even send his composition across the sea to be represented, secure of having trained performers in another country who will understand the dancing and singing. The dialect is correspondingly international. It has Æolic, 'Epic,' and Doric elements, the proportions varying slightly in various writers. These facts suffice to show that the choir-poem which we get even in Alcman, much more that of Simônides, is a highly-developed product. Our chief extant specimens, the prize-songs of Pindar, represent the extreme fulness of bloom upon which decay already presses.

What is the history implied in this mixture of dialects? The Æolic is the language of song, because of Sappho and Alcæus. No singer followed them who was not under their spell. The 'Epic' element comes from the 'Homer' which had by this time grown to be the common property of Greece.[1] The Doric element needs explanation.

The poets, as we have seen, were not especially Dorian; but the patrons of the poetry were, and so to a great extent was its spirit. It was the essence of the Ionian and Æolian culture to have set the individual free; the Dorian kept him, even in poetry, subordinated to a larger whole, took no interest in his private feelings, but required him to express the emotions of the community. The earliest choir-poets, Alcman and Tisias,

---

[1] What this 'Homer' dialect was in Bœotia, or Lesbos, or Argos, we are not able to say. The 'Epic' element in our lyric remains has been Ionised and Atticised just as the *Iliad* has been.

were probably public servants, working for their respective states. That is one Dorian element in the choir-song. Another is that, as soon as it ceases to be genuinely the performance by the community of a public duty, it becomes a professional entertainment for the pleasure of a patron who pays. The non-choral poets, Alcæus, Sappho, Archilochus, wrote to please themselves ; they were 'their own,' as Aristotle puts it, and did not become ἄλλου, 'another's.' Anacreon lived at courts and must really have depended on patronage ; but his poems are ostensibly written at his own pleasure, not at the bidding of Polycrates. The training of a professional chorus, however, means expense, and expense means a patron who pays. Pindar and Simônides with their trained bands of dancers could only exist in dependence on the rich oligarchies.

The richest Ionian state, Athens, looked askance at this late development. Her dithyrambs and tragedies were not composed to the order of a man, nor executed by hired performers ; they were solemnly acted by free citizens in the service of the great Demos. Occasionally a very rich citizen might have a dithyramb performed for him, like a Dorian noble ; but even Megacles, who employed Pindar, cuts a modest and economical figure by the side of the Æginetans and the royalties ; and the custom was not common in Athens. Alcibiades employed Euripides for a dithyramb, but that was part of his ostentatious munificence. The Ionian states in general were either too weak or too democratic to exercise much influence on the professional choir-song.

The choir-song formed a special branch of literature with a unity of its own, but it had no one name. Aris-

totle often uses the special name 'dithyramb' to denote
the whole genus ; this is a popular extension of meaning,
influenced by the growth of the later Attic dithyramb
in the hands of Timotheos and Philoxenos. Even the
names of the different kinds of choir-song are vague.
When Alexandrian scholars collected the scattered works
of Pindar or Simônides, they needed some principle of
arrangement and division. Thus, according to the
subjects, we have drink-songs, marriage-songs, dirges,
victory-songs, &c.; or, by the composition of the choirs,
maiden-songs, boy-songs, man-songs ; or, from another
point of view again, standing-songs, marching-songs,
dancing-songs. Then there come individual names,
not in any classification : a 'pæan' is a hymn to Apollo ;
a 'dithyramb,' to Dionysus ; an 'iâlemos' is perhaps a
lament for sickness, and not for death. The confusion
is obvious. The collectors in part made divisions of
their own ; much more they utilised the local names
for local varieties of song which were not intended to
have any reference to one another. If an 'iâlemos'
really differed from a 'thrênos,' and each from an
'epikêdeion,' it was only that they were all local names,
and the style of dirge-singing happened to vary in the
different localities.

The dithyramb proper was a song and dance to
Dionysus, practised in the earliest times in Naxos,
Thasos, Bœotia, Attica ; the name looks as if it were
compounded of Δι-, 'god,' and some form of *triumphus*,
θρίαμβος, 'rejoicing.' It was a wild and joyous song.
It first appears with strophic correspondence; afterwards
it loses this, and has no more metre than the rhapso-
dies of Walt Whitman. It was probably accompanied
with disguise of some sort ; the dancers represented the

dæmonic followers of Bacchus, whom we find in such hordes on the early Attic drinking-vessels. We call them satyrs; but a satyr is a goat-dæmon, and these have the ears and tail of a horse, like the centaurs. The difference in sentiment is not great: the centaurs are all the wild forces that crash and speed and make music in the Thessalian forests; the satyr is the Arcadian mountain-goat, the personification of the wildness, the music and mystery, of high mountains, the instincts that are at once above and below reason: his special personification is Pan, the Arcadian shepherd-god, who has nothing to do with Dionysus. When we are told that Arîon "invented, taught, and named" the dithyramb in Corinth, it may mean that he first joined the old Dionysus-song with the Pan-idea; that he disguised his choir as satyrs. Corinth, the junction of Arcadia and the sea-world, would be the natural place for such a transition to take place. Thus the dithyramb was a goat-song, a 'tragôidia'; and it is from this, Aristotle tells us, that tragedy arose. It is remarkable that the dithyramb, after giving birth to tragedy, lived along with it and survived it. In Aristotle's time tragedy was practically dead, while its daughter, the new comedy, and its mother the Attic dithyramb, were still flourishing.

THE EARLY MASTERS

ALCMAN

The name ALCMAN is the Doric for Alcmæon, and the bearer of it was a Laconian from Messoa (*circa* 650 B.C.). But Athenian imagination could never assimilate the idea of a Spartan being a poet. In the case of Tyrtæus they made the poet an Athenian; in that of Alcman, some chance words in one of his poems suggested that he or his ancestors came from Lydia. Hence a romance—he was a Lydian, made a slave of war by the wild Kimmerians, and sold across seas to Sparta, where his beautiful songs procured him his freedom. Alcman is very near the Lesbians; he speaks freely in his own person, using the choir merely as an instrument; the personal ring of his love-passages made Archŷtas (4th cent. B.C.) count him the inventor of love-poetry; he writes in a fresh country dialect, as Sappho does, with little literary varnish; his personal enthusiasm for the national broth of Sparta is like that of Carlyle for porridge. His metres are clear and simple; and the fragment imitated by Tennyson in *In Memoriam* shows what his poetry can be: "*No more, oh, wild sweet throats, voices of love, will my limbs bear me; would, would I were a ceryl-bird, that flies on the flower of the wave amid the halcyons, with never a care in his heart, the sea-purple bird of the spring!*"

His longest fragment is on an Egyptian papyrus, found by Mariette in 1855, and containing part of a beautiful 'Parthenion,' or choir-song for girls. It is a dramatic part-song. When we hear first that Agido among the rest of the chorus is like "*a race-horse among cows*," and afterwards that "*the hair of my cousin Agesichora gleams like pure gold*," this does not mean that the 'boorish' poet is expressing his own frank and fickle preferences—would the 'cows' of the choir, in that case, ever have consented to sing such lines?—it is only that the two divisions of the chorus are paying each other compliments. This poem, unlike those of the Lesbians, has a strophic arrangement, and is noteworthy as showing a clear tendency towards rhyme. There are similar traces of intentional rhyme in Homer and Æschylus ; [1] whereas the orators and Sophocles, amid all their care for euphony in other respects, admit tiresome rhyming jangles with a freedom which can only be the result of unsensitiveness to that particular relation of sounds.

ARÎON

ARÎON of Methymna, in Lesbos, is famous in legend as the inventor of the dithyramb, and for his miraculous preservation at sea : some pirates forced him to ' walk the plank ' ; but they had allowed him to make music once before he died, and when he sprang overboard, the dolphins who had gathered to listen, carried him on their backs to Mount Tænarum. It is an old saga-motive, applied to Phalanthos, son of Poseidon, in Tarentum, to Enalos at Lesbos, and to the sea-spirits Palæmon, Melikertes, Glaucus, at other places. Arîon's own works disappeared early ; Aristophanes of Byzantium could not find any (2nd cent. B.C.), though an interesting piece of fourth-century dithyramb in which the singer represents Arîon, has been handed down to us as his through a mistake of Ælian.

STÊSICHORUS

The greatest figure in early choric poetry is that of TÎSIAS, surnamed STÊSICHORUS ('Choir-setter') of Hîmera. The man was a West-Locrian from Matauros, but became a citizen of Hîmera in the long struggles against Phalaris of brazen-bull celebrity. The old fable of the

---

[1] *Sept.* 778 ff., 785 ff.

horse making itself a slave to man in order to be revenged on the stag, was one of his warnings against the tyrant. When Phalaris triumphed, Stêsichorus retired to Catana ; where his octagonal grave outside the gate became in Roman times one of the sights of Sicily. Apart from such possible fragments of good tradition as may survive in the notorious forgeries called the *Letters of Phalaris*, we possess only one personal fact about his life. He was attacked with a disease of the eyes ; and the thought preyed upon his mind that this was the divine wrath of Helen, of whom he had spoken in the usual way in some poem—perhaps the *Helen** or the *Sack of Ilion.** His pangs of conscience were intensified by historical difficulties. It was incredible that all Troy should have let itself be destroyed merely to humour Paris. If the Trojans would not give up Helen, it must have been that they never had her. Tîsias burst into a recantation or ' Palinôdia,' which remained famous : " *That tale was never true ! Thy foot never stepped on the benched galley, nor crossed to the towers of Troy.*" We cannot be sure what his own version was ; it cannot well have been that of Herodotus and Euripides, which makes Helen elope to Egypt, though not to Troy. But, at any rate, he satisfied Helen, and recovered his sight. A very similar story is told of the Icelandic Skald Thormod.

The service that Stêsichorus did to Greek literature is threefold : he introduced the epic saga into the West ; he invented the stately narrative style of lyric ; he vivified and remodelled, with the same mixture of boldness and simple faith as the Helen story, most of the great canonical legends. He is called "the lyric Homer," and described as "bearing the weight of the epos on his lyre." [1]

[1] Quint. x. 1.

The metres specially named 'Stesichorean'—though others had used them before Stêsichorus—show this half-epic character. They are made up of halves of the epic hexameter, interspersed with short variations— epitrites, anapæsts, or mere syncopæ—just enough to break the dactylic swing, to make the verse lyrical. His diction suits these long stately lines ; it is not passionate, not very songful, but easily followed, and suitable for narrative. This helps to explain why so important a writer has left so few fragments. He was not difficult enough for the grammarian ; he was not line by line exquisite enough for the later lover of letters. The ancient critics, amid all their praises of Stêsichorus, complain that he is long ; the *Oresteia** alone took two books, and doubtless the *Sack of Ilion** was equal to it. His whole works in Alexandrian times filled twenty-six books. He had the fulness of an epic writer, not the vivid splendour that Pindar had taught Greece to ex- pect in a lyric. Yet he gained an extraordinary position.[1] Simônides, who would not over-estimate one whom he hoped to rival, couples him with Homer—" So sang to the nations Homer and Stêsichorus." In Athens of the fifth century he was universally known. Socrates praised him. Aristophanes ridiculed him. " Not to know three lines of Stêsichorus " was a proverbial description of illiteracy.[2] There was scarcely a poet then living who was not in- fluenced by Stêsichorus ; scarcely a painter or potter who did not, consciously or unconsciously, represent his version of the great sagas. In tracing the historical

[1] The coins of Hîmera bearing the figure of Stêsichorus are later than 241 B.C., when he had become a legend. *Cf.* also Cic. *Verr.* ii. 35.

[2] No reference, as used to be thought, to the strophe, antistrophe, epode of choric music.

development of any myth, research almost always finds
in Stêsichorus the main bridge between the earliest remains of the story and the form it has in tragedy or in
the late epos. In the Agamemnon legend, for instance,
the concentration of the interest upon Clytæmnestra,
which makes the story a true tragedy instead of an
ordinary tale of blood - feud, is his ; Clytæmnestra's
dream of giving suck to a serpent is his ; the con-
science-mad Orestes is probably his ; so are many of
the details of the sack of Troy, among them, if the
tradition is right, the flight of Æneas to Italy.

This is enough to show that Stêsichorus was a creative
genius of a very high order—though, of course, none of
these stories is absolutely his own invention. Confessed
fiction was not possible till long after Stêsichorus. To
the men of his day all legend was true history ; if it was
not, what would be the good of talking about it ? The
originality lies, partly, in the boldness of faith with which
this antique spirit examines his myths, criticising and
freely altering details, but never suspecting for an instant that the whole myth is an invention, and that he
himself is inventing it. It is the same with Pindar.
Pindar cannot and will not believe that Tantalus offered
his son to the gods as food, and that Demeter ate part
of his shoulder. Therefore he argues, not that the
whole thing is a fable, nor yet that it is beyond our
knowledge ; agnosticism would never satisfy him : he
argues that Poseidon must have carried off Pelops to
heaven to be his cup-bearer, and that during his absence some 'envious neighbour' invented the cannibal-
story. This is just the spirit of the Palinôdia.

But, apart from this, even where Stêsichorus did not
alter his saga-material, he shows the originality of genius

in enlarging the field of poetry. He was the first to feel
the essence of beauty in various legends which lived in
humble places : in the death of the cowherd Daphnis for
shame at having once been false to his love (that rich
motive for all pastoral poetry afterwards) ; in the story
of the fair Kalykê, who died neglected ; of the ill-starred
Rhadina, who loved her cousin better than the tyrant
of Corinth. This is a very great achievement. It is what
Euripides did for the world again a little later, when the
mind of Greece, freeing itself from the stiffer Attic
tradition, was ready to understand.

THE MIDDLE PERIOD

ÎBYCUS

ÎBYCUS of Rhêgion, nearly two generations later than
Stêsichorus, led a wandering life in the same regions
of Greece, passing on to the courts of Polycrates and
Periander. Like Arîon, he is best known to posterity
by a fabulous story—of his murder being avenged by
cranes, 'îbykes.' His songs for boy-choirs are specially
praised. He is said to have shown an 'Æolo-Ionic
spirit' in songs of Dorian language and music, and
the charming fragments full of roses and women's
attire and spring and strange birds,[1] and "*bright sleep-
less dawn awaking the nightingales,*" show well what
this means. It is curious that the works of Stêsichorus were sometimes attributed to him—for instance,
the *Games at Pelias's Funeral.** Our remains of the
two have little in common except the metre.

[1] *Cf.* No. 8.

SIMÔNIDES

On the day, it is said, that Tisias died, there was born in Keos the next great international lyrist of Greece, SIMÔNIDES (556–468 B.C.). A man of wide culture and sympathies, as well as great poetic power, he was soon famous outside the circle of Ionian islands. Old Xenophanes, who lived in Italy, and died before Simônides was thirty, had already time to denounce him as a well-known man. He travelled widely—first, it is said, to Western Greece, at the invitation of Stêsichorus's compatriots ; afterwards to the court of Hipparchus in Athens ; and, on his patron's assassination, to the princes of Thessaly. At one time he crossed to Asia; during the Persian War he was where he should have been—with the patriots. He ended his life with Æschylus, Pindar, Bacchylides, Epicharmus, and others, at the court of Hiero of Syracuse. If he was celebrated at thirty, in his old age he had an international position comparable perhaps to that of Voltaire. He was essentially ὁ σοφός, the wit, the poet, the friend of all the great ones of the earth, and their equal by his sheer force of intellect. His sayings were treasured, and his poems studied with a verbal precision which suggests something like idolatry. Rumour loved to tell of his strange escape from shipwreck, and from the fall of the palace roof at Crannon, which killed most of Scopas's guests. He was certainly a man of rich and many-sided character ; he was trusted by several tyrants and the Athenian democracy at the same time ; he praised Hipparchus, and admired Harmodius and Aristogeiton ; in his old age he was summoned to Sicily to reconcile the two most powerful princes in

Greece, Gelo and Hiero. The charges of avarice which pursue his memory are probably due to his writing at specified terms—not for vague, unspecified patronage, like the earlier poets. The old fashion was more friendly and romantic, but contained an element of servitude. Pindar, who laments its fall, did not attempt to recur to it; and really Simônides's plan was the nearest approach then possible to our system of the independent sale of brain-work to the public. Simônides, like the earlier lyrists, dealt chiefly in occasional poetry — the occasion being now a festival, now a new baby, now the battle of Thermopylæ—and he seems to have introduced the 'Epinîkos,' the serious artistic poem in honour of victories at the games. Not that an 'Epinîkos' is really a bare ode on a victory—on the victory, for instance, of Prince Skopas's mules. Such an ode would have little power of conferring immortality. It is a song in itself beautiful and interesting, into which the poet is paid to introduce a reference to the mules and their master.

Simônides wrote in many styles: we hear of Dithyrambs, Hyporchêmata, Dirges — all these specially admired—Parthenia, Prosodia, Pæans, Encômia, Epigrams. His religious poetry is not highly praised. If one could use the word 'perfect' of any work of art, it might apply to some of Simônides's poems on the events of the great war—the ode on Artemisium, the epitaph on those who died at Thermopylæ. They represent the extreme of Greek 'sôphrosynê'—self-mastery, healthymindedness—severe beauty, utterly free from exaggeration or trick—plain speech, to be spoken in the presence of simple and eternal things : " *Stranger, bear word to the Spartans that we lie here obedient to their charge.*" He is great, too, in the realm of human pity. The little fragment on Danaë adrift in the chest justifies the admiration of ancient critics for his 'unsurpassed pathos.' On the other hand, he is essentially an Ionian and a man of the world, one of the fathers of the Enlightenment. He has no splendour, no passion, no religious depth. The man who had these stood on the wrong side in his country's life-struggle ; and Greece turned to Simônides, not to Pindar, to make the record of its heroic dead.

TIMOCREON

The 'Home for Geniuses' which Hiero's court eventually became, must have been a far from peaceful refuge. Pindar especially was born to misunderstand and dislike Simônides ; and though jealousy is not one of the vices laid to the latter's charge, he was a wit and could be severe. When he was attacked by a low poet from Rhodes, TIMOCREON, who is chiefly known by his indecent song of delight at the condemnation of Themistocles as a traitor—" *Not Timocreon alone makes compacts with the Medes ; I am not the only dock-tail ; there are other foxes too !*" Simônides answered by writing his epitaph : " *Here lies Timocreon of Rhodes, who ate much, drank much, and said many evil things.*" The poet's poetry is not mentioned.

BACCHYLIDES

Simônides's nephew, BACCHYLIDES, lived also at Hiero's court, and wrote under the influences both of his uncle and of Pindar. He was imitated by Horace, and admired for his moral tone by the Emperor Julian—a large share of 'immortality' for one who is generally reckoned a second-class poet. And it appears that more is in store for him. The British Museum has recently acquired a papyrus of the first century B.C., containing several epinikian odes of Bacchylides intact, as well as some fresh fragments. It would be an ungracious reception to a new-comer so illustrious in himself, to wish that he had been some one else—Alcæus, for instance, or Sappho or Simônides. But we may perhaps hope that the odes will not all be about the Games, as Pindar's are. The headings of three of them, 'Theseus,' 'Io,' and 'Idas,' seem to suggest a more varied prospect; but similar titles are sometimes found in MSS. of Pindar, and merely serve to indicate the myths which the particular 'Epinîkoi' contain. The longest of the new odes is in honour of Hiero, and celebrates the same victory as Pindar's first Olympian—a poem, by the way, which has been thought to contain an unkind reflection upon Bacchylides. The style is said to be much simpler than Pindar's, though it shows the ordinary lyric fondness for strange compound words, such as μεγιστοϜάνασσα. The most interesting of the fragments heretofore published is in praise of Peace.

THE FINAL DEVELOPMENT

PINDAR

PINDAR, "by far the chief of all the lyrists," as Quintilian calls him, was born thirty-four years after Simônides, and survived him about twenty (522–448 B.C.). He is the first Greek writer for whose biography we have real documents. Not only are a great many of his extant poems datable, but tradition, which loved him for his grammatical difficulties as well as for his genius, has pre-

served a pretty good account of his outer circumstances.
He was born at the village of Kynoskephalæ, in Bœotia ;
he was descended from the Ægîdæ, a clan of conquering
invaders, probably 'Cadmean,' since the name 'Pindar'
is found in Ephesus and Thêra. The country-bred Bœotian boy showed early a genius for music. The lyre,
doubtless, he learned as a child : there was one
Skopelînus at home, an uncle of the poet, or perhaps
his step-father, who could teach him flute-playing. To
learn choir-training and systematic music he had to go
to Athens, to 'Athênoclês and Apollodôrus.' Tradition
insisted on knowing something about his relation to
the celebrities of the time. He was taught by Lasus of
Hermionê ; beaten in competition by his country-woman
Corinna, though some extant lines of that poetess make
against the story : *"I praise not the gracious Myrtis, not I,
for coming to contest with Pindar, a woman born !"* And
another anecdote only makes Corinna give him good
advice—*" to sow with the hand, not with the whole sack,"*
when he was too profuse in his mythological ornaments.

The earliest poem we possess (*Pyth.* x.), written when
Pindar was twenty — or possibly twenty-four — was a
commission from the Aleuadæ, the princes of Pharsâlus,
in Thessaly. This looks as if his reputation was made
with astonishing rapidity. Soon afterwards we find him
writing for the great nobles of Ægîna, patrons after his
own heart, merchant princes of the highest Dorian
ancestry. Then begins a career of pan-Hellenic celebrity : he is the guest of the great families of Rhodes,
Tenedos, Corinth, Athens ; of the great kings, Alexander
of Macedon, Arkesilâus of Cyrene, Thêro of Acragas,
and Hiero of Syracuse. It is as distinguished as that of
Simônides. though perhaps less sincerely international.

Pindar in his heart liked to write for 'the real nobility,' the descendants of Æacus and Heracles ; his Sicilian kings are exceptions, but who could criticise a friendly king's claim to gentility ? This ancient Dorian blood is evidently at the root of Pindar's view of life ; even the way he asserts his equality with his patrons shows it. Simônides posed as the great man of letters. Pindar sometimes boasts of his genius, but leaves the impression of thinking more of his ancestry. In another thing he is unlike Simônides. Pindar was the chosen vessel of the priesthood in general, a votary of Rhea and Pan, and, above all, of the Dorian Apollo. He expounded the re-habilitation of traditional religion, which radiated from Delphi. He himself had special privileges at Delphi during his life, and his ghost afterwards was invited yearly to feast with the god. The priests of Zeus Ammon in the desert had a poem of his written in golden letters on their shrine.

These facts explain, as far as it needs explanation, the great flaw in Pindar's life. He lived through the Persian War ; he saw the beginning of the great period of Greek enlightenment and progress. In both crises he stood, the unreasoning servant of sacerdotal tradition and racial prejudice, on the side of Bœotia and Delphi. One might have hoped that when Thebes joined the Persian, this poet, the friend of statesmen and kings in many countries, the student from Athens, would have protested. On the contrary, though afterwards when the war was won he could write *Nemean* iv. and the Dithyramb for Athens, in the crisis itself he made what Polybius calls (iv. 31) "a most shameful and injurious refusal" : he wrote a poem of which two large dreamy lines are preserved, talking of peace and neutrality ! It is typical of the man. Often in thinking over the best pieces of Pindar—the majestic organ-playing, the grave strong magic of language, the lightning-flashes of half-revealed mystery—one wonders why this man is not counted the greatest poet that ever lived, why he has not done more, mattered more. The answer perhaps is that he was a poet and nothing else. He thought in music ; he loved to live among great and beautiful images—Heracles, Achilles, Perseus, Iâson, the daughters of Cadmus. When any part of his beloved saga repelled his moral sensitiveness, he glided away from it, careful not to express scepticism, careful also not to speak evil of a god. He loved poetry and music, especially his own. As a matter of fact, there was no poetry in the world like his, and when other people sang they jarred on him, he confesses, '*like crows.*'

He loved religion, and is on the emotional side a great religious poet. The opening of *Nemean* vi. is characteristic ; so is the end of his last dated work (*Pyth.* viii.) : "*Things of a day ! what are we and what not ?   A dream about a shadow is man ; yet when some god-given splendour falls, a glory of light comes over him and his life is sweet.   Oh, Blessed Mother Ægîna, guard thou this city in the ways of freedom, with Zeus and Prince Æacus and Peleus and good Telamon and Achilles !*"—a rich depth of emotion, and then a childlike litany of traditional saints. His religious speculations are sometimes far from fortunate, as in *Olympian* i. ; sometimes they lead to slight improvements. For instance, the old myth said that the nymph Corônis, loved by Phœbus, was secretly false to him ; but a raven saw her, and told the god. Pindar corrects this : "*the god's all-seeing mind*" did not need the help of the raven. It is quite in the spirit of the Delphic movement in religion, the defensive reformation from the inside. Pindar is a moralist: parenthetical preaching is his favourite form of ornament; it comes in perfunctorily, like the verbal quibbles and assonances in Shakespeare. But the essence of his morality has not advanced much beyond Hesiod; save that where Hesiod tells his peasant to work and save, Pindar exhorts his nobleman to seek for honour and be generous. His ideal is derived straight from the Dorian aristocratic tradition. You must start by being well-born and brave and strong. You must then do two things, *work* and *spend:* work with body and soul; spend time and money and force, in pursuit of ἀρετὰ, 'goodness.' And what is 'goodness'? The sum of the qualities of the true Dorian man, descended from the god-born, labouring, fearless, unwearied fighter against the enemies of gods and men, Heracles. It is not absolutely necessary to be rich—there were poor Spartans; nor good-looking—some of his prize boxers were probably the reverse. But honour and renown you must have. Eccentric commentators have even translated ἀρετὰ as 'success in games'—which it implied, much as the ideal of a mediæval knight implied success in the tourney.

Pindar is not false to this ideal. The strange air of abject worldliness which he sometimes wears, comes not because his idealism forsakes him, but because he has no sense of fact. The thing he loved was real heroism. But he could not see it out of its traditional setting; and when the setting was there, his own imagination sufficed to create the heroism. He was moved by the holy splendour of Delphi and Olympia; he liked the sense of distinction and remoteness from the vulgar

H

which hung about the court of a great prince, and he idealised the merely powerful Hiero as easily as the really gallant Chromios. Not that he is ever conscious of identifying success with merit; quite the reverse. He is deeply impressed with the power of envy and dishonest arts—the victory of the subtle Ionian Odysseus over the true Æacid Aias. It was this principle perhaps which helped him to comprehend why Simônides had such a reputation, and why a mob of Athenian sailors, with no physique and no landed property, should make such a stir in the world.

It is a curious freak of history that has preserved us only his ' Epinîkoi'—songs for winners in the sacred games at Olympia, Pytho, Nemea, and the Isthmus. Of all his seventeen books—" Hymns; Pæans; Dithyrambs, 2; Prosodia, 2; Parthenia, 3; Dance-songs, 2; Encômia; Dirges; Epinîkoi, 4 "—the four we possess are certainly not the four we should have chosen. Yet there is in the kind of song something that suits Pindar's genius. For one thing, it does not really matter what he writes about. Two of his sublimest poems are on mule-races. If we are little interested by the fact that Xenophon of Corinth won the Stadium and the Five Bouts at Olympia in the fifth century B.C., neither are we much affected by the drowning of young Edward King in the seventeenth A.D. Poems like *Lycidas* and *Olympian* xiii. are independent of the facts that gave rise to them. And, besides, one cannot help feeling in Pindar a genuine fondness for horses and grooms and trainers. If a horse from Kynoskephalæ ever won a local race, the boy Pindar and his fellow-villagers must have talked over the points of that horse and the proceedings of his trainer with real affection. And whether or no the poet was paid extra for the references to Melêsias the 'professional,' and to the various uncles and grandfathers of his victors, he introduces them with a great semblance of spontaneous interest. It looks as if he was one of those un-self-conscious natures who do not much differentiate their emotions : he feels a thrill at the sight of Hiero's full-dress banquet board, of a wrestling bout, or of a horse-race, just as he does at the thought of the labour and glory of Heracles ; and every thrill makes him sing.

Pindar was really three years younger than Æschylus ; yet he seems a generation older than Simônides. His character and habits of thought are all archaic ; so is his style. Like most other divisions of Greek literature, the lyric had been working from obscure force to lucidity. It had reached it in Simônides and Bacchylides. Pindar throws us back to Alcman, almost. He is hard even to read ; can any one have understood him, sung ? He tells us how his sweet song will "*sail off from Ægina in the big ships and the little fishing-boats*" as they separate homewards after the festival (*Nem.* v.). Yet one can scarcely believe that the Dorian fishermen could catch at one hearing much of so difficult a song. Perhaps it was only the tune they took, and the news of the victory. He was proud of his music ; and Aristoxenus, the best judge we have, cannot praise it too highly. Even now, though every wreck of the music is lost—the Messina musical fragment (of *Pyth.* i.) being spurious—one feels that the words need singing to make them intelligible. The mere meaning and emotion of *Pythian* iv. or *Olympian* ii. —to take two opposite types—compel the words into a chant, varying between slow and fast, loud and low. The clause-endings ring like music : παλίγκοτον δαμασθέν (*Olymp.* ii.) is much more than "*angry and overborne.*" The king of the Epeans, when "*into the deep channel running deathwards, he watched*—ἴζοισαν ἑὰν πόλιν—*his own city sink*" (*Olymp.* x. 38), remains in one's mind by the echoing "*my own*" of the last words ; so Pelops praying "*by the grey sea-surge*—οἶος ἐν ὄρφνᾳ, *alone in the darkness*"—in *Olymp.* i.; so that marvellous trumpet-crash in *Pyth.* iv. (*ant.* 5) on the last great word τιμάν. Many lovers of Pindar agree that the things that stay in one's mind, stay not as thoughts, but as music.

But his worthy lovers are few. He is hard in the original—dialect, connection, state of mind, all are difficult to enter into; ordinary readers are bewildered by the mixture of mules and the new moon and trainers and the Æacidæ. In translations—despite the great skill of some of them—he is perhaps more grotesquely naked than any poet ; and that, as we saw above, for the usual reason, that he is nothing but a poet. There is little rhetoric, no philosophy, little human interest; only that fine bloom— what he calls ἄωτος—which comes when the most sensitive language meets the most exquisite thought, and which "not even a god though he worked hard" could keep unhurt in another tongue.

Pindar was little influenced either by the movements of his own time or by previous writers. Stêsichorus and Homer have of course affected him. There are just a few notes that seem echoed from Æschylus : the eruption of Ætna is treated by both ; but Pindar seems quite by himself in his splendid description (*Pyth.* i.). It is possible that his great line λῦσὲ δε Ζεὺς ἄφθιτος Τιτᾶνας, is suggested by the *Prometheus* trilogy, of which it is the great lesson—"*Everlasting Zeus set free the Titans.*"

V

THE BEGINNINGS OF PROSE

INSCRIPTIONS

IF our earliest specimens of Greek prose are inscribed on stone and bronze, that only means that these are durable materials, and have outlived the contemporary wood and wax and parchment. At the time of the treaty between Elis and Heræa in the sixth century, there must have been plenty of commercial and diplomatic correspondence; far more again, before the later treaty could be made between Oianthê and Chaleion, regulating the right of Forcible Reprisal ($\sigma\hat{v}\lambda a\iota$), and fixing the mild penalty of four drachmæ for exercising that form of piracy in the wrong place. But it looks as if the earliest prose was in essence similar to these inscriptions—a record of plain, accurate statements of public importance, which could not be trusted to the play of a poet's imagination or the exigencies of his metre. The temples especially were full of such writings. There were notices about impiety. At Ialysus, for instance, the goddess Alectrôna announced a fine of 10,000 drachmæ for the entrance into her precinct of horses, mules, asses, and men in pig-skin shoes. There were full public statements of accounts. There were records of the prayers which the god had answered, engraved at the cost of the votary; of the offences he had signally visited, engraved, presumably, by the temple authorities. In the medical temples of Cos, Rhodes, and Cnidus, there were, as early as the sixth century B.C., full notes of interesting diseases, giving the symptoms, the treatment, and the result. There were, doubtless, records of prodigies and their expiations. There were certainly lists of priests and priestesses, sometimes expanding into a kind of chronicle.

These were public and subject to a certain check. But there were also more esoteric books, not exposed to the criticism of the vulgar. The ceremonial rules were sometimes published and sometimes not ; the Exêgêtai at Athens had secret records of omens and judgments on points of law or conscience ; in Delphi and other centres, where the tradition was rich, there were written ὑπομνή-ματα ('memoirs') of the stories which the servants of the god wished to preserve. And, of course, outside and beyond the official temple-worship, there was the private and unauthorised preacher and prophet, the holder of mysteries, the seller of oracles, the remitter of sins—men like Onomacritus, Tisamenus the Iamid, Lampon, and the various Bakides, whose misty and romantic stories can frequently be traced in Herodotus. And there were also the noble families. Their bare genealogies were often in verse, in a form suitable for quoting, and easily remembered among the public. But even in the genealogies other branches of the same stock were apt to have contradictory versions ; and when it came to lives and deeds, which might be forgotten or misrepresented, the family did well to keep authentic records, suitably controlled, in its own hands.

'STORY'

And here we meet the other tendency which goes to the forming of prose history, the old *Lust zum Fabuliren*, taking the form of interest in individuals and a wish to know their characters and their stories. The Story is a younger and lesser sister of the Saga, in some lights not to be distinguished from her. It is impossible to read our accounts of Solon, Crœsus, Demokêdes, Polycrates, Amâsis, without feeling that we are in the realm of imaginative fiction. We are nearer to fact than in the epos; and the fact behind is more a human fact. The characters are not gods or heroes, they are adventurous prophets and sages and discrowned kings; the original speaker is not the Muse, but the Ionian traveller. It may even be supposed that there is a certain truth in the characters, if in nothing else. But that is further than we have a right to go; Sir John Falstaff is not psychologically true to Oldcastle the Lollard; there is no reason to suppose that the farcical king Amâsis resembles any Egyptian Aahmes, or to credit the mellow wisdom of our Crœsus to the real conqueror of Ionia. Once created, it is true, the character generally stays; but that is the case even with the men of the epos.

The story was early fixed as literature. The famous Milesian and Sybarite stories must date from the sixth century B.C., before Sybaris was destroyed and Miletus ruined. Such instances as have been preserved in late tradition—'The Widow of Ephesus' in Petronius, and large parts of Appuleius—are pure fiction, tales in the tone of Boccaccio, with imaginary characters. But everything points to the belief that in their first form they were attached to historical names like the anecdotes of Herodotus; and as a matter of fact the earliest fragment of Greek prose romance known,[1] has for its hero and heroine Ninus and Semiramis.

CHRONICLES

For literature in the narrower sense, the first important prose histories are the chronicles (ὧροι) of Ionian towns, followed closely by those of Sicily. No set of 'Hôroi' is extant, unless one may regard the Parian Marble as an attempted abbreviation of the 'Hôroi' of all Hellas. It still remains for the student of antiquity to make out what data in our tradition go back to the ancient annals of particular towns. Some local genealogies—many, for instance, in the Scholia to Apollonius—clearly do so; so does that meteoric stone which fell at Aigospotamoi in the seventy-eighth Olympiad; and so does that "white swallow no smaller than a partridge" whose appearance in Samos has such a cloud of witnesses.[2] A Syracusan chronicle seems to be the source of the record which Thucydides (vi. 1–5) gives of the foundations of the Italian and Sicilian towns; they are dated by the foundation of Syracuse, which is taken as the great era of the world not needing closer specification. The origin of any given chronicle is of course lost in obscurity. Like the epos in early times, like even the histories and commentaries and the philosophical text-books of the various schools in later antiquity, like the cathedrals of the Middle

---

[1] *Hermes*, xxvii. 161 ff.

[2] The stone is given in the Parian Marble; the swallow's witnesses are Aristotle (fr. 531), Antigonus Carystius, Heraclides Ponticus, and Ælian quoting Alexander Myndius.

Ages, the chronicles were continued and altered and expanded under a succession of editors.

The names of the earliest chroniclers have a mythical ring. The Chronicle of Corinth was written by 'Eumê-lus' himself, the Corinthian Homer; the Ephesian by 'Creophŷlus,' the Cretan by 'Epimenides.' That of Miletus, commonly acknowledged to be the oldest of all, was the first thing written by CADMUS, when he had invented letters! He is called 'Cadmus of Miletus,' though by birth a Phœnician, just as the Argive chronicler is called 'ACUSILÂUS of Argos,' though a native, like Hesiod, of a little village in Bœotia. His chronicle is said to have consisted of Hesiod turned into prose and 'corrected.' But even Acusiláus ('*Hearken-people*') is not misty enough to be its real author; he only transcribed it from the bronze tablets which his father found buried in the earth! The Chronicle of Athens, afterwards worked up by many able men such as Cleidêmus, Androtiôn, Philochorus, has left no tradition of its origin. A certain MELÊSAGORAS, who knows why no crow has ever been seen on the Acropolis, seems to represent the sacred Chronicle of Eleusis, and thus in part that of Athens. There are many important fragments quoted from 'PHEREKŶDES': Suidas distinguishes three of the name, from Syros, Leros, and Athens, respectively; modern scholars generally allow two only—a seventh-century philosopher from Syros, and a fifth-century Athenian historian born in Leros; while a critical study of the evidence will probably reduce the list to one — whose chronicle began with the origin of the gods and contained the 'words of Orpheus'—a half-mythical '*Bring-renown*' parallel to '*Hearken-people*' of Argos.

The first real chroniclers come from Ionia and the islands, thoughtful and learned men, who put into books both the records and the oral tradition — BION of Proconnêsus, who worked over Cadmus ; DIONYSIUS of Miletus, perhaps the first who tempered the records of his unheroic Ionia with the great deeds of Persia ; CHARON of Lampsacus, whose work must have been something like that of Herodotus, taking in Persian and Ethiopian history, details in Themistocles's life, and voyages beyond the pillars of Heracles ; EUGÆON of Samos, XANTHUS of Lydia, and many others leading up to the great triad, Hecatæus, Herodotus, Hellanîcus.

In the West it is a different story. A rich and tragic history was there, and a great imaginative literature ; but the two did not meet. There were no writers of history till after the time when the aged Herodotus went over to finish his days in Thurii. Then ANTIOCHUS of Syracuse published a record of the West reaching at least as far down as the year 424 B.C. The problematic HIPPYS of Rhêgion may have written at the same time. The Westerns had, no doubt, their temple records, and produced a great group of historians in the generation after Thucydides. But in the beginning of prose composition it is significant that they treated literature before history. THEAGENES of Rhêgion (520 B.C.?) is counted as the first Homeric scholar ; we only know that he explained something 'allegorically' and told about the War of the Giants. GLAUCUS of Rhêgion wrote 'About Poets,' giving not only names and dates, but styles and tendencies as well, and stating what original authors each poet 'admired' or followed, from Orpheus onward, who "*admired nobody, because at that time there was nobody.*" It is this tendency, this interest in pure literature, which explains the rise of Gorgias.

If we search in Eastern Greece for critics of Homer, we shall find them only in the chroniclers of the towns which have special connection with him, like ANTIDÔRUS of Kymê, and DAMASTES of Sigêum. Nevertheless the higher prose literature took its rise in the East, in that search for knowledge in the widest sense, which the Ionian called ἱστορίη, and the Athenian apparently φιλοσοφία. We are apt to apply to the sixth century the terminology of the fourth, and to distinguish philosophy from history. But when Solon the philosopher "went over much land in search of knowledge," he was doing exactly the same thing as the historians Herodotus and Hecatæus. And when this last made a 'Table' of the world, with its geography and anthropology, he was in company with the philosophers Anaximander and Democritus. 'Historiê' is inquiry, and 'Philosophia' is love of knowledge. The two cover to a great extent the same field—though, on the whole, philosophy aims more at ultimate truth and less at special facts; and, what is more important, philosophy is generally the work of an organised school with more or less fixed or similar doctrines—Milesians, Pythagoreans, Eleatics— while the 'Historikos' is mostly a traveller and reciter of stories.

A prose book in the sixth century was, except in the case of a text-book for a philosophic school, the result of the author's 'Historiê'; it was his 'Logos,' the thing he had to say. Neither the book itself nor the kind of literature to which it belonged had any name. The first sentence served as a kind of title-page. The simplest form is—"*Alkmæon of Crotôn says this*"; "*This is the*

setting forth of the research of Herodotus of Halicarnassus."
In a more specialised ' Historiê '—*"Antiochus, Xenophanes' son, put these things together about Italy" ;* or without the author's name—*" This I say about the whole world"* (Democritus) ; *" Touching the disease called Holy, thus it is"* (Hippocrates). And what was the man who so wrote ?   He was obviously λογογράφος, or λογοποιός, since he had made a ' Logos.'   He was probably γεωγράφος and θεολόγος ; presumably φιλόσοφος, and in the eyes of his admirers a σοφὸς ἀνήρ. If you wished to quote his nameless and chapterless work you had to use some descriptive phrase.   As you referred to the middle part of τ as " Homer in the Foot-washing," so you spoke of " Hecatæus in Asia," or " in the parts about Asia " ; " Charon in the Persian parts " ; " Anaximander about Fixed Stars," or " in the Description of the World."   Late tradition often took these references for the titles of separate works, and made various early authors write books by the dozen.

The early epos was taken as a fact in itself ; it was either authorless, or the work of an imaginary and semidivine author ; so was the story ; so was the chronicle ; so, of course, were the beginnings of speculation and cosmology. In the next stage a book is the work of a corporation ; a guild of poets ; a school of philosophers ; a sect of votaries ; a board of officials.   First ' Homer,' ' Æsop,' ' Hesiod, "Orpheus,' ' Cadmus' ; next Homeridæ, Pythagoristæ, Orphics, and Ὧροι Μιλησίων. The close bond of the old Greek civic life had to be shattered before an individual could rise in person and express his views and feelings in the sacred majesty of a book.   In poetry Archilochus and others had already done it.   In prose the epoch was made by a book of which the open-

ing words must have rung like a trumpet call in men's
ears : "*Hecatæus of Miletus thus speaks. I write as I deem
true, for the traditions of the Greeks seem to me manifold
and laughable.*"

'HISTORIÊ'

HECATÆUS

HECATÆUS was a man of high rank; descendant of a god
in the sixteenth generation, he had always been told, till
the priests at Egyptian Thebes confuted him [1]; a traveller
of a rare type, like his contemporary Skylax, who sailed
down the Indus to the Erythræan Sea, like Eudoxus of
Cyzicus under Ptolemy II., in a certain degree like
Columbus, men whose great daring was the servant of
their greater intellect.   He travelled all about the Mediterranean coasts, in the Persian Empire, and in Egypt,
perhaps in the Pontus and Libya and Iberia, always
ἱστορέων, 'seeking after knowledge.'   We know him
chiefly from the criticisms and anecdotes of Herodotus
who differs from him about the rise of the Nile (ii. 21) and
the existence of the river Oceanus (ii. 23), and states with
reserve his account of the expulsion of the Pelasgians
from Attica (vi. 137), but invests his general story of the
man with a suggestion of greatness.

In the first brewing of the Ionian revolt (v. 36) Miletus
sought its Wise Man's counsel ; not, however, to follow
it.   He urged them not to rebel, "*telling them all the
nations that Darius ruled and the power of him.*"   The
Wise Man was cold and spoke above their heads !   Then,
if they must revolt, he urged them to seize at once the

---

[1] Hdt. ii. 143.

treasures of Apollo at Branchidæ—the Persians would take them if they did not—and to build a fleet that could command the Ægean. The Wise Man was flecked with impiety ! Aristagoras and the people preferred their own way, were routed everywhere, and saw the treasure fall, sure enough, into the hands of the enemy. One other counsel he gave when things seemed hopeless, urging Aristagoras not to fly altogether, but to fortify the island of Leros, hold the sea, and attempt to win Miletus again. That is, all the things which Ionia wished she had done, in looking back upon her bitter history, became in the story the neglected counsels of her great Hecatæus. And it was he, too, who mediated with Artaphernes for the sparing of the conquered towns — that, at least, successfully.

Hecatæus was not a literary artist like Herodotus : he was a thinker and worker. His style, according to Hermogenes (2nd cent. A.D.), who loved the archaic, was "pure and clear, and in some ways singularly pleasant " ; yet, on the whole, the book had "much less charm than Herodotus—ever so much, though it was mostly myths and the like." One must not lay much stress on the last words ; history, to Hecatæus, lay in the ages which we have now abandoned as mythical, and, while he rejected the Greek traditions, he often followed the Egyptian. But we cannot in the face of his opening words talk of his 'credulity,' or make him responsible for the legend that Oineus's bitch gave birth to a vine-stump[1] ; he may have mentioned the story only to ridicule it. In his geographical work he was the standard authority for many centuries ; and though he is not likely to have been quite consistent in his rationalism, he remains a great

[1] Frag. 341.

figure both in the history of literature and in the march of the human mind. Hecatæus represents the spirit of his age as a whole, the research, the rationalism, the literary habit. Herodotus is the most typical illustration of the last of these tendencies ; for the others we select two of the unpreserved writers, Hêrodôrus and Hellanîcus.

HÊRODÔRUS

HÊRODÔRUS of Heraclêa, father of the sophist Bryson, whose dialogues are said to have influenced Plato, is the typical early rationalist. His work was a critical history of the earliest records, dealing primarily with his native town and its founder, Heracles, but touching, for instance, on the Argonauts and the Pelopidæ. His method is one that has lost its charms for us ; but it meant hard thinking, and it wrought real service to humanity. Prometheus, bound, torn by the eagle, and delivered by Heracles, was really a Scythian chief near the river called Eagle, which, as is well known, makes ruinous floods. The inhabitants, thinking (as Hesiod thought) that floods were a punishment for the sins of princes, bound, *i.e.* imprisoned, Prometheus, till Heracles, who is recorded to have received from Atlas "the pillars of earth and heaven "—*i.e.* the foundations of astronomy, geography, and practical science—engineered the stream into a proper seaward course. Laomedon, again, was said to have defrauded Apollo and Poseidon of their reward after they had built his walls for him. That is the simplest matter : he took money from their temples for the building and did not restore it.[1] It was per-

---

[1] Frag. 23, 24, 18.

haps part of Hêrodôrus's method to state the common story before criticising it, for we find him quoted, like Hecatæus, as an authority for some of the absurdest legends, which almost certainly he must have explained away. He was not an unimaginative sceptic, however : he went so far as to believe the well-authenticated tradition that the Nemean Lion fell from the moon. This was because he believed that the moon was not a small light, but 'another earth' ; that meteorites and the like probably fell from it ; that certain insects, and, more notably, vultures, whose nests, as far as he could discover, had never been seen on earth, were likely to have flown down from there ; he perhaps added that the lion cannot possibly have been born in Nemea, and cannot well have travelled there from Mount Hæmus ; that, moreover, the description of it does not tally with that of any known lion. This is not 'simple credulity' : given that he underrated the distance of the moon from us, it is a very excusable error in rationalism. He tried hard to systematise his chronology—that gigantic labour which no Greek Heracles ever quite accomplished ; his geographical studies were wide and careful,[1] and all he did was subservient to a criticism of early history. How different it is, though not in kind inferior, to the spirit of Herodotus and Thucydides !

THE EARLY 'HISTORIKOI'

HELLANÎCUS

HELLANÎCUS of Lesbos is so far fixed in date, that his *Atthis* * is mentioned by Thucydides (i. 97), and con-

[1] Frag. 20, 46.

tained a mention of the battle of Arginusæ [1]—that is,
it was published shortly after 406 B.C.   Hellanîcus is
younger than Herodotus, older than Thucydides.   The
date is of interest, because the general method of
Hellanîcus's work, whatever it may have been in detail,
is not that of Hecatæus or Hêrodôrus, or either of our
historians, but simply that of a ruder Aristotle.   He
went straight to the local record, inscriptional or oral :
he collected a mass of definite, authorised statements of
fact ; forced them into order by a thorough-going system
of chronology ; made each local history throw light on
the others, and recorded his deductions in a business-like
way.   Unfortunately the material he was treating was
unworthy of his method.   The facts he collected were
not facts ; and the order he produced was worse than the
honest chaos which preceded it.

He began, like so many others, by composing *Per-
sika ;* * the fragments seem to be earlier than Herodotus,
and are full of ordinary Greek 'Stories.'   The middle
part of his activity went to a study of the great groups
of legends, to what seemed to him the valuable stores of
remote history then in danger of passing away.   He
wrote *Aiolika* * and *Troika ;* * the local tendencies of
his Æolian birthplace close to Troy explain the selection.
The Æolian traditions led him inevitably to Thessaly, to
the attempt at a record of the descendants of Deucalion
(*Deucaliôneia* *).   The second richest centre of legends in
Greece was Argos, and its traditions were almost independent of Thessaly.   He betook him to Argos, and not
only wrote *Argolika,* * but, what was now demanded by
his developing method, published a list of the successive
priestesses of Hera at Argos, as the basis of a uniform

---

[1] Schol. Ar. *Ranæ*, 694, 720.

I

system of chronology for all the history of the past. It is perhaps through Hellanîcus that Thucydides uses this record,[1] though it was recognised in the Peloponnese before. Meantime, it would seem, the sophist Hippias had issued his epoch-making list of the Olympiads with their successive victors. Hellanîcus followed him with a list of the victors in the games of Apollo Karneios at Sparta.

Hellanîcus had now written a number of separate books. Unlike Herodotus, he gave his various sources undisguised, and did not attempt to mould them all into a personal 'Logos' of his own. He seems even to have given the books names—'*Phorônis*,' * as the Argive history was called, after the ancient king Phorôneus, is a title pure and simple ; and '*Deucaliôneia*,' * half-way between a description and a title. It was after this, to all appearance, that he came to Athens and wrote his celebrated *Atthis* * (Ἀττικὴ συγγραφή). The Athenians of the past generations had been too busy making history to be able to write it. The foreign savant did it for them. It is unfortunate that his interests were more in the past than the present. He began with Ogygos, who was king a thousand and twenty years before the first Olympiad, and ran mercilessly through all the generations of empty names requisite to fill in the gaping centuries. He had started from the Argive list, which was very full ; and he had to extend the meagre Attic list of kings by supposing duplicates of the same name. When he comes to the times that we most wish to know about—the fifty years after the Persian War—the method which he had laboriously built up for the treatment of legend, leaves him helpless in dealing with concrete fact. "Short, and

[1] ii. 2 ; iv. 133.

in his treatment of dates inexact," is the judgment passed upon him by Thucydides. But dates were the man's great glory ! He reckoned by generations, three to a century, in the earliest times, by the annual archons as soon as they were established. Thucydides, in all probability, means that the system of putting the events down in a lump against the archon's name, was inexact compared with his own division of succeeding summers and winters. Hellanîcus was a widely-read and influential author, but he gets rough handling from his critics : Ephorus " puts him in the first rank of liars." [1] Apollodorus says, " He shows the greatest carelessness in almost every treatise " ; Strabo himself " would sooner believe Homer, Hesiod, and the tragedians." This last statement seems only to mean that the general tradition embodied in the poets is safer than the local tradition followed by Hellanîcus. He was an able, systematic, conscientious historian, though it might possibly have been better for history had he never existed.

[1] ἐν τοῖς πλείστοις ψευδόμενον. *Cf.* Josephus c. Ap. i. 3 ; Strabo, x. 451, and xiii. 612.

VI

HERODOTUS

HERODOTUS, SON OF LYXES OF HALICARNASSUS (484 (?)–425 (?) B.C.)

HERODOTUS, the father of history,[1] was an exiled man and a professional story-teller ; not of course an 'improvisatore,' but the prose correlative of a bard, a narrator of the deeds of real men, and a describer of foreign places. His profession was one which aimed, as Thucydides severely says, more at success in a passing entertainment than at any lasting discovery of truth ; its first necessity was to interest an audience. Herodotus must have had this power whenever he opened his lips ; but he seems to have risen above his profession, to have advanced from a series of public readings to a great history—perhaps even to more than that. For his work is not only an account of a thrilling struggle, politically very important, and spiritually tremendous ; it is also, more perhaps than any other known book, the expression of a whole man, the representation of all the world seen through the medium of one mind and in a particular perspective. The world was at that time very interesting ; and the one mind, while strongly individual, was one of the most comprehensive known to human records.

---

[1] Cic. *de Leg.* i. 1.

Herodotus's whole method is highly subjective. He is too sympathetic to be consistently critical, or to remain cold towards the earnest superstitions of people about him : he shares from the outset their tendency to read the activity of a moral God in all the moving events of history. He is sanguine, sensitive, a lover of human nature, interested in details if they are vital to his story, oblivious of them if they are only facts and figures ; he catches quickly the atmosphere of the society he moves in, and falls readily under the spell of great human influences, the solid impersonal Egyptian hierarchy or the dazzling circle of great individuals at Athens ; yet all the time shrewd, cool, gentle in judgment, deeply and unconsciously convinced of the weakness of human nature, the flaws of its heroism and the excusableness of its apparent villainy. His book bears for good and ill the stamp of this character and this profession.

He was a native of Halicarnassus, in the far south of Asia Minor, a mixed state, where a Dorian strain had first overlaid the native Carian, and then itself yielded to the higher culture of Ionian neighbours, while all alike were subjects of Persia : a good nursery for a historian who was to be remarkable for his freedom from prejudices of race. He was born about 484 B.C. amid the echoes of the great conflict. Artemisia, queen of Halicarnassus, fought for Xerxes at Salamis, and her grandson Lygdamis still held the place as tyrant under Artaxerxes after 460. Herodotus's first years of manhood were spent in fighting under the lead of his relative, the poet and prophet Panyâsis, to free his city from the tyrant and the Persian alike. He never mentions these wars in his book, but they must have marked his character somewhat. Panyâsis fell into the tyrant's

hands and was put to death. Herodotus fled to Samos.
At last, in what way we know not, Lygdamis fell and
Herodotus returned ; but the party in power was for
some reason hostile to him—possibly they were 'auto-
nomists,' while he stood for the Athenian League—and
Herodotus entered upon his life of wandering. He
found a second home in Athens, where he had a friend
in Sophocles, and probably in Pericles and Lampon.
He was finally provided for by a grant of citizenship
in Thurii, the model international colony which Athens
founded in South Italy, in 443, on the site of the twice-
ruined Sybaris. Of his later life and travels we know
little definite. He travelled in Egypt as far as Elephan-
tînê at some time when the country was in the hands
of Persia, and of course when Persia was at peace with
Athens—after 447, that is. He had then already finished
his great Asiatic journey (ii. 150) past Babylon to the
neighbourhoods of Susa and Ecbatana. At some time
he made a journey in the Black Sea to the mouths of
the Ister, the Crimea, and the land of the Colchians.
Pericles went through the Black Sea with a large fleet
in 444 ; perhaps Herodotus had been employed beforehand to examine the resources of the region. Besides
this, he went by ship to Tyre, and seems to have travelled
down the Syrian coast to the boundary of Egypt. He
went to Cyrênê and saw something of Libya. He knew
the coast of Thrace, and traversed Greece itself in all
directions, seeing Dodôna, Acarnania, Delphi, Thebes,
and Athens, and, in the Peloponnese, Tegea, Sparta,
and Olympia.

What was the object of all this travelling ; and how
was a man who had lost his country, and presumably
could not draw on his estate, able to pay for it ? It is a

tantalising question, and the true answer would probably tell us much that is now unknown about Greek life in the fifth century B.C. Herodotus may have travelled partly as a merchant ; yet he certainly speaks of merchants in an external way ; and he not only mentions— as is natural considering the aim of his book—but seems really to have visited, places of intellectual interest rather than trade-centres. In one place (ii. 44) he says explicitly that he sailed to Tyre in order to find out a fact about Heracles. The truth seems to be that he was a professional ' Logopoios,' a maker and reciter of ' Logoi,' ' *Things to tell*,' just as Kynaithos, perhaps as Panyâsis, was a maker and reciter of ' Epê,' ' Verses.' The anecdotic tradition which speaks of his public readings at Athens, Thebes, Corinth, and Olympia, certainly has some substratum of truth. He travelled as the bards and the sophists travelled ; like the Homeridæ, like Pindar, like Hellanîcus, like Gorgias. In Greek communities he was sure of remunerative audiences ; beyond the Greek world he at least collected fresh ' Logoi.' One may get a little further light from the fact attested by Diyllus the Aristotelian (end of 4th cent. B.C.), that Herodotus was awarded ten talents (£2400) on the motion of Anytus by a decree of the Athenian Demos. That is not a payment for a series of readings : it is the reward of some serious public service. And it seems better to interpret that service as the systematic collection of knowledge about the regions that were politically important to Athens— Persia, Egypt, Thrace, and Scythia, to say nothing of states like Argos—than as the historical defence of Athens as the ' *saviour of Hellas*,' at the opening of the Peloponnesian War. Even the published book, as we have it, is full of information which must have been invaluable to an Athenian politician of the time of Pericles ; and it stands to reason that Herodotus must have had masses of further knowledge which he could impart to the Athenian ' Foreign Office,' but decidedly not publish for the use of all Hellas.

The histories of Herodotus are ordinarily divided into nine books, named after the nine Muses. The division is of course utterly post-classic ; Herodotus knew nothing of his ' Muses,' but simply headed his work, " *This is the account of the research of Herodotus of Thurii.*" In our editions it is " *Herodotus of Halicarnassus,*" but he must have written "*of Thurii*" by all analogy, and Aristotle read "*of Thurii.*" The Athenian or Eastern book-trade, appealing to a public which knew the man as a Halicarnassian, was naturally tempted to head its scrolls accordingly. It is like the case of the *Anabasis*, which appeared pseudonymously as the work of Themistogenês of Syracuse (see p. 319) ; but it was known to be really Xenophon's, and the book-trade preferred to head it with the better-known name.

The last three books of Herodotus give the history of the invasion of Xerxes and its repulse ; the first six form a sort of introduction to them, an account of the gradual gathering up of all the forces of the world under Persia, the restive kicking of Ionia against the irresistible, and the bursting of the storm upon Greece. The connection is at first loose, scarcely visible ; only as we go on we begin to feel the growing intensity of the theme—the concentration of all the powers and nations to which we have been gradually introduced, upon the one great conflict.

Starting from the mythical and primeval enmity between Asia and Europe, Herodotus takes up his history with Crœsus of Lydia, the first Asiatic who enslaved Greek cities. The Lydian 'Logoi,' rich and imaginative, saturated with Delphic tradition, lead up to the conquest of Lydia by Cyrus, and the rise of Persia to the empire of Asia. The past history and subjugation of Media and Babylon come as explanations of the greatness of Persia, and the story goes on to the conquest of Egypt by Cambyses. Book II. is all occupied with the Egyptian 'Logoi.' Book III. returns to the narrative, Cambyses' wild reign over Egypt, the false Smerdis, the conspiracy and rise of Darius, and his elaborate organisation of the Empire. In Book IV., Darius, looking for further conquests, marches against the Scythians, and the hand of Persia is thus first laid upon Europe in the north — here come the Scythian 'Logoi'; while meantime at the far south the queen of Cyrênê has called in the Persian army against Barca, and the terrible power advances over Libya as well—here is a place for the Libyan 'Logoi.' In Book V., while a division of the Scythian army is left behind under Megabazos, to reduce Thrace—here come the Thracian 'Logoi'—Aristagoras, tyrant of Miletus, prompted by his father-in-law the ex-tyrant, harassed with debt, and fearing the consequences of certain military failures, plunges all Ionia into a desperate revolt against the Persian. He seeks help from the chief power of Greece, and from the mother-city of the Ionians. Sparta refuses ; Athens consents. Eretria, the old ally of Miletus, goes with Athens ; and in the first heat of the rising the two strike deep into the Persian dominion and burn Sardis, only to beat forthwith an inevitable retreat, and to make their own destruction a necessity for Persian honour. Book VI. gives the steady reduction of Ionia,

the end of Aristagoras, the romantic and terrible
flights of whole communities from the Persian vengeance ; the hand of the king is uplifted over Greece.
In the north the great Mardonius advances, persistently
successful, recovering Thrace and the islands, and
receiving the submission of Macedonia ; in the south,
Datis comes by sea direct upon Eretria and Athens.
And at the same time heralds are sent to the Greek
states demanding 'earth and water,' the token of submission to the king's will.

Through all these books, but in VI. more than any,
the history of the Greek states has been gathered up in
digressions and notes, historically on a higher plane than
the main current of the narrative in Asia. Datis lands in
Eubœa and discharges the first part of his orders by
sweeping Eretria from the face of the earth, then proceeds to Marathon to fulfil the remaining part. He is
met, not by the united Greeks, not even by the great
Dorian cities, only by the Athenians and a band of
heroic volunteers from Platæa—met, and by God's help,
to man's amazement, defeated. After this the progress
of the narrative is steady. Book VII. indeed moves
slowly : there is the death of Darius and the succession
of Xerxes ; the long massing of an invincible army,
the preparations which 'shake Asia' for three years.
There are the heart-searchings and waverings of various
states, the terror, and the hardly-sustained heroism ;
the eager inquiries of men who find the plain facts to
be vaster than their fears ; the awful voice of the
God in whom they trust at Delphi, bidding them only
despair, fly, "*make their minds familiar with horrors.*"
"Athens, who had offended the king, was lost. Argos
and other towns might buy life by submission, by

not joining the fools who dared fight their betters." Then comes the rising of the greater part of Greece above its religion, the gathering of "*them that were better minded*," and thus at last the tremendous narrative of battle.

Much has been written about the composition of the histories of Herodotus. They fall apart very easily, they contain repetitions and contradictions in detail, and the references to events and places outside the course of the story raise problems in the mind of an interested reader. Bauer worked at this question on the hypothesis that the book was made up of separate 'Logoi' inorganically strung together. Kirchhoff held that the work was originally conceived as a whole, and composed gradually. Books I.–III. 119, which show no reference to the West, were written before 447, and before the author went to Thurii; some time later he worked on to the end of Book IV.; lastly, at the beginning of the Peloponnesian War he returned to Athens, and in that stirring time wrote all the second half of his work, Books V.–IX. He had meant to go much further; but the troubles of 431 interrupted the work, and his death left it unfinished. Mr. Macan supposes that the last three books were the first written, and that the rest of the work is a proem, "composed of more or less independent parts, of which II. is the most obvious, while the fourth book contains two other parts, only one degree less obvious"; but that internal evidence can never decide whether any of these parts were composed or published independently.

Some little seems certain : the last events he mentions are the attack on Platæa in 431 B.C., the subsequent invasion of Attica by the Lacedæmonians, and the

execution of the Spartan ambassadors to Persia in 430.[1]
We know he was in Athens after 432, because he had seen
the Propylæa finished. His book must have been fresh
in people's memory at Athens in 425, when Aristophanes
parodied the opening of Book I.[2] Arguing from what he
does not mention, it is probable that he was not writing
after 424, when Nikias took Cythêra (vii. 235), and almost
certain that he did not know of the Sicilian expedition
of 415 or the occupation of Dekeleia in 413. His theme
was the deliverance of Greece and the rise of the
Athenian Empire, and he died before that Empire began
to totter.

For it is clear that he did not live to finish his work.
Kirchhoff argues that he meant to carry the story down
to the Battle of Eurymedon, to the definite point where
the liberated Ionians swore their oath of union under
the hegemony of Athens. That, Kirchhoff holds, is
the real finish of the ' Mêdika' ; not the siege of Sestos,
which is the last event given in our narrative.[3] And
does not Herodotus himself show that he intended to
go further when he promises (vii. 213) to tell ' later '
the cause of the feud in which the traitor Ephialtes
was murdered, an event which occurred some time after
476 ? Kirchhoff says, Yes ; but the conclusion is not
convincing. The cause of the feud may have come
long before the murder, and it is perfectly clear from a
number of passages that Herodotus regards all events
later than 479–8 as not in the sphere of his history. He
dismisses them with the words, *"But these things happened
afterwards."* Thus he does, it seems, reach his last date ;
but he has not finished the revising and fitting. He leaves

[1] vii. 233 ; ix. 73 ; vii. 137 ; *cf.* vi. 91.
[2] *Acharnians*, 524 ff.   [3] Meyer, *Rh. Mus.* xlii. 146.

unfulfilled the promise about Ephialtes; he mentions twice in language very similar, but not identical (i. 175; viii. 104), the fact, not worthy of such signal prominence, that when any untoward event threatened the city of Pêdasus, the priestess of Athena there was liable to grow a beard. More remarkable still, he refers in two places to what he will say in his 'Assyrian Logoi' (i. 106; i. 184), which are not to be found. The actual end of the work is hotly fought over. Can it, a mere anecdote about Cyrus, tacked on to an unimpressive miracle of Protesi-laus's tomb, be the close of the great life-work of an artist in language? It is a question of taste. A love for episodes and anecdotes is Herodotus's chief weakness, and Greek literary art liked to loosen the tension at the end of a work, rather than to finish in a climax.

As to the 'Assyrian Logoi,' the most notable fact is that Aristotle seems to have read them. In the *Natural History* (viii. 18) he says that "crook-clawed birds do not drink. Herodotus[1] did not know this, for he has fabled his ominous eagle drinking, in his account of the siege of Nineveh." That must be in the 'Assyrian Logoi.' *

This clue helps us to a rough theory of the composition of the whole work, which may throw some light on ancient writings in general. If Herodotus was telling and writing his 'Historiai' most of his life, he must have had far more material than he has given us, and parts of that material doubtless in different forms. It is "against nature" to suppose that a 'Logographos' would only utilise a particular 'Logos' once, or never alter the form of it. The treatment of the Pedasus story shows how the anecdote unintentionally varies and gets inserted in

---

[1] Some MSS. 'Ησίοδος, which is hardly possible.

different contexts. Our work clearly seems based on a great mass of material collected and written down in the course of a life-time ; and, on the other hand, it is certainly a unity, the diverse strands being firmly held and woven eventually into the main thread. This view makes it difficult to lay stress on references to later events as proving the late composition of any particular passage. The work as it stands is the composition of the man's last years, though large masses of the material of it may be taken, with hardly a word altered, from manuscripts he has had by him for lustres.

In one important point Meyer and Busolt appear to be right, as against Mr. Macan and most Herodotean authorities—in placing the Egyptian 'Logoi' quite late, after the historian's return from Thurii, rather than before his first settlement there. Book II. stands very much apart from the rest of the work ; it shows signs of a deep inward impression on the mind of the writer made by the antiquity of Egyptian history and culture ; and, with all its helpless credulity on the unarmed side of Herodotus's mind, it shows a freer attitude towards the Greek religion than any other part. If this impression had been early made, it would surely have left more mark upon the general run of the work than is now visible. There is, however, another hypothesis quite probable : he may have utilised a youthful work which he intended to revise. Diels attributes the peculiar tone of Book II. to the author's close dependence upon Hecatæus; he thinks that the plagiarism is too strong for ordinary ancient practice, unless we suppose that these 'Logoi' were intended only for use in public readings, and never received the revision necessary for a permanent book-form.

Our judgments about Herodotus are generally affected

by an implied comparison, not with his precursors and contemporaries, nor even with his average successors, which would be fair, but with one later writer of peculiar and almost eccentric genius, Thucydides. Thus in religious matters Herodotus is sometimes taken as a type of simple piety, even of credulity. An odd judgment. It is true that he seldom expresses doubt on any point connected with the gods, while he constantly does so in matters of human history. He veers with alacrity away from dangerous subjects, takes no liberty with divine names, and refrains from repeating stories which he called 'holy.' Of course he does so ; it is a condition of his profession ; the rhapsode or 'Logopoios' who acted otherwise, would soon have learnt 'wisdom by suffering.' Herodotus was not a philosopher in religion ; he has no theory to preach ; in this, as in every other department of intellect, it is part of his greatness to be inconsistent. But there were probably few high-minded Greeks on whom the trammels of their local worships and their conventional polytheism sat less hamperingly. He has been called a monotheist ; that of course he is not. But his language implies a certain background of monotheism, a moral God behind the nature-powers and heroes, almost as definitely as does that of Æschylus or even of Plato.

Travel was a great breaker of the barriers of belief when the vital creeds of men were still really national, or cantonal, or even parochial. It is surely a man above his country's polytheism who says (ii. 53) that it cannot be more than four centuries since Homer and Hesiod invented the Greek theology, and gave the gods their names, offices, and shapes ! A dangerous saying for the public ; but he is interested in his own speculation, and has not his audience before him. And we may surely combine this with his passing comment on the Egyptian theologies, that (ii. 3) "*about the gods one man knows as much as another.*" There is evident sympathy in his account of the Persian religion as opposed to the Greek : "*Images and temples and altars it is not in their law to set up—nay, they count them fools who make such, as I judge, because they do not hold the gods to be man-shaped, as the Greeks do. Their habit is to sacrifice to Zeus, going up to the tops of the highest mountains, holding all the round of the sky to be Zeus.*" "*They sacrifice,*" he goes on, "*to sun, moon, earth, fire, water, and the winds.*" The feeling of that passage (i. 131) expresses the true Greek polytheism, freed from the accidents of local traditions and anthropomorphism. If you press Herodotus or the average unsacerdotal Greek, he falls back on a One behind the variety of nature and history ; but what comes to him naturally is to feel a divine element here, there, and everywhere, in winds and waters and sunlight and all that appeals to his heart — to single out each manifestation of it, and to worship it there and then.

It is fair to lay stress on these passages rather than on those where Herodotus identifies various foreign deities with known Greek ones under the conventional names (Neith-Athena, Alilat-Ourania, Chem-Pan), or where, after a little excursus into the truth about the life of Heracles, and a conclusion that there were two people of the same name, he prays "the gods and heroes" to take no offence (ii. 43). In those cases he is speaking the language of his audience ; and perhaps, also, the 'safe' professional attitude has become a second nature to him.

With prophecies and omens and the special workings of Providence, the case is different. He is personally interested in prophets, and that for at least two good reasons. The age liked to make the prophets into its heroes of romance, its knights-errant, its troubadours. The mantle of Melampus had fallen in more senses than one on the Acarnanian and Elean seers who passed from army to army, of whom Herodotus "*might tell deeds most wonderful of might and courage*" (v. 72). And besides, as we can see from his marked interest in Heracles, Panyâsis' hero, Herodotus had not forgotten the prophet and patriot who had fought at his side and died for their common freedom in Halicarnassus.

With regard to the oracles and signs, we must always remember his own repeated *caveat*. He relates what he hears, he does not by any means profess always to believe it ; and with regard to the great series of oracles about the war (Book VII.), it is clear that though they were capable of a technical defence—what conceivable oracle was not ?—those who gave them would have preferred to have them forgotten. For the rest, they go with the actions of providence. They greatly heighten the interest of the story, a point which Herodotus would never undervalue ; and without doubt, in looking back on their wonderful victories, all Greeks in their more solemn moments would have the feeling which Herodotus makes Themistocles express in the moment of triumph : "*It is not we who have done this !*" "*The gods and heroes*"—a vague gathering up of all the divine, not really different from Herodotus's favourite phrases 'God' or 'the divine power'—"*grudged that one man should be king both of Europe and Asia, and that a man impious and proud*" (viii. 109). What Englishman did not feel the same at the news of the wreck of the Armada ? What Russian, after the retreat from Moscow ? Nay, in treating the storm

K

that shattered Xerxes' armada (vii. 189, 191), though the Athenians had actually prayed to Boreas to send it, Herodotus refuses to assign it positively to that cause, pointing out that the Magi were praying in the opposite sense for three days, at the end of which time the storm stopped. Herodotus's Godhead is *"jealous and fraught with trouble,"* and *"falls like lightning"* upon human pride — upon the sin, that is, of man making himself equal to God. Aristotle is one of the few theologians who have explained that 'jealousy' is inconsistent with the idea of God, and that in the true sense man should make himself as near God as can be. In that point Herodotus's deity seems to stoop; but it is the Moral Tribunal of the world, and all tribunals are apt to punish wrong more than to reward right. It would be invidious, though instructive, to quote parallels from modern historians on the special workings of Providence upon the weather and such matters, in favour of their own parties; and as for oracles, Herodotus's faith is approved by his standard translator and commentator at the present day, who shows reason to suppose that the Pythia was inspired by the devil![1]

A certain rabies against the good faith of Herodotus has attacked various eminent men in different ages. But neither Ktesias nor Manetho nor Plutarch nor Panovsky nor Sayce has succeeded in convincing many persons of his bad faith. He professes to give the tradition, and the tradition he gives; he states variant accounts with perfect openness, and criticises his material abundantly. He is singularly free from any tendency to glorify past achievements into the miraculous, still more singularly free from national or local

[1] Rawlinson, i. 176 *n.*

prejudice. He admires freedom ; he has a vivid horror
of tyrants. But there is no visible difference in his
treatment of the oligarchic and democratic states ; and
it is difficult to show any misrepresentation of particular
tyrants due to the writer, though it is likely, on the whole,
that the tradition he follows has been unfair to them.
Herodotus is not more severe than Thucydides or Plato.
As to the Persians, he takes evident pleasure in testifying
not only to their courage, as shown, for instance, in
fighting without armour against Greek hoplites, but to
their chivalry, truthfulness, and high political organisation. He is shocked at the harem system, the oriental cruelties, the slave-soldiers driven with scourges,
the sacking of towns, where the Asiatics behaved like
modern Turks or like Europeans in the wars of religion.
He is severe towards the Corinthians and Thebans ;
whose defence, however, it would be difficult to make
convincing. To see really how fair he is, one needs
but to look for a moment at the sort of language such
writers as Froude and Motley use of the average active
Catholic, especially if he be French or Spanish.

In the main, Herodotus is dependent for his mistakes
upon his sources, and in all respects but one he is
closer to the truth than his sources. He had read
nearly all existing Greek literature ; he not only quotes
a great many writers, chiefly poets, but he employs
phrases, "*no poet has mentioned*," and the like, which
imply a control of all literature. He seems for some
reason or other to have avoided using his professional
colleagues, Charon and Xanthus ; he mentions no
logographer but Hecatæus. He refers in some four-
teen passages to monuments or inscriptions, though
he certainly did not employ them systematically. For

the most part, he depends on the oral statements of well-informed persons, both for the older history of Greece and for the '*Mêdika.*' In barbarian countries he was largely dependent on mere dragoman-knowledge, and the careless talk of the Greek quarter of the town.

His frequent expressions, "*the Libyans say,*" "*the Cyrenæans say,*" seem to refer either to the results of his own inquiries in the country referred to, or to the direct statement of some native. Four times we have a personal authority given.[1] "*Archias whom I met at Pitanê*" gives the story of his grandfather; Tymnes, the steward of Ariapeithes, verifies some genealogies; Thersander of Orchomenus, who had dined with Mardonius in Thebes, and Dikaios of Athens, who had lived in exile among the Medes together with Demarâtus the Spartan king, vouch respectively for two stories which tell at least of troubled nerves among the following of Mardonius. A more important source of knowledge lay in the archives of various families and corporations : sometimes, perhaps, Herodotus was allowed to read the actual documents ; more often, probably, he had to question the men who possessed them. That would be the case, for instance, with the Delphic oracle, to whose records he plainly owes an immense amount, especially in the earlier books. He draws from the traditions of the Alcmæonidæ (Pericles), the Philaïdæ (Miltiades), and probably from those of the Persian general Harpagos.

The weakness of these sources may be easily imagined. In his Spartan history Herodotus knows all about Lycurgus, who was of course a fixed saga-figure ; then

[1] iii. 55 ; iv. 76 ; viii. 65 ; ix. 16.

he knows nothing more till he comes to Leon and
Agasicles, some three centuries later, and bursts into a
blaze of anecdote. The non-mythical Spartan tradition
only began there. The weakness of his Athenian record,
apart from the haze of romance which it has in common
with the rest, is due to the bitterness of Athenian feeling
at the time when the last books were writing. When
we hear how the Corinthians fled at Salamis; how
the Thebans were branded on the head with the king's
monogram, those are only the reverberations of the storm
of 432–1 B.C. Somewhat in the same way an older war
of passions has resulted in the condemnation, without
defence, of Themistocles. It could not be denied that
he had saved Hellas, that he loomed the highest man
of the age in all eyes. But he had at the last fled to
Persia! The provocation was forgotten; the stain of
the final treason blackened all his country's memory of
the man; and Herodotus depends for his story upon
the two great houses who had hunted Themistocles to
a traitor's end.[1] Partly they, partly the swing of popular
indignation, had succeeded in fixing Themistocles in the
story as a type of the low-born triumphant trickster.
It was for Ephorus to redeem his memory, till Ephorus,
too, lost his power to speak.

Besides the oral information which came in some
shape or another from records, there was that which
was merely oral, more 'alive' than the other, as Plato
would say, and consequently tending more towards the
mere story. This element is ubiquitous in Herodotus.
Some of his history can be recognised as Eastern and
Germanic folk-lore. Polycrates throwing his ring into
the sea and having it brought back by the fish is an old

---

[1] Busolt, *Griech. Geschichte*, ii. 619.

friend. Amâsis and Rhampsinîtus are all but fairy-tale figures; and two celebrated passages—the speech of the wife of Intaphernes preferring her irreplaceable brother to her replaceable sons (iii. 119); the immortal Hippocleides winning his bride by his prowess and high birth, losing her by dancing on his head, and remarking, as his feet fly, that it is "*all one to Hippocleides!*" (vi. 126 seq.)— these two have been run to ground in Indian literature.[1] Solon cannot have met Crœsus, because the dates do not fit. He cannot have uttered the great speech Herodotus gives him, for it is made up partly from Argive, partly from Delphic legends, legends which clustered in each case around certain unexplained tombs. The dreams that came to lure Xerxes to his ruin, require more personal affidavits to substantiate them. The debate of the seven Persians on Monarchy, Oligarchy, and Democracy, though Herodotus stakes his reputation upon it, has been too much for almost every believer. Conceivably Maass is right in tracing it to a fictitious dialogue by Protagoras. But it is idle to reject only what is grossly improbable, and accept without evidence all that may possibly be true. The most part of the history of Herodotus is mixed up with pure popular story-making in various degrees; the ancient foreign history almost irrecognisably so, the Greek history before Marathon very deeply, while even the parts later than Marathon are by no means untransfigured. In one way, it is true, Herodotus is guilty of personal, though unconscious, deceptiveness; his transitions, his ways of fitting one block of 'Logoi' into another, are purely stylistic. He gets a transition to his Libyan 'Logoi' by saying (iv. 167) that the expedition of Aryandes was

[1] Macan's edition, App. xiv.

really directed against all Libya. There is no reason
to think that it was. He introduces his Athenian history by saying (i. 56) that Crœsus looked for an ally
among the Greeks, and found that two cities stood out—
Sparta, chief of the Dorians; Athens, chief of the Ionians ;
but that the latter was crushed for the time being
under the heel of her tyrant Pisistratus. The tyrant had
not crushed Athens ; he was probably not then reign-
ing ; Athens was a third-rate Ionian state. In framing
these transitions and in getting motives for the insertion
of anecdotes, as when he gives to Gelon Pericles's
famous saying, " *The spring is taken out of the year* " (vii.
162), Herodotus does not expect to be pinned to
conclusions. As Plutarch angrily puts it, he cares for
accuracy in such points "no more than Hippocleides !"
For the rest, his historical faults are the inevitable consequence of his sources—the real untrustworthiness
consisting not in error or inaccuracy here and there,
much less in any deliberate misrepresentation, but in
a deep unconscious romanticising of the past by men's
own memories, and the shaping of all history into an
exemplification of the workings of a Moral Providence.

To his own aim he is singularly true—that " *the real
deeds of men shall not be forgotten, nor the wondrous works
of Greek and barbarian lose their name.*" Plutarch—for
the treatise *On the Malice of Herodotus* is surely Plutarch,
if anything is—does not quarrel with him merely for
the sake of Thebes. To Plutarch the age Herodotus
treated is an age of giants, of sages and heroes in
full dress, with surprising gifts for apophthegm and re-
partee, and he sees all their deeds in a glow of adoring
humility. He hates, he rejects their meaner side ; and
he cannot bear the tolerant gossiping realism of Hero-

dotus. Yet it is this power of truthfulness in the man, combined with his tragic grasp and his wide sympathy— this way of seeing men's hearts just as they are with all their greatness and their failure, that causes a critic who weighs his every word, to claim that "no other Greek writer has covered so large a world with so full a population of living and immortal men and women as Herodotus," [1] and to place his work opposite Homer's, "irremovably and irreplaceably" at the fountain-head of European prose literature.

[1] Macan, lxxiii.

VII

PHILOSOPHIC AND POLITICAL LITERATURE TO THE DEATH OF SOCRATES

EARLY PHILOSOPHY

IN turning abruptly from History to Philosophy, it is well to remember that we are only moving from one form to another of the Ionic 'Historiê,' and that there was, and still is, a considerable Greek literature dealing with other subjects, Science, Medicine, Geographical Discovery, Painting, Sculpture, Politics, and Commerce ; all occupying the best powers of the Greek mind, and all, except Sculpture and Commerce, referred to by extant writers with respect and even enthusiasm. But the plan of this work compels us to omit them almost entirely, and we can only touch on Philosophy so far as is absolutely necessary for the understanding of literature in the narrower sense.

Philosophy first meets us in Miletus, where THALES, son of Examias—a Carian name—sought as a basis for his scientific work some doctrine of the 'Archê,' or origin of the world. He ignored myths and cosmogonies, and sought for an original substance, which he found in what he called ' Moisture.' His disciple ANAXIMANDER preferred to describe it as the ἄπειρον, the Infinite Undefined material, out of which all definite 'things' arise by 'separation.' It is God: by its law all 'things' must be destroyed again into that from which they were made; they meet with 'retribution' for their 'unrighteousness,' *i.e.* their invasions of one another's spheres of being. The third Milesian, ANAXI-MENES, trying to specify what Anaximander left unclear, takes the Infinite to be really Vapour—ἀήρ; while the process of separation by which the various things come into being is really condensation due to change of temperature. The unity of this school lies in its conception of the question to be answered—"What is the world?" means to them, "What is the world made of?"—and in their assumption of a half-materialist hylozoism. 'Air,' for instance, is 'Mind.' The school spent most of its activity on scientific research, till it shared the destruction of its city in 494 B.C. It remained the chief source and stimulus of later philosophy.

Altogether opposite in spirit was the great 'Thiasos' of the West, founded about 530 B.C., by an exiled Samian oligarch, PYTHAGORAS. Its principles seem to have included a religious reformation, hostile both to the theology of the poets and to the local cults; a moral reformation, reacting against the freer life and more complicated social conditions of the time; and a political reaction in support of the aristocratic principle, which was in danger of disappearing before the democracies and tyrannies. In the time of its founder the sect marred its greatness by unusual superstition, and by perpetrating the great crime of the age, the destruction of Sybaris. Later, it did important work in mathematics and astronomy.

The doctrine of the Milesians was spread over Hellas by the minstrel XENOPHANES (see p. 74). A rhapsode had an enormous public, and stood in the central fortress of the poetic religion. From this vantage-ground Xenophanes denounced the 'lies' of Homer and Hesiod, and preached an uncompromising metaphysical monotheism. There was One God, not man-shaped, not having parts, infinite, unchanging, omnipresent, and all of him conscious. He is One and the Whole. He is really, perhaps, Anaximander's Infinite robbed of its mobility ; he is so like the One of Parmenides that tradition makes Xenophanes that philosopher's teacher, and the founder of the Eleatic School.

At Ephesus near Miletus, in the next generation to Anaximenes, the problem of the Milesians receives an entirely new answer, announced with strange pomp and pride, and at the same time bearing the stamp of genius. "*All things move and nothing stays,*" says HERACLÎTUS ; "*all things flow.*" And it is this Flow that is the real secret of the world, the 'Archê' : not a substance arbitrarily chosen, but the process of change itself, which Heraclîtus describes as 'Burning' ($\pi\hat{v}\rho$). Heraclîtus writes in a vivid oracular prose ; he is obscure, partly from the absence of a philosophic language to express his thoughts, but more because of the prophet-like fervour of expression that is natural to him. It must also be remembered that in an age before the circulation of books a teacher had to appeal to the memory. He wrote in verses like Xenophanes and Parmenides, or in apophthegms like Heraclîtus and Democritus. The process of change is twofold—a Way Up and a Way Down—but it is itself eternal and unchanging. There is Law in it ; Fate, determining the effect of every cause ; Justice, bringing retribution on every offence.

The 'offences' appear to be, as in Anaximander, the self-assertive pride of particular things claiming to Be when they only Become and Pass, claiming to be Themselves when they are only a transition of something else into something else. Heraclîtus speaks with a twofold pride—as one who has found truth, and as a nobleman. He would have concurred entirely in Nietzsche's contempt for "shopkeepers, cows, Christians, women, Englishmen, and other democrats." The Milesians are as dirt to him ; so are his fellow-citizens and mankind generally. He condescends to mention Pythagoras, Xenophanes, and Hecatæus with Hesiod, as instances of the truth that *" much learning teaches not wisdom."*

PARMENIDES of Elea answers Heraclîtus ; he finds no solution of any difficulty in Heraclîtus's flow ; there is nothing there but Becoming and Ceasing, and he wants to know what IS—in the sense, for instance, that 2 × 2 *is* 4, absolutely and eternally, though Parmenides would not admit our popular distinction between abstract and concrete.

What is, is ; what is not, is not, οὐκ ἔστι, does not exist. Therefore there is no Change or Becoming, because that would be passage from Not-being to Being, and there is no Not-being. Equally, there is no empty space ; therefore no motion. Also there is only One Thing ; if there were more, there would have to be Not-being between them. He goes on to show that the One Thing is spherical and finite, and of course divine. It is matter, solid ; but it is also Thought, for *" Thought and that of which it is thought are the same."*

What then about the world we know, which has obviously a great many things in it ? Parmenides answers orientally : it is only deceit, what an Indian calls *Maya.*

How the deceit comes, how the unchanging One can deceive, and who there is to be deceived, he does not tell us, though he does in the second part of his poem (see p. 75) give us *"the Way of Falsehood,"* explaining how the mirage works, and what contradictions are necessarily involved in a belief in it. This last line of thought is especially followed by Parmenides's disciple ZENO, who develops the antinomies and inherent contradictions involved in the conceptions of Time, Space, and Number. If the doctrine of the One is hard, he argues, consistent belief in the Multiplicity of things is flatly impossible.

Greek speculation thus reaches a point where two more or less consistent roads of thought have led to diametrically opposite conclusions—the One Unchangeable Being of Parmenides ; the ceaseless Becoming of Heraclîtus. The difficulty first emerges in the case of MELISSUS, the Samian admiral who once defeated Pericles ; he tried to make the One into a Milesian 'Archê,' but found it would not work : you could not possibly develop the one datum of pure thought into an account of the facts of the world. After Melissos the breach is more consciously felt. On the one side, starting from Heraclîtus, the Pythagoreans seek the Real, the thing that *Is* eternally, in the unchanging laws of the Flow ; that is, in proportion, in the eternal facts of Number. Geometry is the truth of which the particular square, round, or triangular objects are imperfect and passing instances ; the laws of harmony are the 'truth' of music, and abstract astronomy the 'truth' of the shifting stars. Thus in Number they found the real essence of the world, a One, eternal and unchangeable, which would fairly satisfy Parmenides's requirements.

From the side of Being there arose three important systems.

EMPEDOCLES of Acragas, whom we have treated above (p. 75), assumes the existence not of one, but of four original ' Roots of Things '—Earth, Water, Air, and Fire, with empty space about them. The roots are unchanging matter in themselves, but moved and mixed—this is perhaps his most important contribution to philosophy —by non-material forces, which he describes as Love and Hate, or Attraction and Repulsion.

ANAXAGORAS of Clazomenæ, the first philosopher to settle permanently in Athens, assumed a very much larger number of original and eternal '*things*' or '*seeds*' (χρήματα, σπέρματα), whose combination and separation make the substances of the world. He means something like the 'Elements' of modern Chemistry. Among them there is Mind, 'Noös,' which is a 'thing' like the rest, but subtler and finer, and able to move of itself. It acts in the various component parts of the world just as we feel it act in our own bodies. It has '*come and arranged*' all the 'things.' Anaxagoras treated the Sun and Moon as spheres of stone and earth, the Sun white-hot from the speed of its movement ; both were enormous in size, the Sun perhaps as big as the Peloponnese ! He gave the right explanation of eclipses.

The other solution offered by this period is the Atomic Theory. It seems to have originated not from any scientific observation, but from abstract reasoning on Parmenidean principles. The ὄν is a πλέον, a Thing is a Solid, and anything not solid is nothing. But instead of the One Eternal Solid we have an immense number of Eternal Solids, too small to be divided any more— 'Atomoi'('Un-cuttables'). Parmenides's argument against empty space is not admitted, nor yet his demand that 'that which is' must be round and at rest. Why should it? As a matter of fact the things have innumerably different shapes and are always moving. Shape, size, and motion are all the qualities that they possess, and these are the only Natural Facts. All else is conventional or derivative. The theory was originated by Leukippus of Abdêra, but received its chief development from his great disciple Democritus, and from Epicurus.

THE ATHENIAN PERIOD OF PHILOSOPHY

Empedocles died about 430 B.C., and Anaxagoras was banished in 432. But for some years before this the reaction against cosmological speculation had begun. It was time to find some smaller truths for certain, instead of speculating ineffectually upon the great ones. The fifth century begins to work more steadily at particular branches of science—at Astronomy, Mathematics, History, Medicine, and Zoology.

This tendency in its turn is met and influenced by the great stream of the time. The issue of the Persian War, establishing Greek freedom and stimulating the sense of common nationality, had let loose all the pent-up force of the nation, military, social, and intellectual. Great towns were appearing. The population of Athens and the Piræus had risen from 20,000 to about 100,000. Property was increasing even faster. The facilities for disposing of money were constantly growing; commercial enterprises were on a larger scale and employed greater numbers both of free workmen and of slaves. Intercourse between the different cities was much commoner; and the foreign residents, at least in Athens and the progressive towns, were well cared for by law and lightly taxed. Local protective tariffs were practically abolished; the general Athenian customs at the Piræus amounted only to 1 per cent. on imports and exports. Compared with other periods, the time after the battle of Mykalê was one-of prolonged peace. The nation was possessed by an enthusiastic belief in itself, in progress, and in democracy. One result of this was the economic movement, which gives the key to so much of Athenian history, the struggle of the free workman to keep up his standard of living by means of his political ascendancy. The other is the demand of the Demos for the things of the intellect, answered by the supply of those things in a shape adapted for popular consumption.

At all times the Greeks had keenly felt the value of personal quality in a man ($\dot{a}\rho\epsilon\tau\dot{\eta}$), and of wisdom or skill ($\sigma o\phi\acute{\iota}a$). How could these things be attained? A 'Hagnistês' could make you pure if you were defiled; an 'Andrapodistês' could make you a slave; was there such a thing as a 'Sophistês' who could make you wise? They came in answer to the demand, men of diverse characters and seeing 'wisdom' in very different lights. Some rejected the name of 'Sophistês': it claimed too much. Some held that wisdom might be taught, but not virtue: that could only be 'learned by practice.' Gorgias doubted if he could teach anything; ne only claimed to be 'a good speaker.' PROTAGORAS boldly accepted the name and professed to teach $\pi o\lambda\iota\tau\iota\kappa\dot{\eta}$ $\dot{a}\rho\epsilon\tau\dot{\eta}$, social virtue; he preached the characteristic doctrine of periods of 'enlightenment,' that vice comes from ignorance, and that education makes character.

The Sophists were great by their lives and influence, more than by their writings, and even what they did write has almost completely perished (see p. 334). We hear of them now only through their opponents : from Aristophanes and the party of ignorance on one side, on the other from the tradition of the fourth century, opposed both in politics and in philosophy to the spirit of the fifth.

If we had any definite statement of Plato's opinion of the great Periclean Sophists, it would probably be like Mr. Ruskin's opinion of Mill and Cobden. But we have no such statement. Plato does not write history; he writes a peculiar form of dramatic fiction, in which the actors have all to be, first, historical personages, and, secondly, contemporaries of the protagonist Socrates. When he really wishes to describe the men of that time, as in the *Protagoras*, he gives us the most delicate and realistic satire ; but very often his thoughts are not with that generation at all. Some orator of 370–360 displeases him ; he expresses himself in the form of a criticism by Socrates on Lysias. He proposes to confute his own philosophical opponents ; and down go all Antisthenes's paradox-mongering and Aristippus's new-fangled anarchism of thought to the credit of the ancient Protagoras.

In these cases we can discover the real author of the doctrine attacked. Sometimes the doctrine itself seems to be Plato's invention. Suppose, for instance, Plato seeks to show that morality has a basis in reason or that the wicked are always unhappy, he is bound to make some one uphold the opposite view. And suppose he thinks—controversialists often do—that the opposite view would be more logical if held in an extreme and shame-

L

less form ; his only resource is to make his puppet, either with cynical coolness or in blind rage, proceed to the necessary extremes, and be there confounded. And who is the puppet to be ? Somebody, if possible, who is not too notoriously incongruous to the part ; whose supposed tenets may vaguely be thought to imply something analogous to the infamous sentiments which have to be defended.

Thrasymachus of Chalkêdon is made in *Republic I.* to advocate absolute injustice, to maintain that law and morality are devices of the weak for paralysing the free action of the strong. It is very improbable that this respectable democratic professor held such a view : in politics he was for the middle class ; and in 411 he pleaded for moderation. He went out of his way to attack the current type of successful injustice, Archelâus of Macedon. He was celebrated as a sentimental speaker ; he says in an extant fragment that the success of the unrighteous is enough to make a man doubt the existence of divine providence. Plato's fiction is, in fact, too improbable ; no wonder he has to make the puppet lose its temper before it will act.

This is the chief crime which has made Thrasymachus the typical " corrupt and avaricious sophist " ; the other is that, being a professional lecturer, he refused to lecture gratuitously and in public to Socrates and his young friends—whose notorious object was to confute whatever he might say.

What Aristophanes says of the Sophists is of course mere gibing ; happily he attacks Socrates too, so we know what his charges are worth. What the Socratics tell us—and they are our chief informants—is coloured by that great article of their faith, the ideal One Righteous

Man murdered by a wicked world : nobody is to stand near Socrates. Socrates himself only tells us that the philosophy of the Sophists would not bear his criticism any more than the sculpture of Pheidias or the statesmanship of Pericles. They were human ; perhaps compared to him they were conventional ; and their real fault in his eyes was the spirit they had in common—the spirit of enlightened, progressive, democratic, over-confident Athens in the morning of her greatness.

Their main mission was to teach, to clear up the mind of Greece, to put an end to bad myths and unproven cosmogonies, to turn thought into fruitful paths. Many of them were eminent as original thinkers : Gorgias reduced Eleaticism to absurdity ; Protagoras cleared the air by his doctrine of the relativity of knowledge. The many sophists to whom 'wisdom' meant knowledge of nature, are known to us chiefly by the Hippocratic writings, and through the definite advances made at this time in the various sciences, especially Medicine, Astronomy, Geometry, and Mechanics. Cos, Abdêra, and Syracuse could have told us much about them ; Athens, our only informant, was thinking of other things at the time—of social and human problems. In this department Protagoras gave a philosophic basis to Democracy. The mass of mankind possesses the sense of justice and the sense of shame—the exceptions are wild beasts, to be exterminated — and it is these two qualities rather than intellectual powers that are the roots of social conduct. Alkidamas, a disciple of Gorgias, is the only man recorded as having in practical politics proposed the abolition of slavery ; in speculation, of course, many did so. Antiphon the sophist represents, perhaps alone, the sophistic view that a wife is a 'second self' and more than any friend.

In history, Hippias laid the foundations of a national system of chronology by publishing the list of Olympian victors. The whole science of language rests on the foundations laid by such men as Prodicus and Protagoras : the former insisting on the accurate discrimination of apparent synonyms ; the latter showing that language is not a divine and impeccable thing, but a human growth with conventions and anomalies. As to morals in general, most of the Sophists were essentially preachers, like Hippias and Prodicus ; others, like Gorgias, were pure artists. The whole movement was moral as well as intellectual, and was singularly free from the corruption and lawlessness which accompanied, for example, the Italian Renaissance. The main fact about the Sophists is that they were set to educate the nation, and they did it. The character of the ordinary fourth - century Greek, his humanity, sense of justice, courage, and ethical imagination, were raised to something like the level of the leading minds of the fifth century, and far above that of any population within a thousand years of him. After all, the Sophists are the spiritual and intellectual representatives of the age of Pericles ; let those who revile them create such an age again.

OCCASIONAL WRITINGS

The real origin of Attic prose literature is not to be found in the florid art of Gorgias, nor yet in the technical rhetoric of Teisias, where Aristotle rather mechanically seeks it : it lies in the political speeches and pamphlets

of Athens herself. If we look for a decisive moment
by which to date it, we may fix upon the transference
of the Federation Treasure from Delos in 454 B.C., the
most typical of all the events which made Athens not
only the Treasury, Mint, and Supreme Court, but
the ordinary legal and commercial centre of Eastern
Hellas. The movement of the time brought an immense amount of legal and judicial work to Athens,
and filled the hands of those who could speak and
write ; it attracted able men from all parts of the
Empire ; it gave the Attic dialect a paramount and
international validity. Athens herself wrote little during
the prime of the Empire ; she governed, and left it for
the subject allies to devote to literature the energies
which had no legitimate outlet in politics.

ION of Chios (before 490–423 B.C.) is an instance. He
was an aristocrat, a friend of Kimôn and King Archidâmus,
and he probably fought in the allied forces against Eiôn
in 470. But there was no career for him except in letters.
He wrote tragedies, of course in Attic, with great success ;
and it is pleasant to see (frag. 63) that he could openly
express enthusiastic admiration of Sparta to an Athenian
audience without any known disagreeable result. He
wrote a *Founding of Chios* * and some books on Pythagorean philosophy. What we most regret is his book
of Memoirs, telling in a frank, easy style of the *Passing
Visits* * (Ἐπιδημίαι) to his island of various notable
foreigners. The long fragment about Sophocles is interesting ; though the idea it gives of contemporary wit
and grace is on the whole as little pleasing to our taste
as the jests of the court of Queen Elizabeth.

An utterly different person was STESIMBROTUS of
Thasos, a man with a pen and some education, and in

place of character a settled bitterness against everything
that represented the Empire. He was like that malcontent
islander whom Isocrates answers in his *Panegyricus*, a
representative of the Oligarchic and Particularist party
in the allied states, the aristocrats and dependents of aristocrats, whose influence and property were lost through
the Athenian predominance, and to whom the Democracy and the Empire were alike anathema. Yet he
came to Athens like every one else, like those 'dozens
of Thasians' mentioned by Hegêmon the satirist :

> " *Close-shorn, not over nice, whom sheer Want ships on the packet,*
> *Damaged and damaging men, to profess bad verses in Athens.*"

Stesimbrotus lectured successfully as a sophist ; wrote
on Homer and on current politics. At last he was able
to relieve his feelings by a perfect masterpiece of libel,
*Upon Themistocles, Thucydides, and Pericles.** The first and
last were his especial arch-fiends; the son of Melêsias,
being Pericles's opponent, probably came off with the
same mild treatment as Kimôn, who, " *although an abject
boor, ignorant of every art and science, had at least the merit
of being no orator and possessing the rudiments of honesty ;
he might almost have been a Peloponnesian !*" If Stesimbrotus were not such an infamous liar, one would have
much sympathy for him. As it is, the only thing to be
urged in his favour is that he did not, as is commonly
supposed, combine his rascality with sanctimoniousness.
His book on the *The Mysteries** must have been an
attack. The mysteries were a purely and characteristically Athenian possession, to which, as Isocrates says,
they only admitted other Greeks out of generosity ; and
Stesimbrotus would have falsified his whole position if
he had praised them. The man is a sort of intransigeant
ultramontane journalist, wearing rather a modern look

among his contemporaries, a man of birth, ability, and learning, shut out by political exigencies from the due use of his gifts.

Similar to Stesimbrotus in general political views, vastly removed from him in spirit, is the 'OLD OLIGARCH,' whose priceless study of the Athenian constitution is preserved to us by the happy accident of the publisher taking it for Xenophon's. It is not only unlike Xenophon's style and way of thinking, but it demonstrably belongs to the first Athenian Empire, before the Sicilian catastrophe. It is, in fact, the earliest piece of Attic prose preserved to us, and represents almost alone the practical Athenian style of writing, before literature was affected by Gorgias or the orators. It is familiar, terse, vivid ; it follows the free grammar of conversation, with disconnected sentences and frequent changes of number and person. It leaves, like some parts of Aristotle, a certain impression of naked, unphrased thought. The Old Oligarch has a clear conception of the meaning of Athenian democracy, and admitting for the moment that he and his friends are the 'Noble and Good,' while the masses are the 'Base and Vile,' he sees straight and clear, and speaks without unfairness. *"I dislike the kind of constitution, because in choosing it they have definitely chosen to make the Vile better off than the Noble. This I dislike. But granted that this is their intention, I will show that they conserve the spirit of their constitution well, and manage their affairs in general well, in points where the Greeks think them most at fault."* There is even a kind of justice in the arrangement ; *"for it is the masses that row the ships, and the ships that have made the Empire."* They do not follow the advice of the Good men—no ; *" the first Vile man who likes, stands up and speaks to the Assembly*," and, as a fact, "*does somehow find out what is to his interest and that of the masses. Ignorance* plus *Vileness* plus *Loyalty is a safer combination in an adviser of the Demos than Wisdom* plus *Virtue* plus *Disaffection.*" As for the undue licence allowed to slaves and resident aliens, it is true that you cannot strike them, and they will not move out of your way ; but the reason is that neither in dress nor in face is the true Athenian commoner at all distinguishable from a slave, and he is afraid of being hit by mistake !

The writer goes over the constitution in detail without finding a serious flaw : everything is so ordered — the elective offices, the arrangements with the allies, the laws about comedy and about the public buildings— as to secure the omnipotence of the Demos. For instance, the system of making the allies come to Athens for their lawsuits is oppressive, and sometimes keeps litigants waiting as long as a year before their cases can be heard. But it provides the pay of the jury-courts ! It enables the Demos to keep an eye on the internal affairs of the whole Empire and see that the 'Good' do not get the upper hand anywhere. It makes the allies realise that the 'Mob' is really their master, and not the rich admirals and trierarchs whom they see representing Athens abroad. Then it brings taxes ; it means constant employment for the heralds, and brisk trade for the lodging-house keepers and the cabmen and those who have a slave to hire out. If only we had a hundred pages of such material as this instead of thirteen, our understanding of Athenian history would be a more concrete thing than it is.

It is hard to see the exact aim of the Old Oligarch. He discusses coolly the prospect of a revolution. No half-measures are of the least use ; and to strike a death-blow at the Democracy is desperately hard. There are not enough malcontents; the Demos has not been unjust enough. On the whole, a land invasion is the only hope; if Athens were an island she would be invulnerable.

The work reads like the address of an Athenian aristo-crat to the aristocrats of the Empire, defending Athens at the expense of the Demos. 'We aristocrats sympathise with you ; your grievances are not the results of de-liberate oppression or of the inherent perversity of the Athenians, they are the natural outcome of the demo-cratic system. If a chance comes for a revolution, we shall take it ; at present it would be madness.'

CRITIAS the 'Tyrant' wrote *Constitutions** ; his style, to judge from the fragments, was like our Oligarch's, and he is quoted as using the peculiar word διαδικάζειν in the exact sense in which it occurs here. The spirit of this tract indeed is quite foreign to the restless slave of ambition whom we know in the Critias of 404. Never-theless, the Critias who objected to action in the revolu-tion of 411, who proposed the recall of Alcibiades, and the banishment of the corpse of Phrynichus, may perhaps lead us back to a moderate and not too youthful Critias of 417–414, the date given to our Oligarch by Müller-Strübing and Bergk.

Among the other political writings of this time were Antiphon's celebrated *Defence,** Critias's *Lives** and *Pamphlets,** Thrasymachus's explanation of the *Consti-tution of our Fathers,** and a history of the events of 411 which serves as the basis of Aristotle's account in his *Constitution of Athens*. It contained a glorification of Theramenes's action, and a bold theory that the revolu-tion he aimed at was really the restoration of the true constitution of Draco. It can scarcely have been by Theramenes himself, since it shows no special hostility to Critias and the Oligarchical extremists. The same pamphleteering spirit infected even Pausanias, the exiled Spartan king, and led him to attack Lysander and the Ephors under the cover of a *Life of Lycurgus.*[*]

SOCRATES, SON OF SOPHRONISCUS FROM ALÔPEKÊ
(468–399 B.C.)

Among the Sophists of the fifth century is one who scarcely deserves that name, or, indeed, any other which classes him with his fellows : a man strangely detached ; living in a world apart from other men a life of incessant moral and intellectual search; in that region most rich to give and hungry to receive sympathy, elsewhere dead to the feelings and conventions of common society. It is this which makes the most earnest of men a centre of merriment, a jester and a willing butt. He analyses life so gravely and nakedly that it makes men laugh, as when he gropes his way to the conclusion that a certain fiery orator's aim in life is "*to make many people angry at the same time.*" The same simpleness of nature led him to ask extraordinary questions ; to press insistently for answers ; to dance alone in his house for the sake of exercise ; to talk without disguise of his most intimate feelings. He was odd in appearance too ; stout, weather-stained, ill-clad, barefooted for the most part, deep-eyed, and almost fierce in expression ; subject to long fits of brooding, sometimes silent for days, generally a persistent and stimulating talker, sometimes amazingly eloquent ; a man who saw through and through other men, left them paralysed, Alcibiades said, and feeling 'like very slaves'; sometimes inimitably humorous, sometimes inexplicably solemn; only, always original and utterly unself-conscious.

The parentage of Socrates was a joke. He was the son of a midwife and a stone-mason; evidently not a successful stone-mason, or his wife would not have continued her profession. He could not manage such little property as he had, and was apt to drop into destitution without minding it. He had no profession. If he ever learned sculpture, he did not practise it. He took no fees for teaching; indeed he could not see that he taught anything. He sometimes, for no visible reason, refused, sometimes accepted, presents from his rich friends. Naturally he drove his wife, Xanthippê, a woman of higher station, to despair; he was reputed henpecked. In the centre of education he was ill educated; in a hotbed of political aspirations he was averse to politics. He never travelled; he did not care for any fine art; he knew poetry well, but insisted on treating it as bald prose. In his military service he showed iron courage, though he had a way of falling into profound reveries, which might have led to unpleasant results. In his later years, when we first know him, he is notorious for his utter indifference to bodily pleasures or pains. But we have evidence to show that this was not always so; that the old man who scarcely knew whether it was freezing or whether he had breakfasted, who could drink all night without noticing it, had passed a stormy and passionate youth. Spintharus, the father of Aristoxenus, one of the few non-disciples who knew him in his early days, says that Socrates was a man of terrible passions, his anger ungovernable and his bodily desires violent, "though," he adds, "he never did anything unfair."

Socrates's positive doctrines amounted to little : he clung to a paradoxical belief that Virtue is Knowledge ; a view refuted before him by Euripides, and after him by Aristotle—in its ordinary sense, at least : to him, of course, it meant something not ordinary. He had no accomplishments, and did not as a rule care to acquire them ; though, when it occurred to him, late in life, to learn music, he went straight to a school and learned among the boys. He was working incessantly at a problem which he never really could frame to himself, which mankind never has been able to frame. He felt that the great truth he wanted must be visible everywhere, if we knew how to look for it. It is not more knowledge that we want : only the conscious realising of what is in us. Accepting the jest at his mother's profession, he described his process of questioning as assisting at the birth of truth from spirits in travail.

Along with this faith in a real truth inside man, Socrates possessed a genius for destructive criticism. Often unfair in his method, always deeply honest in his purpose, he groped with deadly effect for the fundamental beliefs and principles of any philosopher, politician, artist, or man of the world, who consented to meet him in discussion. Of course the discussions were oral ; Athens had not yet reached the time for pamphlet criticism, and Socrates could not write a connected discourse. He objected to books, as he did to long speeches, on the ground that he could not follow them and wanted to ask questions at every sentence.

Socrates was never understood ; it seems as if, for all his insistence on the need of self-consciousness, he never understood himself. The most utterly divergent schools of thought claimed to be his followers. His friends Euclîdes at Megara, and Phædo at Elis, seem to have found in him chiefly dialectic—abstract logic and metaphysics, based on Eleaticism. Two others, Æschines and Apollodôrus, found the essence of the man in his external way of life (see p.340). Antisthenes, the founder of the Cynic school, believed that he followed Socrates in proclaiming the equal nullity of riches, fame, friendship, and everything in the world except Virtue. Virtue was the knowledge of right living; all other knowledge was worthless, nay, impossible. Equally contemptuous of theoretic knowledge, equally restricted to the pursuit of right living, another Socratic, Aristippus of Cyrênê, identified Right Living with the pursuit of every momentary pleasure; which, again, he held to be the only way of life psychologically possible. If one can attempt to say briefly what side of Socrates was developed by Plato, it was perhaps in part his negative criticism, leading to the scepticism of the later Academics; and in part his mystical side, the side that was eventually carried to such excess by the Neo-Platonists of the fourth century A.D. Socrates was subject to an auditory hallucination : a Divine Sign used to 'speak' to him in warning when he was about to act amiss.

But the most fundamental likeness between Plato and Socrates seems to lie in a different point—in their conception of Love. The great link that bound Socrates to his fellows, the secret, perhaps, of the affection and worship with which so many dissimilar men regarded him, was this passionate unsatisfied emotion to which he could give no other name. The Pericleans were 'lovers' of Athens. Socrates 'loved' what he called Beauty or Truth or Goodness; and, through this far-off cause of all Love, loved his disciples and all who were working towards the same end. Plato realises this to the full. Socrates perhaps had only glimpses of it; but it is clear that that intense vibrating personal affection between man and man, which gives most modern readers a cold turn in reading the Platonic dialogues, is in its seed a part of Socrates. It is remarkable, considering the possibilities of Greek life at the time, that this 'Erôs' gave rise to no scandal against Socrates, not even at his trial.[1] In Plato's case it showed itself to be a little imprudent; Aristotle's magnificent conception of Friendship is best explained when we see that it is the Platonic Love under a cooler and safer name.

What was the source of Socrates's immense influence over all later philosophy, since in actual philosophic achievement he is not so great as Protagoras, not comparable with Democritus? It was largely the dæmonic, semi-inspired character of the man. Externally, it was the fact of his detachment from all existing bodies and institutions, so that in their wreck, when Protagoras, Pericles, Gorgias fell, he was left standing alone and undiscredited. And, secondly, it was the great fact that he sealed his mission with his blood. He had enough of the prophet in him to feel that it was well for him to die; that it was impossible to unsay a word of what he believed, or to make any promise he did not personally approve. Of course the Platonic *Apology* is fiction, but there is evidence to show that Socrates's indifference, or rather superiority, to life and death is true in fact. The world was not then familiarised with religious persecutions, and did not know how many people are ready

---

[1] He speaks quite positively on the point: Xen. *Symp.* viii. 32 ff.

to bear martyrdom for what they believe. But there is
one point about Socrates which is unlike the religious
martyr : Socrates died for no supposed crown of glory,
had no particular revelation in which he held a fanatical
belief. He died in a calm, deliberate conviction, that
Truth is really more precious than Life, and not only
Truth but even the unsuccessful search for it. The trial
has been greatly discussed both now and in antiquity.
The Socratics, like Æschines and Antisthenes, poured
out the vials of their wrath in literature. Plato wrote
the *Apology* and the *Gorgias ;* Lysias the orator stepped
in with a defence of Socrates in speech form ; Polycrates
the sophist dared to justify — probably not as a mere
jeu d'esprit — the decision of the court ; Isocrates fell
upon him with caustic politeness in the *Busiris,* and
Xenophon with a certain clumsy convincingness in the
Memorabilia.

The chief point to realise is that the accusers were
not villains, nor the judges necessarily 'lice' as M.
Aurelius tersely puts it. Socrates had always been
surrounded by young men of leisure, drawn mainly
from the richer and more dissolute classes. He had
in a sense 'corrupted' them : they had felt the destructive side of his moral teaching, and failed to grasp
his real aim. His political influence was markedly
sceptical. He was no oligarch ; his oldest apostle
Chairephon fought beside Thrasybûlus at Phŷlê ; but
he had analysed and destroyed the sacred principle of
Democracy as well as every other convention. The
city had barely recovered from the bloody reign of
his two close disciples Critias and Charmides ; could
never recover from the treason of his 'beloved' Alcibiades. The religious terrors of the people were

keenly awake—confusedly occupied with oligarchic plots, religious sins, and divine vengeance.

Of his accusers, the poet Melêtus was probably a fanatic, who objected to the Divine Sign. He was a weak man ; he had been intimidated by the Thirty into executing an illegal arrest at their orders—the same arrest, according to the legend of the Socratics, which Socrates had refused to perform. Lycôn seems to have been an average respectable politician ; the Socratics have nothing against him except that he was once the master's professed friend. These men could hardly have got a conviction against Socrates in the ordinary condition of public feeling ; but now they were supported by Anytus. A little later in the same year, when Melêtus attempted another prosecution for impiety against Andokides, in opposition to Anytus, he failed to get a fifth of the votes. Anytus was one of the heroes of the Restored Democracy, one of the best of that generous band. As an outlaw at Phŷlê he had saved the lives of bitter oligarchs who had fallen into the hands of his men. When victorious he was one of the authors of the amnesty. He left the men who held his confiscated property undisturbed in enjoyment of it.

He had had relations with Socrates before. He was a tanner, a plain well-to-do tradesman, himself ; but he had set his heart on the future of his only son, and was prepared to make for that object any sacrifice except that which was asked. The son wished to follow Socrates. He herded with young aristocrats of doubtful principles and suspected loyalty ; he refused to go into his father's business. Socrates, not tactfully, had pleaded his cause. Had Socrates had his way, or Anytus his, all might have been well. As it was, the young man was left rebellious and hankering; when his father became an outlaw for freedom's sake, he stayed in the city with Socrates and the tyrants; he became ultimately a hopeless drunkard. As the old tradesman fought his way back through the bloody streets of the Piræus, he thought how the same satyr-faced sophist was still in Athens, as happy under the tyrants as under the constitution, always gibing and probing, and discussing ambiguous subjects with his ruined son. It needed little to convince him that here was a centre of pestilence to be uprooted. The death of Socrates is a true tragedy. Both men were noble, both ready to die for their beliefs; it is only the nobler and greater who has been in the end triumphant.

M

VIII

THUCYDIDES

At the time when the old Herodotus was putting the
finish to his history in Athens, a new epoch of struggle
was opening for Greece and demanding a writer. The
world of Herodotus was complete, satisfying. Persia
was tamed ; the seas under one law ; freedom and
order won — " Equal laws, equal speech, democracy."
The culture which, next to freedom, was what Herodotus
cared for most, was realised on a very wide scale : he
lived in a great city where every citizen could read and
write, where everybody was δεινὸς and φιλόκαλος. There
had never been, not even in the forced atmosphere of
tyrants' courts, such a gathering of poets and learned
men as there was in this simply-living and hard-working
city. There was a new kind of poetry, natural only to
this soil, so strangely true and deep and arresting, that
it made other poetry seem like words. And the city
which had done all this—the fighting, the organising, the
imaginative creating alike—was the metropolis of his
own Ionia, she whom he could show to be the saviour
of Hellas, whom even the Theban had hailed, " *O shining,
violet-crowned City of Song, great Athens, bulwark of
Hellas, walls divine.*" [1] That greeting of Pindar's struck
the keynote of the Athenians' own feeling. Again and

[1] Pind. frag. 76.

again the echoes of it come back; as late as 424 B.C.
the word 'violet-crowned' could make an audience sit
erect and eager, and even a judicious use of the adjective 'shining' by a foreign ambassador could do diplomatic wonders.[1]

It was a passionate romantic patriotism. In the best
men the love for their personified city was inextricably
united with a devotion to all the aims that they felt to be
highest—Freedom, Law, Reason, and what the Greeks
called 'the beautiful.' Theirs was a peerless city, and
they made for her those overweening claims that a man
only makes for his ideal or for one he loves. Pericles
used that word : called himself her 'lover' (ἐραστής)—the
word is keener and fresher in Greek than in English—
and gathered about him a band of similar spirits, united
lovers of an immortal mistress. This was why they
adorned her so fondly. Other Greek states had made
great buildings for the gods. The Athenians of this age
were the first to lavish such immense effort on buildings
like the Propylæa, the Docks, the Odeon, sacred only
to Athens. Can Herodotus have quite sympathised with
this ? He cannot at least—who can understand another
man's passion ?—have liked the ultimate claim, definitely
repeated to an indignant world, that the matchless city
should be absolute queen of her 'allies,' a wise and bene-
ficent tyrant, owing no duties except to protect and lead
Hellas, and to beat off the barbarian.[2]

There was a great gulf between Herodotus and the
younger generation in the circle of Pericles, the gulf of
the sophistic culture. The men who had heard Anaxa-

---

[1] Ar. *Eq.* 1329, *Ach.* 637.
[2] Thuc. ii. 63, Pericles ; much more strongly afterwards, iii. 37, Cleon ;
v. 89, at Melos ; vi. 85, Euphêmus ; *cf.* i. 124, Corinthians.

goras, Protagoras, and Hippocrates, differed largely in beliefs, in aims, in interests ; but they had the all-important common principle, that thought must be clear, and that Reason holds the real keys of the world. Among the generation influenced by these teachers was a young man of anti-Periclean family, who nevertheless profoundly admired Pericles and had assimilated much of his spirit ; who was perhaps conscious of a commanding intellect, who had few illusions, who hated haziness, who was also one of the band of Lovers. He compared his Athens with Homer's Mycenæ or Troy ; he compared her with the old rude Athens which had beaten the Persians. He threw the whole spirit of the 'Enlightenment' into his study of ancient history. He stripped the shimmer from the old greatnesses, and found that in hard daylight his own mistress was the grandest and fairest. He saw—doubtless all the Periclean circle saw — that war was coming, a bigger war perhaps than any upon record, a war all but certain to establish on the rock the permanent supremacy of Athens. THUCYDIDES determined to watch that war from the start, mark every step, trace every cause, hide nothing and exaggerate nothing—do all that Herodotus had not done or tried to do. But he meant to do more than study it : he would help to win it. He was a man of position and a distinguished soldier. He had Thracian blood, a northern fighting strain, in his veins, as well as some kinship with the great Kimôn and Miltiades. The plague of 430 came near to crushing his ambitions once for all, but he was one of the few who were sick and recovered. The war had lasted eight years before he got his real opportunity. He was elected general in 423 B.C., second in command, and sent to Chalcidicê. It was close to his own country, where he had some hereditary chieftain-ship among the Thracians, and it was at that moment the very centre of the war. The Spartan Brasidas, in the flush of his enormous prestige, was in the heart of the Athenian dependencies. A defeat would annihilate him, as he had no base to retire upon ; and the conqueror of Brasidas would be the first military name in Greece.

No one can tell exactly what happened. The two towns in especial danger were Amphipolis and Eiôn on the Strymôn. The mere presence of the Athenian ships might suffice to save these two towns, but could do little to hurt Brasidas. Whereas, if only Thucydides could raise the Thracian tribes, Brasidas might be all but annihilated. That is what the Amphipolitans seem to have expected ; and that is perhaps why, when Brasidas, starting unexpectedly and marching all day and all night through driving snow, stormed the bridge of the Strymôn in the winter dawn and appeared under the walls of Amphipolis, Thucydides was half a day's sail away near Thasos, opposite his centre of influence in Thrace. His colleague Eucles was in Amphipolis, and the town could easily have held out. But Brasidas had his agents inside ; his terms were more than moderate, and there had always been an anti-Athenian party. When the first seven ships from Thasos raced into the river at dusk, Amphipolis was lost, and so was Thucydides's great opportunity. He threw himself into Eiôn, had the barren satisfac-tion of beating Brasidas twice back from the walls ; then—all we know is given in his own words (v. 26)— *"It befell to me to be an exile from my country for twenty years after my command at Amphipolis."*

Who can possibly tell the rights of the case?[1] We know only that Athens was a rude taskmaster to her generals. We cannot even say what the sentence was. He may have been banished ; he may have been condemned to death, and fled ; he may have fled for fear of the trial. We do not know where he lived. The ancient Life says, at his estate at Scaptê Hŷlê in Thrace ; but that was in Athenian territory, and no place for an exile. It is certain that he returned to Athens after the end of the war. He says himself that he was often with the Lacedæmonian authorities. He seems to have been at the battle of Mantinea, and possibly in Syracuse. We know nothing even of his death, which probably occurred before the eruption of Etna in 396. His grave was in Athens among those of Kimon's family ; but 'Zopyrus,' confirmed by 'Cratippus'—whoever they are—say that it had an '*ikrion*' —whatever that is—upon it, which was a sign that the grave did not contain the body.

If we knew more of Cratippus we should be able to add much to our life of Thucydides. The traditional lives, one by Marcellînus (5th cent. A.D.), one anonymous, are a mass of conflicting legends, conjectures, and deductions. He wept at hearing Herodotus read, and received the old man's blessing ; he married a Thracian Leiress ; he was exiled by Cleon ; he sat under a plane-tree writing his histories ; he drove all the Æginetans out of their island by his usury ; he was murdered in three places, and died by disease in another. Dionysius of Halicarnassus says in so many words (pp. 143, 144) that Cratippus was Thucydides's contemporary. If that were

---

[1] The case against Thucydides is well given by Grote (vi. 191 ff.), who accepts Marcellînus's story that Cleon was his accuser.

true it would rehabilitate the credit of the tradition, but the evidence is crushing against it. Recent criticism of the Life is all based on an article in *Hermes* xii., where Wilamowitz reduces the conventional structure to its base in the facts given incidentally by Thucydides himself *plus* the existence of a tomb of "Thucydides, son of Olorus, of the deme Halimûs," among the Kimonian graves in Athens; and then rebuilds from the fragments one small wigwam which he considers safe—the conclusion, namely, that Praxiphanes, a disciple of Theophrastus and a first-rate authority, had said that Thucydides, together with certain poets, lived at the court of Archelaus of Macedon. The argument is supported by Thucydides's own remarks (ii. 100) about that king improving the country in the way of organisation and road-making "*more than all the eight kings before him together.*" But it has led irresistibly to a further conclusion.[1] Not only did Praxiphanes say this, but we can find where he said it: it was in his dialogue *About History.** That spoils all. The scenes in dialogues are, even in Plato's hands, admittedly unhistoric; after Plato's death they are the merest imaginary conversations; so that our one wigwam collapses almost as soon as it is built. One corner of it only remains.

The dialogue, in discussing the merits of history and poetry—Aristotle had pronounced poetry to be the 'more philosophic'—pits Thucydides, the truthful historian, alone against five poets of different kinds; and we can probably guess what the decision was, from the fragmentary sentence which states that "*in his lifetime Thucydides was mostly unknown, but valued beyond price by posterity.*"

[1] Hirzel in *Hermes* xiii.

That, then, is one new fact about Thucydides, and it is like the others. His personal hopes were blighted in 423; his political and public ideals slowly broken from 414 to 404. And the man's greatness comes out in the way in which he remains faithful to his ideal of history. He records with the same slow unsparing detail, the same convincing truthfulness, all the triumphs and disasters—his own failure and exile, the awful story of Syracuse, the horrors of the 'Staseis,' the moral poison of the war-spirit throughout Greece, even the inward humiliations and exacerbated tyranny of her who was to have been the Philosopher-Princess among nations.

Our conception, 'the Peloponnesian War,' we owe to Thucydides. There are in it three distinct wars and eight years of unreal peace. The peace after the first war was followed by an alliance, and it looked as if the next disturbance in the air of Hellas would find Athens and Sparta arrayed as allies against some Theban or Argive coalition. Thucydides was still working at his record of the Ten Years' War when fresh hostilities broke out in Sicily, and he turned his eyes to them. The first war is practically complete in our book. The Sicilian Expedition (vi., vii.) is practically finished, too, in itself, though not fully brought into its place in the rest of the history. It has a separate introduction; it explains who Alcibiades is, as though he had not been mentioned before; it repeats episodes from the account of the Ten Years' War, or refers to it as to a separate book. As the Sicilian War drew on, Thucydides realised what perhaps few men could see at the time, the real oneness of the whole series of events. He collected the materials for the time of peace and partly shaped them into history (v. 26 to end); he collected most of the

material for the final Dekelêan or Ionian War (viii.). He
has a second prologue (v. 26) : " *The same Thucydides of
Athens has written these, too, in order, as each thing fell,
by summers and winters, until the Lacedæmonians and allies
broke the empire of the Athenians and took the Long Walls
and the Piræus.*" Those words must have been hard to
write.

He never reached the end. It is characteristic both
of the man and of a certain side of Athenian culture,
that he turned away from his main task of narrative to
develop the style of his work as pure literature. Instead
of finishing the chronicle of the war, he worked over
his reports of the arguments people had used, or the
policies various parties had followed, into elaborate and
direct speeches. Prose style at the time had its highest
development in the form of rhetoric ; and that turn of
mind, always characteristic of Greece, which delighted
in understanding both sides of a question, and would
not rest till it knew every seeming wrongdoer's apology,
was especially strong. The speeches are Thucydides's
highest literary efforts. In some cases they seem to
be historical in substance, and even to a certain extent
in phrasing; the letter of Nikias has the look of reality
(vii. 11 ff.), and perhaps also the speech of Diodotus
(iii. 42). Sometimes the speech is historical, but the
occasion is changed. One great Funeral Oration of
Pericles was made after his campaign at Samos ; [1] he
may have made one also in the first year of the war,
when there were perhaps hardly fifty Athenians to bury.
More probably Thucydides has transferred the great
speech to a time when he could use it in his history. [2]

[1] Ar. *Rhet.* 1365 *a* 31, 1411 *a* 1 ; Plut. *Per.* 28.
[2] W. M. in *Hermes* xii. 365 note.

Sometimes the speakers are vaguely given in the plural —'*the Corinthians said*'—that is, the political situation is put in the form of a speech or speeches showing vividly the way in which different parties conceived it. A notable instance is the imaginary dialogue between the Athenians and the Melians, showing dramatically and with a deep, though perhaps over-coloured, characterisation the attitude of mind in which the war-party at Athens then faced their problems.

This is at first sight an odd innovation to be introduced by the great realist in history. He warns us frankly, however. It was hard for him or his informants to remember exactly what the various speakers had said. He has therefore given the speeches which he thought the situation demanded, keeping as close as might be to the actual words used (i. 22). It is a hazy description. He himself would not have liked it in Herodotus ; and the practice was a fatal legacy to two thousand years of history-writing after him. But in his own case we have seen why he did it, and there is little doubt that he has done it with extraordinary effect. There is perhaps nothing in literature like his power of half personifying a nation and lighting up the big lines of its character. The most obvious cases are actual descriptions, such as the contrast between Athens and Sparta drawn by the Corinthians in I., or the picture of Athens by Pericles in II. ; but there is dramatic personation as well, and one feels the nationality of various anonymous speakers as one feels the personal character of Nikias or Sthenelaïdas or Alcibiades. It would be hard to find a clearer or more convincing account of conflicting policies than that given in the speeches at the beginning of the war.

Of course we should have preferred a verbatim report; and of course Thucydides's practice wants a Thucydides to justify it. But if we compare these speeches with the passages in VIII. where he has given us the same kind of matter in indirect form, one inclines to think that the artificial and fictitious speech is the clearer and more ultimately adequate. The fact is that in his ideal of history Thucydides was almost as far from Polybius as from Herodotus. Carefulness and truth, of course, come absolutely first, as with Polybius. *"Of the things done in the war"* (as distinguished from the speeches) *"I have not thought fit to write from casual information nor according to any notion of my own. Parts I saw myself; for the rest, which I learned from others, I inquired to the fulness of my power about every detail. The truth was hard to find, because eye-witnesses of the same events spoke differently as their memories or their sympathies varied. The book will perhaps seem dull to listen to, because there is no myth in it. But if those who wish to look at the truth about what happened in the war, and the passages like it which are sure according to man's nature to recur in the future, judge my work to be useful, I shall be content. What I have written is a thing to possess and keep always, not a performance for passing entertainment."*

He seeks truth as diligently and relentlessly as a modern antiquary who has no object for concealment or exaggeration. But his aim is a different one. He is not going to provide material for his readers to work upon. He is going to do the whole work himself—to be the one judge of truth, and as such to give his results in artistic and final form, no evidence produced and no source quoted. A significant point, perhaps, is his use of documents on the one hand and speeches on the other. Speaking roughly, one may say that in the finished parts of his work there are no documents ; in the unfinished there are no speeches. With regard to the speeches the case is clear. Nearly all bear the marks of being written after the end of the war. The unfinished Eighth Book has not a single speech ; the unfinished part of Book V. only the Melian Dialogue.

With the documents there is more room for doubt ; but the point is of great inner significance. Of the nine documents embodied verbatim in the text, three are in the notoriously unfinished Eighth Book ; three are in that part of Book V. which deals with the interval of peace; three—a Truce, a Peace, and an Alliance, between Athens and Sparta—belong to the finish of the Ten Years' War. Now, it can be made out that these last three come from Attic, not Spartan, originals ; that they were not accessible to the exile till his return in 403, and that such information as he had of them through third persons was not correct. Where they stand in the text they are *inorganic*. The narrative has been written without knowledge of them; in one case it contradicts them. The Truce shows that a separate truce had been made between Athens and Trœzen, not mentioned in the text. The Peace differs from the narrative about Pteleon and Sermylia, and implies that Athens had recovered the towns in Chalcidicê. The Alliance does *not* contain any clause binding Athens and Sparta to make no separate alliance except by mutual consent, though the surrounding narrative both implies and states that it did (v. 39, 46). Thucydides's documents have all been added to the text after

403, and imply a new and more ambitious aim for his history. When he wrote the Ten Years' War he gave no documents — not the peace of 445, nor the treaties with Rhegion and Leontini in 433, nor even that with Corcȳra. The same with his Sicilian War ; there is not even the treaty with Egesta.

He began his history as a true 'chronicle of the war by summers and winters.' He enlarged it to an attempt at a full and philosophic history of Athens in her diplomatic and imperial relations. When he was cut off from documents he saw their value, and when the opportunity came back, embodied them in his history as they stood recorded on the stones. The great political speeches were not recorded ; he knew that they expressed the inner meaning of the time, and he did his best to remember or recreate them.

Here again his work is unfinished. He has only nine documents in all, and the collection seems to a certain extent fortuitous. Three of them, more interesting than important, are mere abortive and apparently secret treaties between Sparta and Persia. He must have got these through some private channel, perhaps from the same source—Kirchhoff thinks, Alcibiades—as the Argive and Spartan documents in Book V. Many more documents would have been needed to make up his ideal history ; and many more of the dissertations and digressions, the explanations of internal policy and social change, which are now almost confined to the first two books and the introduction to Book VI. Even the documents which he has got, have not, as we have seen, been fully utilised. There were still some small errors in the narrative, which documentary evidence could help him to correct. There were some consider-

able omissions. His account of the tribute is obscure
for want of detail. He says Thêra was not in the
Empire in 432, and does not explain how she came to
be paying tribute in 426.[1] He says little about treaties
and proposals of peace, little of finance, little of Athenian
political development or military organisation. There is
not so much 'background,' to use Mr. Forbes's word,
to his history as to that of Herodotus. But the comparative fulness of Book I. in such matters is perhaps
an indication of what the rest would eventually have
become.

Thucydides's style as it stands in our texts is an extraordinary phenomenon. Undeniably a great style, terse,
restrained, vivid, and leaving the impression of a powerful intellect. Undeniably also an artificial style, obscure
amid its vividness, archaistic and poetic in vocabulary,
and apt to run into verbal flourishes which seem to have
little thought behind them. Part of this is explicable
enough. He writes an artificial semi-Ionic dialect, ξὺν
for μετὰ, ἢν for ἐὰν, πράσσω for πράττω. The literary
tradition explains that. Literature in Greek has always
a tendency to shape itself a language of its own. He is
overladen with antitheses, he instinctively sees things
in pairs; so do Gorgias and Antiphon. He is fond
of distinguishing between synonyms ; that is the effect
of Prodicus. He is always inverting the order of his
words, throwing separate details into violent relief,
which makes it hard to see the whole chain of
thought. This is evidently part of the man's peculiar
nature. He does it far more than Antiphon and Gorgias,
more even than Sophocles. His own nature, too, is
responsible for the crowding of matter and thought that

[1] C. I. A. 38 ; cf. 37.

one feels in reading him—the new idea, the new logical distinction, pressing in before the old one is comfortably disposed of. He is by nature '*Semper instans sibi*' (Quintilian). A certain freedom in grammar is common to all Greek, probably to all really thoughtful and vivid, writers : abstract singular nouns with plural verbs, slight anacolutha, intelligible compressions of speech. But what is not explicable in Thucydides is that he should have fallen into the intermittent orgies of ungrammatical and unnatural language, the disconcerting trails of comment and explanation, which occur on every third page.

Not explicable if true; but is it true? The answers arise in a storm. "No; our text is utterly corrupt." "It is convicted of gross mistakes by contemporary inscriptions. It is full of glosses. It has been filled with cross - references and explanatory interpolations during its long use as a school-book." "Intentional forgers in late times have been at it" (Cobet, Rutherford). "One of them was 'blood-thirsty,' and one talked 'like a *cretin*'!" (Müller-Strübing). "Nay, the work itself being notoriously unfinished, it was edited after the author's death by another" (Wilamowitz) ; or by various others, who interpolated so freely, and found the MSS. in such a state of confusion, that the "unity of authorship is as hopelessly lost in the Thucydidean question as in the Homeric" (Schwartz).

Against this onslaught, it is not surprising that the average scholar has taken refuge in deafness, or looked on with sympathetic hope while Herbst does his magnificent gladiator-work in defence of everything that he believed in the happy sixties—the time, as he says plaintively, when he felt, in opening his Thucydides, that he was "resting in Abraham's bosom." It is not surprising that conservative editors have even adopted the extraordinary theory—merely in defence against the development theories of Ullrich, Kirchhoff, and Cwiklinski—that Thucydides did not write a word between 432 and 404, and then apparently did the whole book at a sitting.

This is not the place to discuss the text, except in the broadest manner, and for the sake of its significance in the history of literature and in our conception of Thucydides. In the first place, the general line of Cobet followed by Rutherford, that the text is largely defaced by adscripts and glosses, and that Thucydides, a trained stylist at a time when style was much studied, did not, in a work which took twenty-nine years' writing, mix long passages of masterly expression with short ones of what looks like gibberish — thus much seems morally certain. The mere comparison of the existing MSS. and the study of Thucydides's manner show it. But that takes us very little way. Dr. Rutherford's valuable edition of Book IV., attempting to carry these results to a logical conclusion, has produced a text which hardly a dozen scholars in Europe would accept. We can see that the original wording has been tampered with ; we can see to a certain extent the lines of the tampering. We cannot from that restore the original.

But we have some concrete facts by which to estimate our tradition. We have part of the original text of one of Thucydides's documents extant on an Attic stone.[1] We have some significant quotations in the late geographer Stephen of Byzantium.

The inscription, according to Kirchhoff, taking the twenty-five lines alone, but allowing for restorations,

---

[1] The treaty, Thuc. v. 47 = C. I. A. iv. 46 *b*.

shows our Thucydides text to be wrong in thirty-two small points of detail; or not counting repetitions, in twenty; not counting conjectural restorations of the stone, in thirteen. The details are in spelling, in the order of the words, in the use of different prepositions or verb-forms, or in the omission of formal phrases. There is no difference in meaning. There is evidence to make it practically certain that Thucydides copied from an Athenian original verbally identical with our original—almost certain that he took his copy from our very stone.

Now, dismissing the desperate theory that Thucydides was consciously improving the style of his document (Herbst), the errors in our text will naturally be attributed to divers and various of the many scribes who have mediated between Thucydides and us. In that case our text is a seriously-damaged article. To save the vulgate some have sacrificed Thucydides. ' He did not care for verbal accuracy. He lived before the age of precision in literary matters.' Very probable; but a suicidal defence. For if Thucydides, the pupil of the Sophists, did not care for verbal accuracy in his documents, is it likely that the contemporary journey-man scribe cared for verbal accuracy in copying him ?

The evidence of Stephen is different, but points in the same direction. Our text of Thucydides gives foreign proper names in a more or less consistently Atticised form, and it has been thought the height of pedantry to suspect them. Stephen in five places where he quotes Thucydides in his Geography spells the names in the correct and ancient way,[1] which of

---

[1] Γραϊκὴν, ii. 23; Κοτύρταν, Ἀφροδιτίαν, Κυνουρία, iv. 56; Μεταπίους, iii. 101.

course he cannot have known by his own wits. In another passage (iii. 105), where our text says that Olpæ, a place on the extreme border of Acarnania towards Amphilochia, was "*the common tribunal of the Acarnanians*," Stephen quotes it as "*of the Acarnanians and Amphilochians*," which is just what its position demands.

The upshot of this is that all criticism of Thucydides must recognise the demonstrable imperfection of our text. For instance, in the well-known Mitylenæan story, when the Assembly has condemned the whole military population to death in a moment of passion, repented the same day, and, by the tremendous exertion of the galley-rowers who bore the reprieve, saved them, it proceeds to condemn and execute the ringleaders of the rebellion, "*those most guilty*." "*They numbered rather more than* 1000" (iii. 50)! Is that number remotely credible? There is nothing in which MSS. are so utterly untrustworthy as figures, the Greek numeral system lending itself so easily to enormous mistakes. The ringleaders were in Athens at the time. It was a deliberate execution of prisoners, not a hot-blooded massacre; and nobody, either in Thucydides or for centuries after him, takes the least notice of it! Diodôrus, with his Thucydides before him, makes Hermocrates of Syracuse deliver a speech upon all the crimes of Athens; he tells of many smaller things; he tells of the cruel decision of the first Assembly and of the enormity which the Athenians *thought of committing*— and omits to mention that they executed 1000 of their subjects in cold blood. It is clear that Diodôrus did not read our story. It all rests on the absolute correctness of the figure ϙ; and our editors cry aloud and cut themselves with knives rather than admit that the *ą* can possibly be wrong ! [1]

In the same way, in i. 51 our text can be checked by a contemporary inscription.[2] The stone agrees exactly with Thucydides in the names of the first set of generals mentioned ; in the second it gives "Glaukon (Metage)nês and Drakonti(dês)." Our text gives "*Glaukon, son of Leagros ; Andokidês, son of Leôgoras*"—that is, Andokidês the orator. Is this a mere mistake of the historian's ? Not necessarily. Suppose the owner of some copy in which there was a blot or a tear was not sure of the form 'Leagros'; "Leôgoras," he would reflect, "is a real name ; Andokidês was son of a Leôgoras." Hence enters the uninvited orator and ousts the two real but illegible names. Something of that sort is far more likely than such a mistake on the part of Thucydides.

In a passage at the end of Book I. where the narrative is easy and the style plain, the scholiast observes that "here the lion laughs." The lion would laugh more often and more pleasantly if we could only see his real expression undistorted by the accidents of tradition.

To return from this inevitable digression, we see easily how Thucydides was naturally in some antagonism to Herodotus's whole method of viewing things. Thucydides had no supernatural actors in his narrative. He sees no suggestion—how could he in the wrecked world that lay before him ?—of the working of a Divine Providence. His spirit is *positif ;* he does not speak of things he knows nothing about. He is a little sardonic about

---

[1] Müller-Strübing of course thinks the passage an interpolation. Thucydides used the decadic system of numerals, not that of the Attic inscriptions.

[2] C. I. A. 179.

oracles, which of course filled the air at the time. He instances their safe ambiguity (ii. 17, 54), and mentions as a curiosity the only one he had ever known to come definitely true (v. 26). He speaks little of persons. He realises the influence of a great man such as Pericles, a mere demagogue such as Cleon, an unscrupulous genius such as Alcibiades. Living in a psychological age, he studies these men's characters and modes of thought, studies them sometimes with vivid dramatic personation, in the speeches and elsewhere ; but it is only the mind, never the manner or the matter, that he cares for, and he never condescends to gossip. He cares for great movements and organised forces. He believes above all things in reason, brain-power, intelligence.

There is another point in which he is irritated by Herodotus. He himself was a practical and highly-trained soldier. Herodotus was a man of letters who knew nothing of war except for some small Ionian skirmishing in his youth. Herodotus speaks of the 'regiment of Pitanê,' showing that he thought Spartan regiments were raised by localities ; it makes Thucydides angry that a professed historian should not know better than that.[1] Except in topography, which is always difficult before the era of maps, Thucydides is very clear and pointed in his military matters ; and it is interesting to observe that he lays his hand on almost all the weaknesses of Greek military organisation which were gradually made clear by experience in the times after him. In the Peloponnesian War the whole strength of the land army was in the heavy infantry. Thucydides shows the helplessness of such an army against adequate light infantry.[2] Iphicrates and Xenophon learned the lesson. He shows

[1] i. 20 ; cf. Hdt. ix. 53.   [2] iii. 102 ; iv. 39.

the effect of the Syracusan superiority in cavalry, both for scouting and foraging and in actual engagements. It was cavalry that won Chæronea for Philip, and the empire of Darius for Alexander. He points out, too, the weakest spot of all in Greek strategy, the hampering of the general's action in the field by excessive control at home. The Sicilian Expedition was lost, not by Nikias, but by the Athenian Assembly ; or if Nikias also made grave errors, they were largely due to the state of paralysing subjection in which he was kept by that absent body. The Roman Senate, composed so largely of military men, was as sympathetic to its generals' failures as it was to their extortions. The Athenian Assembly was largely affected by the private soldier and the man, who, though liable to serve, was in reality no soldier at all. Sparta was almost as bad for a different reason. Only an exceptional position like that of Brasidas in Chalcidicê, or Agis at Dekeleia, enabled a general to act with real freedom,[1] though even Agis was materially hindered by jealousy. Here again we see one of the secrets of the power of Philip and Alexander.

Like most thoughtful soldiers—Bauer [2] quotes parallels from Moltke and others — Thucydides is consistently impressed with the uncertainty of war, the impossibility of foreseeing everything, or of knowing in a battle what exactly is being done. He does not judge men, as the stupid do, by their success. He had personal reasons, of course, for not doing so in military matters ; but this principle, one of the greatest marks of the real thinker, is with him all through his work. Pericles was convinced from the facts before him that Athens would win the war ; and she lost it. Pericles was profound and correct

[1] viii. 5, Agis.   [2] *Philologus*, l. 401.

in his reckoning, but he could not foresee the plague, nor
be responsible for the abandonment of his policy after
his death.   It is very remarkable, indeed, how Thucydides
never expresses a personal judgment which could be de-
duced from the facts he has given.   He only speaks when
he thinks the facts likely to be misinterpreted.   Cleon's
undertaking (iv. 28) to capture Sphactêria in less than
twenty days was fulfilled.   It was nevertheless an insane
boast, says Thucydides.   At the end of the Sicilian Expedition, we are full of admiration for Demosthenes ;
our pity for Nikias is mingled with irritation, and even
contempt.   Thucydides sobers us : *"Of all the Greeks of
my time, he least deserved so miserable an end, for he
lived in the performance of all that was counted virtue"*
(vii. 86).   Generous praise ; but the man's limitations
are given — *" all that was counted virtue."*   We should
never have discovered this about Nikias from the mere
history.   But Thucydides knew the man ; is perfectly,
almost cruelly, frank about him ; and that is Thucydides's final judgment.   It is the same with Antiphon.
He is a sinister figure : he was responsible for a reign
of terror.   But Thucydides, who knew him, admired
him, while he deliberately recorded the full measure
of his offences.   Macchiavelli's praise of Cæsar Borgia
suggests itself.   Antiphon's ἀρετή was perhaps rather
like Borgia's *Virtù*, and Macchiavelli had a great ideal
for Italy, something like that of Thucydides for Athens.
Or one might think of Philippe de Commines' praise
of Louis XI.   But Thucydides, though in intellect not
unlike these two, is a much bigger man than De Commines, a much saner and fuller man than Macchiavelli,
and a much nobler man than either.   He is very chary
of moral judgments, but surely it needs some blindness

in a reader not to feel the implication of a very earnest moral standard all through. It has been said that he attributes only selfish motives even to his best actors, a wish for glory to Brasidas, a desire to escape punishment to Demosthenes. But he seldom mentions personal motives at all, and when such motives do force their way into history they are not generally unselfish. He certainly takes a high standard of patriotism for granted. One would not be surprised, however, to learn that Thucydides's speculative ethics found a difficulty in the conception of a strictly 'unselfish' action.

Of course Thucydides is human ; he need not always be right. For instance, the 'Archæologia,' or introduction to ancient history in Book I., is one of the most striking parts of his whole work. For historical imagination, for breadth of insight, it is probably without a parallel in literature before the time of the Encyclopédistes ; and in method it is superior even to them. Nevertheless it is clear that Thucydides does not really understand Myth. He treats it merely as distorted history, when it often has no relation to history. Given Pelops and Ion and Hellên, his account is luminous ; but he is still in the stage of treating these conceptions as real men.

Of course in the 'Archæologia' there is no room for party spirit ; but even where there is, the essential fairness and coolness of the writer's mind remain unbroken. He is often attacked at the present day. But the main facts—that most antiquity took him as a type of fair-mindedness, while some thought him philo-Spartan and some philo-Athenian ; that Plato and Aristotle censured him for being too democratic, while his modern opponents complain that he is not democratic enough—

speak volumes. His own politics are clearly moderate. The time when Athenian political affairs pleased him best, he tells us—not counting, presumably, the exceptional 'Greatest-Man-Rule' of Pericles—was during the first months of the Restored Constitution in 411. It was "*a fair combination of the rights of the Few and the Many*."[1] He seems to be a man with strong personal opinions, and a genius for putting them aside while writing narrative. His reference to '*a certain*' Hyperbolus (viii. 73)—when Hyperbolus had been for some time the most prominent politician in Athens—is explicable when one realises that his history was addressed to the whole Greek world, which neither knew nor cared about Athenian internal politics. The contemptuous condemnation of the man which follows, is written under the influence of the spirit current in Athens at the end of the century. His tone about Cleon is certainly suggestive of personal feeling. But the second introduction of him[2] is obviously due to some oversight either of author or scribe; and the astounding sentence in iv. 28, 5, becomes reasonable when we realise that "*the Athenians*" who "*would sooner be rid of Cleon than capture Sphactêria*," are obviously the then majority of the Assembly, the party of Nikias. After all, his account of Cleon is the least unfavourable that we possess; and if it is harsh, we should remember that Thucydides was under a special obligation to show that Cleon is not Pericles.

It must be borne in mind that Thucydides returned to Athens in 403 like a ghost from the tomb, a remnant of the old circle of Pericles. He moved among men who were strangers to him. His spirit was one which had practically died out of Athens nearly a generation

[1] viii. 97; *cf.* ii. 65, 5, and iii. 82, 8.   [2] iv. 21 = iii. 36.

before, and the memory of it vanished under the strain
and bloodshed and misery of the last fifteen years. The
policy of Pericles, the idea of the Empire, the Democracy itself, was utterly, hopelessly discredited in the
circles where Thucydides naturally moved. The thinkers
of the day took the line of the oligarchical writers,
the line of Aristotle afterwards. Athenian history was
the 'succession of demagogues,' Aristeides, Ephialtes,
Pericles, Cleon, Cleophôn, Callicrates—"*and from that
time on in succession all who were ready for the greatest
extremes in general recklessness, and in pandering to the
people for their immediate advantage.*"[1] The Democracy,
in a moderate and modified form, had to be accepted;
but it was, as Alcibiades had pronounced it, '*folly confessed,*'[2] and its leaders were all so many self-seeking
adventurers. 'Pericles — why, look at Stesimbrotus
and the comedies of that day — he was just as bad
as the worst of them; and Aristeides the Just, we
could tell some queer stories about him!' The men
of the early fourth century are living among ruins,
among shattered hopes, discredited ideals, blunted and
bewildered aims. The best of them[3] "*has seen the
madness of the multitude. He knows that no politician is
righteous, nor is there any champion of justice at whose
side he may fight and be saved.*" In public life he would
be "*a man fallen among wild beasts.*" It is better that
he "*retires under the shelter of a wall while the hurrying
wind and the storm of dust and sleet go by.*" Testifying
solitarily among these is the old returned exile of the
time of Pericles. His life is over now, without distinction, his Athens ruined beyond recognition, the old
mistress of his love dead and buried. But he keeps

[1] Ar. *Ath. Pol.* xxviii.   [2] Thuc. vi. 89.   [3] Plato, *Rep.* 496 D.

firm the memory of his real city and his leader—the man whom they called a demagogue because he was too great for them to understand; who never took a gift from any man; who dwelt in austere supremacy; who, if he had only lived, or his counsels been followed, would have saved and realised the great Athens that was now gone from the earth. Other men of the day wrote pamphlets and arguments. Thucydides has not the heart to argue. He has studied the earlier and the mythical times, and prepared that marvellous introduction. He has massed all the history of his own days as no man ever had massed history before. He knows ten times more than any of these writers, and he means to know more still before he gives out his book. Above all, he is going to let the truth speak for itself. No man shall be able to contradict him, no man show that he is ever unfair. And he will clothe all his story in words like the old words of Gorgias, Prodicus, Antiphon, and Pericles himself. He will wake the great voices of the past to speak to this degenerate world.

His death came first. The book was unfinished. Even as it stood it was obsolete before it was published. As a chronicle it was continued by Xenophon, and as a manifesto on human vanity by Theopompus; but the style and the spirit of it passed over the heads of the fourth century. Some two hundred years later, indeed, he began to be recognised among the learned as the great truthful historian. But within fifty years of his death Ephorus had rewritten, expanded, popularised, and superseded him, and left him to wait for the time of the archaistic revival of the old Greek literature in the days of Augustus Cæsar.

IX

THE DRAMA

INTRODUCTION

LOOKING at the Drama of Sophocles as a finished product, without considering its historical growth, we are constantly offended by what seem to be inexplicable pieces of conventionalism. From some conventional elements, indeed, it is singularly free. There are one or two traditional *ficelles*—oracles, for instance, and exposure of children ; but on the whole the play of incident and character is as true as it is unostentatious. There is no sham heroism, no impossible villainy, no maudlin sentiment. There is singular boldness and variety of plot, and there is perfect freedom from those pairs of lovers who have been our tyrants since modern drama began.

One group of alleged conventions may be at once set aside. We must for the present refuse to listen to those who talk to us of masks and buskins and top-knots and sacerdotal dress, repeat to us the coarse half-knowledge of Pollux and Lucian, show us the grotesques of South Italy and the plasterer's work of Pompeian degradation, compile from them an incorrect account of the half-dead Hellenistic or Roman stage—the stage that competed with the amphitheatre—and bid us construct an idea of the drama of Euripides out of the ghastly farrago. It is one of the immediate duties of archæological research to set us right again where archæological text-books have set us so miserably wrong.

Still our undoubted literary tradition does contain strong elements of conventionalism. The characters are all saga-people ;[1] they all speak in verse ; they tend to speak at equal length, and they almost never interrupt except at the end of a line. Last and worst, there is eternally present a chorus of twelve or fifteen homogeneous persons—maidens, matrons, elders, captives, or the like—whose main duty is to minimise the inconvenience of their presence during the action, and to dance and sing in a conventional Doric dialect during the intervals. The explanation of this is, of course, historical.

We have seen above (p. 99) how the Silenus-choir of the Centaur-like followers of Dionysus was merged into the Satyr-choir of wild mountain-goats in the suite of the Arcadian mountain-god Pan. 'Tragos' is a goat; 'tragikos choros' a goat-choir; and 'tragôidia' a goat-song. The meaning of the word only changed because the thing it denoted changed. Tragedy developed from the Dorian goat-choirs of the Northern Peloponnese—those of Arîon at Corinth, and of the precursors of Pratînas at Phlius, and those which the tyrant Cleisthenes suppressed at Sikyon for "celebrating the sufferings of Adrastus."[2]

---

[1] The best known exception is the *Antheus* * (not *Flower*) of Agathon. Agathon left Athens (about 407) at the age of forty, when he had already won a position inferior only to that of Sophocles and Euripides, but before his individual originality and his Socratic or Platonic spirit had a permanent effect on the drama. Aristophanes had assailed him vehemently in the *Thesmophoriazusæ* and *Gerytades* *—a testimony to his 'advanced' spirit in art.

[2] Hdt. v. 67.

Of course, other influences may also have helped. There was a mimetic element in the earliest popular poetry, and we hear of '*drômena*' (things performed) —the word lies very near '*drâma*' (performance)—in many religious cults. The birth of Zeus was acted in Crete; his marriage with Hera, in Samos, Crete, and Argos. There were sacred puppets, '*Daidala*,' at Platæa. The 'Crane-Dance' of Delos showed Theseus saving the children from the Labyrinth; and even the mysteries at Eleusis and elsewhere made their revelations more to mortal eyes by spectacle than to mortal ears by definite statement.

The first step in the transformation of the goat-choir took place on Attic soil, when the song poetry of the Dorian met the speech poetry of Ionia. A wide-spread tradition tells us that Thespis of the village Icaria was the first poet who, " to rest his dancers and vary the entertainment," came forward personally at intervals and recited to the public a speech in trochaic tetrameters, like those metrical harangues which Solon had declaimed in the market-place.[1] His first victory was in 534 B.C. His successors were Choirilus and a foreigner who performed in Attica, Pratînas of Phlius.

The choir were still satyrs at this stage. What was the poet? Probably he represented the hero of the play, the legendary king or god. An old saying, not understood afterwards, speaks of the time " when Choirilus was a king among satyrs." But if the poet represented one character, why should he not represent more ? If he

---

[1] Aristotle does not mention Thespis; and the pseudo-Platonic dialogue *Minos* says expressly that tragedy did not start, " as people imagine," with Thespis, nor yet with Phrynichus, but was much older. See Hiller in *Rh. Mus.* xxxix. 321.

came on first, say, as the King Lycurgus, let him change his dress during the next song and re-enter as the priest whom Lycurgus has scorned; next time he may be a messenger announcing the tyrant's death. All that is needed is a place to dress in. A section of the round dancing-floor ('orchêstra') is cut off; a booth or '*skênê*' is erected, and the front of it made presentable. Normally it becomes a palace with three doors for the actor-poet to go in and out of. Meantime the character of the dancing is somewhat altered, because there is no longer a ring to dance in; the old ring-dance or 'cyclic chorus' has turned into the 'square' chorus of tragedy.

Of course, the choir can change costume too: Pratînas once had a choir representing Dymanian dancing girls. But that was a more serious business, and seems to have required a rather curious intermediate stage. There are titles of plays, such as *The Huntsmen-Satyrs*,* *Herald-Satyrs*,* *Wrestler-Satyrs*.* Does not this imply[1] something like the *Maccus a Soldier*, *Maccus an Innkeeper*, of the Italian 'Atellanæ,' like *The Devil a Monk* in English? The actor does not represent a soldier simply; he represents the old stage buffoon Maccus pretending to be a soldier. The choir are not heralds; they are satyrs masquerading as such. It is the natural end of this kind of entertainment to have the disguise torn off, and the satyrs, or Maccus, or the Devil, revealed in their true characters. In practice the tragic choirs were allowed three changes of costume before they appeared as satyrs confessed. That is, to use the language of a later time, each performance was a 'tetralogy'— three 'tragedies' ('little myths,' Aristotle calls them by comparison with the

[1] W. M. *Herakles*, i. p. 88.

longer plays of his own day), followed by a satyric drama. The practice did not die till the middle period of Euripides. His *Cyclops* is the one satyr-play extant, while his *Alkêstis* is a real drama acted as a concluding piece to three tragedies.

The Greek word for actor, 'hypocritês,' means 'answerer.' The poet was really the actor ; but if he wanted to develop his solitary declamation into dialogue, he needed some one to answer him. The chorus was normally divided into two parts, as the system of strophe and antistrophe testifies. The poet perhaps took for answerers the leaders of these two parts. At any rate, 'three actors' are regularly found in the fully-developed tragedy. The old round choir consisted of fifty dancers and a poet : the full tragic company of forty-eight dancers, two 'answerers,' and a poet. That was all that the so-called '*chorêgus*' — the rich citizen who undertook the expenses of the performance — was ever bound to supply ; and munificent as this functionary often was in other respects, his '*parachorêgêmata*,' or gifts of supererogation, never took the form of a fourth actor in the proper sense. Nor did he provide four changes of costume for the whole forty-eight dancers ; they appeared twelve at a time in the four plays of the tetralogy. The tradition says loosely that Thespis had one actor, Æschylus two, and Sophocles three, though sometimes it is Æschylus who introduced the third. As a matter of fact, it was the state, not the poet, which gave fixed prizes to the actors, and settled the general conduct of the Dionysus Feast. Accordingly, when we find an ancient critic attributing particular scenic changes to particular poets, this as a rule only means that the changes appeared to him to occur for

the first time in their works. A mutilated inscription[1]
seems to give us the date of some important altera-
tion or ratification of stage arrangements. It admitted
Comedy to the great Dionysia ; it perhaps established
the 'three actors,' perhaps raised the tragic chorus from
twelve to fifteen, and perhaps made the palace-front
scene a permanency. The poets tended naturally to
retire from acting. Æschylus ceased in his later life.
Sophocles is said to have found his voice too weak.
The profession of actor must have been established
before 456 B.C., when we first find the victorious
actors mentioned officially along with the poet and the
'chorêgus.'

The chorus was the main substance of the tragedy.
Two main processes were needed to make a complete
performance : the 'chorêgus' 'provided a chorus,' the
poet 'taught the chorus'—those were the difficult things.
The mere composition was a matter of detail, which any
good poet was ready to do for you. All the technical
terms are formed with reference to the chorus. The
'prologue' is all that comes before their entrance ; an
'episodion' is the 'entry to' the chorus of any fresh
character ; the close of the play is an 'exodus,' because
they then depart. But the chorus was doomed to
dwindle as tragedy grew. Dialogue is the essence of
drama ; and the dialogue soon became, in Aristotle's
phrase, 'the protagonist.' We can see it developing
even in our scanty remains. It moves from declaimed
poetry to dramatic speech ; it grows less grand and
stiff, more rapid and conversational. It also increases
in extent. In the *Suppliants* of Æschylus (before
470 B.C.) the chorus are really the heroines of the

[1] C. I. A. ii. 971.

play. They are singing for two-thirds of it. They are present from the first line to the last. In the *Philoctêtês* of Sophocles (409 B.C.) they are personally unimportant, they do not appear till the play is well in train, and their songs fill about one-sixth of the whole. This is one reason why the later plays are so much longer than the earlier: they were quicker to act.

There was, however, another influence affecting the musical side of tragedy in a very different manner. The singing gradually ceased to be entirely in the hands of the chorus. The historical fact is that with the rise of the Athenian Democracy the chorus ceased to be professional. It consisted of free burghers who undertook the performance of the public religious dances as one of their privileges or duties.[1] The consequence was that the dancing became less elaborate. The metres and the singing had to be within the capabilities of the average musical man. But meanwhile the general interest in music was growing deeper, and the public taste more exacting in its demands. The average choir-song lost its hold on the cultivated Athenian of the war time. If he was to have music, let him have something more subtle and moving than that, something more like the living music of the dithyramb, which was now increasingly elaborate and professional. So while between Æschylus and the later plays of Sophocles the musical side of the drama is steadily falling back, between the earlier and later plays of Euripides it is growing again. But it is no longer the music of the chorus. Euripides used 'answerers' who were also trained singers; he abounds in 'monodies' or solos. In the *Medea* (431 B.C.) the lyrical part is about a fifth

---

[1] *Resp. Ath.* i. 13.

of the whole ; in the *Ion* (414 B.C.) it is nearly half, but
the monodies and part-songs amount to half as much
again as the choir-songs. In the *Orestes* (408 B.C.) the
solo parts are three times as long as the choral parts.
One apparent exception to this rule really illustrates
its meaning. The *Bacchæ*, one of the very latest plays,
has a large choral element and no monodies. Why ?
Because when Euripides wrote it he had migrated to
Macedonia, and apparently had not taken his operatic
actors with him. Macedonia had no drama ; but it had
a living dithyramb with professional performers, and it
was they who sang in the *Bacchæ*.

This upward movement of the satyr-song was due to
various causes—to the spiritual crises that ennobled the
Athenian people ; to the need for some new form of art
to replace the dying epos as a vehicle for the heroic
saga ; to the demand made by Dionysus-worship for
that intensity of emotion which is almost of necessity
tragic. The expropriated satyrs were consigned, with
their quaint old-world buffoonery, to a private corner at
the end of the three tragedies, and the comic element
was left to develop itself in a separate form of art.

To us in our reflective moods comedy and tragedy
seem only two sides of the same thing, the division
between them scarcely tangible ; and so thought the
Athens of Menander. But historically they are of
different pedigree. Tragedy springs from the artistic
and professional choir-song ; comedy, from the mumming of rustics at vintage and harvest feasts. "Tragedy
arose from the dithyramb," says Aristotle ; "comedy,
from the phallic performances." These were celebrated
in honour of the spirits of fructification and increase
in man, beast, or herb, which were worshipped under

various names in different parts of Greece. It was
Dionysus at Acharnæ, in Rhodes, and in Delos. It
was the sisters Dâmia and Auxêsia in Ægina ; Demeter
in some parts of Attica ; Pan in the Northern Peloponnese.
It is always a shock to the modern imagination
to come upon the public establishment of such monstrously
indecent performances among a people so far
more simple and less self-indulgent than ourselves.
But, apart from possible elements of unconscious
hypocrisy on our own part, there are many things
to be borne in mind. In dealing with those elements
in human nature which are more permanent than respectable,
the characteristic Greek method was frank
recognition and regulation. A pent-up force becomes
dangerous ; let all natural impulses be given free play in
such ways and on such occasions as will do least damage.
There were the strictest laws against the abuse of these
festivals, against violence, against the undue participation
of the young ; but there was, roughly speaking, no shame
and no secrecy. We have, unfortunately, lost Aristotle's
philosophy of comedy. It was in the missing part of the
Poetics. But when he explains the moral basis of tragedy
as being "to purge our minds of their vague impulses of
pity and terror" by a strong bout of these emotions ;
when he justifies 'tumultuous' music as affording a
'purgation' of the wild emotional element in our
nature which might else break out in what he calls
'*enthousiasmos*' ; it is easy to see that the licences in
comedy might be supposed to effect a more obvious
and necessary purgation.[1] Besides this, we must not

---

[1] The definition in frag. 3, Vahlen, says this directly : "$\dot{\eta}\delta o\nu\dot{\eta}$ and $\gamma\epsilon\lambda\omega s$
are to be so purged by comedy." But is the whole passage a genuine quotation,
or is it rather a deduction of Aristotle's views ?

forget that there was always present in Greece an
active protest against these performances ; that even
absolute asceticism was never without its apostles ;
and, lastly, that where religion gives sanctity to a bad
custom it palsies the powers of the saner intellect.
Without a doubt many a modest and homely priestess
of Dionysus must have believed in the beneficial effects
both here and hereafter of these ancient and symbolical
processions.

One of the characteristics of the processions was
'*parrhêsia*' ('free speech') ; and it remained the proud
privilege of comedy. You mocked and insulted freely
on the day of special licence any of those persons to
whom fear or good manners kept you silent in ordinary
life. In some of the processions this privilege was specially granted to women. As soon as comedy began to be
seriously treated, the central point of it lay in a song,
written and learned, in which the choir, acting merely
as the mouthpiece of the poet, addressed the public on
'topical' subjects. This became the '*parabasis*' of the
full-grown comedy. For the rest, the germ of comedy is
a troop of mummers at the feast of Dionysus or some
similar god, who march with flute and pipe, sing a
phallic song, and amuse the onlookers with improvised
buffoonery. They are unpaid, unauthorised. It was not
till about 465 B.C. that public recognition was given to
the '*kômoi*,' or revel-bands, and '*komôidia*' allowed to
stand by the side of '*tragôidia*.' It came first at the
Lenæa, afterwards at other Dionysiac festivals. But it
was not till the beginning of the Peloponnesian War that
two gifted young writers, Eupolis and Aristophanes,
eventually gave the Old Comedy an artistic form, wove
the isolated bits of farce into a plot, and more or less

abolished or justified the phallic element.[1] After that comedy develops even more rapidly than tragedy. The chorus takes a more real and lifelike part in the action ; its inherent absurdity does much less harm, and it disappears more rapidly. The last work of Aristophanes is almost without chorus, and marks the intermediate development known as the Middle Comedy, tamer than the Old, not so perfect as the New. Then comes, in weaker hands, alas ! and brains less 'dæmonic,' the realisation of the strivings of Euripides, the triumph of the dramatic principle, the art that is neither tragic nor comic but both at once, which aims self-consciously at being "the imitation of life, the mirror of human intercourse, the expression of reality."[2] This form of art once established lasted for centuries. It began shortly after 400 B.C., when public poverty joined with artistic feeling in securing the abolition of the costly chorus, and when the free libel of public persons had, after long struggles and reactions, become finally recognised as offensive. It reached its zenith with Menander and Philêmon about 300 B.C. ; while inscriptions of various dates about 160 have recently taught us that even at that time five original comedies a year were still expected at the great Dionysia, besides the reproduction of old ones. It is a curious irony of fortune that has utterly obliterated, save for a large store of 'fragments' and a few coarse Latin adaptations, the whole of this exceptionally rich department of ancient literature.

[1] Abolished in the *Clouds*, justified in the *Lysistrata*.
[2] Cic. *de Repub.* iv. 11, quoting a Peripatetic (?).

PHRYNICHUS, SON OF POLYPHRADMON (*fl.* 494 B.C.)

The least shadowy among the pre-Æschylean dramatists is PHRYNICHUS. Tradition gives us the names of
nine of his plays, and tells us that he used the trochaic
tetrameter in his dialogue, and introduced women's
parts. We hear that he made a play on the *Capture
of Milêtus;* * that a fine was put on him for doing so,
and notice issued that the subject must not be treated
again. The fall of Miletus was a national grief, and
perhaps a disgrace ; at any rate, it involved party politics
of too extreme a sort. Phrynichus had better fortune
with his other play from contemporary history, the
Phœnissæ; * its chorus representing the wives of Xerxes'
Phœnician sailors, and its opening scene the king's
council-chamber, with the elders waiting for news of
the great war. He won the prize that time, and probably
had for 'chorêgus' Themistocles himself, the real, though
of course unmentioned, hero of the piece. It is the
lyrics that we most regret to have lost, the quaint
obsolete songs still hummed in the days of the Peloponnesian War by the tough old survivors of Marathon,
who went about at unearthly hours of the morning—

> " *Lights in their hands, old music on their lips,*
> *Wild honey and the East and loveliness.*" [1]

A certain grace and tenderness suggested by our remains
of Phrynichus enable us to realise how much Æschylus's
grand style is due to his own character rather than to the
conditions of the art in his time ; though it remains true
that the Persian War did for tragedy what the Migrations
seem to have done for Homer, and that Phrynichus and
Æschylus are both of them 'men of Marathon.'

[1] Aristoph. *Vesp.* 220.

X

ÆSCHYLUS

ÆSCHYLUS, SON OF EUPHORION, FROM ELEUSIS (525–456 B.C.)

ÆSCHYLUS was by birth an Eupatrid, of the old nobility. He came from Eleusis, the seat not only of the Demeter Mysteries, but also of a special worship of Dionysus-Zagreus, and close to Thespis's own deme Icaria. We hear that he began writing young ; but he was called away from his plays, in 490, to fight at Marathon, where his brother Kynêgeirus met a heroic death, and he won his first victory in the middle of the nine years of peace which followed (484). Four years later he joined in the general exodus to the ships and Salamis, leaving the stones of Athens for the barbarians to do their will upon. These were years in which tragedies and big thoughts might shape themselves in men's minds. They were not years for much actual writing and play-acting. In 476 Æschylus seems to have been at the wars in Thrace ; we have echoes of them in the *Lycurgus* * Trilogy and in the *Persæ* (esp. 866). Soon after that again he was in Syracuse, perhaps on a diplomatic mission, and wrote his *Women of Etna*,* in honour of the town of that name which Hiero had just founded (476–475) on the slopes of the mountain.

From 484 onwards he was probably the chief figure

in Attic letters; though his old rivals Pratînas and Phrynichus, and their respective sons Aristias and Polyphradmon, among others, doubtless won prizes over his head from time to time, and, for all we know, deserved them. The earliest play we possess is the *Suppliant-Women;* the earliest of known date is the *Persæ,* which won the first prize in 472.

In 470 he was again in Syracuse, and again the reason is not stated, though we hear that he reproduced the *Persæ* there. In 468 he was beaten for the first time by the young Sophocles. The next year he was again victor with the *Seven against Thebes.* We do not know the year of his great *Prometheus* Trilogy, but it and the *Lykurgeia* * seem to have come after this. His last victory of all was the *Oresteia* (*Agamemnon, Choëphoroi,* and *Eumenides*) in 458. He was again in Sicily after this—the little men of the Decadence suggest that he was jealous of Sophocles's victory of ten years back!—and died suddenly at Gela in 456. His plays went in and out of fashion at Athens, and a certain party liked to use him chiefly as a stick for beating Euripides; but a special law was passed after his death for the reproduction of his tragedies, and he had settled into his definite place as a classic before the time of Plato. The celebrated bronze statue of him was made for the stone theatre built by Lycurgus about 330.

The epitaph he is said to have written for his tomb at Gela is characteristic: no word of his poetry; only two lines, after the necessary details of name and birthplace, telling how the "*grove of Marathon can bear witness to his good soldierhood, and the long-haired Mede who felt it.*" It is very possible that the actual facing of death on that first great day remained with him as the supreme moment of his life, and that his poetry had failed to satisfy him. It often leaves that impression, even at its most splendid heights.

Of the ninety plays Æschylus wrote, we possess seven. The earliest, on internal grounds, is the *Suppliant-Women* —a most quaint and beautiful work, like one of those archaic statues which stand with limbs stiff and coun- tenance smiling and stony. The subject, too, is of the primitive type, more suited for a cantata than for a play. The suppliants are the fifty daughters of Danaus, who have fled to Argos to avoid marrying their cousins, the fifty sons of Ægyptus. Their horror is evidence of a time when the marriage of first cousins was counted incestuous. They appeal for protection to Pelasgus, king of Argos, who refers the question to the Demos. The Demos accepts the suppliants, and the proud Egyptian herald is defied. The other plays of the trilogy had more action. In the *Makers of the Bride-Bed,** the sons of Ægyptus follow the Danaids, conquer Danaus in battle, and insist on the marriage. Danaus, preferring murder to incest, com- mands his daughters to stab their husbands on their bridal night ; all do so except Hypermêstra, who is put on trial in the *Danaides** for marriage with a cousin and for filial disobedience, and is acquitted by the help of Aphrodite. Our play seems to have been acted on the old round dancing-floor, with a platform in the middle, and images round it. There is no palace front ; and the permanent number of fifty in the chorus throughout the trilogy suggests the idea that the old round choir may have been still undivided.

The *Persæ* (472) was the second piece of a trilogy. The first had the name of *Phîneus,** the blind prophet of the Argonaut legend, who probably prophesied something about the greater conflict between Europe and Asia, of which that expedition was a type. The third was *Glaucus ;* * but there were two pieces of that name, and the plot is not certain. The *Persæ* itself is modelled on the *Phœnissæ* * of Phrynichus : the opening words of the two are almost identical, and the scene in both is in the council-chamber of Susa, though in the *Persæ* it afterwards changes to the tomb of Darius. The *Persæ* has not much plot-interest in the ordinary sense ; but the heavy brooding of the first scenes, the awful flashes of truth, the evocation of the old blameless King Darius, who had made no Persians weep, and his stern prophecy of the whole disaster to come, all have the germ of high dramatic power : one feels the impression made by " *the many arms and many ships, and the sweep of the chariots of Syria,*" both in the choir-songs and in the leaping splendour of the descriptions of battle. The external position of the *Persæ* as the first account of a great piece of history by a great poet who had himself helped to make the history, renders it perhaps unique in literature ; and its beauty is worthy of its eminence.

The *Seven against Thebes* came third in the trilogy after the *Laïus* * and the *Œdipus.* * One old version of the saga allowed Œdipus to put away Iocasta after the discovery of their relationship, and marry Euryganeia ; there was no self-blinding, and the children were Euryganeia's. But Æschylus takes the story in the more gruesome form that we all know. The *Seven* gives the siege of Thebes by the exiled Polyneîkes, the battle, and mutual slaying of the two brothers. It was greatly admired in antiquity — " *a play full of Ares,*

*that made every one who saw it wish forthwith to be
a 'fiery foe,'"* as Aristophanes puts it (*Ranæ*, 1002).
The war atmosphere is convincing, the characters plain
and strong. Yet, in spite of a certain brilliance and
force, the *Seven* is perhaps among Æschylean plays
the one that bears least the stamp of commanding
genius. It is like the good work of a lesser man.

Very different is the *Prometheus*, a work of the same
period of transition as the *Seven*, and implying the
use of three actors in the prologue, as the *Seven*
probably does in the 'exodus.' The trilogy seems
to have consisted of *Prometheus Bound, Prometheus
Freed,** and *Prometheus the Fire-Carrier.** The subject
is Titanic ; it needs a vast and 'winged' imagination.
But it has produced in the hands of Æschylus and
of Shelley two of the greatest of mankind's dramatic
poems. Prometheus is the champion of man against
the Tyrant Power that sways the world. He has
saved man from the destruction Zeus meant for him,
taught him the arts of civilisation, and, type of all
else, given him fire, which was formerly a divine
thing stored in heaven. For this rebellious love of
mankind he is nailed to a storm-riven rock of the
Caucasus ; but he is not conquered, for, in the first
place, he is immortal, and besides he knows a secret
on which the future of heaven and earth depends.
Zeus tries by threats and tortures to break him, but
Prometheus will not forsake mankind. And the
daughters of Ocean, who have gathered to comfort
him, will not forsake Prometheus. They face the
same blasting fire, and sink with him into the abyss.
There is action at the beginning and end of the play;
the middle part, representing, apparently, centuries

rather than days, is taken up with long narratives of Prometheus to the Oceanides, with the fruitless intercession of Oceanus himself, and the strange entry of another victim of Zeus, the half-mad Moon-maiden Io, driven by the gadfly, and haunted by the ghost of the hundred-eyed Argos. The chorus of the *Prometheus* is perhaps in character and dramatic fitness the most beautiful and satisfying known to us on the Greek stage. The songs give an expression of *Weltschmerz* for which it would be hard to find a parallel before the present century. The whole earth is in travail as Prometheus suffers : "*There is a cry in the waves of the sea as they fall together, and groaning in the deep ; a wail comes up from the cavern realms of Death, and the springs of the holy rivers sob with the anguish of pity.*" In another place the note is more personal : "*Nay, thine was a hopeless sacrifice, O beloved; speak—what help shall there be, and where ? What succour from things of a day ? Didst thou not see the little-doing, strengthless, dream-like, wherein the blind race of man is fettered ? Never, never shall mortal counsels outpass the great Harmony of Zeus !*" Zeus is irresistible : those who obey him have peace and happiness such as the Ocean-Daughters once had themselves. Yet they feel that it is better to rebel.

There is perhaps no piece of lost literature that has been more ardently longed for than the *Prometheus Freed*.* What reconciliation was possible ? One can see that Zeus is ultimately justified in many things. For instance, the apparently aimless persecution of Io leads to great results, among them the birth of Heracles, who is another saviour of mankind and the actual deliverer of Prometheus. Again, it seems that Prometheus does not intend to overthrow the 'New Tyrant,' as Shelley's

Prometheus does.   He had deliberately helped him against the old blind forces, Kronos and the Titans ; but he means, so to speak, to wring a constitution out of him, and so save mankind. But it needs another Æschylus to loose that knot in a way worthy of the first. We have some external facts about the second play. It opened when Prometheus came back to the light after thirty thousand years ; the chorus was of Titans. The last play, the *Fire-Carrier*,* seems to have explained the institution of the Festival of Prometheus at Athens. Such ' origins ' formed a common motive for drama.

The *Oresteia* represents the highest achievement of Æschylus, and probably of all Greek drama. It has all the splendour of language and the lyrical magic of the early plays, the old, almost superhuman grandeur of outline, while it is as sharp and deep in character-drawing, as keenly dramatic, as the finest work of Sophocles. The Cassandra scene in the *Agamemnon*, where the doomed prophetess, whom none may believe, sees the vision of her own death and the king's, await-ing her in the palace, is simply appalling on the stage, while in private study many a scholar will testify to its eternal freshness. The first play deals with the murder of Agamemnon on his triumphant return from Troy by a wife deeply sinned against and deeply sin-ning. The *Choëphoroi* (' Libation-Bearers ') gives the retribution. Orestes, a child at the time of his father's death, has grown up in exile ; he returns secretly to execute the blood-feud on Ægisthus, and, by special command of Apollo, to slay also his mother.

The *Choëphoroi* is in some ways the most complex of the dramas of Æschylus. There is a recognition scene (see p. 259), impossible in detail, but grand and moving; there is a definite plot by which the ministers of vengeance enter the palace; there is great boldness of drawing in all the characters down to the pathetic and ludicrous old nurse; there is the haunting shadow of madness looming over Orestes from the outset, and deepening through the hours that the matricide is before him and the awful voice of Apollo in his ears, and he struggles helplessly between two horrors, up to the moment when his mother's curses take visible form to him, and he flies from the grey snake-locked faces.

The *Eumenides* is dramatic in its opening, merely spectacular in its close. There is a certain grandeur in the trial scene where Orestes is accused by the Curse-Spirits, defended by Apollo, and acquitted by the voice of Athena. The gods, however, are brought too close to us, and the foundation of the Areopagus has not for us the religious reality it had for Æschylus. But the thing that most disappoints us, the gradual slackening of the interest till the 'pity and terror' melt away in gentle artistic pleasure, was, as every choric ode and most tragedies testify, one of the essential principles of Greek art. Shakespeare was with the Greeks. He ends his tragedies by quiet scenes among minor characters, and his sonnets with a calm generalising couplet. We end our plays with a point, and our sonnets with the weightiest line.

The general spirit of Æschylus has been much misunderstood, owing to the external circumstance that his life came at the beginning of an age of rapid progress. The pioneer of 490 is mistaken for a reactionary of 404. Æschylus is in thought generally a precursor of the

sophistic movement, as Euripides is the outcome of it.
He is an enthusiastic democrat of the early type. Listen
to the pæans about freedom in the *Persæ*. That is the
very spirit recorded by Herodotus as having made
Athens rise from a commonplace Ionian state to be
the model and the leader of Hellas. And the *Persæ* is
not isolated. The king in the *Suppliants* is almost
grotesquely constitutional; the *Prometheus* abounds in
protests against despotism that breathe the true
Athenian spirit; a large part of the *Agamemnon* is a
merciless condemnation of the ideal of the conquering
monarch. In the *Eumenides*, it is true, Æschylus definitely glorifies the Areopagus at a time when Ephialtes and Pericles were removing most of its jurisdiction.
He was no opponent of Pericles, who was his 'chorêgus,'
at least once;[1] but he was one of the men of 490. To
that generation, as Aristotle's *Constitution* has taught us,
the Areopagus was the incarnation of free Athens in
battle against Persia; to the men of 460 it was an obsolete and anomalous body.

As to the religious orthodoxy of Æschylus, it appears
certain that he was prosecuted for having divulged or
otherwise offended against the mysteries, which suggests
that he was obnoxious to the orthodox party. We may
possibly accept the story, stated expressly by Clement,
and implied by Aristotle (1111 *a*), that he escaped by
proving that he had not been initiated, and consequently
had nothing to divulge. For a distinguished Eleusinian
not to have been initiated — if credible at all—would
imply something like an anti-sacerdotal bias. Certainly
he seems to have held no priesthoods himself, as Sophocles and Pindar did; and his historical position may

[1] C. I. A. 971.

well have been that of those patriots who could not
forgive or forget the poltroonery of Delphi before the
war (see p. 138). However this may be, he is in religious
thought generally the precursor of Euripides. He stands
indeed at a stage where it still seems possible to reconcile
the main scheme of traditional theology with morality
and reason. Euripides has reached a further point,
where the disagreement is seen to be beyond healing.
Not to speak of the *Prometheus*, which is certainly sub-
versive, though in detail hard to interpret, the man who
speaks of the cry of the robbed birds being heard by
"*some Apollo, some Pan or Zeus*" (*Ag.* 55) ; who prays
to "*Zeus, whoe'er he be*" (160) ; who avows "*there is no
power I can find, though I sink my plummet through all
being, except only Zeus, if I would in very truth cast off
this aimless burden of my heart*"—is a long way from
Pindaric polytheism. He tries more definitely to grope
his way to Zeus as a Spirit of Reason, as opposed to the
blind Titan forms of Hesiodic legend. "*Lo, there was one
great of yore, swollen with strength and lust of battle, yet it
shall not even be said of him that once he was ! And he
who came thereafter met his conqueror, and is gone. Call
thou on Zeus by names of Victory. . . . Zeus, who made
for Man the road to Thought, who stablished 'Learn by
Suffering' to be an abiding Law!*" That is not written in
the revelations of Delphi or Eleusis ; it is true human
thought grappling with mysteries. It involves a practical discarding of polytheism in the ordinary sense, and
a conception—metaphorical, perhaps, but suggestive of
real belief—of a series of ruling spirits in the government
of the world—a long strife of diverse Natural Powers,
culminating in a present universal order based on reason,
like the political order which Æschylus had seen estab-

lished by Athenian law. Compare it with the passage in
Euripides (*Tro.* 884) :—

> "*Base of the world and o'er the world enthroned,*
> *Whoe'er thou art, Unknown and hard of surmise,*
> *Cause-chain of Things or Man's own Reason, God,*
> *I give thee worship, who by noiseless paths*
> *Of justice leadest all that breathes and dies !*"

That is the same spirit in a further stage : further, first
because it is clearer, and because of the upsetting alternative in the third line ; but most, because in the actual
drama the one rag of orthodoxy which the passage
contains is convicted as an illusion ! The Justice for
which thanks are given conspicuously fails : the 'noise-
less paths' lead to a very wilderness of wrong—at least,
as far as we mortals can see.

The only orthodox Greek writer preserved to us is
Pindar. Sophocles held a priesthood and built a chapel,
but the temper of his age was touched with rationalism,
and the sympathetic man was apt unconsciously to
reflect it.

About the positive ideas, religious and moral, implied
in the plays of Æschylus, too much has been written
already ; it is difficult to avoid overstatement in criticism of the kind, and the critics have generally been
historians of philosophy rather than lovers of Greek
poetry. One may perhaps make out rather more
strongly in Æschylus than in other writers three
characteristic ways of looking at life. His tragedies
come, as perhaps all great tragedies do, from some
'Hubris,' some self-assertion of a strong will, in the
way of intellect or emotion or passion, against stronger
outside forces, circumstances or laws or gods. Æschylus
was essentially the man to feel the impassable bars

P

against which human nature battles; and the over-throw of the Great King was the one thought that was in every Greek mind at the time. Thus the peril of human 'Hubris' and the 'jealousy of God'—*i.e.* the fact that man's will aims further than his power can reach—is one rather conspicuous principle in Æschylus.

Another is a conviction of the inevitableness of things; not fatalism, nor any approach to it, in the vulgar sense, but a reflection that is borne in on most people in considering any grave calamity, that it is the natural consequence of many things that have happened before. The crimes in Æschylus are hereditary in two senses. In the great saga-houses of Thebes and Mycenæ there was actually what we should call a taint of criminal madness—it is brought out most explicitly in Euripides's *Electra*. Orestes was the son of a murderess and a man who had dealt much in blood (πολυκτόνος). His ancestors had been proud and turbulent chieftains, whose passions led them easily into crime. But the crime is hereditary in itself also. The one wild blow brings and always has brought the blow back, "the ancient blinded vengeance and the wrong that amendeth wrong." This, most people will admit, is a plain fact; of course the poet puts it in a mystical or symbolical form. The old blood remains fresh on the ground, crying for other blood to blot it out. The deed of wrong begets children in its own likeness. The first sin produces an 'Arâ,' a Curse-Spirit, which broods over the scene of the wrong, or over the heart and perhaps the race of the sinner. How far this is metaphor, how far actual belief, is a problem that we cannot at present answer.

This chain of thought leads inevitably to the question, What is the end of the wrong eternally avenged and regenerated? There may of course be no end but the extinction of the race, as in the *Theban Trilogy;* but there may come a point where at last Law or Justice can come in and pronounce a final and satisfying word. Reconciliation is the end of the *Oresteia,* the *Prometheia,* the *Danaid Trilogy.* And here, too, we get a reflection of the age in which Æschylus lived, the assertion over lawless places of Athenian civilisation and justice.

In looking over the plays and fragments as a whole, one notices various marks both of the age and of the individual. It is characteristic of both that Æschylus wrote satyr-plays so much, and, it would seem, so well. These Titanic minds—Æschylus and Heraclitus among Greeks; men like Victor Hugo and Carlyle among ourselves—are apt to be self-pleasing and weird in their humour. One of the really elemental jokes of Æschylus is in the *Prometheus Firekindler,** a satyr-play, where fire is first brought into the world, and the wild satyrs go mad with love for its beauty, and burn their beards in kissing it! The thing is made more commonplace, though of course more comic, in the Sophoclean satyr-play *Helen's Marriage,** where they go similarly mad about Helen. A definite mark of the age is the large number of dramas that take their names from the chorus, which was still the chief part of the play — *Bassaræ,** *Edôni,** *Danaides,** &c. Another is the poet's fondness for geographical disquisitions. Herodotus had not yet written, and we know what a land of wonder the farther parts of the world still were in his time. To the Athens of Æschylus the geographical interest was partly of this imaginative sort; in part it came from the impulse given by the rise of Athens to voyages of discovery and trade adventure. Of our extant plays, the *Prometheus* is full of mere declamations on saga-geography ; the *Persæ* comes next, then the *Suppliants;* and even the *Agamemnon* has the account of the beacon stations. *Glaucus of the Sea,** *Niobe,** and probably the *Mysians,** were full of the same thing. The impulse did not last in Greek tragedy. Sophocles has his well-known burst of Herodotean quotation, and he likes geographical epithets as a form of ornament, but he keeps his interest in ' historiê' within due limits. Euripides, so keenly alive to all other branches of knowledge, is quite indifferent to this.

In the choice of subjects Æschylus has a certain preference for something superhuman or unearthly, which combines curiously with this geographical interest. The *Prometheus* begins with the words : *" Lo, we are come to the farthest verge of the world, to where the Scythians wander, an unearthly desolation."* That is the region where Æschylus is at home, and his ' large utterance ' natural and unhampered. Many of his lost plays move in that realm which Sophocles only speaks of, among

> *" The last peaks of the world, beyond all seas,*
> *Well-springs of night and gleams of opened heaven,*
> *The old garden of the Sun."* [1]

It is the scene of the *Daughters of the Sun,** treating of the fall of Phaëthon ; of the *Soul-Weighing,** where Zeus balances the fates of Hector and Achilles ; of the *Ixion ; ** of the *Memnon ; ** and the numerous plays on Dionysiac subjects show the same spirit.

It is partly the infancy of the art and partly the intensity of Æschylus's genius that makes him often choose subjects that have apparently no plot at all, like our

[1] Soph. frag. 870.

Suppliants and *Persæ*. He simply represents a situation, steeps himself in it, and lights it up with the splendour of his lyrics. Euripides tried that experiment too, in the *Suppliants* and *Heracleidæ*, for instance. Sophocles seems never to have risked it, except perhaps in the *Demanding of Helen*.* It is curious that Æschylus, unlike his successors, abstained entirely from the local legends. Perhaps it was that he felt the subjects to be poor, and that the realities of the Persian War had blotted out all less vivid things from the horizon of his patriotism.

It is interesting to compare the fragments of the three tragedians : fragments are generally 'gnomic,' and tend to show the bent of a writer's mind. Sophocles used gnomes but little. Reflection and generalisation did not interest him, though he has something to say about the power of wealth (frag. 85) and of words (frag. 192) and of wicked women (frag. 187). Euripides notoriously generalises about everything in heaven and earth. He is mostly terse and very simple—so simple that an unsympathetic reader misses the point.

"*Love does not vex the man who begs his bread*" (frag. 322).
"*The things that must be are so strangely great*" (frag. 733).
"*Who knoweth if we quick be verily dead,*
And our death life to them that once have passed it ?" (frag. 638).

Sometimes, as in the opening speeches of Phædra and Medea, he treats subtly a point in psychology. He has much to say about wealth and slavery and power of speech. Æschylus simply never thinks about such things. He has some great lines on love (frag. 44), but his typical gnome is like that in the *Niobe :* *—

"*Lo, one god craves no gift. Thou shalt not bend him:*
By much drink-offering and burnt sacrifice.
He hath no altar, hearkeneth to no song,
And fair Persuasion standeth far from Death."

It does "somehow spoil one's taste for twitterings." And so, above all, do his great dramatic speeches, so ruggedly grand that at first sight one is often blind to the keen psychology of passion in them—for instance, that in which Clytæmestra gives public welcome to her husband. She does not know whether he has been told of her unfaithfulness; she does know that she is utterly friendless, that the man whom she dreaded in her dreams is returned, and that the last hour for one or other of them has come. She tries, like one near to death, to leave some statement of her case. She is near breaking down more than once; but she gathers courage as she speaks, and ends in the recklessness of nervous exaltation :—

> " *Freemen of Argos, and ye gathered Elders,*
> *I shall not hold it shame in the midst of you*
> *To outspeak the love ye well know burns within me.*
> *There comes a time when all fear fades and dies.*
> *Who else can speak? Does any heart but mine*
> *Know the long burden of the life I bore*
> *While he was under Troy? A lonely woman*
> *Set in a desolate house, no man's arm near*
> *To lean on—Oh, 'tis a wrong to make one mad!*
> *Voices of wrath ring ever in her ears:*
> *Now, he is come! Now, 'tis a messenger:*
> *And every tale worse tidings than the last,*
> *And men's cries loud against the walls that hold her!*
> *If all the wounds that channelled rumour bore*
> *Have reached this King's flesh—why, 'tis all a net,*
> *A toil of riddled meshes! Died he there*
> *With all the deaths that crowded in men's mouths,*
> *Then is he not some Gêryon, triple-lived,*
> *Three-bodied, monstrous, to be slain and slain*
> *Till every life be quelled? . . . Belike ye have told him*
> *Of my death-thirst—the rope above the lintel,*
> *And how they cut me down? True: 'twas those voices,*
> *The wrath and hatred surging in mine ears.*

Our child, sire, is not here : I would he were :
Orestes, he who holds the hostages
For thee and me. Yet nowise marvel at it.
Our war-friend Strophios keeps him, who spoke much
Of blows nigh poised to fall,—thy daily peril,
And many plots a traitorous folk might weave,
I once being weak, manlike, to spurn the fallen.

But I—the stormy rivers of my grief
Are quenched now at the spring, and no drop left.
My late-couched eyes are seared with many a blight,
Weeping the beacon fires that burned for thee
For ever answerless. And did sleep come,
A gnat's thin song would shout me in my dreams,
And start me up seeing thee all girt with terrors
Close-crowded, and too long for one night's sleep !
And now 'tis all past ! Now with heart at peace
I hail my King, my watch-dog of the fold,
My ship's one cable of hope, my pillar firm
Where all else reels, my father's one-born heir,
My land scarce seen at sea when hope was dead,
My happy sunrise after nights of storm,
My living well-spring in the wilderness !
Oh, it is joy, the waiting-time is past !
Thus, King, I greet thee home. No god need grudge—
Sure we have suffered in time past enough—
This one day's triumph. Light thee, sweet my husband,
From this high seat : yet set not on bare earth
Thy foot, great King, the foot that trampled Troy !
Ho, thralls, why tarry ye, whose task is set
To carpet the King's way ? Bring priceless crimson :
Let all his path be red, and Justice guide him,
Who saw his deeds, at last, unhoped for, home !"

XI

SOPHOCLES

SOPHOCLES, SON OF SOPHILLOS, FROM COLONUS
(496–406 B.C.)

SOPHOCLES is formed by the legend into a figure of
ideal serenity and success. His life lay through the
period of his country's highest prosperity. He was
too young to suffer much in the flight of 480, and he
died just before Athens fell. He was rich, pious, good-
looking, good-tempered, pleasure-loving, witty, "with
such charm of character that he was loved by everybody wherever he went." He held almost the only
two sources of income which did not suffer from the
war—the manufacture of weapons, and the state-paid
drama. He won a prodigious number of first prizes—
twenty as against the five of Euripides. The fifteen of
Æschylus were gained in times of less competition. He
dabbled in public life, and, though of mediocre practical ability, was elected to the highest offices of the
state. He was always comfortable in Athens, and had
no temptation to console himself in foreign courts as
his colleagues did. We may add to this that he was
an artist of the 'faultless' type, showing but few
traces of the 'divine discontent.' His father was a
rich armourer, and a full citizen—not a 'Metœcus' like
Kephalus (p. 337). Sophocles learned music from Lam-

pros, and we hear of him at the age of sixteen leading a choir as harper in the thanksgiving for Salamis. His first victory was in 468, when he was eight and twenty. The play was perhaps the *Triptolemus*.* [1] If so, it was a success to the patriotic drama on its first appearance ; for Triptolemus was a local hero with no real place in the Homeric legend.[2] Our account of the victory is embroidered by a strange anecdote : there were such hot factions in the theatre that the archon suddenly set aside the regular five judges, and called on the ten generals, who had just returned from campaigning, to provide a fresh board. The first defeat of Æschylus by a younger generation which knew not Marathon and Salamis, would produce the same bitterness as was felt in modern Greece and Italy against the first Prime Ministers who had not fought in the wars of independence.

One of Sophocles's very earliest plays was probably the *Women Washing*.* The scene, Nausicaa and her maidens on the sea-shore, seems meant for the old dancing-floor before the palace front had become a fixed tradition ; and the poet himself acted Nausicaa, which he can only have done in youth. His figure in middle life was far from girlish, as even the idealised statue shows. The earliest dated play is the *Antigone;* it was produced immediately before the author's appointment as admiral in the Samian War of 440, and constituted in the opinion of wits his chief claim to that office. The poet Ion, who met him at Chios, describes him as "merry and clever over his cups," and charming in conversation ; of public affairs he

---

[1] Plin. *Hist. Nat.* 18, 65.
[2] The *Hymn to Demeter* is no evidence to the contrary.

"understood about as much as the average educated Athenian." In 443 he had been 'Hellênotamias' (Treasurer of the Empire) with no bad results. His fame and popularity must have carried real weight, or he would not have been one of ten Commissioners ('Probouloi') appointed after the defeat of the Sicilian Expedition in 413. And it is significant that, when he was prosecuted along with his colleagues for agreeing to the Oligarchical Constitution of 411, he was acquitted on the naïve defence that he "had really no choice!"

An authorless anecdote speaks of some family difficulties at the end of his life, attributing them to his connection with an 'hetaira' named Theôris. His legitimate son Iophon tried to get a warrant for administering the family estate, on the ground of his father's incapacity. Sophocles read to the jury an ode from the *Œdipus at Colônus*, which he was then writing, and was held to have proved thereby his general sanity! The story smacks of the comic stage; and the references to the poet at the time of his death, especially by Aristophanes in the *Frogs*, and Phrynichus, son of Eunomides, in the *Muses*,* preclude the likelihood of any serious trouble having occurred shortly before. He died in 406, a few months after his great colleague Euripides, in whose honour he introduced his last chorus in mourning and without the usual garlands.[1] His tomb lay on the road to Dekeleia, and we hear that he was worshipped as a hero under the name of 'Dexiôn' ('Receiver'), on the curious ground that he had in some sense 'received' the god Asclêpius into his house. He was a priest of the Asclepian hero Alcon, and had built a chapel to

---

[1] At the '*pro-agôn*' or introductory pageant. At the actual feast such conduct would probably have been 'impiety.'

'The Revealer' — Mênûtes, identified with Heracles ;
but the real reason for his own worship becomes clear
when we find in another connection that he had
founded a 'Thiasos of the Muses,' a sort of theatrical
club for the artists of Dionysus. He thus became
technically a ' Hero - Founder,' like Plato and Epicurus, and doubtless was honoured with incense and
an ode on his birthday. He was 'Dexiôn' perhaps as
the original 'host.'

Sophocles was writing pretty continuously for sixty
years, and an interesting citation in Plutarch[1] purports
to give his own account of his development. That the
words are really his own is rather much to believe ; but
the terms used show the criticism to be very ancient.
Unfortunately the passage is corrupt. He began by
having some relation—is it 'imitation' or is it 'revolt' ?
—towards the 'magniloquence of Æschylus' ; next came
'his own 'stern' and artificial period of style' ;[2] thirdly,
he reached more ease and simplicity, and seems to have
satisfied himself. Bergk finds a trace of the ' Æschylean
period' in some of the fragments ; and it is a curious
fact that ancient critics found in the pseudo-Euripidean
Rhesus a 'Sophoclean character.' It is not like the
Sophocles of our late plays, but does suggest a fourth-
century imitation of Æschylus. One form of the 'artificial' tendency—it might as well be translated 'technical'
or 'professional'—is expressed in the scenic changes with
which Sophocles is particularly associated ; though, of
course, it must be borne in mind that the actual admission of 'three actors and scene-painting'[3] to the

---

[1] *De Profect. Virt.* 7.
[2] Πικρὸν καὶ κατάτεχνον. Πικρὸν is early Greek for the later αὐστηρόν.
[3] Ar. *Poet.* 4.

sacred precinct must have been due to a public enactment, and not to the private innovation of a poet.

Perhaps the most important change due to Sophocles
himself took place in what the Greeks called the
'economy' of the drama.   He used up all his myth
material in one well-constructed and complex play, and
consequently produced three separate plays at a time
instead of a continuous trilogy.[1]   But, in general, Sophocles worked as a conscious artist improving details,
demanding more and smoother tools, and making up,
by skilful construction, tactful scenic arrangement, and
entire avoidance of exaggeration or grotesqueness, for
his inability to walk quite so near the heavens as his
great predecessor.   The 'stern and artificial' period is
best represented by the *Electra*.   The *Electra* is 'artificial' in a good sense, through its skill of plot, its
clear characterisation, its uniform good writing.   It is
also artificial in a bad sense.   For instance, in the
messenger's speech, where all that is wanted is a false
report of Orestes's death, the poet chooses to insert a
brilliant, lengthy, and quite undramatic description of
the Pythian Games.   It is also 'stern.'   Æschylus in
the *Choëphoroi* had felt vividly the horror of his plot :
he carries his characters to the deed of blood on a
storm of confused, torturing, half - religious emotion ;
the climax is, of course, the mother-murder, and Orestes
falls into madness after it.   In the *Electra* this element
is practically ignored.   Electra has no qualms ; Orestes
shows no sign of madness ; the climax is formed, not
by the culminating horror, the matricide, but by the
hardest bit of work, the slaying of Ægisthus !   Æschylus

---

[1] It was his contemporary Aristarchus of Tegea who first " made plays of
their present length " (Suidas).

had kept Electra and Clytæmestra apart: here we see them freely in the hard unloveliness of their daily wrangles. Above all, in place of the cry of bewilderment that closes the *Choëphoroi*—"*What is the end of all this spilling of blood for blood?*"—the *Electra* closes with an expression of entire satisfaction. It is this spirit that makes the *Electra*, brilliant as it is, so typically uncharming. The explanation may partly lie in some natural taste for severity and dislike of sentiment in Sophocles; it seems certainly also to be connected with his archaism. His language is archaistic through and through; and it seems as if his conceptions were.

All three tragedians have treated the Electra-saga, and treated it in characteristically different ways. The realistic spirit of Euripides's *Electra* is obvious to every one —the wolfish Pelopidæ, the noble peasant, the harrowing scene of remorse and mutual reproach between the murderers. But the truth is that Æschylus has tried to realise his subject too. He takes the old bloody saga in an earnest and troubled spirit, very different from Homer's, though quite as grand. His Orestes speaks and feels as Æschylus himself would. It is only Sophocles who takes the saga exactly as he finds it. He knows that those ancient chiefs did not trouble about their consciences: they killed in the fine old ruthless way. He does not try to make them real to himself at the cost of making them false to the spirit of the epos. The same objectiveness of treatment appears in another characteristic of Sophocles—the stress he lays on mere physical horror in the *Œdipus*, on physical pain in the *Trachiniæ* and the *Philoctêtes*. It is the spirit of the oldest, most savage epos.[1]

[1] *Cf.* p. 41 on the *Niptra.**

Something of the same sort keeps him safe in the limits of convention. A poet who is uncompromisingly earnest in his realism, or unreserved in his imagination, is apt to jar upon his audience or to make them laugh. Sophocles avoids these dangers. He accepts throughout the traditional conception of heroes and saga-people. The various bits of criticism ascribed to him—"I draw men as they ought to be drawn ; Euripides draws them as they are"; "Æschylus did the right thing, but without knowing it"—all imply the 'academic' standpoint. Sophocles is the one Greek writer who is 'classical' in the vulgar sense—almost in the same sense as Vergil and Milton. Even his exquisite diction, which is such a marked advance on the stiff magnificence of his predecessor, betrays the lesser man in the greater artist. Æschylus's superhuman speech seems like natural superhuman speech. It is just the language that Prometheus would talk, that an ideal Agamemnon or Atossa might talk in their great moments. But neither Prometheus nor Œdipus nor Electra, nor any one but an Attic poet of the highest culture, would talk as Sophocles makes them. It is this characteristic which has established Sophocles as the perfect model, not only for Aristotle, but in general for critics and grammarians ; while the poets have been left to admire Æschylus, who "wrote in a state of intoxication," and Euripides, who broke himself against the bars both of life and of poetry.

The same limitation comes out curiously in points where his plays touch on speculation. For one thing, his piety makes him, as the scholiast quaintly puts it,[1] "quite helpless in representing blasphemy." Contrast, for instance, the similar passages in the *Antigone* (l. 1043)

[1] *Electra*, 831.

and the *Heracles* of Euripides (l. 1232). In the *Heracles*, the hero rebukes Theseus for lifting him from his despair and unveiling his face ; he will pollute the sunlight ! That is not a metaphor, but a real piece of superstition. Theseus replies that a mortal cannot pollute the eternally pure element. Later he asks Heracles for his hand. "*It is bloody,*" cries Heracles ; "*it will infect you with my crime !*" "*Let me clasp it,*" answers Theseus, "*and fear not.*" Now, Sophocles knew of these ideas—that the belief in a physical pollution of blood is a delusion, and that a man cannot, if he tries, make the sun impure ; but to him they reeked of scepticism—or else of prosiness. He uses them as blasphemy in the mouth of the offending Creon ! No impulse to reason or analyse was allowed to disturb his solemn emotional effects. Another typical difference between the two poets is in their treatment of the incest of Œdipus. Sophocles is always harping on it and ringing the changes on the hero's relationships, but never thinks it out. Contrast with his horrified rhetoric, the treatment of the same subject at the end of Euripides's *Phœnissæ*, the beautiful affection retained by the blind man for Iocasta, his confidence that she at any rate would have gone into exile at his side uncomplaining, his tender farewell to her dead body. What was the respectable burgher to say to such a thing ? It was defrauding him of his right to condemn and abominate Iocasta. No wonder Sophocles won four times as many prizes as Euripides ! A natural concomitant of this lack of speculative freedom is a certain bluntness of moral imagination which leads, for instance, to one structural defect in the *Œdipus Tyrannus*. That piece is a marvel of construction : every detail follows naturally, and yet every detail depends on the characters being exactly what they were, and makes us understand them. The one flaw, perhaps, is in Teiresias. That aged prophet comes to the king absolutely determined not to tell the secret which he has kept for sixteen years, and then tells it—why ? From uncontrollable anger, because the king insults him. An aged prophet who does that is a disgrace to his profession ; but Sophocles does not seem to feel it.

Sophocles is thus subject to a certain conventional idealism. He lacks the elemental fire of Æschylus, the speculative courage and subtle sympathy of Euripides. All else that can be said of him must be unmixed admiration. Plot, characters, atmosphere are all dignified and 'Homeric' ; his analysis, as far as it goes, is wonderfully sure and true ; his language is a marvel of subtle power ; the music he gets from the iambic trimeter by his weak endings and varied pauses is incomparable ; [1] his lyrics are uniformly skilful and fine, though they sometimes leave an impression of laboured workmanship ; if they have not the irresistible songfulness of Æschylus and Euripides, they are safe from the rhodomontade of the one, and the inapposite garrulity of the other. And it is true that Sophocles shows at times one high power which but few of the world's poets share with him. He feels, as Wordsworth does, the majesty of order and well-being ; sees the greatness of God, as it were, in the untroubled things of life. Few hands but his could have shaped the great ode in the *Antigone* upon the Rise of Man, or the description in the *Ajax* of the 'Give and Take' in nature. And even in the

---

[1] W. M. *Heracles*, i. p. 21. It is Ionic style : weak endings, elisions at the end of the verse (like Achaios of Eretria), ἡμίν for ἡμῖν, shortening of a long vowel or diphthong before another vowel.

famous verdict of despair which he pronounces upon
Life in the second *Œdipus*[1] there is a certain depth
of calm feeling, unfretted by any movement of mere
intellect, which at times makes the subtlest and boldest
work of Euripides seem 'young man's poetry' by
comparison.

Utterly dissimilar as the two dramatists are, the construction of the *Œdipus Tyrannus* reminds one strongly
of Ibsen's later plays. From the very first scene the
action moves straight and undistracted towards the
catastrophe. The interest turns, not on what the characters do, but on their finding out what they have done.
And one of the strongest scenes is made by the husband and wife deliberately and painfully confessing to
one another certain dark passages of their lives, which
they had hitherto kept concealed. The plot has the
immense advantage of providing a deed in the past—
the involuntary parricide and incest—which explains the
hero's self-horror without making him lose our sympathies. And, as a matter of fact, the character of Œdipus,
his determination to have truth at any cost, his utter
disregard of his own sufferings, is heroic in itself, and
comes naturally from the plot. Iocasta was difficult
to treat : the mere fact of her being twice as old as
her husband was an awkwardness ; but there is a stately
sadness, a power of quiet authority, and a certain stern
grey outlook on life, which seem to belong to a woman
of hard experiences. Of course there are gross im-
probabilities about the original saga, but, as Aristotle
observes, they fall outside the action of the play. In
the action everything is natural except the very end.
Why did Œdipus put out his eyes ? Iocasta realised

[1] *Antigone*, 332 ff. *Ajax*, 669 ff. *Œdipus Col.*, 1211 ff.

that she must die, and hanged herself. Œdipus himself meant to slay her if she had not anticipated him. Why did he not follow her? Any free composition would have made him do so; but Sophocles was bound to the saga, and the saga was perfectly certain that Œdipus was alive and blind a long time afterwards. Euripides avoided the awkwardness in an ingenious way. In his *Œdipus*[1] the hero is overpowered and blinded by the retainers when he has murdered Iocasta and is seeking to murder his children and himself. As a mere piece of technique, the *Œdipus* of Sophocles deserves the position given to it by Aristotle, as the typical example of the highest Greek tragedy. There is deep truth of emotion and high thought; there is wonderful power of language, grasp of character, and imagination; and for pure dramatic strength and skill, there are few things in any drama so inexpressibly tragic as the silent exit of Iocasta, when she alone sees the end that is coming.

The *Ajax*—called by the grammarians *Ajax the Scourge-Bearer*, in distinction to another *Ajax the Locrian*[*]—is a stiff and very early play. It is only in the prologue and in the last scene that it has three actors, and it does not really know how to use them, as they are used, for instance, in the *Electra* and the *Antigone*. Ajax, being defeated by Odysseus in the contest for the arms of Achilles, nursed his wrath till Athena sent him mad. He tried to attack Odysseus and the Atridæ in their tents, and, like Don Quixote, fell on some sheep and oxen instead. He comes to his mind again, goes out to a solitary place by the sea, and falls upon his sword. All the last five hundred lines

---

[1] Frag. 541, which seems misplaced in Nauck.

are occupied with the question of his burial, his great
enemy Odysseus being eventually the man who pre-
vails on the angry generals to do him honour. The
finest things in the play are the hero's speeches in his
disgrace, and the portraiture of his concubine, the
enslaved princess Tecmessa, whom he despises, and
who is really superior to him in courage and strength
of character, as well as in unselfishness. It is difficult
to believe that the *Ajax* is uniform as we have it.
Not only does the metrical technique vary in different
parts, but both the subtly-drawn Tecmessa and the
fiendish Athena seem to come from the influence of
Euripides ; while other points of late style, such as
the abuse of heralds, and the representation of Menelaus as the wicked Spartan, combine with the dis-
proportionate length of the burial discussion to suggest
that there has been some late retouching of this very
old play.

The *Antigone* is perhaps the most celebrated drama
in Greek literature. The plot is built on the eternally-
interesting idea of martyrdom, the devotion to a higher
unseen law, resulting in revolt against and destruction
by the lower visible law. Polyneikes has been slain
fighting against his usurping brother Eteocles and
against his country ; and Creon — the name merely
means 'ruler,' which accounts for its commonness for
the official kings of the saga—commands that he be
cast out to the dogs and birds as a traitor. Any one
who attempts to bury him shall suffer instant death.
His sister Antigone determines to bury him ; the other
sister, Ismênê, hesitates and shrinks. Antigone is discovered, refuses to make any kind of submission, and is
condemned. Ismênê tries to share her suffering ; her

lover Hæmon, son of Creon, intercedes for her : both in vain. Hæmon forces his way into the tomb where she has been immured alive, finds her dead, and slays himself.

Apart from the beauty of detail, especially in the language, one of the marks of daring genius in this play is Antigone's vagueness about the motive or principle of her action : it is because her guilty brother's cause was just ; because death is enough to wipe away all offences ; because it is not her nature to join in hating, though she is ready to join in loving (l. 523) ; because an unburied corpse offends the gods ; because her own heart is really with the dead, and she wishes to go to her own. In one passage she explains, in a helpless and pathetically false way, that she only buries him because he is her brother ; she would not have buried her husband or son ! It is absolutely true to life in a high sense ; like Beatrice Cenci, she "cannot argue : she can only feel." And another wonderful touch is Antigone's inability to see the glory of her death : she is only a weak girl cruelly punished for a thing which she was bound to do. She thinks the almost religious admiration of the elders is mockery (l. 839).

Creon also is subtly drawn. He is not a monster, though he has to act as one. He has staked his whole authority upon his edict. Finding it disobeyed, he has taken a position from which it is almost impossible to retreat. Then it appears that his niece is the culprit. It is hard for him to eat up his words forthwith ; and she gives him no faintest excuse for doing so. She defies him openly with a deep dispassionate contempt. Ismênê, bold in the face of a real crisis, joins her sister ; his own son Hæmon, at first moderate, becomes presently violent and insubordinate. Creon seems to be searching for a loophole to escape, subject only to the determination of an obstinate autocrat not to unsay what he has said. After Hæmon leaves him, he cries desperately that he sticks to his decision. Both the maidens must die ! *" Both,"* say the chorus—*"you never spoke of Ismênê !"* *" Did I not ?"* he answers, with visible relief—*"no, no ; it was only Antigone !"* And even on her he will not do the irreparable. With the obvious wish to leave himself breathing time, he orders her to be shut in a cave without food or water *" till she learns wisdom."* When he repents, of course, it is too late.

There are several similarities between this, perhaps the sublimest, and the *Electra,* perhaps the least sublime, of Sophocles's plays. The strong and the weak sister stand in exactly similar contrast ; indeed in the passages where Antigone defies Creon and where she rejects Ismênê's claim to share her martyrdom, we seem to have a ring of the old 'harshness.' There are marks of early date also. The question Τίς ἀνδρῶν ;—*" What man hath dared ?"*—when the real sinner is of course a woman, is a piece of well-worn dramatic effect which the Attic stage soon grew out of. The love of antithesis, always present in Sophocles, is dominant in the *Antigone*—*" Two brothers by two hands on one day slain" ;* or finer :

> *" Be of good cheer, thou livest; but my life*
> *For the dead's sake these many days is dead."*

The claims of the dead form, in fact, a note common to this play and the *Electra.* They repeat the protest already uttered by Æschylus in the *Choëphoroi,* against treating wrong done merely as it affects the convenience of the living. The love-motive in Hæmon is not likely to be due to Sophocles's invention ; it is unlike his spirit, and he makes little use of it, much less than Euripides did in his lost *Antigone*.* The idea would naturally come from Mimnermus or one of the erotic elegists.

The *Trachiniæ* and the *Philoctêtes* show clearly the influence of Euripides. The former deals with the death of Heracles by the coat of burning poison which his enemy the centaur Nessus has given to the hero's wife Dêianîra, professing that it is a love - charm. Dêianîra finds that Heracles is untrue to her, and that an unhappy princess whom he has sent as captive of war to her house is really the object for whom he made the war. She bethinks her of the love-charm and sends it, and the burly demi-god dies raging. The Dorian hero, a common figure in satyr-plays, had never been admitted to tragedy till Euripides's *Heracles*, where he appears as the lusty conquering warrior, jovial and impulsive, with little nobleness of soul to fall back upon. There are some definite imitations of the *Heracles* in the *Trachiniæ*, apart from the Euripidean prologue and the subtly dramatic situation between Dêianîra and her husband's unwilling mistress. One would like to know if there can be any connection between the writing of this play and the history contained in Antiphon's speech *On Poisoning* (p. 335).

The *Philoctêtes* (409 B.C.) is markedly a character-play. The hero, once the companion of Heracles, and now owner of his unerring bow, had been bitten by a noxious snake. The festering wound seemed about to breed a pestilence, and the Greeks left the sick man marooned on Lemnos. Long years afterwards an oracle reveals that the bow, and Philoctêtes with it, must come to Troy, if the town is to be taken. It is all but impossible to approach the injured man; but Odysseus, the great contriver, agrees to try it, and takes with him the son of Achilles, Neoptolemus. Odysseus himself is known to Philoctêtes; so he keeps in the background, and puts Neoptolemus forward to entrap the man on board his ship by ingenious lies. The young soldier reluctantly consents. He wins entirely the confidence of the old broken-hearted solitary; everything is in train for the kidnapping, when a spasm of agony from the incurable wound comes on Philoctêtes. Neoptolemus does his best to tend him, and cannot face his victim's gratitude. At the last moment he confesses the truth. Philoctêtes has taken him for his single friend; he is really a tool in the hand of his cruellest enemy. A profoundly tragic situation, lit up by the most thrilling beauty of verse; it ends in Euripidean style by Heracles appearing as a Divine Reconciler " ex machinâ " (see p. 268).

The *Œdipus at Colônus* is a play of the patriotic-archæological type, of which our earliest example is the *Heracleidæ* of Euripides. It turns on the alleged possession by Attica of the grave of Œdipus—evidently only 'alleged,' and that not in early tradition, for we find in the play that no such supposed grave was visible. When Œdipus is an old man, and has, as it were, worn out the virulence of the curse upon him by his long innocent wanderings with his daughter Antigone, news is brought to him from Thebes by Ismênê of a new oracle. His body is to keep its 'hagos' or *taboo* — the power of the supernaturally pure or supernaturally polluted — and will be a divine

bulwark to the country possessing it. Consequently
the Thebans intend to capture him, keep him close
to their border till he dies, and then keep control
of his grave. Œdipus meantime has reached Colônus,
in Attica, the seat of the 'Semnai,' 'Dread Goddesses,'
where he knows that he is doomed to die. Theseus
accepts him as a citizen, and he passes mysteriously
away. This is the only play in which Sophocles has
practically dispensed with a plot, and it is interesting
to see that the experiment produces some of his
very highest work. The poetry leaves an impression
of superiority to ordinary technique, of contentment
with its own large and reflective splendour. But
the time was past when a mere situation could by
imaginative intensity be made to fill a whole play.
Sophocles has to insert 'epeisodia' of Creon and
Polyneikes, and to make the first exciting by a futile
attempt to kidnap the princesses, the second by the
utterance of the father's curse. The real appeal of
the play is to the burning, half-desperate patriotism
of the end of the War Time. The glory of Athens,
the beauty of the spring and the nightingales at Colônus, the holy Acropolis which can never be conquered,
represent the modern ideals of that patriotism : the
legendary root of it is given in the figure of Theseus,
the law-abiding, humane, and religious king ; in the
eternal reward won by the bold generosity of Athens ;
in the rejection of Argos and the malediction laid
for ever on turbulent and cruel Thebes. The piece
is reported to be effective on the stage. Certainly
the spiritual majesty of Œdipus at the end is among
the great things of Greek poetry ; and the rather
harsh contrast which it forms with the rage of the

curse-scene, could perhaps be made grand by sympathetic acting.

The play is said by the 'didascaliæ'[1] to have been produced after the poet's death by his grandson of the same name. The verse, however, seems decidedly earlier than that of the *Philoctêtes* (409), and the political allusions have led to various unconvincing theories about its composition at earlier dates. Prof. L. Campbell's (411) is perhaps the most probable.

Though not one of the most characteristic of the poet's plays, it is perhaps the most intimate and personal of them ; and it would be hard to find a more typical piece of Sophoclean writing than the beautiful lines of Œdipus to Theseus :

> " *Fair Aigeus' son, only to gods in heaven*
> *Comes no old age nor death of anything ;*
> *All else is turmoiled by our master Time.*
> *The earth's strength fades and manhood's glory fades,*
> *Faith dies, and unfaith blossoms like a flower.*
> *And who shall find in the open streets of men*
> *Or secret places of his own heart's love*
> *One wind blow true for ever ?* "

---

[1] Catalogues of the annual performances, collected from the official lists by Aristotle and others.

XII

EURIPIDES

EURIPIDES, SON OF MNESARCHIDES OR MNESARCHUS, FROM PHLYA (*ca.* 480–406 B.C.)

WE possess eighteen plays from the hand of Euripides, as against seven each from the other two tragedians; and we have more material for knowledge about him than about any other Greek poet, yet he remains, perhaps, the most problematic figure in ancient literature. He was essentially representative of his age, yet apparently in hostility to it; almost a failure on the stage—he won only four[1] first prizes in fifty years of production—yet far the most celebrated poet in Greece. His contemporary public denounced him as dull, because he tortured them with personal problems; as malignant, because he made them see truths they wished not to see; as blasphemous and foul-minded, because he made demands on their religious and spiritual natures which they could neither satisfy nor overlook. They did not know whether he was too wildly imaginative or too realistic, too romantic or too prosaic, too childishly simple or too philosophical —Aristophanes says he was all these things at once. They only knew that he made them angry and that they could not help listening to him. Doubtless they realised that he had little sense of humour and made a good butt;

---

[1] The fifth was after his death.

and perhaps, on the other hand, they felt that he really was what they called him in mockery, 'wise.' At any rate, after the great disaster of Syracuse he was the man they came to, to write the epitaph on the hopes of Athens.

The tradition, so gentle to Sophocles, raves against Euripides. "He was a morose cynic, privately vicious for all his severe exterior." "He did not write his plays; they were done by his slaves and casual acquaintances." "His father was a fraudulent bankrupt; his mother a greengroceress, and her greens bad. His wife was called Choirilê ('Sow'), and acted up to her name; he divorced her, and his second wife was no better." It delights in passages between the two tragedians in which the poverty-stricken misanthrope is crushed by the good Sophocles, who took to his cups and their bearers like a man, and did not profess to be better than his neighbours.

A few of these stories can be disproved; some are grossly improbable; most are merely unsupported by evidence. It can be made out that the poet's father, Mnesarchides, was of an old middle-class family owning land and holding an hereditary office in the local Apollo-worship at Phlya. His mother, Kleito the 'green-groceress,' was of noble family. Our evidence suggests that her relation towards her son was one of exceptional intimacy and influence; and motherly love certainly forms a strong element in his dramas. Of Euripides's wife we only know that her name was not Choirilê, but Melitê, and that Aristophanes in 411 could find no ill to say of her. Of his three sons, we hear that Mnesar-chus was a merchant, Mnesilochus an actor, Euripides apparently a professional playwright; he brought out the *Iphigenia*, *Bacchæ*, and *Alcmeon* * after his father's death. The poet lived, so Philochorus says, on his own estate at Salamis, and worked in a cave facing the sea, which was shown to tourists down to Pliny's time. He avoided society and public life—as much, that is, as an Athenian of that day could avoid them. He served in the army. He had at least once to perform a 'liturgy' of some sort, perhaps fitting out a trireme; he was a 'Proxenus' of Magnesia, an office which resembled that of a modern consul, and involved some real political work. These expensive posts must have come to him early in his life; he was reduced to poverty, like all the landed proprietors, towards the end of the war. For the rest, he was the first Greek who collected a library, the writer and thinker, not the man of affairs.

At one time, indeed, we find him taking at least an indirect part in politics. About 420, at the end of the Ten Years' War, he wrote a play with a definite 'tendency.' The *Suppliants* not only advocates peace with Sparta—that was the case with the *Cresphontes** and the *Erechtheus** as well — it also advocates alliance with Argos, and proclaims the need in Athens of "*a general young and noble.*" "A general young and noble" was at that moment coming to the front, and especially pressing forward the Argive alliance—Alcibiades. Next year he was appearing at Olympia with that train of four-horse chariots which made such a noise in Greece, and winning the Olympian victory for which Euripides wrote a Pindaric ode. This lets us see that the philosophic poet, like Socrates and most other people, had his period of Alcibiades-worship. We do not know how long it lasted. Euripides was for peace, and Alcibiades for war; and by the time of the Sicilian Expedition, it would seem, Euripides had lost faith in the 'dæmonic' leader. The *Trôiades* (415 B.C. ?) starts by describing a great fleet sailing triumphantly to sea, unconscious of the shadow of blood-guiltiness that rests upon it, and the gods who plot its destruction as it goes.

The plays from this time on, all through the last agony of the war, are written in fever, and throw a strong though distorting light on the character of the man behind them. His innermost impulses betray themselves at the expense of his art, and he seems to be bent on lacerating his own ideals. Patriotism, for instance, had always been a strong feeling in Euripides. In 427 we had the joyous self-confident patriotism of the *Heracleidæ*, the spirit of a younger Pericles. Earlier still there had been the mere sentimental patriotism of the *Hippolytus* (428 B.C.) Later came the *Erechtheus*,* *Theseus*,* *Suppliants* (421 B.C.). But in the last plays the spirit has changed. Dying Athens is not mentioned, but her death-struggle and her sins are constantly haunting us ; the joy of battle is mostly gone, the horror of war is left. Well might old Æschylus pray, " *God grant I may sack no city !*" if the reality of conquest is what it appears in the later plays of Euripides. The conquerors there are as miserable as the conquered ; only more cunning, and perhaps more wicked.

Another motive which was always present in him, and now becomes predominant, is a certain mistrust of the state and all its ways—the doctrine explicitly preached to the present generation by Tolstoi. The curse of life is its political and social complication. The free individual may do great wrongs, but he has a heart somewhere ; it is only the servant of his country, the tool of the 'compact majority,' who cannot afford one. Odysseus in the *Trôiades* and *Palamêdes* * (415 B.C.) has got beyond even

the Odysseus of the *Hecuba* (424 ?), where the type is
first sketched clearly. He is not personally blood-thirsty,
but he is obliged to put the interest of the Achaioi
before everything. The most disagreeable consequences
are to be apprehended if he does not lie, murder, and
betray ! It is the same with Menelaus in the *Orestes*,
and, above all, with Agamemnon in the *Iphigenia in
Aulis*. They are so placed that ordinary social considerations seem to make justice and honour impossible.

Another note which marks the last years of the war is a
tendency to dwell on the extreme possibilities of revenge.
It was an old theme of Euripides—the *Medea* had taught
it in 431—but he now saw all about him instances of the
rule that by wronging people beyond a certain point you
make them into devils. It is this motive which gives unity
to the *Hecuba*, the gradual absorption of the queen's whole
nature into one infinite thirst for vengeance ; which
answers the scholiast's complaint about the *Orestes*, that
"everybody in it is bad." Another deepening sentiment
in Euripides is his aversion to the old tales that call
themselves heroic. His *Electra* was enough to degrade
for ever the blood-feud of the Atridæ. Read after it
what any other poet says on the subject, Sophocles or
Æschylus or Homer, and the conviction forces itself
upon you : "It was not like this ; it was just what
Euripides says it was. And a δολοφονία, a 'craft-murder,'
is not a beautiful thing after all."

It is at this last period of his life at Athens that we
really have in some part the Euripides of the legend—
the man at variance with his kind, utterly sceptical, but
opposed to most of the philosophers, contemptuous of
the rich, furious against the extreme democracy,[1] hating

[1] *Or.* 870-930.

all the ways of men, commanding attention by sheer force of brain-power. He was baited incessantly by a rabble of comic writers, and of course by the great pack of the orthodox and the vulgar. He was beaten. After producing the *Orestes* in 408, he left Athens for the court of Archelaus of Macedon. We hear that he went "because of the malicious exultation of almost everybody," though we have no knowledge of what the exultation was grounded on. In Macedon he found peace, and probably some congenial society. Agathon the tragedian and Timotheus the musician were there, both old friends of his, and the painter Zeuxis, and probably Thucydides. Doubtless the barbarism underneath the smooth surface of the Macedonian court, must sometimes have let itself appear. The story of Euripides being killed by the king's hounds is disproved by the silence of Aristophanes; but it must have produced a curious effect on the Athenian when one of the courtiers, who had addressed him rudely, was promptly delivered up to him to be scourged! He died about eighteen months after reaching Macedon; but the peace and comfort of his new surroundings had already left their mark upon his work. There is a singular freshness and beauty in the two plays, *Bacchæ* and *Iphigenîa in Aulis*, which he left unfinished at his death; and the former at any rate has traces of Macedonian scenery (565 ff.). Of the *Archelaus,** which he wrote in his host's honour, but few fragments survive.

Not that in the last period of Euripides's work at Athens his gloom is unmixed. There is nothing that better illustrates the man's character than the bright patches in these latest plays, and the particular forms taken by his still-surviving ideals. In his contempt for society and statecraft, his iconoclastic spirit towards the all-admired Homeric demi-gods, his sympathy with the dumb and uninterpreted generally, he finds his heroism in quiet beings uncontaminated by the world.   The hero of the *Electra* is the Working Peasant, true-hearted, honourable, tactful, and of course as humbly conscious of his inferiority to all the savage chieftains about him as they are confident of their superiority to him.   But, above all, Euripides retains his old belief in the infinite possibilities of the untried girl.   To take only the complete plays, we have a virgin-martyr for heroine in the *Heracleidæ*, *Hecuba*, *Iphigenîa in Aulis;* we have echoes of her in the *Trôiades* and the *Suppliants*.   She is always a real character and always different.   One pole perhaps is in the *Trôiades*, where the power to see something beyond this coil of trouble, the second sight of a pure spirit, gets its climax in Cassandra.   The other, the more human side, comes out in the *Iphigenîa*.   The young girl, when she first finds that she has been trapped to her death, breaks down, and pleads helplessly, like a child, not to be hurt; then when the first blinding shock is past, when she has communed with herself, when she finds that Achilles is ready to fight and die for her, she rises to the height of glad martyrdom for Hellas' sake.   The life of one Achilles is worth that of a thousand mere women, such as she !   That is her feeling at the moment when she has risen incomparably beyond every one in the play and made even her own vain young hero humble.   Aristotle—such are the pitfalls in the way of human critics—takes her as a type of inconsistency! [1]

An element of brightness comes also in the purely romantic plays of the last years, the *Helena* and *Andromeda.** One is reminded of the *Birds* (p. 286).   Euripides

[1] *Poetics, cap.* xv.

can be happy if he turns entirely away from πράγματα, from *affaires*, from the things that weighed on all Athens. The *Helena* is a light play with a clear atmosphere and beautiful songs; Helen and Menelaus are both innocent. The *Andromeda*** was apparently the one simple un-clouded love-story that Euripides wrote. It was very celebrated. Lucian has a pleasant story of the tragedy-fever which fell upon the people of Abdêra: how they went about declaiming iambics, "and especially sang the solos in the *Andromeda* and went through the great speech of Perseus, one after another, till the city was full of seven-day-old tragedians, pale and haggard, crying aloud, '*O Love, high monarch over gods and men*,' and so on." The *Andromeda*** opened (without a prologue?) giving the heroine chained on the cliff, and watching for the first glimmer of dawn with the words, "*O holy Night, how long is the wheeling of thy chariot!*" Some little fragments help us to see the romantic beauty of the play as a whole : the appeal of the chorus to the echo of the sea-cliffs "*by Aidôs that dwelleth in caves*"; and the words of Andromeda to her lover and deliverer :

> "*Take me, O stranger, for thine handmaiden,*
> *Or wife or slave.*"

The love-note in this pure and happy sense Euripides had never struck before ; and the note of superhuman mystery, of sea-cliff and monsters and magic, not since the *Phaëthon.***

This, of course, is the Euripides of the end of the war, when his antagonisms had become more pro-nounced. But from his first appearance in 455 with the *Daughters of Pelias*,* the man must have impressed people as unlike anything they had known before. He showed himself at once as the poet of the Sophistic

R

Movement, of the Enlightenment; as the apostle of clearness of expression, who states everything that he has to say explicitly and without bombast. His language was so much admired in the generations after his death that it is spoilt for us. It strikes us as hackneyed and undistinguished, because we are familiar with various commonplace fellows who imitated it, from Isocrates to Theodore Prodromus. He probably showed even in the *Daughters of Pelias** his power to see poetry everywhere. His philosophical bent was certainly fore-shadowed in lines like "*in God there is no injustice*" (frag. 606); his quick sympathy with passion of every sort, in the choice of the woman Medea for his chief figure.

But the most typical of the early plays, and the one which most impressed his contemporaries, was the *Telephus** (438 B.C.). It has a great number of the late characteristics in a half-developed state, overlaid with a certain externality and youthfulness. It is worth while to keep the *Telephus** constantly in view in tracing the gradual progress of Euripides's character and method. The wounded king of Mysia knows that nothing but the spear of Achilles, which wounded him, can cure him; the Greeks are all his enemies; he travels through Greece, lame from his wound, and disguised as a beggar; speaks in the gathering of hostile generals, is struck for his insolence, but carries his point; finally, he is admitted as a suppliant by Clytæmestra, snatches up the baby Orestes, reveals himself, threatens to dash out the baby's brains if any of the enemies who surround him move a step, makes his terms, and is healed. The extraordinarily cool and resourceful hero —he recalls those whom we meet in Hugo and Dumas

—was new to the stage, and fascinating. There was originality, too, in his treatment of 'anagnôrisis' or 'recognition' as a dramatic climax — the overturning of a situation by the discovery *who* some person really is—the revelation, in this case, that the lame beggar is Têlephus. This favourite Euripidean effect had become by Aristotle's time a common and even normal way of bringing on the catastrophe. Of our extant plays, the *Ion*, *Electra*, *Helena*, *Iphigenîa in Tauris* contain 'recognitions.' A celebrated instance among the lost plays was in the *Cresphontes*.* That hero, son of the murdered king of Messenia, had escaped from the usurper Polyphontes, and was being reared in secret. His mother, Meropê, was in the tyrant's power. He comes back to save her, gains access to Polyphontes by pretending that he has slain Cresphontes, and asks for a reward. Meropê hears that a stranger is in the house claiming a reward for having murdered her son. She sends quickly to her son's refuge and finds that he has disappeared. In despair she takes an axe and goes to where the boy sleeps. At the last instant, while she is just speaking the words, "*Infernal Hades, this is mine offering to thee,*" her husband's old slave, who holds the light for her, recognises the youth, and rushes in to intercept the blow. Even in Plutarch's time this stage effect had not lost its power.

Apart from the technical 'recognition,' the *Têlephus* * gave the first sign of a movement towards melodramatic situations, the tendency which culminates in the *Orestes*. That play opens some days after the slaying of Clytæmestra and Aigisthus. Orestes and Electra are besieged in the castle by the populace, and the Assembly is at the moment discussing their doom. Orestes is ill and mad ; Electra wasted with watching and nursing. If she saves him, the two will probably be stoned. News comes of safety. Menelaus, their father's brother, has sailed into the harbour with Helen. Helen comes to the castle, and Menelaus's veterans guard the entrances. Orestes gradually recovers his mind ; it seems as if he and his sister were saved. But Menelaus is the natural heir to the kingdom after Orestes ; and he has always disapproved of deeds of violence ; he will not thwart the will of the people ; and cannot offend his father-in-law Tyndareus, who claims vengeance for Clytæmestra. In short, he means to let the brother and sister be stoned. Scenes of vivid contrast and strain succeed one another, till the two see that all is lost. The blood-madness comes on Orestes. He gets possession of his sword and turns upon Helen and Hermione. To take one touch from many : to escape stoning, Electra and Orestes are resolved to die. She begs him to kill her. He turns from her : "*My mother's blood is enough. I will not kill thee. Die as best thou mayest.*"

The *Têlephus* * was in these several respects the typical play of Euripides's early period, but it strikes one as a young play. The realism, for instance, was probably not of the subtle type we find in the *Electra*. The great mark of it was the disguised beggar's costume, which threw stage convention to the winds. In the *Acharnians* of Aristophanes the hero has to make a speech for his life, and applies to Euripides for some 'tragic rags' which will move the compassion of his hearers. He knows just the rags that will suit him, but cannot remember the name of the man who wore them. "*The old unhappy Oineus appeared in rags,*" says Euripides. "*It was not Oineus; some one much wretcheder.*"   "*The blind Phœnix perhaps?*"

" Oh, much, much wretcheder than Phœnix !"   " Possibly you mean Philoctêtes the beggarman?"   " No, a far worse beggar than Philoctêtes."   " The cripple Bellerophon?"   " No, not Bellerophon; though my man was a cripple too, and a beggar and a great speaker."   " I know; Têlephus of Mysia!—Boy, fetch Têlephus's beggar-clothes; they are just above Thyestes's rags, between them and Ino's."[1]

It is difficult, too, to make out any subtlety or delicacy of situation in the *Têlephus*,* such as we have ten years after, for instance, in the *Hippolytus* (ll. 900–1100), when Hippolytus returns to find his father standing over Phædra's body, and reading the tablet which contains her accusation against him. He does not know the contents of the tablet, but he can guess well enough why Phædra died. He is inevitably unnatural in manner, and his constraint inevitably looks like guilt. That is one subtlety ; and there is another a moment afterwards, where Hippolytus is on his defence, and has sworn not to tell the one thing that will save him. His speeches get lamer and more difficult. At least twice it seems as if he is at the point of giving way—why should he not ? The oath was forced from him by a trick, and he had rejected it at the time : *" My tongue hath sworn; there is no bond upon my heart."* Nevertheless he keeps silence, as he promised; appeals desperately to the gods, and goes forth convicted.[2]

There is another subtlety of Euripidean technique in the *Hippolytus*, and one which is generally misunderstood. The main difficulty to the playwright is to carry

---

[1] *Ach.* 418 f.

[2] There was a similar scene in *Melanippe the Wise*,* where Melanippe has to plead for the life of her own secretly-born children, saying everything but the truth ; even hinting that 'some damsel' may have borne them and hidden them from shame.

the audience with Phædra on the wave of passion which leads to her murderous slander. It can only be done at the expense of Hippolytus, and it is hard to make a true and generous man do right and be odious for doing so. The long speech of Hippolytus (ll. 616 ff.) manages it. At his exit the spectator is for the moment furious, and goes whole-heartedly with Phædra.

It was in 431, before the *Hippolytus*, but seven years after the *Telephus*,* that Euripides first dealt with the motive of baffled or tragic love, which he afterwards made peculiarly his own. The *Medea* is, perhaps, the most artistically flawless of his plays; though, oddly enough, it was a failure when first acted. The barbarian princess has been brought from her home by Jason, and then deserted, that he may marry the daughter of the king of Corinth. She feigns resignation; sends to the bride "a gift more beautiful than any now among men, which has come from the fiery palaces of her ancestor the sun." It is really a robe of burning poison. The bride dies in torture. Medea murders her children for the sake of the pain it will be to their father, and flies.

This is the beginning of the wonderful women-studies by which Euripides dazzled and aggrieved his contemporaries. They called him a hater of women; and Aristophanes makes the women of Athens conspire for revenge against him (see p. 288). Of course he was really the reverse. He loved and studied and expressed the women whom the Socratics ignored and Pericles advised to stay in their rooms. Crime, however, is always more striking and palpable than virtue. Heroines like Medea, Phædra, Stheneboia, Aërope, Clytæmestra, perhaps fill the imagination more than those of the angelic or devoted type—Alcestis, who died to save her husband, Evadne and Laodamia, who could not survive theirs, and all the great list of virgin-martyrs. But the significant fact is that, like Ibsen, Euripides refuses to idealise any man, and does idealise women. There is one youth-martyr, Menoikeus in the *Phœnissæ*, but his martyrdom is a masculine business-like performance—he gets rid of his prosaic father by a pretext about travelling-money (ll. 990 ff.)— without that shimmer of loveliness that hangs over the virgins. And again, Euripides will not allow us to dislike even his worst women. No one can help siding with Medea ; and many of us love Phædra—even when she has lied an innocent man's life away.

It is a step from this championship of women to the other thing that roused fury against Euripides—his interest in the sex question in all its forms. There are plays based on questions of marriage-breaking, like the *Hippolytus* and *Stheneboia**—in which the heroine acted to Bellerophon as Potiphar's wife to Joseph. There was one, the *Chrysippus,** in condemnation of that relation between men and boys which the age regarded as a peccadillo, and which Euripides only allowed to the Cyclops. There was another, the *Æolus,** which made a problem out of the old innocent myth of the Wind-god with his twelve sons and twelve daughters married together and living in the isle of the Winds. It is Macareus in this play who makes the famous plea : " *What thing is shameful if a man's heart feels it no shame ?* " But more important than the special dramas is the constant endeavour of this poet to bring his experiences into relation with those of people whom he is trying to understand, especially those of the two silent classes, women and slaves. In the sweat of battle, perhaps when he was wounded, he had said to himself, " *This must be like child-bearing, but not half so bad!* " [1] No wonder the general public did not know what to do with him! And how were they to stand the man who was so severe on the pleasures of the world, and yet did not mind his heroes being bastards? Nay, he made the priestess Augê, whose vow of virginity had been violated, and who was addressed in terms of appropriate horror by the virgin warrior Athena, answer her blasphemously:

> " *Arms black with rotted blood*
> *And dead men's wreckage are not foul to thee—*
> *Nay, these thou lovest : only Augê's babe*
> *Frights thee with shame!* "

And so with slavery : quite apart from such plays as the *Archelaus* * and *Alexander*,* which seem to have dealt specially with it, one feels that Euripides's thought was constantly occupied with the fact that certain people serve and belong to certain others, and are by no means always inferior to them.

Towards religion his attitude is hard to define. Dr. Verrall entitles his keen-sighted study of this subject, *Euripides the Rationalist ;* and it is clear that the plays abound in marks of hostility towards the authoritative polytheism of Delphi, and even to the beliefs of the average Athenian. And further, it is quite true that in the generation which condemned Protagoras and Socrates, and went mad about the Hermæ, the open expression of freethinking views was not quite safe for a private individual in the market-place ; very much less so for the poet of an officially accepted drama of Dionysus, on the

[1] *Med* 250.

feast-day and in the sacred precinct. Any view of
Euripides which implies that he had a serious artistic
faith in his "gods from the mêchanê"—a form of superstition too gross even for the ordinary public—is practically out of court. His age held him for a notorious
freethinker, and his stage gods are almost confessedly
fictitious. Yet it is a curious fact that Euripides is
constantly denouncing the inadequacy of mere rationalism. There is no contrast more common in his plays
than that between real wisdom and mere knowledge or
cleverness; and the context generally suggests that the
cleverness in question includes what people now call
'shallow atheism.' He speaks more against the σοφοὶ
than with them. It seems, in fact, that here, as in the
rest of his mental attitude, he is a solitary rebel.

He is seldom frankly and outspokenly sceptical; when
he is so, it is always on moral grounds. No stress can
be laid on mere dramatic expressions like the famous
" *They are not, are not!* " of Bellerophon (frag. 286),
or the blasphemies of Ixion, or the comic atheism of the
Cyclops. There is more real character in the passages
which imply a kind of antitheism. In the *Bellerophon*,*
for instance (frag. 311), the hero, bewildered at the
unjust ordering of things, attempts to reach Zeus and
have his doubts set at rest, whereupon Zeus blasts him
with a thunderbolt. He sees that he is θεοῖς ἐχθρὸς and
condemned, yet he cannot seriously condemn himself.
He speaks to his heart :

> " *Reverent thou wast to God, had he but known ;*
> *Thy door oped to the stranger, and thine help*
> *For them that loved thee knew no weariness.*"

One cannot take these for the poet's actual sentiments,
but the fact that such thoughts were in his mind has

its significance. One of the rare instances of a plain personal statement is in the *Heracles* (ll. 1341 ff.):

> " *Say not there be adulterers in heaven,*
> *Nor prisoner gods and gaolers :—long ago*
> *My heart hath named it vile and shall not alter !—*
> *Nor one god master and another thrall.*
> *God, if he be God, lacketh naught. All these*
> *Are dead unhappy tales of minstrelsy.*"

These words seem clearly to represent the poet himself, not the quite unphilosophic hero who utters them. They read like the firm self-justification of a man attacked for freethinking. That was written about 422, before the time of bitterness. For the most part, Euripides is far from frank on these subjects. The majority of the plays draw no conclusions, but only suggest premises. They state the religious traditions very plainly, and leave the audience to judge if it believes in them or approves of them. His work left on his contemporaries, and, if intelligently read, leaves on us, an impression of uneasy, half-disguised hostility to the supernatural element which plays so large a part in it. It is a tendency which makes havoc in his art. Plays like the *Ion*, the *Electra*, the *Iphigenîa in Tauris*, the *Orestes*, have something jarring and incomprehensible about them, which we cannot dispose of by lightly calling Euripides a 'botcher,' or by saying, what is known to be untrue in history, that he was the poet of the 'ochlocracy' and played to the mob.

For one thing, we must start by recognising and trying to understand two pieces of technique which are specially the invention or characteristic of Euripides, the Prologue and the *Deus ex machinâ*. The Prologue is easily explained. There were no playbills, and it was well to let the audience know what saga the play was to treat. The need was the more pressing if a poet was apt, like Euripides, to choose little-known legends or unusual versions of those that were well known. The Prologue was invented to meet this need. But, once there, it suggested further advantages. It practically took the place of an explanatory first act. Euripides uses it to state the exact situation in which he means to pick up his characters; the *Orestes* and the *Medea*, for instance, gain greatly from their prologues. They are able to begin straight at the centre of interest. It must, of course, be fully recognised that our existing prologues have been interpolated and tampered with. Euripides held the stage all over the Hellenistic world for centuries after his death, and was often played to barbarian audiences who wanted everything explained from the beginning. Thus the prologue of the *Electra*, to take a striking example, narrates things that every Athenian knew from his infancy. But the Prologue in itself is a genuine Euripidean instrument.

If we overcome our dislike for the Prologue, we are still offended by the way in which Euripides ends his plays. Of his seventeen genuine extant tragedies, ten close with the appearance of a god in the clouds, commanding, explaining, prophesying. The seven which do not end with a god, end with a prophecy or something equivalent — some scene which directs attention away from the present action to the future results. That is, the subject of the play is really a long chain of events; the poet fixes on some portion of it—the action of one day, generally speaking—and treats it as a piece of vivid concrete life, led up to by a merely narrative introduction, and melting away into a merely narrative close.

The method is to our taste quite undramatic, but it is explicable enough : it falls in with the tendency of Greek art to finish, not with a climax, but with a lessening of strain.

There is a growth visible in this method of ending. In the earliest group of our extant plays, there is, with the merely apparent exception of the *Hippolytus* (see p. 270), no *deus ex machinâ*. From about 420 to 414 the god appears, prophesies, or pronounces judgment, but does not disturb the action ; in the 'troubled period' he produces what is technically called a 'peripeteia,' a violent reversal of the course of events.[1] Now, if Pindar had done this, we might have said that his superstition was rather gross, but we could have accepted it. When it is done by a man notorious for his bold religious speculation, a reputed atheist, and no seeker of popularity, then it becomes a problem. Let any one who does not feel the difficulty, read the *Orestes*. Is it credible that Euripides believed that the story ended or could end as he makes it ; that he did not see that his *deus* makes the whole grand tragedy into nonsense? Dr. Verrall finds the solution of this knot in a bold theory that Euripides, writing habitually as a freethinker, under circumstances in which outspokenness was impossible, deliberately disguised his meaning by adding to his real play a sham prologue and epilogue, suitable for popular consumption, but known by those in the poet's confidence to have no bearing on his real intent. The difficulties in this view are obvious.

---

[1] (1) No *deus ex machinâ*: *Alcestis* (438), *Cyclops*, *Medea* (431), *Heracleidæ* (427), *Heracles* (422), and *Hecuba* (424 ?); also *Trôiades* (415) and *Phœnissæ* (410). (2) *Deus* with mere prophecy or the like : *Andromache* (424), *Supplices* (421), *Ion*, *Electra* (413 ?). (3) *Deus* with 'peripeteia': *Iphigenîa in Tauris* (413), *Helena* (412), *Orestes* (408). *Iphigenîa in Aulis* and *Bacchæ* doubtful ; probably 'peripeteia' in each.

It is safer to confine ourselves to admitting that, as a thinker, Euripides was from the outset out of sympathy with the material in which he had to work. He did not believe the saga, he did not quite admire or like it; but he had to make his plays out of it. In his happier moods this dissonance does not appear—as in the *Medea* or *Hippolytus;* sometimes it appears and leaves us troubled, but is overcome by the general beauty of treatment. That is the case with the *Alcestis,* where the heroine's devotion suggests at once to Euripides, as it does to us, the extreme selfishness of the husband who let her die for him. Sophocles would have slurred or explained away this unpleasantness. Euripides introduces a long and exquisitely hard-hitting scene merely for the purpose of rubbing it in (*Alc.* 614 f.). In a third stage the dissonance runs riot : he builds up his drama only to demolish it. What can one make of the *Ion?* "A patriotic play celebrating Ion, the Attic hero, the semidivine son of Creusa and Apollo." That is so. But is it really a celebration or an exposure ? The old story of the divine lover, the exposed child, the god saving his offspring—the thing Pindar can treat with such reverence and purity—is turned naked to the light. "If the thing happened," says Euripides—"and you all insist that it did—it was like this." He gives us the brutal selfishness of Phœbus, the self-contempt of the injured girl, and at last the goading of her to the verge of a horrible murder. If that were all the play has to say, it would be better ; but it is not all. It is inextricably and marringly mixed with a great deal of ordinary poetic beauty, and the play ends in a perfunctory and unreal justification of Apollo, in which the culprit does not present himself, and his representative, Athena, does not seem to be telling the exact truth! In this point, as in others, the over-comprehensiveness of Euripides's mind led him into artistic sins, and made much of his work a great and fascinating failure.

There are two plays, one early and one late, in which the divine element is treated with more consistency, and, it would seem, with some real expression of the poet's thought—the *Hippolytus* and the *Bacchæ*. The Love-goddess in the former (428 B.C.) is a Fact of Nature personified ; her action is destructive, not (l. 20) personally vindictive ; her bodily presence in the strangely-terrible speech which forms the prologue, is evidently mere symbolism, representing thoughts that are as much at home in a modern mind as in an ancient. Hippolytus is a saint in his rejection of the Cyprian and his cleaving to the virgin Artemis ; it is absurd to talk of his 'impiety.' Yet it is one of the poet's rooted convictions that an absolute devotion to some one principle—the 'All or nothing' of Brand, the 'Truth' of Gregers Werle—leads to havoc. The havoc may be, on the whole, the best thing : it is clear that Hippolytus 'lived well,' that his action was καλόν ; but it did, as a matter of fact, produce malediction and suicide and murder. Very similar is the unseen Artemis of the end, so beautiful and so superhumanly heartless. The fresh virginity in nature, the spirit of wild meadows and waters and sunrise, is not to be disturbed because martyrs choose to die for it.

The *Bacchæ* is a play difficult to interpret. For excitement, for mere thrill, there is absolutely nothing like it in ancient literature. The plot is as simple as it is daring. The god Dionysus is disowned by his own kindred, and punishes them. There comes to

Thebes a 'Bacchos'—an incarnation, it would seem, of the god himself—preaching the new worship. The daughters of Cadmus refuse to accept his spirit ; he exerts it upon them in strength amounting to madness, and they range the hills glorifying him. The old Cadmus and the prophet Teiresias recognise him at once as God ; the unearthly joy fills them, and they feel themselves young again. The king Pentheus is the great obstacle. He takes his stand on reason and order : he will not recognise the 'mad' divinity. But Pentheus is the wrong man for such a protest ; possibly he had himself once been mad—at least that seems to be the meaning of l. 359, and is natural in a Bacchic legend—and he acts not calmly, but with fury. He insults and imprisons the god, who bears all gently and fearlessly, with the magic of latent power. The prison walls fall, and Dionysus comes straight to the king to convince him again. Miracles have been done by the Mænads on Cithæron, and Dionysus is ready to show more ; will Pentheus wait and see ? Pentheus refuses, and threatens the 'Bacchos' with death ; the god changes his tone (l. 810). In a scene of weird power and audacity, he slowly controls—one would fain say 'hypnotises'—Pentheus : makes him consent to don the dress of a Mænad, to carry the thyrsus, to perform all the acts of worship. The doomed man is led forth to Cithæron to watch from ambush the secret worship of the Bacchanals, and is torn to pieces by them. The mad daughters of Cadmus enter, Agavê bearing in triumph her son's head, which she takes for a lion's head, and singing a joy-song which seems like the very essence of Dionysiac madness expressed in music. The story is well known how this play was acted at the Parthian capital after the defeat of Crassus at Carrhæ. The actor who represented Agavê, entered bearing the actual head of Crassus; and the soldier who had really slain Crassus broke out in the audience, clamouring for the ghastly trophy. That was what semi-Hellenised savages made out of the *Bacchæ!*

What does it all mean? To say that it is a reactionary manifesto in favour of orthodoxy, is a view which hardly merits refutation. If Dionysus is a personal god at all, he is a devil. Yet the point of the play is clearly to make us understand him. He and his Mænads are made beautiful; they are generally allowed the last word (except 1. 1348); and the swift Ionic-a-minore songs have, apart from their mere beauty, a certain spiritual loftiness. Pentheus is not a 'sympathetic' martyr. And there is even a certain tone of polemic against 'mere rationalism' which has every appearance of coming from the poet himself.[1] The play seems to represent no *volte-face* on the part of the old free-lance in thought, but rather a summing up of his position. He had always denounced common superstition; he had always been averse to dogmatic rationalism. The lesson of the *Bacchæ* is that of the *Hippolytus* in a stronger form. Reason is great, but it is not everything. There are in the world things not of reason, but both below and above it; causes of emotion, which we cannot express, which we tend to worship, which we feel, perhaps, to be the precious elements in life. These things are Gods or forms of God: not fabulous immortal men, but 'Things which Are,' things utterly non-human and non-moral, which bring man bliss or tear his life to shreds without a break in their own serenity. It is a

[1] See, *e.g.*, Bruhn's Introduction.

religion that most people have to set themselves in some relation to ; the religion that Tolstoi preaches against, that people like Paley and Bentham tried to abolish, that Plato denounced and followed. Euripides has got to it in this form through his own peculiar character, through the mixture in him of unshrinking realism with unshrinking imaginativeness ; but one must remember that he wrote much about Orphism in its ascetic and mystic side, and devoted to it one complete play, the *Cretans.* *

In the end, perhaps, this two-sidedness remains as the cardinal fact about Euripides : he is a merciless realist ; he is the greatest master of imaginative music ever born in Attica. He analyses, probes, discusses, and shrinks from no sordidness ; then he turns right away from the world and escapes " *to the caverns that the Sun's feet tread,*" [1] or similar places, where things are all beautiful and interesting, melancholy perhaps, like the tears of the sisters of Phaëthon, but not squalid or unhappy. Some mysticism was always in him from the time of the *Hippolytus* (l. 192): " *What-ever far-off state there may be that is dearer to man than life, Darkness has it in her arms and hides it in cloud. We are love-sick for this nameless thing that glitters here on the earth, because no man has tasted another life, because the things under us are unrevealed, and we float upon a stream of legend.*" There is not one play of Euripides in which a critic cannot find serious flaws and offences ; though it is true, perhaps, that the worse the critic, the more he will find. Euripides was not essentially an artist. He was a man of extraordinary brain-power,

---

[1] *Hip.* 733. The cavern in question was in the moon. *Cf.* Apollonius, *Arg.* iii. 1212, and Plutarch *On the Face in the Moon,* § 29, *Hym. Dem.* 25.

dramatic craft, subtlety, sympathy, courage, imagination; he pried too close into the world and took things too rebelliously to produce calm and successful poetry. Yet many will feel as Philêmon did: "*If I were certain that the dead had consciousness, I would hang myself to see Euripides.*"

XIII

COMEDY

Before Aristophanes

ANCIENT comedy, a development from the mumming of the vintage and harvest feasts, took artistic form in the two great centres of commercial and popular life, Syracuse and Athens. The Sicilian comedy seems to have come first. EPICHARMUS is said to have flourished in 486. He was a native of Cos, who migrated first to Sicilian Megara, and then to Syracuse. His remains are singularly scanty compared with his reputation, and it is hard to form a clear idea of him. He was a comedy-writer and a philosopher, apparently of a Pythagorean type. His comedies are partly burlesques of heroic subjects, like the *Cyclops*,* *Busîris*,* *Promâtheus*,* resembling the satyric dramas of Athens, and such comedies as the *Odyssês** and *Chirônes** of Cratînus. Others, like the *Rustic** and the *Sight-Seers*,* were mimes, representing scenes from ordinary life. In this field he had a rival, SOPHRON, who wrote 'Feminine Mimes' and 'Masculine Mimes,' and has left us such titles as the *Tunny-Fisher*,* the *Messenger*,* the *Seamstresses*,* the *Mother-in-Law*.* A third style of composition followed by Epicharmus was semi-philosophical, like the discussion between 'Logos' and 'Logîna,' Male and Female Reason, or whatever the words mean. And he wrote one strictly philosophical poem, *On Nature.** We hear that the comedies were rapid and bustling; but, of course, the remnants that have survived owe their life merely to some literary quality, whether pithiness of thought or grammatical oddity. His description of a parasite—the thing existed in his time, though not the word—is excellent.[1] It is interesting to find him using puns of the most undisguised type, as where one speaker describes Zeus as Πέλοπι γ' ἔρανον ἱστιῶν, and the other hears γ' ἔρανον as γέρανον, and supposes that the god fed his guest on a crane. A typical piece of conversation is the following:[2] "A. *After the sacrifice came a feast, and after the feast a drinking-party.* B. *That seems nice.* A. *And after the drinking-party a revel, after the revel a swinery, after the swinery a summons, after the summons a condemnation, and after the condemnation fetters and stocks and a fine.*" The other side of the man is represented by his philosophical sayings: "*Mind hath sight and Mind hath hearing; all things else are deaf and blind*"; "*Character is destiny to man*"; or, one of the most frequently-quoted lines of antiquity, "*Be sober, and remember to disbelieve: these are the sinews of the mind.*" The metre of Epicharmus is curiously loose; it suggests the style of a hundred years later, but his verbose and unfinished diction marks the early craftsman. He often reminds one of Lucilius and Plautus.

The Attic comedy was developed on different lines, and, from about 460 B.C. onwards, followed in the steps of tragedy. The ground-form seems to be a twofold division, with the 'parabasis' between. First comes a

---

[1] P. 225, Lorenz, *Leben*, &c. [2] *Fr. incert.* 44.

general explanation of the supposed situation and the meaning of the disguises ; then the 'parabasis,' the 'coming-forward' of the whole choir as the author's representative, to speak in his name about current topics of interest ; then a loose string of farcical scenes, illustrating, in no particular order or method, the situation as reached in the first part. The end is a 'cômos' or revel, in which the performers go off rejoicing. For instance, in our earliest surviving comedy, the *Acharnians* of Aristophanes, the first part, which has become genuinely dramatic by this time, explains how the hero contrives to make a private peace with the Peloponnesians ; then comes the 'parabasis' ; then a series of disconnected scenes showing the fun that he and his family have, and the unhappy plight of all the people about them.

Of the oldest comic writers—Chionides, Ecphantides, Magnes—we know little. The first important name is CRATÎNUS, who carried on against Pericles—"*the squill-headed God Almighty*," "*the child of Cronos and Double-dealing*"—the same sort of war which was waged by Aristophanes against Cleon. Critics considered him incomparable in force, but too bitter. Aristophanes often refers to him : he was "*like a mountain-torrent, sweeping down houses and trees and people who stood in his way.*" He was an initiated Orphic, who had eaten the flesh of the bull Bacchus,[1] and also a devotee of Bacchus in the modern sense. In the *Knights* (424 B.C.) his younger rival alluded to him pityingly as a fine fellow quite ruined by drink. The reference roused the old toper. Next year he brought out the *Pytîne** ('Wine-Flask'), a kind of outspoken satire on himself, in which his wife Comedy

---

[1] Or is so called in jest. Ar. *Frogs*, 357. See Maass, *Orpheus*, p. 106.

redeems him from the clutches of the designing Pytîne. He won the first prize, and Aristophanes was last on the list.   But a wreck he was after all, and was dead by 421. One of his actors—he employed three—was Crates, who wrote with some success, and has the distinction of having first produced drunken men on the stage.

PHEREKRATES, who won his first victory in 437, was a praiseworthy but tiresome writer, to judge by his very numerous fragments.   He had better plots than his contemporaries, and approached the manner of the later comedy.   He treats social subjects, such as the impudence of slaves and the ways of 'hetairai'; he has a violent attack on Timotheus and the new style of music. He also shows signs of the tendency which is so strong in Aristophanes, to make plays about imaginary regions of bliss ; in his *Miners*,* for instance, a golden age is found going on somewhere deep in or under the earth, and in his *Ant-Men** there was probably something similar.   We only know of one political drama by him —an attack on Alcibiades.

EUPOLIS is the most highly praised of the contemporaries of Aristophanes.   His characteristic was χάρις, 'charm' or 'grace,' as contrasted with the force and bitterness of Cratînus, and the mixture of the two in Aristophanes.   These three formed the canon of comic writers in Alexandria.   It is said that the death of Eupolis in battle at the Hellespont was the occasion of exemption from military service being granted to professional poets.   His political tendencies were so far similar to those of Aristophanes that the two collaborated in the most savage piece of comedy extant, the *Knights*, and accused one another of plagiarism afterwards.   That play was directed against Cleon.   In the *Marikâs**

Eupolis wrote against Hyperbolus; in the *Dêmoi* * he spoke well of Pericles as an orator (frag. 94), but this was after his death and probably did not mean much. In reviling Cleon it was well to praise Pericles, just as in reviling Hyperbolus it was well to praise Cleon. Comedy was an ultra-democratic institution, as the Old Oligarch remarked, yet all the comic writers have an aristocratic bias. This is partly because their province was satire, not praise : if they were satisfied with the course of politics, they wrote about something else which they were not satisfied with. Partly, perhaps, it is that they shared the bias of the men of culture. But Eupolis was more liberal than Aristophanes. Aristophanes does not seem ever to have violently attacked rich people.[1] Eupolis wrote his *Flatterers* * against ' Money-bag Callias' and his train, and his *Baptai* * or *Dippers* * against Alcibiades. The latter piece represented one of those mystical and enthusiastic worships which were so prominent at the time, that of a goddess named Cotytto. Baptism was one of the rites ; and so was secrecy, unfortunately for the reputation of those concerned. The Greek layman attributed the worst possible motives to any one who made a secret of his religious observances or prayed in a low voice.

PHRYNICHUS, son of Eunomides, who won his first prize in 429, and PLATO, of whom we know no piece certainly earlier than 405, bridge the transition to the comedy of manners, which arose in the fourth century. The *Solitary* * of Phrynichus is an instance of a piece which was a failure because it was produced some twenty years before the public were ready for it. We have no purely political play from Phrynichus ; from Plato we

---

[1] Alcibiades had fallen at the time of the *Triphales.* *

have a *Hyperbolus*,* a *Cleophon*,* and one called the *Alliance*,* dealing with the alleged conspiracy of Nikias, Phæax, and Alcibiades to get Hyperbolus ostracised.

ARISTOPHANES, SON OF PHILIPPUS, FROM KYDATHENAION
(*ca.* 450 B.C. to *ca.* 385 B.C.)

By far the most successful of the writers of the old comedy was ARISTOPHANES ; and though he had certain external advantages over Cratînus, and enjoyed a much longer active life than Eupolis, he seems, by a comparison of the fragments of all the writers of this form of literature, to have deserved his success. He held land in Ægîna. There is no reason to doubt his full Athenian citizenship, though some lines of Eupolis (frag. 357), complaining of the success of foreigners, have been supposed to refer to him. He probably began writing very young. At least he explains that he had to produce his first piece, the *Daitalês* * ('Men of Guzzleton') under the name of his older friend the actor Callistratus ; partly because he was too young for something or other—perhaps too young to have much chance of obtaining a chorus from the archon ; partly because, though he had written the play, he had not enough experience to train the chorus. This manner of production became almost a habit with him. He produced the *Daitalês*,* *Babylonians*,* *Acharnians*, *Birds*, and *Lysistrata* under the name of Callistratus ; the *Wasps*, *Amphiarâus*,* and *Frogs* under that of Philônides. That is, these two persons had the trouble of teaching the chorus, and the pleasure of receiving the state payment for the production. They also had their names proclaimed as authors, though every one knew that they were not so. Whatever monetary arrangement the poet eventually made, this process meant the payment of money for the saving of trouble ; and, taken in conjunction with his land in Ægina, and his general dislike for the poor, it warrants us in supposing that Aristophanes was a rich man. He had the prejudices and also the courage of the independent gentleman. His first piece (427 B.C.) was an attack on the higher education of the time, which the satirist, of course, represented as immoral in tendency. The main character was the father of two sons, one virtuous and old-fashioned, the other vicious and new-fashioned. The young poet obtained the second prize, and was delighted.[1] Next year (426) he made a violent attack, with the vigour but not the caution of the Old Oligarch, on the system of the Democratic Empire. The play was called the *Babylonians ;* * the chorus consisted of the allies represented as slaves working on the treadmill for their master Demos. The poet chose for the production of this play the midsummer Dionysia when the representatives of the allies were all present in Athens. He succeeded in making a scandal, and was prosecuted by Cleon, apparently for treason. We do not know what the verdict was. In the *Acharnians*, Aristophanes makes a kind of apology for his indiscretion, and remarks that he had had such a rolling in dirt as all but killed him. He afterwards reserved his extreme home-truths for the festival of the Lenæa, in early spring, before the season for foreigners in Athens.

The *Acharnians* was acted at the Lenæa of 425 ; it is the oldest comedy preserved, and a very good one (see p. 277). It is political in its main purpose, and is directed

[1] *Clouds*, 529.

against Cleon and Lamachus, as representing the war
party ; but the poet handles his formidable enemy with
a certain caution ; while, on the other hand, he goes out
of his way to attack Euripides (p. 260), whom he had
doubtless already made responsible for the 'corruption of the age' in the *Daitalês*.* We do not know
of any personal cause of enmity between the two men ;
but it is a fact that, in a degree far surpassing the other
comic writers, Aristophanes can never get Euripides
out of his head.   One might be content with the fact
that Euripides was just the man to see how vulgar and
unreal most of the comedian's views were, and that
Aristophanes was acute enough to see that he saw it.
But it remains a curious thing that Aristophanes, in the
first place, imitates Euripides to a noteworthy extent—
so much so that Cratînus invented a word 'Euripid-
aristophanize' to describe the style of the two ; and,
secondly, he must, to judge from his parodies, have
read and re-read Euripides till he knew him practically
by heart.

In 424 Aristophanes had his real fling.   The situation
assumed in the *Knights* is that a crusty old man called
Demos has fallen wholly into the power of his rascally
Paphlagonian slave ; his two home-bred slaves get hold
of an oracle of Bakis, ordaining that Demos shall be
governed in turn by four 'mongers' or 'chandlers'—
the word is an improvised coinage—each doomed to
yield to some one lower than himself.   The 'hemp-
chandler' has had his day, and the 'sheep-chandler' ;
now there is the Paphlagonian 'leather-chandler,' who
shall in due time yield to—what ?   A 'black-pudding
chandler !'   "*Lord Poseidon, what a trade !*" shouts the
delighted house-slave, and at the critical instant there

appears an abnormally characteristic costermonger with a tray of black-puddings. The two conspirators rouse the man to his great destiny. The rest of the play is a wild struggle between the Paphlagonian and the black-pudding man, in which the former is routed at his own favourite pursuits—lying, perjury, stealing, and the art of 'cheek.' The Paphlagonian, of course, is Cleon, who owned a tannery; the two slaves are Nikias and Demosthenes; the previous 'chandlers' were apparently Lysicles and Eucrates. But the poet tells us that, in the first place, he could get no actor to take the part of Cleon, and, secondly, that when he took the part himself the mask-painters refused to make a mask representing Cleon. The play is a perfect marvel of rollicking and reckless abuse. Yet it is wonderfully funny, and at the end, where there is a kind of trans-formation scene, the black-pudding man becoming a good genius, and Demos recovering his senses, there is some eloquent and rather noble patriotism. The attack is not exactly venomous nor even damaging. It can have done very little to spoil Cleon's chances of election to any post he desired. It is a hearty deluge of mud in return for the prosecution of 426. Such a play, if once accepted by the archon, and not interrupted by a popular tumult, was likely to win frantic applause; as a matter of fact, the *Knights* won the first prize.

The next year there was a reaction. The *Clouds*, attacking the new culture as typified in Socrates, was beaten, both by the *Wine-Flask* * of the 'wreck' Cratînus, and by the *Connus* * of Ameipsias. Aristo-phanes complains of this defeat[1] in a second version of the play, which has alone come down to us. He

---

[1] *Clouds*, 'parabasis.'

considered it the best thing he had ever written. Besides the 'parabasis,' two scenes in our *Clouds* are stated not to have occurred in the original play—the dialogue between the Just Cause and the Unjust Cause, and the rather effective close where Socrates's house is burnt. The present play is manifestly unfinished and does not hang together, but the interest taken by posterity in the main character has made it perhaps the most celebrated of all Aristophanes's works. The situation— an old man wishing to learn from a sophist the best way to avoid paying his debts—is not really a very happy one ; and, in spite of the exquisite style which Aristophanes always has at command, and the humour of particular situations, the play is rather tame. Socrates must have done something to attract public notice at this time, since he was also the hero of the *Connus.**
Ameipsias described him as a poor, hungry, ragged devil, who 'insulted the bootmakers' by his naked feet, but nevertheless 'never deigned to flatter.' That caricature is nearer to the original than is the sophist of the *Clouds*, who combines various traits of the real Socrates with all the things he most emphatically disowned—the atheism of Diagoras, the grammar of Protagoras, the astronomy and physics of Diogenes of Apollonia. However, the portrait is probably about as true to life as those of Cleon, Agathon, or Cleonymus, and considerably less ill-natured.

In 422 Aristophanes returned again from the movement of thought to ordinary politics. The *Wasps* is a satire on the love of the Athenians for sitting in the jury courts and trying cases. It must have been a fascinating occupation to many minds : there was intellectual interest in it, and the charm of conscious power.

But it is hard to believe that too many difficulties were settled by 'Justice,' and too few by force, even in the last quarter of the fifth century. Nor is it necessary to conclude that Aristophanes would really have liked a return to the more primitive methods which the growth of Athenian law had superseded. The *Wasps* probably[1] won the first prize. Its political tendency is visible in the names of the insane old judge Philocleon and his wiser son Bdelycleon—'Love-Cleon' and 'Loathe-Cleon' respectively. And the sham trial got up for the entertainment of Philocleon is a riddle not hard to read : the dog Labes is vexatiously prosecuted by a dog ('Kuôn') from Kydathenaion for stealing a cheese, just as the general Laches had been prosecuted by Cleon from Kydathenaion for extortion. The various ways in which Philocleon's feelings are worked upon, his bursts of indignation and of pity, look like a good parody of the proceedings of an impulsive Athenian jury. Racine's celebrated adaptation, *Les Plaideurs*, does not quite make up by its superior construction for its loss of 'go' and naturalness. The institutions of the *Wasps* are essentially those of its own age.

In 421 Aristophanes produced the *Peace*, a *rechauffé* of the *Acharnians*, brilliantly redeemed by the parody of Euripides's *Bellerophon** with which it opens. The hero does not possess a Pegasus, as Bellerophon did, but he fattens up a big Mount Etna beetle—the huge beast that one sees rolling balls in the sandy parts of Greece and Italy—and flies to heaven upon it, to the acute annoyance of his servants and daughters. The *Peace* won the second prize.

After 421 comes a gap of seven years in our records.

---

[1] The ' Hypothesis ' is corrupt. *Cf.* Leo in *Rh. Mus.* xxxiii.

We may guess that the *Old Age*,* in which some old men were rejuvenated, was produced in the interval, and also the *Amphiaràus*,* in which some one goes to ' dream a dream' in the temple of the hero at Orôpus. The same subject is satirised in the *Plutus* many years after (*cf. also* p. 328). The next play in our tradition is Aristophanes's unquestioned masterpiece, the *Birds* (414 B.C.). It has perhaps more fun, certainly more sustained interest, and more exquisite imagination and lyric beauty, than any of his other works. It is a revelation of the extraordinary heights to which the old comedy with all its grotesqueness could rise. The underlying motive is the familiar desire to escape from the worry of reality, into some region of a quite different sort. Two Athenians, Peithetairus ('Persuader') and Euelpidês ('Hopefulson'), having realised the fact that Têreus was a king of Athens before he was turned into a hoopoe and became king of the Birds—a fact established beyond doubt by Sophocles and other highly-respected poets— determine to find him out, and to form a great Bird-commonwealth. Peithetairus is a splendid character, adapting himself to every situation and converting every opponent. He rouses the melancholy Têreus ; convinces the startled and angry Birds ; gets wings made ; establishes a constitution, public buildings, and defences ; receives and rejects multitudes of applicants for citizenship, admitting, for instance, a lyric-poet and a 'father-beater,' who seems to be the ancient equivalent for a wife-beater, but drawing the line at a prophet, an inspector, and a man of science. Meantime the new city has blocked the communication of the gods with Earth, and cut off their supplies of incense. Their messenger Iris is arrested for trespassing on the Birds' territory, and Peithetairus makes the poor girl cry! At last the gods have to propose terms. But a deserter has come to Peithetairus beforehand: it is Prometheus, the enemy of Zeus, hiding from 'Them Above' under a large umbrella—how much further can cheery profanity go?—and bringing information about the weakness of the gods. When the embassy comes, it consists of one wise man, Poseidon; one stupid man, who is seduced by the promise of a good dinner, Heracles; and one absolute fool, Triballos, who cannot talk intelligibly, and does not know what he is voting for. Zeus restores to the Birds the sceptre of the world, and gives to Peithetairus the hand of his beautiful daughter Basileia ('Sovereignty'), and 'Cloudcuckootown' is established for ever. A lesser man would have felt bound to bring it to grief; but the rules of comedy really forbade such an ending, and Aristophanes is never afraid of his own fancies. There is very little political allusion in the play. Aristophanes's party were probably at the time content if they could prevent Athens from sending reinforcements to Sicily and saving the army that was during these very months rotting under the walls of Syracuse. The whole play is a refusal to think about such troublous affairs. It was beaten by Ameipsias's *Revellers*,* but seems to have made some impression, as Archippus soon after wrote his *Fishes** in imitation of it.

The next two plays of our tradition are written under the shadow of the oligarchy of 411. Politics are not safe, and Aristophanes tries to make up for them by daring indecency. The *Lysistrata* might be a very fine play; the heroine is a real character, a kind of female Peithetairus, with more high principle and less sense of humour. The main idea—the women strike in a body and refuse to have any dealings with men until peace is made—was capable of any kind of treatment; and the curious thing is that Aristophanes, while professing to ridicule the women, is all through on their side. The jokes made by the superior sex at the expense of the inferior—to give them their Roman names—are seldom remarkable either for generosity or for refinement. And it is our author's pleasant humour to accuse everybody of every vice he can think of at the moment. Yet with the single exception that he credits women with an inordinate fondness for wine-parties—the equivalent, it would seem, of afternoon tea—he makes them, on the whole, perceptibly more sensible and more 'sympathetic' than his men. Of course the emancipation of women was one of the ideas of the time. Aristophanes wrote two plays on the subject. Two other comedians, Amphis and Alexis, wrote one each, and that before Plato had made his famous pronouncement, or the Cynics started their women-preachers. It was an instinct in Aristophanes to notice and superficially to assimilate most of the advanced thought of his time; if he had gone deeper, he would have taken things seriously and spoilt his work. He always turns back before he has understood too much, and uses his half-knowledge and partial sympathy to improve his mocking.

The *Thesmophoriazusæ*, written in the same year and under the same difficulties, is a very clever play. The women assembled at the feast of Thesmophoria, to which no men were admitted, take counsel together how to have revenge on Euripides for representing such 'horrid' women in his tragedies. Euripides knows of the plan, and persuades his father-in-law to go to the meeting in disguise and speak in his defence. The intruder is discovered and handed over to a policeman; he eventually escapes by his son-in-law's help. Euripides hums fragments of his own plays behind the scenes, and the prisoner hums answering fragments under the policeman's nose, till the plot is arranged. The play was acted twice in slightly different versions.

In the next few years we have the *Lemnian Women*,* about the newly-established worship of Bendis at the Piræus; the *Gêrȳtadês*,* which seems to have been similar in plot to the *Frogs*; and the *Phœnissæ*,* in mere parody—a new departure this—of Euripides's tragedy of that name. We have also a play directed against Alcibiades, the *Triphalês*.* It dealt certainly with his private life, and possibly with his public action. If so, it is the last echo of the political drama of the fifth century, a production for which the world has never again possessed sufficient ' parrhêsia '—' free-spokenness.'

The death of Euripides in 406 gave Aristophanes the idea of founding a whole play, the *Frogs*, on the contrast between the poetry of his childhood and that which was called new—though, as a matter of fact, this latter was passing swiftly out of existence. Æschylus and Euripides were dead, Sophocles dying; Agathon had retired to Macedonia. The patron-god of the drama, Dionysus, finds life intolerable with such miserable poets as now are left him. He resolves to go to Hades and fetch Euripides back. When he gets there—his adventures on the way, disguised as Heracles, but very unworthy of the lion's skin, are among the best bits of fun in Aristophanes—he finds that after all Euripides is not alone. Æschylus is there too; and the position becomes delicate. The two were already disputing about the

T

place of honour when he came. The death of Sophocles must have occurred when the play was half written : he has to be mentioned, but is represented as having no wish to return to earth ; while Dionysus himself affects to be anxious to see what sort of work Iophon will do without his father's help. His poetry is not criticised or parodied. On the arrival of Dionysus, there follows a long contest between the two poets. It seems a pedantic subject, and it is certainly wonderful that an Athenian audience can have sat listening and laughing for hours to a piece of literary criticism in the form of a play. But the fact remains that the play makes even a modern reader laugh aloud as he reads. As to the judgments passed on the two poets, one may roughly say that the parodies are admirable, the analytical criticism childish.[1] Aristophanes feels all the points with singular sensitiveness, but he does not know how to name them or expound them, as, for instance, Aristotle did. The choice is hard to make : " *I think the one clever, but I enjoy the other,*" says Dionysus. Eventually he leaves the decision to his momentary feelings and chooses Æschylus. It would be quite wrong to look on the play as a mere attack on Euripides. The case would be parallel if we could imagine some modern writer like the late Mr. Calverley, a writer of comedy and parody with a keen and classic literary taste, sending Dionysus to call Browning back to us, and deciding in the end that he would sooner have Keats.

There comes another great gap before we meet, in 392, the poorest of Aristophanes's plays, the *Ecclêsiazûsæ* or 'Women in Parliament.' It reads at first like a parody of the scheme for communism and abolition of the

---

[1] The musical criticism, which is plentiful, of course passes over our heads.

family given by Plato in *Republic V*. The dates will not allow this ; but it is, of course, quite likely that Plato had expressed some such views in lectures or conversation before he put them in writing. The schemes are far from identical. In Plato the sexes are equal ; in Aristophanes the men are disfranchised. The marriage system is entirely different. The communism and the simplification of life might be sympathetic parodies of Plato, but Aristophanes will not have the severe training or the military saints at any price. The *Ecclêsiazûsæ* has a larger subject than the merely political *Lysistrata*, but it is a much tamer play.

The *Plutus* (388 B.C.) is the last play of Aristophanes preserved, and is very different from the rest. It may almost be called a play without personalities, without politics, without parabasis ; that is, it belongs practically not to the old but to the middle comedy—the transition to the pure comedy of manners. It is, indeed, still founded on a sort of 'hypothesis,' like the *Birds* or the *Acharnians*. Plutus ('Wealth') is a blind god ; if we could catch him and get his eyesight restored by a competent oculist or a miracle-working temple, what a state of things it would be ! The main lines of the play form merely the working out of this idea. But the new traits appear in many details ; we have the comic slave, impudent, rascally, but indispensable, who plays such an important part in Menander and Terence, and we have character-drawing for its own sake in the hero's friend Blepsidêmus. We hear of two later plays called *Aiolosikon* * and *Côcalus*,* which Aristophanes gave to his son Arârôs to make his début with. Sikon is a cook's name ; so, presumably, the first represented the old Wind-god acting in that capacity. The second, like so many of the new comedy plays, contained a story, not comic but romantic, with a seduction and a recognition.

Aristophanes is beyond doubt a very great writer. The wisdom of his politics, the general value of his view of life, and, above all, the '*Sittliche Ernst*' which his admirers find in his treatment of his opponents' alleged vices, may well be questioned. Yet, admitting that he often opposed what was best in his age, or advocated it on the lowest grounds ; admitting that his slanders are beyond description, and that as a rule he only attacks the poor, and the leaders of the poor— nevertheless he does it all with such exuberant high spirits, such an air of its all being nonsense together, such insight and swiftness, such incomparable direct- ness and charm of style, that even if some Archelaus had handed him over to Euripides to scourge, he would probably have escaped his well-earned whipping. His most characteristic quality, perhaps, is his combina- tion of the wildest and broadest farce on the one hand, with the most exquisite lyric beauty on the other. Of course the actual lyrics are loose and casual in work- manship ; it argues mere inexperience in writing lyric verse for a critic seriously to compare them in this respect with the choruses of Sophocles and Euripides. But the genius is there, if the hard work is not.

As a dramatist, Aristophanes is careless about construc- tion ; but he has so much 'go' and lifting power that he makes the most absurd situations credible. He has a real gift for imposing on his audience's credulity. His indecency comes partly, no doubt, from that peculiarly Greek *naïveté*, which is the result of simple and un- affected living ; partly it has no excuse to urge except that it is not deliberately vicious (and *cf.* p. 211). It is instructive to know that Plato liked Aristophanes. Of course their politics agreed; but if there is any truth in the anecdote [1] that Plato made Dionysius of Syracuse read the *Knights* in order to see what Athenian political life was like, it was merely the free-speaking that he wished to illustrate. The comedian's speech in the *Symposium* shows the inner bond which united these two great princes of imagination. But only his own age could really stand Aristophanes. The next century wanted more refinement and character-work, more plot and sentiment and sobriety. It got what it wanted in Menander. The Alexandrians indeed had enough of the genuine antiquarian spirit to love the old comedy. It was full of information about bygone things, it was hard, it belonged thoroughly to the past; they studied Aristophanes more than any poet except Homer. But later ages found him too wild and strong and breezy. Plutarch's interesting criticism of him as compared with Menander is like an invalid's description of a high west wind. At the present day he seems to share with Homer and Æschylus and Theocritus the power of appealing directly to the interest and sympathy of almost every reader.

[1] *Vita* xi. in Duebner's *Scholia.*

XIV

PLATO

PLATO, SON OF ARISTON, FROM KOLLŶTUS (427-347 B.C.)

DESCENDED by his father's side from Codrus, the last
king of Attica, through his mother from Solon ; a cousin
of Critias and nephew of Charmides ; an accomplished
gymnast and wrestler, a facile and witty writer ; with
a gift for occasional poems and an ambition towards
tragedy, with an unusually profound training in music,
mathematics, and letters, as well as a dash of Heraclitean
philosophy ; Plato must have seemed in his first youth a
type of the brilliant young Athenian aristocrat. He might
have aspired to a career like that of Alcibiades, but his
traditions and preferences made him turn away from legitimate political action. He despised the masses, and was
not going to flatter them. He went in sympathies, if not
in action, with his relatives along the road dimly pointed
by the Old Oligarch—the road of definite conspiracy with
help from abroad. When he first met Socrates he was
twenty, and not a philosopher. He was one of the
fashionable youths who gathered about that old sage to
enjoy the process of having their wits sharpened, and
their dignified acquaintances turned into ridicule. These
young men were socially isolated as well as exclusive.
They avoided the Ecclesia, where oligarchism was not
admitted ; their views were as a rule too 'advanced' for

official exposition on the stage. They mostly read their
tragedies to one another.

Plato amused his friends with a new kind of literature,
the mime. It was a form which seems to be introducing itself among ourselves at the present moment
—the close study of little social scenes and conversations, seen mostly in the humorous aspect. The two
great mime-writers, Epicharmus and Sophron, had by
this time made their way from Sicily to all the cultured circles of Greece. Plato's own efforts were in
prose, like Sophron's, though we hear that he slept
with the poems of Epicharmus under his pillow. A
mass of material lay ready to hand—one Tisamenus of
Teos had perhaps already utilised it—in the conversations of Socrates with the divers philosophers and dignitaries. Plato's earliest dialogue [1] seems to be preserved.
In the *Laches* Socrates is formally introduced to the
reader as a person able, in spite of his unpromising
appearance, to discuss all manner of subjects. Two
fathers, who are thinking of having their sons trained
by a certain semi-quackish fencing-master, ask the great
generals Laches and Nikias to see one of his performances and advise them. Socrates is called into the
discussion, and after some pleasant character-drawing
it is made evident that the two generals have no notion
what courage is, nor consequently what a soldier ought
to be. The *Greater Hippias* is more outspokenly humo-

---

[1] I follow mainly the linguistic tests as given in C. Ritter's statistical
tables. The chief objections to this method are—(1) the statistics are not yet
sufficiently comprehensive and delicate ; (2) it is difficult to allow for the fact,
which is both attested by tradition and independently demonstrable, that
Plato used to work over his published dialogues. But I do not expect the
results of Campbell, Dittenberger, Schanz, Gomperz, Blass, Ritter, to be
seriously modified.

rous. Socrates applies to the sophist to know what 'the beautiful' (τὸ καλὸν) is ; he has a 'friend' at home 'with a big stick' who asks him questions of this sort, and will not let him sleep of nights till he answers them. The point of the dialogue lies in the utter incapacity of Hippias, for all his wide information and practical ability, to grasp an abstract idea, and in his gradual disgust at the coarse language and outrageous conduct which Socrates imputes to the imaginary friend.

A change in the manner of these mimes comes with the events of 404–403 B.C. We could be sure even without the testimony of *Letter VII.* that Plato must have looked with eager expectation at the attempt of the Thirty to "stay but for a moment the pride of the accursed Demos,"[1] and introduce a genuine aristocracy ; he must have been bitterly disappointed when their excesses "*made the Demos seem gold in comparison.*" His two kinsmen fell in the streets fighting against their country-men ; their names were universally execrated by the Athens of the Restoration. Plato had loved Charmides, and chooses a characteristic imaginative way to defend his memory. The Thirty were guilty of ὕβρις—'pride,' 'intemperance,' whatever we call it. Admitted ; what is their excuse ? That they never knew any more than any one else what σωφροσύνη ('soberness,' 'healthy-minded-ness') was. Plato goes back from the slain traitor Char-mides to the Charmides of 430 ; a boy full of promise and of all the ordinary qualities that men praise—nobly born, very handsome, docile, modest, eager to learn. Socrates affects to treat him for a headache ; but you cannot treat the head without the body, nor the body without the soul. Is his soul in health ? Has he

[1] Alleged epitaph of Critias.

σωφροσύνη ? In the result, of course, it appears that
no one knows what this health of soul is. Charmides
seems to be full of σωφροσύνη ; his friends are sure of
it ; but his hold must be precarious of a thing which he
does not really know. " *The sorrow of it is to think how
you, being so fair in shape, and besides that so sober in soul,
will perhaps have no help in life from that Soberness*." He
determines to come to Socrates and try with him to
learn the real nature of it. Critias agrees ; but Critias
himself is an influence as well as Socrates, and "*when
Critias intends to make some attempt and is in the mood for
violence, no man living can withstand him*."

In 399 came the event which shadowed all Plato's
life, the execution of Socrates. We do not know what
he did at the time ; the *Phædo* says that "*Plato was
away through sickness*," but that may be merely due
to the artistic convention which did not allow the
writer himself to appear in his work. For us Socrates's
death means an outburst of passionate and fiery writing
from Plato, and an almost complete disappearance of
the light-hearted mockery of his earlier dialogues. His
style was practically at its perfection by 399 : the
linguistic tests seem to show that he had already composed his skit on Rhetorical Showpieces, the *Menexenus ;*
his masterpiece of mere dramatic work, the *Protagoras*,
with its nine characters, its full scenic background, its
subtle appreciation of different points of view ; the
Euthydêmus, with its broadly-comic satire on the Eristic
sophists ; and the *Cratylus*, which discusses the nature
of language in as serious a spirit as could be expected
before the subject had become a matter of science.

The *Apology, Crito, Euthyphro, Gorgias, Phædo,* are all
directly inspired by Socrates's death. The first, the only

philosophical work of Plato that is not a dialogue, purports to be Socrates's defence at his trial, but is, in
fact, neither a speech for a real court nor an answer
to a legal accusation, but a glorification of a great
man's whole character in the face of later Athenian
rumours. It cannot have been written for some years
after 399. The *Crito* is in the same spirit; it tells how
Crito had arranged for Socrates to escape from prison,
and how Socrates would not evade or disobey the laws.
The *Euthyphro* is a slight sketch, framed on the usual
plan : people were ready to put Socrates to death for
impiety, when no one really knew what piety was. The
Phædo gives the last hours in prison, the discourse on the
immortality of the soul, and the drinking of the poison.
It is realistic in every detail, but the realism is softened
partly by the essential nobleness of the actors, partly
by an artistic device which Plato loved in the middle
period of his work : the conversation is not given
directly, it is related by Phædo, who had been present,
to one Echecrates of Phlius, some years after, and far
from Athens. "There is nothing in any tragedy ancient
or modern," says the late Master of Balliol, "nothing
in poetry or history (with one exception), like the last
hours of Socrates in Plato." Very characteristic is the
lack of dogmatism or certainty : one argument after
another is brought up, followed intently, and then, to
the general despair, found wanting ; that which is ultimately left unanswered is of a metaphysical character,
like the Kantian position that the Self, not being in
Time, cannot be destroyed in Time. 'Soul' is that by
which things live ; when things die, it is by being
separated from Soul : therefore Soul itself cannot be
conceived dead. It is an argument that carries conviction

to minds of a particular quality in speculative moments. The ordinary human comment upon it is given by Plato in that last moment of intolerable strain, when Phædo veils his face, and Crito starts to his feet, and *"Apollodôrus, who had never ceased weeping all the time, burst out in a loud and angry cry which broke down every one but Socrates."*

As for the *Gorgias*, it seems to fulfil a prophecy put into the mouth of Socrates in the *Apology*: *"You have killed me because you thought to escape from giving an account of your lives. But you will be disappointed. There are others to convict you, accusers whom I held back when you knew it not; they will be harsher inasmuch as they are younger, and you will wince the more."* The *Gorgias* is full of the sting of recent suffering. It begins by an inquiry into the nature of Rhetoric; it ends as an indictment of all '*rhêtores*' and politicians and the whole public life of Athens. Rhetoric is to real statesmanship as cookery is to medicine; it is one of the arts of pleasing or 'flattery.' There are two conceivable types of statesman : the true counsellor, who will oppose the sovereign when he goes wrong; and the false, who will make it his business from childhood to drink in the spirit of the sovereign, to understand instinctively all his likes and dislikes. He will be the tyrant's favourite, or the great popular leader, according to circumstances, but always and everywhere a mere flatterer, bad and miserable. *"He will kill your true counsellor, anyhow,"* retorts Callicles, the advocate of evil, *"if he gives trouble!"* *"As if I did not know that,"* answers Socrates—*"that a bad man can kill a good!"* Callicles admits that all existing politicians are of the worse type, imitators of the sovereign, but holds that Themistocles and Kimôn and Pericles were true statesmen. "*All flatterers, cooks, confectioners, tavern-keepers!*" answers Socrates; "*Whom have they made better? They have filled the city with harbours, docks, walls, tributes, and such trash, instead of temperance and righteousness!*" They have made the city bloated and sick; when the crisis comes, the city will know how it has been deceived, and tear in pieces its present flatterers! The dialogue breaks into four main theses: It is worse to do than to suffer wrong; it is better to be punished for wrong done than not to be punished; we do not what we will, but what we desire; to be, and not to seem, is the end of life. It is characteristic of Plato that anger against the world never makes him cynical, but the reverse: he meets his griefs by harder thinking and more determined faith in his highest moral ideal. He speaks in the *Phædo* of men who are made misanthropic by disappointments; "*It is bad that, to hate your fellow-men; but it is worse to hate Reason and the Ideal.*" He fell, like Carlyle, and perhaps like Shakespeare, into the first error; he never came near the second.

The next dialogue, *Meno*, on the old question "whether Goodness is Teachable," still bears the stamp of Socrates's death in the introduction of Anytus and the rather cruel references to his son (see above, p. 176). But pure speculation predominates, especially the theory of Ideas, which was already prominent in the *Phædo*. The *Lysis*, on Friendship, is an unimportant work; Plato could only treat that subject under the deeper name of Love. This he does in two dialogues which stand apart, even in Plato, for a certain glamour that is all their own. The *Phædrus* comes later; the *Symposium* marks the close of this present period. If the claim were advanced that

the *Symposium* was absolutely the highest work of prose
fiction ever composed, most perfect in power, beauty,
imaginative truth, it would be hard to deny it; nor is
it easy to controvert the metaphysician who holds it
to be the deepest word yet spoken upon the nature
of Love; but in it, as in almost all Plato, there is no
enjoyment for him who has not to some extent learnt
'*Hellenisch zu empfinden.*' We will only notice one
point in its composition; it is the last echo of 399.
The spirit of the *Charmides* has come back, in a stronger
form; we reach all the splendour of the *Symposium* only
by crossing the gulf of many deaths, by ignoring so-
called facts, by seeing through eyes to which the things
of the world have strange proportions. Of the characters,
some are as little known to us as Callicles was; of the
rest, Agathon, the triumphant poet, the idol of Athens,
who gives the banquet in honour of his first tragic victory, has died long since, disappointed and a semi-exile,
in Macedon; Phædrus has turned false to philosophy
—'lost,' as Plato says in another place; Socrates has
been executed as a criminal; Alcibiades shot to death
by barbarian assassins. Aristophanes had been, in Plato's
belief, one of the deadliest of Socrates's accusers. It is
a tribute to that Periclean Athens which Plato loves to
blacken, that he always goes back to it to find his ideal
meetings and memories. The *Symposium* seems like
one of those "*glimpses of the outside of the sky*" in the
Phædrus, which the soul catches before its bodily birth,
and which it is always dimly struggling to recover. We
get back to it through that Apollodôrus whose sobs
broke the argument of the *Phædo;* he is nicknamed
'the Madman' now, a solitary man, savage against all
the world except Socrates. It is he who tells Glaucon,

Plato's brother, the story of the Banquet. Not that he was there himself ; it was long before his time, as it was before Glaucon's; but he heard it from Aristodêmus, "*a little unshod man*" who had followed Socrates. So, by indirect memories, we reach the Banquet. We hear the various accounts of the origin and meaning of Love, at last that learnt by Socrates from the Mantinean prophetess Diotîma. Love is the child of Poverty and Power (πόρος); the object of Love is not Beauty but Eternity, though it is only in that which is beautiful that Love can bear fruit. The lover begins by loving some one beautiful person ; then he feels bodily beauty everywhere, then "*beautiful souls and deeds and habits*," till at last he can open his eyes to "*the great ocean of the beautiful*" in which he finds his real life. The passion of his original earthly love is not by any means dulled, it persists in intensity to the end, when at last he sees that ultimate cause of all the sea of beautiful things, Perfect Beauty, never becoming nor ceasing, waxing nor waning ; "*it is not like any face or hands or bodily thing; it is not word nor thought ; it is not in something else, neither living thing, nor earth nor heaven ; only by itself in its own way in one form it for ever Is* (αὐτὸ καθ᾽ αὑτὸ μεθ᾽ αὑτοῦ μονοειδὲς ἀεὶ ὄν)." If a man can see that, he has his life, and nothing in the world can ever matter to him. Suddenly at this point comes a beating on the door, and enters Alcibiades, revelling, "*with many crowns in his hair*" ; we have his absorption into the Banquet, and his speech in praise of Socrates, the brave, wise, sinless. Then—we hear—came a second and louder noise, an inroad of cold night air and unknown drunken revellers. Most of the guests slipped away. Aristodêmus, who was waiting for Socrates, drew back and fell asleep, till he woke in grey dawn to find the feast over, only Socrates still unchanged, discoursing to Agathon and Aristophanes. Aristodêmus was weary and could not follow the whole argument ; he only knew that it showed how comedy and tragedy are the same thing.

But by this time new influences were at work in Plato's development. On his master's death he had retired with other Socratics to Megara, where the whole-hearted protection of Eucleides laid the seeds in Plato's mind of a life-long respect and friendliness towards the barren Megaric dialectics. The *Gorgias* can scarcely have been written in Athens. We hear vaguely of travels in Egypt and Cyrene. But Plato seems to have returned home before 388 B.C., when he made his first fateful expedition to Sicily. Most of Sicily was at this time a centralised military despotism in the hands of Dionysius I., whose brother-in-law, Dion, was an enthusiastic admirer of Plato. It was partly this friend, partly the Pythagorean schools, and partly interest in the great volcano, which drew Plato to Syracuse ; and he probably considered that any tyrant's court was as fit a place for a philosopher as democratic Athens. But he was more a son of his age and country than he ever admitted. He could not forgo the Athenian's privilege of παρρησία (free speech), and he used it in the Athenian manner, on politics. The old autocrat put him in irons, and made a present of him—so the legend runs—to the Spartan ambassador Pollis. Pollis sold him as a slave in Ægîna, where one Annikeris of Cyrene—a follower of Aristippus apparently, heaping coals of fire on the anti-Hedonist's head—bought him into freedom, and refused to accept repayment from Plato's friends ; who, since the subscriptions had been already collected, devoted the money to buying the philosopher a house and garden to teach in, about twenty minutes' walk from Athens, near the gymnasium sacred to the hero Acadêmus. This was in 387, at least two years before the *Symposium*. But every detail in this story varies, and our oldest evidence, the *Seventh Letter*, gives nothing beyond the fact of a disappointing visit.

The founding of the school was a return to the habit of the older philosophers. The Academy was technically a ' *Thiasos*,' or religious organisation, for the worship of the Muses, with officers, a constitution, and landed property. The head was elected ; mathematics, astronomy, and various sciences were taught, as well as philosophy. The lecturers overflowed from the 'Scholarch's' modest house and library into the garden and public gymnasium; it was only later that they acquired adequate buildings. Women students attended as well as men. The institution preserved its unity, and regularly burned incense to Plato as 'hero-founder' upon his birthday, amid the most complete changes of tendency and doctrine, till it was despoiled and abolished by Justinian in 529 A.D. as a stronghold of Paganism. The early fourth century was a great period for school-founding. Antisthenes had begun his lectures in Kynosarges, the gymnasium of the base-born, soon after Socrates's death. Isocrates had followed with his system of general culture about 390 B.C. The next generation saw the establishment of the Lyceum or Peripatos by Aristotle, the Stoa by Zeno, and the Garden by Epicurus.

Whatever the date of the founding of the Academy, after the *Symposium* there appears, on internal evidence, to be a marked interval in Plato's literary work. The next two dialogues, *Parmenides* and *Theætêtus*, bear the stamp of the recognised philosophical 'Scholarch.' The former is unmixed metaphysics : a critical examination, first, of the kind of Being possessed by what Plato calls 'Ideas'—our 'General Conceptions'; and, secondly, of the Absolute Being of Parmenides. The attacks on the authenticity of this dialogue are merely due to the difficulty which critics have found in fitting it into any consistent theory of Plato's philosophy; it is impossible that the author of the *Parmenides* can have held that crude 'Theory of Ideas' which Aristotle has taught us to regard as Platonic. The *Theætêtus* condescends to a dramatic introduction : Eucleides has just been to the Piræus to meet Theætêtus, who is returning, dangerously wounded and ill, from the Corinthian War, when he meets Terpsion, and they talk of the celebrated meeting long ago between Theætêtus and Socrates. But the introduction has become an external thing, and the dialogue itself is severe reasoning upon the Theory of Knowledge. Plato remarks that he has purposely left out the tiresome repetitions of 'he said' and 'I said'; that is, he has taken away the scenery and atmosphere, and left the thought more bare.

The next dialogue of this period is apparently the *Phædrus;* the evidence is as conclusive as such evidence can ever be. The technical terms which Plato coined, the ways of avoiding hiatus, the little mannerisms which mark his later style, are palpably present in the *Phædrus.* The statistics will not allow it to be earlier than 375. On the other hand, it not only leaves an impression of imaginative and exuberant youthfulness, but it demonstrably bears some close relation to Isocrates's speech *Against the Sophists*, which was written about 390, at the opening of his school. We cannot tell which was originally the provocation and which the answer ; controversial writings in antiquity were generally worked over and over till each side had answered the other to its own satisfaction. But the tone of mutual criticism is clear, and the *Phædrus* ends with a supposed message to Isocrates from the master. ' Isocrates is young yet' —that is, of course, at the imaginary date of the conversation—' and is too fine material to be a mere orator ; if he will turn to philosophy, he has the genius for it.' " *Take that message from me, Phædrus, to Isocrates whom I love.*" If this is 'polemic,' it is not living polemic ; it is the tone of an old friend letting bygones be bygones, and agreeing to respect a difference of opinion. The probability is that we have the *Phædrus* in a late revision. The first publication was perhaps the occasion of Isocrates's outburst; our *Phædrus* is rewritten fifteen years later, answering gently various points of criticism, and ending with this palpable olive-branch.

During these years Plato was working out his most elaborate effort, the *Republic.* He used for the introduction a little dialogue in the early humorous style, ' on Righteousness,' between Socrates and Thrasymachus. This is now Book I. of the *Republic ;* the rest is by the language-tests uniform, and the various theories for dividing the long work into ' strata' are so far discountenanced. The main subject of this great unity is δικαιοσύνη—what Righteousness is, and whether there is any reason to be righteous rather than unrighteous. This leads to the discussion and elaboration of a righteous community ; not, as a modern would expect, because Justice is a relation between one man and another— Plato emphatically insists that it is something in the individual's own character—but because it is easier to see things on a large scale. We must not here attempt any analysis of this masterpiece of sustained argument, of observation, wit, imagination, and inspired eloquence. To say that it involves Socialism and Communism, the equalising of the sexes, the abolition of marriage, the crushing of commerce, the devotion of the whole resources of the state to education, a casual and unemphasised abolition of slavery, and an element of despotism in the hands of a class of soldier-saints—such a description results in caricature. The spirit of the *Republic* can naturally only be got from itself, and only then by the help of much study of the Greek mind, or else real power of imaginative sympathy. It yields as little to skimming as do most of the great living works of the past.

Plato's gifts of thought and expression are at their highest in the *Republic*, but several of the notes of his later years are beginning to be heard—the predominant political interest ; the hankering after a reformed and docile Dionysius ; the growing bitterness of the poet-philosopher against the siren who seems to keep him from Truth. Plato speaks of poetry as Mr. Ruskin speaks of literary form. "I show men their plain duty ; and they reply that my style is charming !" 'Poetry is utter delusion. It is not Truth nor a shadow of Truth : it is the third remove, the copy of a shadow, worthless ; and yet it can intoxicate people, and make them mad with delight ! It must be banished utterly from the righteous city.' Aristotle and the rest of us, who are not in peril from our excess of imagination, who have not spent years in working passionately towards an ideal of Truth for which poetry is always offering us a mirage, will very properly deplore Plato's want of appreciation. We try to excuse him by saying that when he spoke of poetry he was thinking of Chærêmon, and the sons of Carkinus. But he was not. It is real poetry, it is Homer and Æschylus and himself that he turns against; and he would have been disloyal to his philosophy if he had done otherwise. Plato had based his life on the belief that hard thinking can lead men to salvation; that Truth and the Good somehow in the end coincide. He meant to work towards that end, come what might; and if Poetry interfered, he must throw Poetry overboard. After the *Republic* she has almost gone; the *Sophistes, Politicus, Laws*, know little of her, and even the myths become more abstract and didactic, except, possibly, that of Atlantis in the *Critias*.

It is curious that Plato does not include his myths in his condemnation of poetry, since it was as poetry that he originally justified them. A divine vision in the *Phædo* commissions Socrates just before his death to 'practise poetry' (μουσική); the oracle from Delphi in the *Apology* proclaims Socrates the wisest of men, because he knows his own ignorance. Both vision and oracle are apparently fictions: they are Plato's way of claiming a divine sanction for his two-sided Socrates, the inspired Questioner and the inspired Story-teller.[1]

It is in later life also that Plato turns seriously to politics. A younger generation of philosophers was then growing up, the future Cynics, Stoics, Epicureans, who turned utterly away from the State, and devoted themselves to the individual soul. Once Plato was ready to preach some such doctrine himself: he had begun life in reaction against the great political period. But he was, after all, a child of Periclean

[1] Schanz, *Herm.* xxix. 597.

Athens, and the deliberate indifference of the rising schools must have struck him as a failure in duty. Three-fourths of his later writings are about politics, and the ruling aspiration of his outer life is the conversion of Dionysius II. This latter thought makes its first definite appearance in that '*third wave*' which is to make the *Republic* possible (p. 473)—the demand that either philosophers shall be kings, or those who are now kings take to philosophy; and the insistence there upon the tyrant's inevitable wretchedness may have been partly meant for a personal exhortation. For some twenty years the great old man clung to his hope of making a philosopher-king out of that vicious dilettante! The spirit of illusion which he had 'expelled with a pitch-fork' from his writings, had returned the more fiercely into his life.

Dion had called him a second time to Sicily in 367, immediately on the succession of Dionysius II., and he went. The result was a brief outburst of philosophic enthusiasm in the court of Syracuse; the air was choked, we are told, with the sand used by the various geometers for their diagrams. Then came coolness, quarrels, Dion's banishment, and Plato's disappointed return. But, of course, a young prince might forget himself and then repent; might listen to evil counsellors, and afterwards see his error. Plato was ready, on receiving another invitation in 361, "*yet again to fathom deadly Charybdis*," as *Letter VII.* Homerically puts it. He failed to reconcile the king with Dion, and only escaped with his life through the help of the Pythagorean community at Tarentum. Dion resorted to unphilosophic methods; drove Dionysius from the throne in 357, and died by assassination in 354. In the Fourth Book of the *Laws*,

Plato could still write (709 f.) : " *Give me a tyrant-governed city to form our community from ; let the tyrant be young, docile, brave, temperate, and so far fortunate as to have at his side a true thinker and lawgiver.*" That is just at the end of the first half of the long work: the *Laws* must have taken years in writing, and there is a demonstrable change of style after Book IV. In the second half we have nothing more of Plato's hopes for a kingdom of this world, unless we connect with them that sad passage where he faces and accepts a doctrine that he would have denied with his last breath ten years before—that there is, after all, an Evil World-Soul ! (p. 896). The other writings of the late period are pure philosophy. The *Sophistes* and *Politicus* are sequels to the *Theœtêtus;* they follow in method the unattractive 'dichotomy' of the *Parmenides.* The *Sophistes* is a demonstration of the reality of Not-Being, the region in which the Sophist, who essentially Is-Not whatever he professes to be, has his existence. The *Philêbus*, an inquiry into the Good —it is neither Knowledge nor Pleasure, but has more analogy to Knowledge—is remarkable for conducting its metaphysics without making use of the so-called Theory of Ideas ; its basis is the union of Finite and Infinite, of Plurality and Unity. It appears from the statistics of language to have been composed at the same time as the first half of the *Laws.*

The *Timœus*, on the origin of the world, and the *Critias*, on that of human society, go with the second half of the *Laws.* The *Timœus* is either the most definitely futile, or the least understood of Plato's speculations ; an attempt to construct the physical world out of abstract geometrical elements, instead of the atoms of Democritus. The *Critias* fragment treats of the glory and downfall of the isle Atlantis, an ideal type of mere material strength and wealth, with marked resemblances to Athens. There was to have been another dialogue, *Hermocrates*, in this series, but it was never written. Plato died, leaving the *Laws* unrevised—still on the wax, tradition says, for Philip of Opus to transcribe and edit—and the *Critias* broken in the midst of a sentence.

Plato had failed in the main efforts of his life. He was, indeed, almost worshipped by a large part of the Greek world ; his greatness was felt not only by philosophers, but by the leading generals and statesmen. The Cyrenaics might be annoyed by his loftiness ; the Cynics might rage at him for a false Socratic, a rich man's philosopher speculating at ease in his garden, instead of making his home with the disinherited and crying in the streets against sin. But at the end of his lifetime he was almost above the reach of attack. Even comedy is gentle towards him ; and the slanders of the next generation are only the rebound against previous exaggerations of praise. It is significant of the vulgar conception of him, that rumour made him the son of Apollo, and wrapped him in Apolline myths ; of the philosophic feeling, that Aristotle—no sentimentalist certainly, and no uncompromising disciple—built him an altar and a shrine.

But the world was going wrong in Plato's eyes : those who praised, did not obey ; those who worshipped, controverted him. He had set out expecting to find some key to the world—some principle that would enable him to operate with all mental concepts as one does with the concepts of mathematics. It is the knowledge of this principle which is to make the Rulers' of the *Laws* and the *Republic* infallible and

despotic.   Plato himself knew that he had not found
it.   The future was for the men who had more mere
grit and less self-criticism.   Aristippus could teach and
act unshrinking hedonism ;   Democritus could organise
science and form a definite dogmatic materialism ;
Antisthenes could revile the world — art, learning,
honour included—without misgiving.   These were the
authors of the great consistent schools.   Platonism had
no form of its own.   Plato's nephew and successor,
Speusippus, merely worshipped his uncle, and thought
all detailed knowledge impossible till one could know
everything; Aristotle developed his own system, practical, profound, encyclopædic, but utterly apart and
un-Platonic ; Heraclides ran to death his master's spirit
of fiction and mysticism, and became a kind of reproach
to his memory.

But it is just this inconclusiveness of Plato's thought
that has made it immortal.   We get in him not a system
but a spirit, and a spirit that no discoveries can super-
sede.   It is a mistake to think of Plato as a dreamer ;
he was keen and even satirical in his insight.   But he
rises beyond his own satire, and, except in the *Gorgias*
period, cares always more for the beauty he can detect
in things than for the evil.   It is equally a mistake to
idealise him as a sort of Apolline hero, radiant and untroubled, or to take that triumphant head of the Indian
Bacchus to be his likeness.   He was known for his
stoop and his searching eyes ; the *Letters* speak often
of illness ; and Plato's whole tone towards his time is
like Carlyle's or Mr. Ruskin's.   He is the greatest master
of Greek prose style, perhaps of prose style altogether,
that ever lived.   The ancient critics, over-sensitive to
oratory, put Demosthenes on a par with him or above

him. Dionysius's criticism (see pp. 325, 326) actually takes the sham speech of the *Menexenus* to compare with that *On the Crown!* But Plato's range is longer; he has more delicacy and depth, and a wider imaginative horizon than was possible to the practical statesman and pleader. You feel in reading him, that, in spite of all the overstatements and eccentricities into which his temperament leads him, you stand in the presence of a mind for which no subtlety is too difficult, no speculative or moral air too rarefied. The accusations against him come to nothing. His work in the world was to think and write, and he did both assiduously at a uniform level of loftiness. Little call was made upon him for action in the ordinary sense; when a call did come, as in Dion's case, he responded with quixotic devotion. But if a man's life can be valued by what he thinks and what he lives for, Plato must rank among the saints of human history. His whole being lay ἐν τῷ καλῷ; and there is perhaps no man of whom one can feel more certainly that his eyes were set on something not to be stated in terms of worldly success, and that he would without hesitation have gone through fire for the sake of it.[1]

---

[1] *As to the Platonic Letters, each must be judged on its own merits. I believe, for instance, that* xiii. *is probably genuine (so W. Christ), and that* vii. *is an early compilation from genuine material. The tendency to reject all ancient letters as forgeries (see, e.g., Hercher's preface to Epistolographi Græci) is a mere reaction from the old Phalaris controversy.*

XV

XENOPHON

XENOPHON, SON OF GRYLLUS, FROM ERCHIA
(434–354 B.C.)

AMONG Socrates's near companions were two young
cavalrymen of about the same age, both of aristocratic and semi-treasonable traditions, which seriously
hampered any political ambition they might entertain,
and neither quite contented to be a mere man of letters.
Plato stayed on in Athens, learning music, mathematics,
rhetoric, philosophy ; performing his military duties ;
writing and burning love-poems ; making efforts at
Euripidean tragedy. XENOPHON went to seek his fortune abroad.

The story goes that Socrates, on first meeting Xenophon in his boyhood, stopped him with his stick and
asked abruptly where various marketable articles were
to be had. The boy knew, and answered politely,
till Socrates proceeded : "And where can you get men
καλοὶ κἀγαθοί (*beaux et bons*) ? "—that untranslatable
conception which includes the 'fine fellow' and the
'good man.' The boy was confused ; did not know.
"Then follow me," said the philosopher. The legend
is well fitted. Xenophon was never a philosopher, but
he was a typical καλὸς κἀγαθός : a healthy-minded man,
religious through and through ; a good sportsman and

soldier ; a good husband and father ; with no speculative power, and no disposition to criticise current beliefs about the gods or the laws, though ready enough to preach and philosophise mildly on all less dangerous topics.

He is said to have been strikingly handsome, and he had in him a dash of romance. A Bœotian friend, Proxenus, had been engaged by the satrap Cyrus, brother to the Great King, to lead a force of Greek mercenaries on an inland march towards Cilicia. The aim of the expedition was not divulged, but the pay was high, and there was every opportunity for adventure. Proxenus offered to take Xenophon with him. Xenophon would not actually take service under Cyrus, who had so recently been his country's enemy, but obtained an introduction to the prince, and followed him as an independent cavalier. The rest of the story is well known. The troops marched on and on, wondering and fearing about the real object of their march. At last it was beyond concealment that they were assailing the Great King. Some fled ; most felt themselves committed, and went forward. They fought the King at Cunaxa ; Cyrus was killed. The Greeks were gradually isolated and surrounded. Their five commanders, including Xenophon's gentle friend Proxenus, the Spartan martinet Clearchus, the unscrupulous Thessalian Menôn, were inveigled into a parley, seized, and murdered. The troops were left leaderless in the heart of an enemy's country, over a thousand miles from Greek soil. Xenophon saved them. In the night of dismay that followed the murder of the generals, he summoned the remaining leaders, degraded the one petty officer who advised submission—a half-Lydian creature, who wore ear-rings !

—had new generals elected, himself one of them, and directed the march, fighting and flying, towards the unexplored Northern mountains. There was scarcely a day or night without adventure, till the memorable afternoon of January 27, 400 B.C., when they caught sight of the sea near Sinôpê ; and not much peace of mind for Xenophon till he handed his army over to the Spartan Harmost Thibron in the March of 399.

It was a brilliant and heroic achievement. True, the difficulties were not so great as they seemed ; for this march itself was the first sign to Europe of that internal weakness of the Oriental Empires which was laid bare by Alexander, Pompey, Lucullus, and the various conquerors of India. But Xenophon's cheery courage, his comparatively high intellect and culture, his transparent honour, his religious simplicity, combined with great skill in managing men and a genuine gift for improvising tactics to meet an emergency, enabled him to perform an exploit which many an abler soldier might have attempted in vain. He was not ultimately successful as a *condottiere*. His Ten Thousand, proud as he is of their achievements afterwards, must have contained some of the roughest dare-devils in Greece ; and Xenophon, like Proxenus, treated them too much like gentlemen. Old Clearchus, knout in hand and curse on lips, never lightening from his gloom except when there was killing about, was the real man to manage them permanently.

For Xenophon the 'Anabasis' was a glory and a *faux pas*. He found a halo of romance about his head, and his occupation gone. He remembered that Socrates had never liked the expedition ; that the god at Delphi had not been fairly consulted ; and he consoled himself with the reflection that if he had been more pushing he would have been more prosperous. His family soothsayer had told him so. The expedition had left in him some half-confessed feeling that he was an ἀρχικὸς ἀνήρ, a man born to command. He wrote a long romance, the *Cyropædeia*, or training of Cyrus, about this ideal ἀρχικὸς ἀνήρ, in which a slight substratum of the history of Cyrus the Great was joined with traits drawn from the younger Cyrus and from Xenophon's own conception of what he would like to be. That was later. At this time he more than once had dreams of founding a colony in Asia, and being a philosophic soldier-king. Failing that, he wanted to have a castle or two near the Hellespont, and act as an independent champion of Hellas against the barbarian. But nobody else wished it, and Xenophon would not push or intrigue. He drifted. He could not return to Athens, which was then engaged in putting his master to death, and would probably meet him with a charge of high treason. Besides, there were no adventures forward in Athens ; they were all in Asia. Meanwhile the Knight-Errant of Hellas was in the position of a filibuster at the head of some eight thousand ruffians under no particular allegiance. Some of them, he found, were discussing the price of his assassination with the Harmost Thibron, who naturally was disinclined to tolerate an independent Athenian in possession of such great and ambiguous powers. The born Ruler might have done otherwise. Xenophon handed over his army and took service under the Spartans, then allies of Athens, against Persia.

It was weary work being bandied from 'harmost' to 'harmost,' never trusted in any position of real power. However, he married happily, had good friends in the Chersonnese, and tried to be resigned. At length in

396 came a general of a better sort, the Spartan king
Agêsilâus, commissioned to wage a more decisive war
against Artaxerxes. Xenophon joined his staff, and the
two became warm friends. But fortune was capricious.
In 395 Athens made an alliance with Artaxerxes; in 394
she declared war on Sparta, and condemned Xenophon
for 'Laconism,' an offence like the old 'Medism,' involving banishment and confiscation of goods. If Xenophon
had drifted before, he had now no choice. He formally
entered the Spartan service, returned to Greece with
Agêsilâus, and was actually with him, though perhaps as
a non-combatant, when he defeated the Thebo-Athenian
alliance at Coronea.

Xenophon was now barely forty-one, but his active
life was over. The Spartans gave him an estate at
Skillûs, near Elis, and perhaps employed him as their
political agent. He spent the next twenty years in
retirement, a cultured country gentleman; writing a
good deal, hunting zealously, and training his two
brilliant sons, Gryllus and Diodorus—the 'Dioscuri,' as
they were called—to be like their father, patterns of the
chivalry of the day. The main object of Xenophon's
later life was probably to get the sentence of banishment
removed, and save these sons from growing up without
a country. He was successful at last. When Athens re-
joined the Spartan alliance the 'Laconist' ceased to be a
traitor, and his sons were admitted into his old regiment;
and when Gryllus fell at Mantinea, all Greece poured poems
and epitaphs upon him. At that time Xenophon was no
longer in the Spartan service. He had been expelled from
Skillûs by an Elean rising in 370, and fled to spend the
rest of his life in the safe neutrality of Corinth.

Of the literary fruits of his retirement, the most im-

portant and the best written is undoubtedly his record
of the *Anabasis*. It also seems to be one of the earliest,
though some passages—such as v. 3. 9, where he refers
to his past employments at Skillûs—have been added
much later. Autobiographical writing was almost unknown at the time; but the publication was partly forced
on Xenophon by the misrepresentations of his action
current in Athens, and perhaps especially by the record
of the expedition already published by Sophainetus of
Stymphâlus. We read in Xenophon that Sophainetus
was the oldest of the officers; that he had once almost
refused to obey Xenophon's command to cross a certain
dangerous gully; that he was fined ten minæ for some
failure in duty.[1] That is Xenophon's account of him.
No doubt his account of Xenophon required answering.
But why did Xenophon publish his book under an assumed name, and refer to it himself in the *Hellenica* as
the work of '*Themistogenes of Syracuse*'? It is not a
serious attempt at disguise. The whole style of writing
shows that the 'Xenophon of Athens,' referred to in
the third person, is really the writer of the book. The
explanation suggests itself, that the 'pseudonymity' was a
technical precaution against possible συκοφαντία dictated
by Xenophon's legal position. He was ἄτιμος—an out-
lawed exile. He was forbidden λέγειν καὶ γράφειν, 'to
speak or write,' in the legal sense of the words, in Attica.
He could hold no property. What was the position of a
book written by such a man? Was it liable to be burnt
like those of Protagoras? Or could the bookseller be
proceeded against? It may well have been prudent,
for the sake of formal legality, to have the book passing
under some safer name.

[1] *Anab.* v. 3. 1, 8. 1; vi. 5. 13.

The style of the *Anabasis* is not very skilful, and the narrative is sometimes languid where the actual events are stirring. Still, on the whole, one feels with Gibbon that "this pleasing work is original and authentic," and that constitutes an inestimable charm. The details are most vivid—the officer pulled over the cliff by catching at the fine cloak of one of the flying Kurds; the Mossyn-dwellers exhibiting their fat babies fed on chestnut-meal to the admiration of the Greeks; the races at Trebizond conducted on the principle that "you could run any-where"; the Thynians waking the author up with the invitation to come out and die like a man, rather than be roasted in his bed—there are literally hundreds of such things. Of course Xenophon is sometimes wrong in his distances and details of fact, and the tendency to romance which we find in the *Cyropædeia* has a slight but visible effect on the *Anabasis*. The ornamental speeches are poor and unconvincing. Still, on the whole, it is a fresh, frank work in which the writer at least succeeds in not spoiling a most thrilling story.

To touch briefly on his other works. When Socrates was attacked and misunderstood, when Plato and the other Socratics defended him, Xenophon, too, felt called upon to write his *Memoirs of Socrates*. His remarkable memory stood him in good stead. He gives a Socrates whom his average contemporary would have recognised as true to life. Plato, fired by his own speculative ideas, had inevitably altered Socrates. Xenophon's ideas were a smaller and more docile body : he seldom misrepresents except where he misunderstood. In the later editions of the *Memorabilia* he inserts a detailed refutation of the charges made by 'the Accuser,' as he calls Polycrates, against Socrates's memory ; and he seems to allow his own imagination more play. When Plato wrote the *Apology*, Xenophon found some gaps which it did not fill. He made inquiries, and published a little note of his own *On the Apology of Socrates*.[1] When Plato wrote the *Symposium*, Xenophon was not entirely satisfied with the imaginative impression left by that stupendous masterpiece. He corrected it by a *Symposium* of his own, equally imaginary — for he was a child when the supposed banquet took place — but far more matter-of-fact, an entertaining work of high antiquarian value.

Another appendix to Xenophon's Socratic writings, the *Oikonomikos*, where Socrates gives advice about the management of a household and the duties of husband and wife, makes a certain special appeal to modern sympathies. The wife is charming—rather like Thackeray's heroines, though more capable of education—and the little dialogue, taken together with the corresponding parts of the *Memorabilia* and *Cyropædeia*, forms almost the only instance in this period of Attic thought of the modern 'bourgeois' ideal of good ordinary women and commonplace happy marriages. Antiphon the sophist, who seems at first sight to write in the same spirit, is really more consciously philosophical.

The *Hiero* is a non-Socratic dialogue on government between the tyrant Hiero and the poet Simonides. The *Agêsilâus* is an eulogy on Xenophon's royal friend, made up largely of fragments of the *Hellenica*, and showing a certain Isocratean tendency in language.

Xenophon's longest work, the *Hellenica*, falls into two parts, separated by date and by style. Books I. and II. are obviously a continuation of Thucydides to the end of

---

[1] On its genuineness, see Schanz, Introduction to Plato's *Apology*.

the Peloponnesian War.   Books III.–VII. contain the
annals of Greece to the battle of Mantinea, ending with
the sentence : *"So far I have written ; what came after
will perhaps be another's study."*   The first part, though
far below Thucydides in accuracy, in grasp, in unity of
view, and in style, is noticeably above the rest of the
work.   The *Hellenica*, though often bright and clear in
detail, forms a weak history.   Outside his personal experience, Xenophon is at sea.   The chronology is faulty;
there is little understanding of the series of events as a
whole ; there is no appreciation of Epaminondas.   The
fact that the history is the work of an able man with
large experience and exceptional opportunities for getting
information, helps us to appreciate the extraordinary
genius of Thucydides.

We possess a tract on the *Constitution of Lacedæmon*,[1]
an essay on *Athenian Finances*, a *Manual for a Cavalry
Commander*, and another for a *Cavalry Private*, and a
tract on *Hunting with Hounds*, bearing the name of
Xenophon.   The last is suspected on grounds of style,
but may be a youthful work.   The genuineness of the
Finances depends partly upon chronological questions
not yet definitely settled : it is an interesting book, and
seems to be written in support of the peace policy
of Eubûlus.   The cavalry manuals do not raise one's
opinions of Greek military discipline, and are less
systematic than the *Manual for Resisting a Siege* by
Xenophon's Arcadian contemporary, ÆNEAS TACTICUS.

The *Cyropædeia* is not a historical romance ; if it were,
Xenophon would be one of the great originators of
literary forms : it is a treatment of the Ideal Ruler and
the Best Form of Government, in the shape of a history

---

[1] For *The Constitution of Athens*, see above, p. 167.

of Cyrus the Great, in which truth is subordinated to edification.[1]   The form is one followed by certain of the Sophists.   Xenophon perhaps took it from Prodicus in preference to the usual Socratic expedient of an imaginary dialogue.   The work was greatly admired in antiquity and in the last century.   The style is more finished than in any of Xenophon's other works.   The Oriental colour is well kept up.   The incidents contain masses of striking tragic material, which only fail to be effective because modern taste insists on more working up than Xenophon will consent to give.   The political ideal which forms the main object of the book, is happily described by Croiset as " a Versailles of Louis XIV. revised and corrected by Fénelon."   It was actually intended— if we may trust the authority of the Latin grammarian, Aulus Gellius—as a counterblast to Plato's *Republic* !

Xenophon was an amateur in literature, as he was in war, in history, in philosophy, in politics, in field-sports. He was susceptible to every influence which did not morally offend him.   His style is simple, but unevenly so.   He sometimes indulges in a little fine writing ; the eulogy on Agêsilâus tries to avoid hiatus, and shows the influence of Isocrates ; the speeches in his histories, and the whole conception of the *Hellenica*, show the influence of Thucydides.   The influence of Plato leads Xenophon into a system of imitation and correction which is almost absurd.   His language has the same receptivity. It shows that colloquial and democratic absence of exclusiveness which excited the contempt of the Old Oligarch ;[2] it is affected by old - fashioned country

---

[1] Contrast, *e.g.*, the historical account of Cyrus's death in Hdt. i. 214, and the romantic one in *Cyrop*. viii. 7.

[2] *Rep. Ath.* 2, 8.

idioms, by the *lingua franca* of the soldiers in Asia, perhaps by long residence in foreign countries—though Doricisms are conspicuous by their absence. If, in spite of this, Xenophon became in Roman times a model of 'Atticism,' it is due to his ancient simplicity and ease, his *inaffectata jucunditas*. He is Attic in the sense that he has no bombast, and does not strive after effect, and that he can speak interestingly on many subjects 'without raising his voice.'

XVI

THE 'ORATORS'

GENERAL INTRODUCTION

MOST students of Greek literature, however sensitive to the transcendent value of the poets and historians, find a difficulty in admiring or reading Lysias, Isocrates, and Isæus. The disappointment is partly justified; Greek orators are not so much to the world as Greek poets are. But it is partly the result of a misunderstanding. We expect to find what we call 'oratory' in them, to declaim them as we would Burke and Grattan and Bossuet; and we discover that, with a few exceptions, the thing cannot be done. Demosthenes indeed is overpoweringly eloquent, and when he disappoints the average modern, it is merely because the modern likes more flamboyance and gush, and cannot take points quickly enough. But many a man must rise in despair from the earlier orators, wondering what art or charm it can be that has preserved for two thousand years Lysias *Against the Corn-Dealers* or Isæus *On the Estate of Cleonymus.*

The truth is that we look upon these writers as orators because we are at the mercy of our tradition. Our tradition comes partly from the Romans, who based all their culture on oratory; partly from the style-worship of the late Greek schools. The typical school critic is Dionysius of Halicarnassus; he was a professional teacher of rhetoric in Cicero's time, a man of some genius and much enthusiasm, but with no interest in anything but rhetorical technique. He criticises Thucydides the historian, Plato the philosopher, Isocrates the publicist, Isæus the acute lawyer, Lysias the work-a-day persuader of juries, all from practically the same stand-point—that of a man who had all his life studied style and taught style, who had written twenty volumes of history with a view to nothing but style. In his own province he is an excellent critic. He sees things which we do not see, and he feels more strongly than we feel. He speaks with genuine hatred of the Asiatic or late and florid style, the 'foreign harlot' who has crept into the place of the true and simple Attic. Our tradition has thus neglected historians, playwrights, philosophers, men of science, and clung to the men who wrote in speech-form ; and these last, whatever the aim and substance of their writing, are all judged as technical orators.

The importance to us of the 'orators' lies in three things. First, they illustrate the gradual building up of a normal and permanent prose style. The earliest artists in prose had been over-ornate ; Gorgias too poetical, Antiphon too formal and austere, Thucydides too difficult. THRASYMACHUS of Chalcêdon (p. 162) probably gave the necessary correction to this set of errors so far as speaking went. His style was 'medium' between the pomp of Gorgias and the colloquialness of ordinary speech. His terse periods and prose rhythms pleased Aristotle. But he was a pleader, not a writer. The next step appears in LYSIAS. He had an enormous practice as a writer of speeches under the Restored Democracy, and, without much eloquence or profound knowledge of the law, a reputation for almost always winning his cases. His style is that of the plain clear-headed man, who tells his story and draws his deductions so honestly, that his adversary's version is sure to seem artificial and knavish. Within his limits Lysias is a perfect stylist ; but he is a man of little imaginative range, and he addresses a jury. He does not develop a normal literary prose. ISÆUS, a lawyer of great knowledge and a powerful arguer, is still further from this end. ISOCRATES achieves it. The essay-writing of his school—men broadly trained in letters, philosophy, and history, and accustomed to deal with large questions in a liberal, pan-Hellenic spirit—forms in one sense the final perfection of ancient prose, in another the ruin of what was most characteristically Attic or indeed Hellenic. It is smooth, self-restrained, correct, euphonious, impersonal. It is the first Greek prose that is capable of being tedious. It has lasted on from that day to this, and is the basis of prose style in Latin and in modern languages. It has sacrificed the characteristic charms of Greek expression, the individuality, the close relation between thought and language, the naturalness of mind which sees every fact naked and states every thought in its lowest terms. Isocrates's influence was paramount in all *belles lettres ;* scientific work and oratory proper went on their way little affected by him.

Secondly, the orators have great historical value. They all come from Athens, and all lived in the century between 420 and 320 B.C. Other periods and towns were either lacking in the combination of culture and freedom necessary to produce political oratory, or else, as happened with Syracuse, they have been neglected by our tradition. The Attic orators are our chief 'source' for Attic law, and they introduce us to the police-court population of a great city — the lawyers, the judges, the ne'er-do-weels, the swindlers, and the 'syko-phantai,' or vexatious accusers trying to win blackmail or political capital by discovering decent people's pecca-dilloes. The Athenian records are less nauseous than most, owing to the mildness of the law and the com-parative absence of atrocious crime. The most painful feature is the racking of slave-witnesses; though even here extreme cruelty was forbidden, and any injury done to the slave, temporary or permanent, had to be paid for. Attic torture would probably have seemed child's play to the rack-masters of Rome and modern Europe. Happily also the owners seem more often than not to refuse to allow examination of this sort, even to the prejudice of their causes. All kinds of argumentative points are made in connection with the worth or worth-lessness of such evidence, and the motives of the master in allowing or refusing it. Perhaps the strangest is where a litigant demands the torture of a female slave in order to suggest that his opponent is in love with her when he refuses.

But the orators have a much broader value than this. The actual words of Demosthenes, and even of Isocrates, on a political crisis, form a more definitely first-hand document than the best literary history. They give us in a palpable form the actual methods, ideals, political and moral standards of the early fourth century—or, rather, they will do so when fully worked over and understood. There are side-lights on religion, as in the case (Lysias, vii.) of the man accused of uprooting a sacred olive stump from his field, and that of Euxenippus (Hyperîdes, iii.) and his illegal dream. A certain hill at Orôpus was alleged by some religious authority to belong to the god Asclêpius, and one

Euxenippus was commissioned to sleep in a temple and report his dream. His dream apparently was in favour of the god. The politician Polyeuctus made a motion in accordance with it ; but the Assembly over-ruled the dream, decided that the motion was illegal, and fined Polyeuctus twenty-five drachmæ. In pardonable irritation he turned on the dreamer, and prosecuted him for reporting to the Assembly "things not in the public interest."

There are innumerable side-lights on politics, especially in Lysias as to the attitude of parties after the revolution of 404. To take one instance, his short speech *Against the Corn-Dealers* throws a vivid light on the economic condition of the time and the influence of the great guild of wholesale importers. The democratic leader Anytus was corn-warden of the Piræus in the year of scarcity 388. In a praiseworthy attempt to keep the price down, he had apparently authorised the retail corn-dealers of the Piræus to form a 'ring' against the importers, and buy the whole stock cheap. The dealers did so ; but 'rings' in corn were expressly forbidden in Attic law, and the importers took action. They were too powerful to be defied ; they could at any time create an artificial famine. And we find the great democratic advocate making the best of a bad business by sacrificing the unhappy dealers and trying to screen Anytus !

Thirdly, it would be affected to deny to Greek oratory a permanent value on the grounds of beauty. The *Philippics*, the *Olynthiacs*, and the *De Corona* have something of that air of eternal grandeur which only belongs to the highest imaginative work. Hyperîdes, Æschines, Andocides are striking writers in their different styles.

The average speech of Lysias has a real claim on the world's attention as a model of what Dionysius calls the 'plain' style of prose—every word exact, every sentence clear, no display, no exaggeration, no ornament except the inherent charm and wit of natural Attic. It is not, of course, a work of art in the same sense as a poem of Sophocles. Speech-writing was a 'technê' in the sense that it had rules and a purpose, but its purpose was to convince a jury, not to be beautiful. We are apt to be misled by Cicero and the late writers on rhetoric. They talk in technical language ; "This ditrochæus brought down the house," says Cicero, when probably the house in question hardly knew what a ditrochæus was, or even consciously noticed the rhythm of the sentence. They tell us of the industry of great men, and how Isocrates took ten years composing the *Panegyricus*. This is edifying, but cannot be true ; for the *Panegyricus* contemplates a particular political situation, which did not last ten years.

The tone of the orators themselves is quite different from that of the rhetoricians, whether late like Dionysius, or early like Alkidamas and Gorgias. Except in Isocrates, who, as he repeatedly insists, is a professor and not an orator, we find the current convention about oratory to be the same in ancient times as in modern—that a true speech should be made extempore, and that prepared or professional oratory is matter for sarcasm. If Æschines likes to quote an absurd phrase from Demosthenes, it is no more than a practical politician would do at the present day. The points in ancient prose which seem most artificial to a modern Englishman are connected with euphony. Ancient literature was written to be read aloud, and this reading aloud gives the clue to the rules about

rhythm and hiatus, just as it explains many details in the
system of punctuation—for instance, the dash below the
line which warns you beforehand of the approach of the
end of the sentence. We are but little sensible to rhythm
and less to hiatus or the clashing of two vowel-sounds
without a dividing consonant ; we are keenly alive to
rhyme. The Greeks generally did not notice rhyme, but
felt rhythm strongly, and abhorred hiatus. In poetry
hiatus was absolutely forbidden. In careful prose it was
avoided in varying degrees by most writers after about
380 B.C. Isocrates is credited with introducing the fashion.
He was followed by all the historians and philosophers
and writers of *belles lettres*, and even, in their old age, by
Plato and Xenophon.[1] The orators who 'published'
generally felt bound to preserve the prevailing habit.
In the real debates of the Assembly, of course, such
refinement would scarcely be either attainable or notice-
able, but a published speech had to have its literary
polish. A written speech, however, was an exceptional
thing. The ordinary orators—Callistratus, Thrasybulus,
Leodamas — were content simply to speak. Even
Demosthenes must have spoken ten times as much as
he wrote.

The speeches we possess are roughly of three kinds.
First, there are the bought speeches preserved by the
client for whom they were written : such are the seven

---

[1] There is indeed some doubt about this avoidance of hiatus. Our earliest
papyri give texts which admit hiatus freely. The funeral speech of Hyperîdes,
for instance, abounds in harsh instances, and the pre-Alexandrian papyri of
Plato have more hiatus than our ordinary MSS. Does this mean that the
Alexandrian scholars deliberately doctored their classical texts and removed
hiatus ? Or does it mean that our pre-Alexandrian remains are generally inaccurate ? The former view must be dismissed as flatly impossible, though
there are some difficulties in the latter.

speeches *For Apollodôrus* in the Demosthenic collection, those of Hyperîdes *For Lycophron* and *Against Athenogenes*, and most of the will cases of Isæus.   Very similar is the case of Lysias, viii., in which some person unnamed renounces the society of his companions—retires from his club, as we should say—on the ground that they have spoken ill of him, have accused him of intruding upon them, and have persuaded him to buy a bad horse. There were doubtless other versions of the affair in existence, and the motive for having the protest copied and circulated is obvious.   Another Lysian fragment has a somewhat similar origin.   The second part of the speech for Polystratus (§ 11 to the end) is not a defence of Polystratus at all, but a moral rehabilitation of the speaker himself, the defendant's son.

Again, there are the orators' own publications—sometimes mere pamphlets never spoken, sometimes actual speeches reissued in permanent form as an appeal to the widest possible circle.   Andocides's publication *On the Mysteries* is a defence of his career, without which he could scarcely have lived safely in Athens.   It was the same with the rival speeches *On the Crown*.   Æschines had lost his case and his reputation ; in self-defence he published a revised and improved version of his speech, answering points which he had missed at the actual trial.   This compelled Demosthenes, who at the time had almost entirely ceased writing, to revise and publish his reply.   Most of our political speeches, however, such as the *Olynthiacs* and *Philippics*, seem to have been circulated to advocate a definite policy ; and it is noteworthy that publication is almost always the resort of the Opposition, not condescended to by the men in power.

There remain a few cases where the object of publication was merely literary or educational. The alleged remains of Gorgias, two speeches of Alkidamas, and two of Isocrates are 'mere literature.' The tetralogies of Antiphon are educational exercises with a political object. The great Epideictic 'Logoi' — 'speeches of display'—really deserve a better name. They express the drift of the pan-Hellenic sentiment of the time, and are only unpractical in the sense that internationalism has no executive power. Gorgias, in his *Olympiacus* * of 408, urged a definite pan-Hellenic policy against Persia. Lysias in 388 compromised the Athenian Democracy by a generous but wild onslaught on Dionysius of Syracuse. Two Olympiads later Isocrates gave the world a masterpiece of political criticism, the *Panegyricus*. The funeral speeches which were delivered yearly on those slain in war, were religious sermons of a somewhat formal type, and were seldom published. Our only genuine example has a practical interest as giving Hyperîdes's defence of his war policy in 323. And doubtless the lost Funeral Speech of Demosthenes contained a similar justification of Chæronea.

The publication of a speech, then, depended chiefly on practical considerations, very little on the artistic value of the speech itself. The preservation of what was published was very largely a matter of accident. The movement for preserving and collecting books may be roughly dated from the founding of Aristotle's school in 335 B.C. The Peripatetics formed the beginning of the scholarly or Alexandrian movement in antiquity. They sought out remarkable books as they sought out facts of history and nature, to catalogue and understand them. And though it is not probable that Aristotle

attached much value to the works of Demosthenes and
Hyperîdes, or even Lysias, the tendency he had set
going secured to some extent the preservation of every
manuscript current under a distinguished name.   The
very idea of the great libraries of the next century
would never have been conceived had there not already
existed a number of small libraries and a wide-spread
spirit of book-preserving.

LIVES OF THE ORATORS

Up to Isocrates

A canonic list of uncertain origin — it appears in
Cæcilius of Calê-Actê, but not in his contemporary
Dionysius — gives us ten Attic orators *par excellence :*
Antiphon, Andocides, Lysias, Isocrates, Isæus, Lycurgus,
Æschines, Hyperîdes, Demosthenes, Deinarchus.   Arbi-
trary as it is, this list determined what orators should
be read for educational purposes from the first century
onward, and has, of course, controlled our tradition.
Outside of it we possess only one important fragment by
Alkidamas, on " *The Sophists, or Those who compose Written
Speeches,*" and some rather suspicious *jeux d'esprit*—
speeches of *Odysseus* by the same Alkidamas, of *Ajax* and
Odysseus by Antisthenes the cynic, a *Praise of Helen* and
a speech of *Palamêdes* by Gorgias. The genuineness
of these is on the whole probable, but they have little
more than an antiquarian value. Happily some speeches
by other writers have been preserved by being erroneously ascribed to one of the canonical ten. In the
Demosthenic collection, for instance, the accusation of

Neæra is the work of some able and well-informed
Athenian, and the speech *On the Halonnese* is perhaps
by Hêgêsippus.

Of ANTIPHON little is known beyond the narrative of
Thucydides mentioned above (p. 198). He had worked
all his life preparing for the revolution of 411. He led
it and died for it, and made what Thucydides considered
the greatest speech in the world in defence of his action
in promoting it. We possess three real speeches of
Antiphon, and three tetralogies. These latter are exercises in speech-craft, and show us the champion of the
oppressed aristocrats training his friends for legal practice, as Thucydides tells us he did. He takes an imaginary case, with as little positive or detailed evidence as
possible, and gives us two skeleton speeches—they are
not more—for the accusation, and two for the defence.
Considering the difficulty of the game, it is well played.
The arguments are necessarily inconclusive and often
sophistical, but they could not be otherwise when real
evidence was against the rules. Minute legal argument
is also debarred. In fact the law contemplated in the
tetralogies is not Attic, but a kind of common-sense
system. It may be that Antiphon, like many of his
party, was really trying to train the aristocrats of the
subject states more than his compatriots. The real
speeches are all on murder cases, the finest being the
defence of Euxitheus (?) the Mitylenean on the charge
of having murdered his shipmate Herôdes. The first
speech, *On a Charge of Poisoning*, deals with a singularly
tragic story. A slave-girl was about to be sold by a
ruffianly master, with whom she was in love ; a woman
who wished to be rid of her own husband, induced the
girl to give the two men, at a dinner which they had

together in a Piræus tavern, something which she alleged to be a love-philtre. Both men died. The girl confessed forthwith, and was executed ; proceedings now being taken against the real culprit.

ANDOCIDES, son of Leôgoras, of the family of the Sacred Heralds, comes to us as a tough, enterprising man, embittered by persecution. In the extraordinary panic which followed the mutilation of the figures of Hermes in 415, Andocides was among the three hundred persons denounced by the informer Diocleides, and, unlike most of the rest, was in a sense privy to the outrage. It was merely a freak on the part of some young sceptics in his own club, who probably thought the Hermæ both ridiculous and indecent. To stop the general panic and prevent possible executions of the innocent, he gave information under a promise of indemnity. It is one of those acts which are never quite forgiven. In spite of the indemnity, he was driven into banishment by a special decree excluding from public and sacred places "those who had committed impiety and confessed it." His next twelve years were spent in adventurous trading, and were ruled by a constant effort to procure his return. The first attempt was in 411, after he had obtained rights of timber-cutting from Archelaus of Macedon, and sold the timber at cost price to the Athenian fleet. He was promptly re-expelled. The second return was the occasion of the speech *About Returning Home*, and took place after 410, when he had used his influence at Cyprus to have corn-ships sent to relieve the scarcity at Athens. He returned finally with Thucydides and all the other exiles, political and criminal, after the amnesty in 403 (see p. 338). He spent his money lavishly on public objects, and escaped prosecution till 399, when the notorious Melêtus, among others, charged him with impiety, raking up the old scandal of 415, and accusing him further of having profaned the Mysteries. Andocides was acquitted. His speech has its name from the accusation, but its main object is really to give the speaker's own version of that youthful act for which he had been so long persecuted. The third speech, advocating the peace with Lacedæmon in 390, failed in its purpose, and was apparently published afterwards as a justification of the writer's policy.

LYSIAS was a Syracusan, born probably about 450, though his extant work lies entirely between 403 and 380. His father Kephalus, known to us from the charming portrait in Plato's *Republic*, was invited to Athens by Pericles. He owned several houses and a large shield-factory in the Piræus. Lysias went to Thurii at the age of fifteen, and had his first opportunity of suffering for the Athenian Democracy in 412, after the defeat of the Sicilian Expedition. Expelled from South Italy, he returned to Athens, and continued his father's business in partnership with his brother Polemarchus. He composed speeches for amusement, and possibly gave lectures on rhetoric. We hear that he was not successful as a teacher compared with Theodôrus and Isocrates ; which is not surprising if either the *Eroticus* attributed to him by Plato in the *Phædrus*, or the *Epitaphius* extant in his remains, is a genuine type of his epideictic style.

In 404 things changed with Lysias. The Thirty Tyrants took to plundering the rich ' Metoikoi ' or resident aliens. The two brothers were arrested. Lysias escaped, Polemarchus was put to death, and what could be found of the property was confiscated. Evidently not all ; for

Y

Lysias, throwing himself with vigour into the democratic cause, was able to supply the army with 200
shields, 2000 drachmæ in money, and large indirect
assistance as well. On the return of the Demos, Lysias
was accepted as a full citizen on the proposal of Thrasybûlus himself. He made his one extant 'Dêmêgoria'
or Parliamentary speech (34) in protest against the
proposal of one Phormisius to limit the franchise to
house or land holders.[1]   Phormisius's policy would
have been that of Thucydides, Isocrates, Theramenes,
and, of course, that of Plato and Aristotle. But Lysias
was an unabashed 'ochlocrat.' He was at this time
poor, and his citizenship was shown to be illegal almost
as soon as it was granted. It was annulled on the
motion of Archînus, a democrat who had fought with
Thrasybûlus but favoured the moderates. Lysias was
debarred from direct political ambition, but repaired
his fortunes and worked well for his party by ceaseless
activity in the law-courts. On the expulsion of the
tyrants in 403, when the various factions were ignorant
of their comparative strength and tired of strife, an
amnesty had been passed, including all except the actual
tyrants, and allowing even these either to leave the
country unmolested, or to be tried individually on their
personal acts. When the extreme democrats realised
their strength, they regretted this amnesty, and some
of the chief speeches of Lysias are attempts to make it
nugatory. Thus in the speech *Against Eratosthenes*, who
had been one of the tyrants, but claimed to be tried,
according to the amnesty, for his personal acts only,
Lysias insists on the solidarity of the whole body of
tyrants. The man had been implicated in the arrest

[1] *Cf.* W. M. *Aristotles und Athen*, ii. 226.

of Polemarchus, though not in his condemnation to death. There was nothing else against him, and he seems to have been acquitted.

The speech *Against Agorâtus* takes a curious ground about the amnesty. Agorâtus had practised as an informer in 405 and 404, and falsely claimed the reward for slaying Phrynichus. This shows, argues Lysias, that he was a democrat. The amnesty was only made by the Demos with the oligarchs, and does not apply between two democrats! In a similar partisan spirit Lysias persecutes the younger Alcibiades. His offence was that he served in the cavalry instead of the heavy infantry. He claims that he had special permission, and it would be hard to imagine a more venial offence. But the father's memory stank in the nostrils of the radicals, and the act savoured of aristocratic assumption. Lysias indicts him in two separate speeches—first, for desertion, and secondly, for failure to serve in the army, invoking the severest possible penalty! After these speeches, and that *Against the Corn-Dealers*, and the markedly unfair special pleading *Against Euandros*, it is difficult to reject other documents in the Lysian collection on the ground of their 'sycophantic tone.'

Lysias is especially praised in antiquity for his power of entering into the character of every different client and making his speech sound 'natural,' not bought. His catholicity of sympathy may even seem unscrupulous, but it has limits. He cannot really conceive an honest oligarch. When he has to speak for one, as in 25, he makes him frankly cynical: *"I used to be an oligarch because it suited my interests; now it suits me to be a democrat. Every one acts on the same principle. The important point is that I have not broken the law."*

He speaks well for the clients of the moderate party, like *Mantitheos*, who had trouble from sycophants, and especially well against the hunger for confiscation of property which marked the worst type of extremist (18, 19). The speech *For the Incapable Man*, a cripple pauper whose right to state relief had been disputed, is good-natured and democratic. The pauper cannot have paid for the speech ; and, even if some one else did, the care taken with it shows real sympathy. On the whole, considering that we have thirty-four more or less complete speeches of Lysias—the ancients had 425, of which 233 were thought genuine !—and some considerable fragments; considering, too, that he was a professional lawyer writing steadily for some twenty-five years—he comes out of his severe ordeal rather well. It is no wonder that Plato disliked him. He was a type of the adroit practical man. He was an intemperate democrat. Above all, he had handled the Socratic Æschines (frag. 1) very roughly. That philosopher had tried to live as a moneyless sage like his master, his simple needs supported by the willing gifts of friends and disciples. Unfortunately he fell on hard times. His friends did not appreciate his gospel ; his neighbours fled from their houses to avoid him. At last they prosecuted him for debt, and the unfortunate priest of poverty had to marry the septuagenarian widow of a pomatum-seller, and run the business himself ! The jest may have been pleasing to the court; but not to Plato. And still less can he have liked the turbulent success of the Olympian oration, when Lysias took his revenge for the enslavement of his native city by calling Hellas to unite and sail against Dionysius —which Hellas never thought of attempting—and inciting the crowd to burn and pillage the tents of the tyrant's legation, which the crowd proceeded to do. The act must have lowered Athens in the eyes of Greece. It is valuable to us as showing that there was a real Lysias capable of passion and indiscretion beneath that cloak of infinite tact and good temper, and "remoteness from the possibility of making a mistake," which is preserved to us in the speeches.

ISÆUS of Chalkis was, like Lysias, a foreigner, but, unlike him, accepted frankly his exclusion from political life. We possess ten complete speeches of his, and large fragments of two more. All are about inheritances, and all effective ; though the ancient judgment is true, which says that while Lysias preserves an air of candour when his processes are most questionable, Isæus hammers so minutely at his arguments that he generally rouses distrust. His extant speeches fall between 390 and 340 B.C.

ISOCRATES, SON OF THEODÔRUS, FROM ERCHIA (436–338 B.C.).

ISOCRATES'S century of life reaches through the most eventful century of Greek history, from Pericles to Alexander. He was the son of a rich flute-maker, and held the views of the cultivated middle class. He was in close relation with the great orator and statesman of the moderates, Theramenes, and his successor Archînus, the disfranchiser of Lysias. He was an enthusiast for education. He heard Protagoras, Prodicus, and Socrates. In his old age he speaks with pride of his school-days, and in a sense he spent all his life in school as learner and teacher. He never looked to a public career. His views were unpopular. He was scrupulous and sensitive ; even in later life his shyness was an amusement to his pupils. However, towards the end of the war, when his father was dead, and every one alike in straits for money, Isocrates had to support himself by his wits. As soon as peace was made and he was free to leave Athens, he went to Thessaly and learned from the great Gorgias—a singular step for a poor man, if we accept the current myth of the 'grasping sophists.' But doubtless the old man was ready to help a promising pupil without a fee.

He was back in Athens by 400, a professional speech-writer and teacher of rhetoric. The latter profession cannot have paid under the circumstances, but the former did. Aristotle says that the booksellers in his time had 'rolls and rolls' of legal speeches bearing the name of Isocrates. He himself disliked and ignored this period of 'doll-making' in contrast to the 'noble sculpture' of his later life,[1] and his pupils sometimes denied its existence altogether. It was at Chios, not Athens, that he first set up a formal school of rhetoric, probably in 393, when, in consequence of Conon's victories, Chios returned to the Athenian alliance. Conon was a friend of Isocrates, and may have given him some administrative post there. The island had long been famous for its good laws and peaceful life. Speech-writing for courts of law was obviously not permissible in an administrator ; even for an Athenian politician it was considered questionable. But there could be no objection to his teaching rhetoric if he wished. Isocrates had nine pupils in Chios, and founded his reputation as a singularly gifted teacher. When

---

[1] Dionys. *Isocr.* 18, *Antid.* 2.

he returned to Athens (391 ?) he did no more law-court work. He established a school, not of mere rhetoric, but of what he called philosophy.

He is at great pains to explain himself, both in the fragment *Against the Sophists*, which formed a sort of prospectus of his system, and afterwards in the elaborate defence of his life and pursuits, which goes by the name of the *Speech on the Exchange of Property*. His philosophy is not what is sometimes so called—paradoxical metaphysics, barren logomachies, or that absolutely certain knowledge *a priori* about all the world, which certain persons offer for sale at extremely reasonable prices, but which nobody ever seems to possess. Nor, again, is it the mere knack of composing speeches for the law-courts, like Lysias, or of making improvisations, like Alkidamas. Isocrates means by philosophy what Protagoras and Gorgias meant—a practical culture of the whole mind, strengthening the character, forming a power of 'generally right judgment,' and developing to the highest degree the highest of human powers, Language. He requires in his would-be 'philosopher' a broad amateur knowledge of many subjects—of history, of dialectics and mathematics, of the present political condition of all Greece, and of literature. He is far more philosophic and cultured than the average orator, far more practical and sensible than the philosophers. It is a source of lifelong annoyance to him that both philosophers and practical men despise his middle course, and that the general public refuses to understand him. Plato in two passages criticises the position very lucidly. In the *Phædrus* (see above, p. 305) he expresses his sympathy with Isocrates as compared with the ordinary speech-writers. In the epilogue to the *Euthydêmus*,[1] Crito mentions the criticisms of a certain nameless person upon Socrates :—"What sort of man was the critic ?"—"Not a philosopher, not a speaker." Crito doubts if he has ever been into a lawcourt; but he understands the art of speech, and writes wonderfully.—"*Ah*," answers Socrates, "*he is what Prodicus used to call a Boundary Stone, half philosopher and half practical statesman. The Boundary Stones believe themselves to be the wisest people in the world ; but probably are not so. For practical statesmanship may be the right thing, or philosophy may be the right thing, or conceivably both may be good, though different. But in none of these cases can that which is half one and half the other be superior to both. Perhaps in our friend's eyes both are positively bad ?*" The likeness to Isocrates is beyond dispute. Isocrates had an easy reply : both practical man and philosopher are one-sided ; the one wants culture and breadth of imagination, the other loses his hold of concrete life. As a matter of fact his answer was his success. His school became the University of Greece. It satisfied a wide-spread desire for culture on the part of men who did not mean to become professional mathematicians or philosophers in the stricter sense. The leading names of the next generation come chiefly from the school of Isocrates—the statesmen Timotheus and Leôdamas, the tragic poet Theodectes, the historians Ephorus and Theopompus, the orators Isæus, Lycurgus, Æschines, Hyperîdes, and some hundred more. The Alexandrian scholar Hermippos wrote a book on *The Disciples of Isocrates*.

---

[1] Though the general statistics of the *Euthydêmus* show it to be a very early work, the epilogue is obviously separable in composition from the rest, and, as a matter of fact, contains some slight marks of lateness (ἐχόμενον φρονήσεως πρᾶγμα, and perhaps ὄντως), and none of earliness.

Soon after opening the school he probably wrote the two slight displays in the style of Gorgias, which have come down to us—the paradoxical *Praise of Busiris,* in which he champions the Socratics, and the fine *Helenê,* in which he speaks sharply of all philosophers. The passage (54–58) of the *Helenê* on Beauty and Chastity is almost Platonic, as profound as it is eloquent. The *Panegyricus,* an address written for the 'Panêgyris,' or General Gathering of all Hellas at the hundredth Olympiad, 380 B.C., is Isocrates's masterpiece. Quite apart from its dignity of form, it shows the author as a publicist of the highest power. It combines a clear review of the recent history and present condition of Greece with an admirable justification of Athens, and an appeal to the sympathies of Greece in favour of renewing the Sea Federation. It is not, indeed, quite impartially pan - Hellenic. The comparison of the Spartan and Athenian rule was inevitable, and the tone of §§ 122–132 cannot have pleased the Peloponnese ; but in maritime Greece the appeal was irresistible. Two years afterwards, his own Chios leading the way, seventy cities joined the Athenian alliance, and Isocrates accompanied the general Timotheus on a two years' commission to organise the terms of the federation in the different islands and coast towns. It was probably at this time that he formed his friendship with Euagoras, king of Salamis in Cyprus, who had been fighting almost single - handed against Persia for eight years. Cyprus was the frontier where Greek and Oriental met. Every step gained by Euagoras was an advance of culture and humanity ; every step lost meant the re-establishment of barbarous laws and bloody superstitions. The sight kindled a lasting fervour in Isocrates.

In 374 Euagoras was conquered and assassinated; his son Nicocles succeeded him. Isocrates has left us an '*Exhortation to Nicocles*,' summoning him with tact and enthusiasm to discharge the high duties of an Hellenic king; a '*Nicocles*,' or an address from that king to his subjects demanding their co-operation and loyal obedience; and an *Encômion on Euagoras*—the first, it is said, ever written upon a character of current history.

Meantime the political situation in Greece proper had changed. The league of Athens and Thebes against Sparta had enabled Thebes to resume more than her old power, while it involved Athens in heavy expense. The anti-Theban sentiment in Athens, always strong, became gradually unmanageable. One crisis seems to have come in 373, when the Thebans surprised and destroyed Platæa. The little town was nominally in alliance with Thebes, but it was notoriously disaffected; so the act was capable of different interpretations. The remnant of the Platæans fled to Athens and asked to be restored to their country. Such a step on the part of Athens would have implied a declaration of war against Thebes and an alliance with Sparta. The *Plataïcus* of Isocrates is a glowing plea for the Platæan cause, a pamphlet in the usual speech form. The chief real speakers on the occasion were Callistratus for Platæa-Sparta, and the great Epaminondas for Thebes. In 366 Isocrates strikes again on the same side. Thebes, in 'her Leuctric pride'—as Theopompus seems to have called it—had established the independence of Messenia, and insisted on the recognition of this independence as a condition of peace. Most of the Spartan allies were by this time anxious for peace on any terms. The liberation of the much-wronged province did not hurt them, and it had roused the enthusiasm of Greece in general, voiced by Alkidamas in his *Messêniacus.** But Sparta could never acquiesce in giving up the richest third of her territory, and seeing her old subjects and enemies established at her doors. She let the allies make peace alone; and Isocrates, in what purports to be a speech of the Spartan king Archidâmus, supports her cause. It was an invidious cause to plead. Principle is really against Isocrates, but he makes a strong case both in practical expediency and in sentiment. The speech is full of what the Greeks called ' êthos' (character). It has a Spartan ring, especially when Archidâmus faces the last alternative. They can leave Sparta, ship the non-combatants to Sicily or elsewhere, and become again what they originally were—a camp, not a city, a home-less veteran army of desperate men which no Theban coalition will care to face (71–79).

This time, again, Isocrates saw his policy accepted and his country in alliance with Sparta. But meanwhile his greater hopes for Athens had been disappointed. The other cities of the Maritime League were sus-picious of her, and the hegemony involved intoler-able financial burdens to herself. Isocrates had seen Euagoras, and formed more definitely his political ideal—peace for Hellas, the abolition of piracy on the seas, the liberation of the Greek cities in Asia, the opening of the East to emigration, and the spread of Hellenism over the world. As early as 367 he had sent a public letter to Dionysius of Syracuse, who had just saved Western Hellas from the Etruscans and Carthaginians, inviting him to come East and free the Greek cities from Persia. Dionysius died the next year, and Isocrates continued hoping the best he

could from the Maritime League. In 357 the league
broke up in open war, which only ended in the abandonment by Athens of all her claims. She sank to
the level of an ordinary large Greek town, and, under
the guidance of Eubûlus, devoted her energies to
financial retrenchment and the maintenance of peace.
Isocrates was one of the few men who saw what the
policy meant—a final renunciation of the burden of
empire. In the treatise *On the Peace*, he pleads for
the autonomy of the allies, and actually uses some of
the arguments of that anti-Athenian party in the islands
which he had confuted in the *Panegyricus.*

About the same time, in the *Areopagiticus*, he preaches
the home policy of the moderates, of Phokion and
Aristotle—a return to the habits of old Athens, to the
πάτριος πολιτεία, which he associates with the Areopagus. In its more obvious aspect, the speech is a
manifesto in support of Eubûlus, like Xenophon's
Finances. But it is at the same time an interesting
illustration of the moral sensitiveness and self-distrust
of the age — the feeling which leads Demosthenes to
denounce all Hellas, and Demâdes to remark that the
Virgin of Marathon is now an old woman, with no
thought beyond slippers, gruel, and dressing-gown !
It was just before the end of the Social War that
Isocrates turned to Archidâmus of Sparta with the
same invitation as he had addressed before to Dionysius. Who else could so well lead the crusade against
barbarism ? Agêsilâus, his father, had made the attempt, and won great glory. He had failed because
he had been interrupted, and because he had tried to
reinstate exiles of his own party in their cities. Archidâmus should confine himself to the one great task of

liberating all Greeks in Asia, and not set Greek against Greek. Isocrates was eighty years of age now (356), and most of his writing is subject to a certain peevish garrulity, of which he seems himself to be conscious ; but his political insight remains singularly deep and unprejudiced. He clings always to his essential idea, and he changes the external clothing of it dexterously. He has already abandoned the hope of Athenian hegemony. He has relaxed—perhaps with less reluctance than he professes [1]—his faith in constitutional government. When Archidâmus failed him he turned towards Philip of Macedon. He saw as well as Demosthenes, that Philip was the rising power ; but he did not therefore count him an enemy. He had made up his mind long ago that the empire was a delusion to Athens, and must not be fought for. He strove to keep on good terms with Philip, to use personal friendship in mitigation of public war. It is hard to read without emotion his *Philippus*, an address to Philip immediately after the first peace in 346. He had loyally kept from treating with his country's enemy during the war. Now he speaks with perfect frankness, and yet with tact. He tells Philip of his past hopes of a leader for Greece, of Jason of Pheræ, Dionysius, Archidâmus. None of these had such an opportunity as Philip now has. He must choose the nobler ambition, not the lower. He must first reconcile Athens, Sparta, Thebes, and Corinth, then make himself the champion of liberty and humanity, the leader of free Hellas, and benefactor of the world. We must not imagine that this was mere dreaming on the part of Isocrates. The aims he had in view were

[1] *Areop.* 56 f.

perfectly real, and proved, in fact, to be nearer the eventual outcome than those of any contemporary. The evils he sought to remove were practical—the financial distress, the over-population, the hordes of mercenaries, and the pirates, who, excepting for the brief supremacies of Athens and Rhodes, and perhaps of Venice, have scourged the Eastern Mediterranean from the times of Homer to the present century.

But Athens was intent on her last fatal war, and was not going to palter with her enemy. Isocrates fell into extreme unpopularity. It is remarkable that even in that suspicious time no enemy ever hinted that he was bribed. They only called him an unpatriotic sophist, a perverter of the statesmen who had been his pupils. Against these attacks we have two answers : the *Panathenaicus*—composed for the Panathenæa of 342, but not finished in time — a confused *rechauffé* of the patriotism of the *Panegyricus*, to which the author no longer really held ; and the speech *On the Exchange of Property*, mentioned above, defending his private activity as a teacher.

One letter more, and the long life breaks. The battle of Chæronea in 338 dazed the outworn old man. It was the triumph of his prophecies ; it made his great scheme possible. Yet it was too much to bear. His country lay in the dust. His champion of united Hellas was rumoured to be sitting drunk on the battle-field among the heroic dead. Isocrates did the last service he could to his country and the world. Philip was absolute victor. No one knew what his attitude would be to the conquered. There is no word of baseness in Isocrates's letter. He does not congratulate Philip on his victory ; he only assumes his good intentions towards Greece, and urges him, now that Hellas is at his feet, to take the great task upon him at last. He saw neither the fulfilment nor the disappointment. Did he commit suicide ? Late tradition says so — Dionysius, Pausanias, Philostratus, Lucian, pseudo-Plutarch, and the *Life*, in unison. At any rate, it is certain that nine days—Aristotle says five days—after Chæronea, Isocrates was dead.

His seven legal speeches are able, and free from chicanery, but they are too 'full-dress' and they do not bite. His letters to the sons of Jason, to Timotheus, and the rulers of Mitylênê, show the real influence which this secluded teacher possessed ; and one inclined to accuse him of servility to his royal correspondents will do well to read the letter of his enemy (Speusippus ?), numbered 30 in the Socratic collection.

We have noticed briefly his relation with Plato.[1] With Aristotle it was something the same. The pupils of the two men developed eventually a violent feud ; the masters respected one another. Plato moved mostly in a different sphere from the teacher of style ; but Aristotle taught rhetoric himself, and is said, in justifying his enterprise, to have parodied a line of Euripides, "*Base to sit dumb, and let barbarians speak*," by substituting 'Isocrates' for 'barbarians.' The strictly scientific method of the *Rhetoric* implies, of course, a criticism of the half-scientific, half-empirical method of Isocrates. But if Aristotle criticises, he also follows. Not only did his first great work, the *Exhortation to Philosophy*,* definitely prefer the Isocratic model to the Platonic, but whenever in his later life he strives after style, it is style according to Isocrates. Also, among previous teachers of rhetoric, Isocrates, though not philosophical enough

---

[1] I cannot think that the 'bald-headed tinker' of *Rep.* vi. is Isocrates.

for Aristotle, was far the most philosophical. In this department, as in every other, he followed the moderate course—he avoided the folly of extremes, or fell between two stools, as one may prefer to phrase it. In a sense his cardinal fault lies in this double-mindedness. Is he a stylist, or is he a political thinker? Is he really advising his country, or is he giving a model exercise to his school? The criticism is not quite fair. It would apply to every orator and stylist, to Grattan, Burke, Cicero, Demosthenes himself. Perhaps the real reason for that curious weariness and irritation which Isocrates generally produces, is partly the intolerance of our own age to formal correctness of the easy and obvious sort. The eighteenth century has done that business for us, and it interests us no longer. Partly it is the real and definite lack in Isocrates of the higher kind of inspiration. He is conceited. He likes a smooth, sensible prose better than Homer. He does not understand poetry, and does not approve of music. It is sins of this kind that mankind ultimately cannot forgive, because they are offences against the eternal element in our life. As to religion in the more definite sense, Isocrates is an interesting type; a moderate as usual, eminently pious, but never superstitious, using religion effectively as an element in his eloquence, and revealing to a close inspection that profound unconscious absence of belief in anything—in providence, in Zeus himself, in philosophy, in principle—which is one of the privileges of the moderate and practical moralist. Yet he was a good and sagacious man, an immense force in literature, and one of the most successful teachers that ever lived.

XVII

DEMOSTHENES AND HIS CONTEMPORARIES

DEMOSTHENES, SON OF DEMOSTHENES, FROM PAIANIA (383–322 B.C.)

DEMOSTHENES lost his father when a boy of seven. His three guardians made away with his property and failed to provide for his mother. It was she that brought him up, a delicate, awkward, and passionate boy, industrious and unathletic. Doubtless the two brooded on their wrongs; and as soon as Demosthenes was legally competent he brought actions against the guardians. They were men of position, connected with the moderate party then in power. They may possibly have had some real defence, but, instead of using it, they tried to browbeat and puzzle the boy by counter-actions and chicanery. When at last he won his case, there was not much property left to recover. The chief results to him were a certain practical skill in law and in speaking, enhanced, it is said, by the lessons of Isæus; a certain mistrust of dignitaries, and a contempt for etiquette. The sordidness, also, of the long quarrel about money offended him. He was by nature lavish; he always gave largely in charity, helped poor citizens to dower their daughters, and ransomed prisoners of war. On this occasion he spent his damages on fitting out a trireme—one of the costliest public services that Athens demanded of her rich citizens; then he settled down to poverty as a speech-writer, and perhaps as a teacher. He succeeded at once in his profession, though his hesitating and awkward delivery interfered with his own speaking. His practice was of the highest kind. He did not deal with 'hetaira' suits like Hyperîdes, and he steadily avoided 'sykophantic' prosecutions, though he both wrote and spoke for the Opposition in cases of political interest.

His first personal appearance was perhaps in 355, *Against Leptines*,[1] who had proposed to abolish public grants of immunity from taxation. It was a prudent financial step, and hard to attack; but these grants were generally rewards for exceptional diplomatic services, and formed an important element in the forward policy advocated by the Opposition.

Eubûlus had taken office after the Social War of 357, when the time called for retrenchment and retreat. His financial policy was an unexampled success; but it meant the resignation of the Empire, and perhaps worse. He had inherited a desultory war with Philip, in which Athens had everything against her. Philip was step by step seizing the Athenian possessions on the shores of Thrace. Eubûlus, since public opinion did not allow him to make peace, replied by a weak blockade of the Macedonian coast and occasional incursions. The hotter heads among the Opposition demanded an army of 30,000 mercenaries to march upon Pella forthwith. This was folly. Demosthenes's own policy was to press the war vigorously until some marked advantage could be gained on which to make a favourable treaty.

But Philip did not yet fill the whole horizon. In the speech *For the Rhodians* (? 351 or 353 B.C.) Demosthenes

[1] Probably Leptînes : see *Class. Review*, Feb. 1898.

urges Athens to help a democratic rising in Rhodes, in the hope of recovering part of her lost influence in the Ægean. Eubûlus was against intervention. In the speech *For Megalopolis* (? 353 B.C.) Demosthenes merely objects to taking a definite side in favour of Sparta. It would have been impossible at the time to give active help to Megalopolis; though perhaps it would have prevented one of the most fatal combinations of the ensuing years, the reliance of the anti-Spartan parts of the Peloponnese upon Philip's support. In 352 Philip had attempted to pass Thermopylæ into Lower Greece; Eubûlus, for once vigorous, had checked him. But the danger had become obvious and acute, and Demosthenes urges it in the *First Philippic*. The king retired northwards and laid siege to Olynthus. Athens knew the immense value of that place, and acted energetically; but the great diplomat paralysed her by stirring up a revolt in Eubœa at the critical moment. Demosthenes, in his three *Olynthiacs*, presses unhesitatingly for the relief of Olynthus. The government took the common-sense or unsanguine view, that Eubœa, being nearer, must be saved first. Eubœa was saved; but Olynthus fell, and Athens was unable to continue the war. When Philocrates introduced proposals of peace, Demosthenes supported him, and was given a place on the commission of ten sent to treat with Philip for terms. He was isolated among the commissioners. The most important of these, after Philocrates, was ÆSCHINES of Kothôkidæ (389–314 B.C.). He was a man of high culture and birth, though the distresses of the war compelled all his family to earn their own livelihood. His father turned schoolmaster; his mother did religious work in connection with some

Mysteries. Æschines himself had been an actor, a profession which carried no slur, and a clerk in the public service. He was a hater of demagogues and a follower of Eubûlus. The three speeches of his which we possess are all connected with Demosthenes and with this embassy.

The negotiations were long. Eventually a treaty was agreed to, containing at least two dangerous ambiguities : it included Athens *and her allies*, and it left each party in possession of what it actually held *at the time*. Now Athens was anxious about two powers, which were allies in a sense, but not subject allies—Kersobleptes, king of a buffer state in Thrace, and the Phokians, any attack on whom would bring Philip into the heart of Greece. Philip's envoys refused to allow any specific mention of these allies in the treaty ; the Athenian commissioners were left to use their diplomacy upon the king himself. And as to the time of the conclusion of the treaty, Athens was bound to peace from the day she took the oaths. Would Philip admit that he was equally bound, or would he go on with his operations till he had taken the oaths himself ? Philocrates and Æschines considered it best to assume the king's good faith as a matter of course, and to conduct their mission according to the ordinary diplomatic routine. Demosthenes pressed for extreme haste. He insisted that they should not wait for Philip at his capital, but seek him out wherever he might be. When the commissioners' passports did not arrive, he dragged them into Macedonia without passports. However, do what he might, long delays occurred ; and, by the time Philip met the ambassadors, he had crushed Kersobleptes and satisfactorily rounded his eastern frontier. Demosthenes made an open breach both with his colleagues and with the king : he refused the customary diplomatic presents, which Philip gave on an exceptionally gorgeous scale ; he absented himself from the official banquet ; he attempted to return home separately. When he reached Athens he moved that the usual ambassador's crown should be withheld from himself and his colleagues.

Before the end of the month Philip had passed Thermopylæ, conquered Phokis, and got himself recognised as a member of the Amphictyonic League with a right to interfere in the politics of Central Greece. The same year (346) he presided at the Pythian Games. The first impulse at Athens was to declare the peace broken ; but that would have been suicidal, as Demosthenes shows in his speech *On the Peace* after the settlement. Still indignation was hot against the ambassadors, and their opponents became active in the law-courts. Demosthenes associated himself with one Timarchus in prosecuting Æschines for misconduct as ambassador. Æschines was in great danger, and retorted by a sharp counter-action against Timarchus,[1] who, though now a leading and tolerably respected politician, had passed an immoral youth. In modern times it would perhaps only have caused a damaging scandal. In Athens it deprived him of all public rights. The unfortunate man collapsed without a word, and Æschines was safe, though it went less well with his friends. Philocrates fled from trial and was condemned. His accuser was HYPERÎDES, son of Glaukippus, an orator considered only second to Demosthenes in power and superior to him in charm. He was an extremist in politics. In private life his wit and his loose ways made him a favourite topic for comedy. The

---

[1] The speech is extant.

traditional *Life* is a mere hash of hostile anecdotes, and a current jest accused him of trying to influence a jury by partially undressing a certain Phrynê in court. His works were absolutely lost till this century, when large parts of five speeches—not eloquent, but surpassing even Lysias in coolness and humour, and a frank dislike of humbug—have been recovered in papyri from Upper Egypt.

Demosthenes himself was engaged in preparing for the future war and trying to counteract Philip's intrigues in the Peloponnese (*Phil. II.*). It was a pity that in 344 he revived the old action against Æschines (*On Misconduct of Ambassadors*). The speeches of both orators are preserved. Æschines appears at his best in them, Demosthenes perhaps at his worst. His attack was intemperate, and his prejudice led him to combine and colour his facts unfairly. He could have shown that Æschines was a poor diplomat; but, in spite of his political ascendency, he could not make the jury believe that he was a corrupt one. Æschines was acquitted, and Demosthenes was not yet secure enough of his power to dispense with publishing his speeches.

We possess one (*On the Chersonnese*) in which he defends the irregularities of his general Diopeithes on Philip's frontier ; and another (*Phil. III.*) in which he issues to all Greece an arraignment of Philip's treacherous diplomacy. Most of Demosthenes's public speeches have the same absence of what we call rhetoric, the same great self-forgetfulness. But something that was once narrow in his patriotism is now gone, and there is a sense of imminent tragedy and a stern music of diction which makes the *Third Philippic* unlike anything else in literature. War was declared in 340, and at first Athens was successful. It was a stroke of religious intrigue that turned the day. The Locrians were induced to accuse Athens of impiety before the Amphictyonic council. Impiety was in Greece, like heresy afterwards, an offence of which most people were guilty if you pressed the inquiry. The Athenians had irregularly consecrated some Theban shields. But the Locrians themselves had profanely occupied the sacred territory of Kirrha. Æschines, who was the Athenian representative, contrived to divert the warlike bigotry of the council against the Locrians. He is very proud of his achievement. But either turn served Philip equally well : he only desired a sacred war of some sort, in order that the Amphictyons, who were without an army, might summon him into Greece as defender of religion. Once inside Thermopylæ, he threw off the mask. Demosthenes obtained at the last moment what he had so long sought, an alliance between Athens and Thebes ; but the Macedonian generalship was too good, and the coalition of Greece lay under Philip's feet at Chæronea in 338.

Athens received the blow with her usual heroism. Lycurgus the treasurer was overwhelmed with voluntary offerings for the defence fund, and the walls were manned for a fight to the death. But that was not Philip's wish. He sent Demâdes the orator, who had been made captive in the battle, to say that he would receive proposals for peace. The friends of Macedon, Phokion, Æschines, and Demâdes, were the ambassadors, and Athens was admitted on easy terms into the alliance which Philip formed as the basis of his march against Persia. Then came a war of the law-courts, the Macedonian party straining every nerve to get rid of the war element. Hyperîdes had proposed, in the first excitement of the defeat, to arm and liberate all slaves. This was unconstitutional, and he was prosecuted by Aristogeiton. His simple confession : "*It was the battle of Chæronea that spoke, not I . . . The arms of Macedon took away my sight*"—was enough to secure his acquittal. A desperate onslaught was made against Demosthenes ; Aristogeiton, Sosicles, Philocrates, Diondas, and Melanthus, among others, prosecuted him. But the city was true to him. Some of the accusers failed to get a fifth of the votes, and he was chosen to make the funeral speech over those slain at Chæronea.[1] Then came the strange counter-campaign of LYCURGUS against the Macedonian party. The man was a kind of Cato. Of unassailable reputation himself, he had a fury for extirpating all that was corrupt and unpatriotic, and his standard was intolerably high. The only speech of his preserved to us is *Against Leocrates*, a person whose crime was that he had left the city after Chæronea, instead of staying to fight and suffer. The penalty demanded for this slight lack of patriotism was death, and the votes were actually equal.

This shows the temper of the city ; but resistance to Macedon was for the time impossible. Athens was content with an opportunist coalition directed by Demosthenes and Demâdes. On Philip's murder a rising was contemplated, but checked by Alexander's promptitude. Soon after, on a rumour that Alexander had been slain in Illyria, Thebes rebelled, and Demosthenes carried a motion for joining her. Army and fleet were prepared, money despatched to Thebes, and an embassy sent to the Great King for Persian aid, when Alexander returned, razed Thebes to the ground, and

---

[1] The extant speech is spurious.

demanded the persons of ten leaders of the war party at Athens, Demosthenes among them. Demâdes, the mediator after Chæronea, acted the same part now. Alexander was appeased by the condemnation of the general Charidêmus ; the other proclaimed persons were spared (335 B.C.).

These repeated failures made Demosthenes cautious. He drew closer to the patient opportunism of Demâdes and gradually alienated the extreme war party. This gave his old enemies the opening for their most elaborate attack. It was indirect and insidious in more ways than one. A certain Ctesiphon—celebrated, according to Æschines, as being the only man who laughed at Demosthenes's jokes—had proposed soon after Chæronea to crown Demosthenes in the theatre of Dionysus in recognition of his public services. Æschines had in the same year indicted Ctesiphon for illegality, but for some reason the trial did not take place till 330. The speech *Against Ctesiphon* rests on three charges : it was illegal to crown an official during his term of office, and Demosthenes held two offices at the time ; secondly, it was against precedent to give crowns in the theatre ; thirdly, Demosthenes was a bad citizen and ought not to be crowned. Obviously, if the third point was to be considered at all, the other two sank into insignificance. The action was a set challenge to Demosthenes, and he came forward as counsel for Ctesiphon (*On the Crown*), to meet it by a full exposition of his political life.

But here comes the insidiousness of Æschines's attack. In the real points at issue between the two policies the country was overwhelmingly on the side of Demosthenes. The burning question was whether the

Demosthenes of the last eight years was true to the
Demosthenes of the *Philippics*. Æschines knows that
the issue of the trial lies with Hyperîdes and the radical
war party, and he plays openly for their support. He
emphasises Demosthenes's connection with the Peace
in the first part of his life. He has the audacity to
accuse him of having neglected three opportunities of
rising against Alexander in the last part! It was well
enough for Alexander's personal friend and tried sup-
porter to use such accusations. Demosthenes could
only answer them by an open profession of treason,
which would doubtless have won his case, and have
sent him prisoner to Macedon. He does not answer
them. He leaves the war party to make its judgment
in silence on the question whether he can have been
false to the cause of his whole life, whether the tone
in which he speaks of Chæronea is like that of a
repentant rebel. It was enough. Æschines failed to
get a fifth of the votes, and left Athens permanently
discredited. He set up a school in Rhodes, and it is
said that Demosthenes supplied him with money when
he was in distress.

But the hostile coalition was not long delayed. In
324 Harpalus, Alexander's treasurer, decamped with a
fleet and 720 talents—full materials for an effective
rebellion. He sought admission at Athens, and the
extremists were eager to receive him. But the time
was in other ways inopportune, and Demosthenes
preferred a subtler game. He carefully avoided any
open breach of allegiance to Alexander. He insisted
that Harpalus should dismiss his fleet, and only agreed
to receive him as a private refugee. When Alexander
demanded his surrender, Demosthenes was able to

refuse as a matter of personal honour, without seriously compromising his relations with the king. The Macedonians insisted that Harpalus should be detained, and the treasure stored in the Parthenon in trust for Alexander. Demosthenes agreed to both proposals, and moved them in the Assembly himself. What happened next is not known, but Harpalus suddenly escaped, and the Macedonians insisted on having the treasure counted. It was found to be less than half the original sum. That it was going in secret preparations for war, they could have little doubt. They would have liked a state trial and some instant executions. Demosthenes managed to get the question entrusted to the Areopagus, and the report deferred. It had to come at last. The Areopagus made no statement of the uses to which the money was applied, but gave a list of the persons guilty of appropriating it, Demosthenes at the head. His intrigue had failed, and he had given the friends of Macedon their chance. He was prosecuted by Hyperîdes on the one side, DEINARCHUS on the other. The latter, a Corinthian by birth, rose into fame by this process, and nothing has survived of him except the three speeches relating to it. Dionysius calls him a 'barley Demosthenes,' whatever that may mean—the suggestion is probably 'beer' as opposed to 'wine'— and his tone in this speech is one of brutal exultation. Very different, suspiciously different, is Hyperîdes, who not only says nothing to make a permanent breach, but even calls attention to Demosthenes's great position, to the unsolved problem of what he meant to do with the money, to the possibility that his lips are in some way sealed. For his own part, Hyperîdes talks frank treason with a coolness which well bears out the stories of his courage. Demosthenes was convicted, and condemned to a fine of fifty talents. Unable to pay such an enormous sum, he withdrew to Troizên.

Nine months after, Alexander died and Greece rose. Demosthenes joined his accuser Hyperîdes in a mission to rouse the Peloponnese, and was reinstated at Athens amid the wildest enthusiasm. The war opened well. The extant *Funeral Speech* of Hyperîdes was pronounced after the first year of it. In 322 came the defeat at Crannon. The Macedonian general Antipater demanded the persons of Demosthenes and Hyperîdes. Old Demâdes, unable to mediate any more, now found himself drawing up the decree sentencing his colleague to death. Demosthenes had taken refuge in the temple of Poseidon at Calauría, where he was arrested, and took poison. Hyperîdes is said to have been tortured, a statement which would be incredible but for the flood of crime and cruelty which the abolition of liberty, and the introduction of Northern and Asiatic barbarism, let loose upon the Greek world in the next centuries.

Demosthenes has never quite escaped from the stormy atmosphere in which he lived. The man's own intensity is infectious, and he has a way of forcing himself into living politics. The Alexandrian schools were monarchical, and thought ill of him. To Grote he was the champion of freedom and democracy. To Niebuhr (1804), Philip was Napoleon, and Demosthenes the ideal protest against him. Since 1870, now that monarchical militarism has changed its quarters, German scholars[1] seem oppressed by the likeness between Demosthenes and Gambetta, and denounce the policy of '*la revanche*';

[1] *E.g.* Rohrmoser, Weidner, and even Beloch and Holm. The technical critics are Spengel and Blass.

one of them is reminded also of 'the agitator Gladstone.' In another way the technical critics have injured the orator's reputation by analysing his methods of arrangement and rhythm, and showing that he avoids the concourse of more than two short syllables. There is a *naïf* barbarism in many of us which holds that great pains taken over the details of a literary work imply insincerity.

It is not for us to discuss the worth of his policy. It depends partly on historical problems, partly on the value we attach to liberty and culture, and the exact point of weakness at which we hold a man bound to accept and make the best of servitude to a moral inferior. Athens, when she had suffered the utmost, and when the case for submission had been stated most strongly, decided that it was well to have fought and failed.

As for his methods, the foolish tendency to take his political speeches as statements of historical fact, has produced a natural reaction, in which critics pounce fiercely upon the most venial inaccuracies. Holm, for instance, finds "three signal falsehoods" in "that masterpiece of sophistry, the third *Philippic*" : viz., the statement that when Philip took certain towns he had already sworn the truce—whereas really he had only made the other side swear it ; the suggestion that Philip's rapid movements were due to his using light-armed troops— which is true, but seems to ignore his heavy phalanx ; and the charge that he came to the Phokians 'as an ally,' when in truth he had left his intentions designedly ambiguous. The critic who complains of such misstatements as these, must have somewhat Arcadian notions of political controversy.

Demosthenes is guilty, without doubt, of breaches of etiquette and convention. He prosecuted his fellow-ambassadors.   He appeared in festal attire on hearing of Philip's assassination, though he had just lost his only daughter.   In the prelude to the last war, Philip's action was often the more correct, as was that of another Philip in dealing with William of Orange.   In Demosthenes's private speech-writing we are struck by one odd change of front.   In 350 he wrote for Phormio against Apollodôrus in a matter of the great Bank with which they were both connected, and won his case.   Next year he wrote for Apollodôrus, prosecuting one of his own previous witnesses, Stephanus, for perjury, and making a violent attack on Phormio's character. The probability is that Demosthenes had made discoveries about his previous client which caused him to regret that he had ever supported him—among them, perhaps, the discovery that Stephanus was giving false evidence.   The only external fact bearing on the problem is the coincidence that in the same year Apollodôrus, at some personal risk, proposed the measure on which Demosthenes had set his heart—the use of the Festival Fund for war purposes—and that he remained afterwards attached to Demosthenes.   The Mîdias case is a clear instance of the subordination of private dignity to public interest.   Mîdias was a close friend of Eubûlus, and had both persecuted and assaulted Demosthenes when he was Chorêgus at the great Dionysia.   Demosthenes prepared to take action, and wrote the vehement speech which we possess (*Against Mîdias*), in which he declares that nothing will satisfy him but the utmost rigour of the law.   But meantime there arose the negotiations for the peace of 346, and Demosthenes had to act in concert with Eubûlus.   He accepted an apology and compensation, and let the matter drop.

We must never forget in reading Demosthenes and Æschines, that we are dealing with an impetuous Southern nation in the agony of its last struggle. The politenesses and small generosities of politics are not there. There is no ornamental duelling. The men fight with naked swords, and mean business. Demosthenes thought of his opponents, not as statesmen who made bad blunders, but as perjured traitors who were selling Greece to a barbarian. They thought him, not, indeed, a traitor—that was impossible—but a malignant and insane person who prevented a peaceful settlement of any issue. The words 'treason' and 'bribe' were bandied freely about; but there is hardly any proved case of treason, and none of bribery, unless the Harpalus case can by a stretch of language be called so. There are no treasury scandals in Athens at this time. There is no legal disorder. There is a singular absence of municipal corruption. The Athenians whom Demosthenes reproaches with self-indulgence, were living at a strain of self-sacrifice and effort which few civilised communities could bear. The wide suspicion of bribery was caused chiefly by the bewilderment of Athens at finding herself in the presence of an enemy far her superior both in material force and in diplomacy. Why was she so incomprehensibly worsted in wars, where she won most of the battles? Why were her acutest statesmen invariably outwitted by a semi-barbarous king? Somebody must be betraying her! Demosthenes on this point loses all his balance of mind. He lives in a world peopled by imaginary traitors. We hear how he rushed at one Antiphon in the streets, and seized him with his own hands. Happily the jurors did not lose their sanity. There were almost no convictions. It was very similar in Italy before and after 1848. People whose patriotism was heroic went about accusing one another of treason. The men of 404, 338, and even 262, will not easily find their superiors in devotion and self-sacrifice.

Another unpleasant result of this suspicion and hatred is the virulence of abuse with which the speakers of the time attack their enemies. Not, indeed, in public speeches. In those of Demosthenes no opponent is even mentioned. But in the law-courts, which sometimes gave the finishing stroke to a political campaign, the attacks on character are savage. The modern analogue is the raking up of more or less irrelevant scandals against both witnesses and principals in cases at law, which custom allows to barristers of the highest character. The attack on Æschines in the *De Corona* is exceptional. Demosthenes had a real and natural hatred for the man. But he would never have dragged in his father and mother and his education, if Æschines had not always prided himself on these particular things —he was distinctly the social superior of Demosthenes, and a man of high culture—and treated Demosthenes as the vulgar demagogue. Even thus, probably Demosthenes repented of his witticisms about the old lady's private initiations and 'revivals.' It is to be wished that scholars would repent of their habit of reading unsavoury meanings into words which do not possess them.

Demosthenes can never be judged apart from his circumstances. He is no saint and no correct mediocrity. He is a man of genius and something of a hero; a fanatic, too, no doubt, and always a politician. He represents his country in that combination of intellectual subtlety and practical driving power with fervid idealism, that union of passion with art, and that invariable insistence on the moral side of actions, on the Just and the Noble, that characterises most of the great spirits of Greek literature. To say with Quintilian that Demosthenes was a 'bad man,' is like saying the same of Burke or even of Isaiah. It implies either that noble words and thoughts are not nobility, or else, what is hardly more plausible, that the greatest expressions of soul in literature can be produced artificially by a dodge. Two sentences of Demosthenes ring in the ears of those who care for him, as typical of the man : *" Never, never, Athenians, can injustice and oath - breaking and falsehood make a strong power. They hold out for once and for a little; they blossom largely in hopes, belike; but time finds them out and they wither where they stand. As a house and a ship must be strongest at the lowest parts, so must the bases and foundations of a policy be true and honest; which they are not in the diplomatic gains of Macedon."* [1]

" It cannot be, Athenians, that you did wrong when you took upon you the battle for the freedom and safety of all. No, by our fathers who first met the Mede at Marathon, by the footmen of Plataea, by the sailors of Salamis and Artemisium, by all the brave men lying in our national sepulchres—whom the city has interred with honour, Æschines, all alike, not only the successful or the victorious !" [2]

---

[1] *Olynth.* 2. 10.   [2] *Crown*, 208.

XVIII

THE LATER LITERATURE, ALEXANDRIAN AND ROMAN

I

FROM THE DEATH OF DEMOSTHENES TO THE BATTLE OF ACTIUM

AMONG the many stereotyped compliments which we are in the habit of paying to Greek literature, we are apt to forget its singular length of life. From the prehistoric origins of the epos to Paul the Silentiary and Musæus in the sixth century after Christ there is not an age devoid of delightful and more or less original poetry. From Hecatæus to the fall of Byzantium there is an almost uninterrupted roll of historians, and in one sense it might be held that history did not find its best expression till the appearance of Polybius in the second century B.C. Philosophy is even more obviously rich in late times ; and many will hold that if the greatest individual thinkers of Greece are mostly earlier than Plato, the greatest achievements of speculation are not attained before the times of Epictêtus and Plotînus. The literature of learning and science only begins at the point where the present book leaves off. It may even be said that the greatest factor in imaginative literature, Love, has been kept out of its rights all through the

Attic period, and that Mimnermus and Sappho have to wait for Theocritus to find their true successor.

Yet the death of Demosthenes marks a great dividing line. Before it Greek literature is a production absolutely unique ; after it, it is an ordinary first-rate literature, like Roman or French or Italian. Of course it is impossible to draw a strict line between creation and adaptation ; but, in the ordinary sense of the words, the death of Demosthenes forms a period before which Greek poets, writers, thinkers, and statesmen were really creating, were producing things of which there was no model in the world ; after which they were only adapting and finishing, producing things like other things which already existed.

That is one great division ; the other is similar to it. We have seen how the crash of 404 B.C. stunned the hopes of Athens, dulled her faith in her own mission and in human progress generally. Chæronea and Crannon stamped out such sparks as remained. Athens and intellectual Greece were brought face to face with the apparent fact that Providence sides with the big battalions, that material force is ultimately supreme. Free political life was over. Political speculation was of no use, because the military despots who held the world were not likely to listen to it. Even Aristotle, who had been Alexander's tutor, and was on friendly terms with him, treats him and his conquests and his system as utterly out of relation to any rational constitution of society. The events of the next two centuries deepened this impression, and political aspirations as a motive in life and literature came to an end for Greece. Of course many ages and peoples have done very well without any freedom in public action or speech or thought.

But these things were in the heart fibres of the Greek race, and it pined when deprived of them.

The middle ages and the East made up for their absence of public interests by enthusiastic religious faith. But this solace likewise was denied the later Greek. The traditional religion was moribund among educated men in the fifth century ; after the fourth it was hardly worth attacking. People knew it was nonsense, but considered it valuable for the vulgar ; and, above all, they asked each thinker if he had anything to put in its place. Much of the intellect of the fourth century is thrown into answering this demand. On the one hand we find Athens full of strange faiths, revived or imported or invented ; superstition is a serious fact in life. One could guess it from the intense earnestness of Epicurus on the subject, or from the fact that both Antiphanes and Menander wrote comedies upon *The Superstitious Man*. But the extant inscriptions are direct evidence. On the other hand came the great philosophical systems. Three of these were especially religious, resembling the sixth century rather than the fifth. The Cynics cared only for virtue and the relation of the soul to God ; the world and its learning and its honours were as dross to them. The Stoics and Epicureans, so far apart at first sight, were very similar in their ultimate aim. What they really cared about was ethics—the practical question how a man should order his life. Both indeed gave themselves to some science —the Epicureans to physics, the Stoics to logic and rhetoric—but only as a means to an end. The Stoic tried to win men's hearts and convictions by sheer subtlety of abstract argument and dazzling sublimity of thought and expression. The Epicurean was determined to make Humanity go its way without cringing to capricious gods and without sacrificing Free-Will. He condensed his gospel into four maxims : "God is not to be feared ; death cannot be felt ; the Good can be won ; all that we dread can be borne and conquered."

Two great systems remained, more intellectual and less emotional : the Academy, which, after the death of its founder and Speusippus, turned from paradoxical metaphysics in the direction of a critical and sceptical eclecticism ; and the Lyceum or Peripatos, whose organisation of knowledge formed the greatest intellectual feat of the age. Its founder, ARISTOTELES of Stagîros, in Chalcidice (384–322 B.C.), stands in character, as well as in date, midway between the Athenian philosopher and the Alexandrian *savant*. He came to Athens at the age of seventeen, and stayed for twenty years. But he had grown up under the shadow of Macedon, his father having been physician to Amyntas II.; he had no democratic sympathies, and the turmoil of Athenian politics was unmeaning to him. In his first published work, a letter in the style of Isocrates, he declared for the 'contemplative life' as opposed to the practical, and remained true to his principles all his days.[1] Plato was his chief philosophical teacher ; but he was an omnivorous lover of knowledge, and spent his energies not only on the history of previous philosophy, on the mathematical researches of Eudoxus and the mysticism of the Pythagoreans, but on such detailed studies as the compilation of the Didascaliæ (see p. 249) and the morphological structure of gourds. His relations with his master are illustrated by the celebrated sentence in the *Ethics* about Plato and Truth : *"Both being dear, I am*

[1] προτρεπτικὸs εἰs φιλοσοφίαν.

bound to prefer Truth."   A more fervid or less original
disciple, Speusippus, for instance, would not have treated
the two as antithetic.   On Plato's death in 347, Speusippus was chosen head of the Academy ; and Aristotle
found it tactful to leave Athens, accompanied by Xenocrates, who afterwards succeeded Speusippus.   He spent
three years at Assos, in Mysia, and married Pythias, the
niece of the dynast there, under romantic circumstances,
having somehow rescued her during a revolt.   It was in
343 that he was invited to Pella by Philip, and became
tutor to the young Alexander, then aged seventeen.

Nothing is known of those lessons.   One fears there
was little in common between the would-be rival of
Achilles and the great expounder of the ' contemplative
life,' except the mere possession of transcendent abili-
ties.   Aristotle's real friend seems to have been Philip.
He had perhaps caught something of that desire for a
converted prince which played such tricks with Plato
and Isocrates.   He had made attempts on two small
potentates before Philip—Themison of Cyprus, and his
wife's uncle, Hermeias.   A year after Philip's death,
Aristotle returned to Athens, and Alexander marched
against the Persian Empire.   Aristotle had always disapproved of the plan of conquering the East.   It was
not 'contemplative.'   And even his secondary piece of
advice, that the conqueror should be a ' leader ' to the
Greeks and a ' master ' to the barbarians, was rejected
by Alexander, who ostentatiously refused to make any
difference between them.   There was a private difficulty,
too, of a worse kind : one Callisthenes, whom Aristotle
left as spiritual adviser in his stead, was afterwards implicated in a supposed conspiracy and put to death.
But there was no open quarrel.   It was probably at this

time (335) that Aristotle founded his school of philosophy
in a building with a ' peripatos' or covered walk, near the
grove of Apollo Lykeios, just outside Athens. It was an
institution in some respects less near to the Academy than
to the Alexandrian libraries, and, like them, was probably
helped by royal generosity. Aristotle's omnivorous learning and genius for organisation had their full scope. He
surrounded himself with fellow - students—συμφιλοσοφοῦντες—directed them to various special collections and
researches ; admitted differences of opinion in them, and
exercised the right of free criticism himself ; and so built
that gigantic structure of organised and reasoned knowledge which has been the marvel of succeeding ages.

Aristotle's writings were divided by the later Peripatetics into ἐξωτερικοὶ and ἀκροαματικοὶ λόγοι—works for
publication and lecture materials. His reputation in
antiquity was based entirely on the former class, especially on the semi-popular dialogues; and it is a curious
freak of history that, with the possible exception of the
Constitution of Athens, not one work of this whole class
is now preserved. In our Aristotle we have no finished
and personal works of art like the dialogues of Plato.
We have only ὑπομνήματα—the notes and memoranda
of the school. That explains the allusive and elliptical
style, the anecdotes and examples, which are suggested
but not stated ; it also explains the repetitions and
overlappings and occasional contradictions. Divers of
the συμφιλοσοφοῦντες have contributed matter, and the
lectures have been repeated and worked over by various
'scholarchs.' Aristotle's *Rhetoric*, for instance, was based
on the collections of his disciple Theodectes, and expanded again by his successor Theophrastus. The
Physics count as Aristotle; the *Botany* and *Mineralogy*,

as Theophrastus; but both men were obviously concerned in both. In the *Ethics* there are clear traces of three separate teachers—the master himself, Eudêmus, and another. The *Metaphysics* and *Logic* must have had their main speculative lines laid by Aristotle's original speculations. The *Poetics* seem to give his personal reply to the challenge which Plato had thrown to "some one not a poet, but a friend of poetry, to give in plain prose" some justification of the senseless thing.[1] But in all of these works there are additions and comments by other teachers. In political science the school collected and analysed 158 different existing constitutions. Aristotle himself did Athens and Sparta; but he published his great theoretic treatise on *Politics* before his collectors had nearly finished their work.

Fifty years after Aristotle's death the 'Peripatos' had become an insignificant institution, and the master's writings were but little read till the taste for them revived in the Roman period. For one thing, much of his work was of the pioneer order, the kind that is quickly superseded, because it has paved the way by which others may advance. Again, organised research requires money, and the various 'diadochi,' or successors of Alexander, kept their endowments for their own capitals. Above all, the aim of universal knowledge was seen—nay, was proved by Aristotle's own experience—to be beyond human powers. The great organisations of Alexandria were glad to spend upon one isolated subject, such as ancient literature or mechanics, more labour and money than the Lyceum could command in its search for Encyclopædic wisdom. Even a great 'polymath' like Eratosthenes is far from Aristotle.

[1] *Rep.* 607.

Athens remained the headquarters of philosophy; but literature in the ordinary sense was gradually attracted to places where it could find high salaries and repose. Even in the great period, poets had collected in the courts of Hiero at Syracuse and Archelaus at Pella. The real superiority of Athens to such retreats was the freedom which it allowed in thought and speech, and the close sympathy and community of culture between the writer and his public; and, moreover, through most of the fifth century Athens must have been the safest and most orderly place of residence in the world. It was less so in the fourth century. There was more safety in the capitals of the great monarchs, behind line upon line of trained armies. Pella was safe; so was Antioch; so, after the expulsion of the Gauls, was Pergamus; so, above all, was Alexandria. And as for the sympathetic public, it was ceasing to exist anywhere. It was always incumbent on a writer to be cultured, and the standard of culture had by this time become uncomfortably high. Books were increasingly written for those who had read all the existing books, and were scarcely intelligible to those who had not. The poet of the third century—nay, even a man like Antimachus long before—only expected to be read by people of his own sort, people with enough leisure and learning to follow easily his ways of thought.

One form of pure literature, Comedy, was faithful to its birthplace. The Athenian lightness of wit, freedom of speech, and dramatic spirit could not bear transplanting. The Middle and New Comedy represented, probably, the most spontaneous and creative work of their age in the domain of pure literature. The division between the two periods is not well marked. The Middle

Comedy is dated roughly from 400 to the death of Alexander, in 336, and is characterised by a love of parody and the ridicule of poets and myths. The New, as we have said above, extended its sphere to all the subjects of ordinary life. The plots are well constructed, and often convincing. The reigns of the 'diadochi' formed a time full of adventure and intrigue, and real life supplied the stage with soldiers of fortune, kidnapped maidens, successful adventurers, and startling changes of fate, as well as with parasites and 'hetairai.' The diction, too, has an air of reality. It is a language based on life, and keeping close to life, utterly remote from the artificial beauty of the contemporary epics and elegies. It aims at being 'urbane and pure' as well as witty; but it is not highly studied. ANTIPHANES and ALEXIS, of the Middle Comedy, wrote over two hundred plays each; MENANDER and PHILÊMON, over two hundred between them. Much is said about the low moral tone of the New Comedy—on the whole, unjustly. The general sympathies of the poets are healthy enough; only they shrink from all high notes, and they do perhaps fail to see the dramatic and imaginative value of the noblest sides of life. Menander himself was a close friend of Epicurus, and shocked people by 'praising pleasure.' The talent and energy devoted to descriptions of eating and drinking in the Middle Comedy are sometimes cited as a symptom of the grossness of the age. But a feast was one of the traditional elements in comedy; how could a 'kômôidia' go without its 'kômos'? Our evidence, too, is misleading, because it comes chiefly from the *Banquet-Philosophers* of Athenæus, a book which specially ransacked antiquity for quotations and anecdotes upon convivial subjects. And, above all, it is well to remember that the Middle Comedy began in years of dearth, and all literature shows us how half-starved men gloat upon imaginary banquets. There is as much suffering as jollification behind some of these long lists of fishes and entrées.

Romantic and adventurous love formed a prominent motive in the plots of the New Comedy, and such love, under the conditions of the time, was generally found among troubled circumstances and damaged characters. In satirical pieces the heroine herself is often a 'hetaira.' In a great many more she is rescued from the clutches of 'hetairai' and their associates. In a few, it would seem, she has 'a past,' but is nevertheless allowed to be 'sympathetic.' In one or two, like the *Amastris* of Diphilus, she is a virtuous, or at least a respectable, princess, and the play itself is really a historic drama. Certainly the sentimental interest was usually greater than the comic.

Philêmon ultimately went to Alexandria, and Machon lived there ; but they were exceptions. Menander himself stayed always in Athens. Our conception of the man is drawn as much from his famous statue, and from the imaginary letters written in his name by the sophist Alkiphron (about 200 A.D.), as from his own numerous but insignificant fragments. Very skilful the letters are, and make one fond of the cultured, critical, easy-natured man, loving nothing much except literature and repose and his independence, and refusing to live at the Alexandrian court for any salary, or to write down to the public in order to win as many prizes as Philêmon.

The same adventurous love interest which pervaded comedy also raised the elegiac and epic poetry of the

time to its highest imaginative achievements. The late
Greek elegy was not only a thing of singular beauty, it
was also a great literary influence ; and Callimachus,
Euphorion, and Philêtas are the chief inspirers of the
long-lived Roman elegy. PHILÊTAS, a younger contemporary of Demosthenes, is perhaps the first typical
Alexandrian elegist ; a pale student, wasted in body,
who "would have been blown away if he had not
worn leaden soles to his boots" ; a Homeric critic ;
tutor to Ptolemy II. and to Theocritus ; a writer of
love elegies, which he called by the name of his own
beloved 'Bittis,' and of an idyll about Odysseus and
Polymêlê. He and ASCLÊPIADES, whose graceful love-
verses are well represented in the Anthology, were the
only poets of this age whom Theocritus frankly confessed to be his superiors. A friend of Philêtas, HERMÊ-
SIANAX, has left us one long fragment, giving little more
than a list of bygone lovers, which will have startled
many readers of Athenæus by a certain echoing and
misty charm. CALLIMACHUS, librarian, archæologist,
critic, and poet, was perhaps the most influential per-
sonality in literature between Plato and Cicero. He
realised and expressed what his age wanted, and what
it was able to achieve. The creative time had gone ;
it was impossible to write like Homer or Hesiod or
Æschylus ; they suited their epoch, we must suit ours,
and not make ourselves ridiculous by attempting to
rival them on their own ground. What we can do is to
write short unambitious poems, polished and perfected
in every line. The actual remains of Callimachus are disappointing, save for a few fine epigrams, and the elegy on
the *Bathing of Pallas*. For the rest, a certain wit and
coldness, a certain obviousness in reaching effects, spoil

the poetry of the great critic ; and after ages, on the whole, will care more for the unsuccessful rebel, Apollonius, who refused to accept his veto.

APOLLONIUS attempted an epic in the old style, long, rather ambitious, absolutely simple in construction, and unepigrammatic in language. That was the kind of poetry he liked, and he meant to write it himself. The *Argonautica* failed in Alexandria, and Apollonius left the country for Rhodes, where he worked up a second version of his poem. He had a small band of admirers in his lifetime ; but taste in general followed Callimachus in favour of the brief and brilliant style. Even Catullus and Propertius were Callimacheans. It was for Vergil to conquer the world with a poem in Apollonius's spirit, with much of its structure and language borrowed line by line from him. Of course Vergil had in a sense a 'call' to write the national epic of his country, whereas no one had called upon Apollonius to celebrate the Argonauts ; and this in itself gives Vergil a superior interest. But the Medea and Jason of the *Argonautica* are at once more interesting and more natural than their copies, the Dido and Æneas of the *Æneid*. The wild love of the witch-maiden sits curiously on the queen and organiser of industrial Carthage ; and the two qualities which form an essential part of Jason —the weakness which makes him a traitor, and the deliberate gentleness which contrasts him with Medea —seem incongruous in the father of Rome. There are perhaps two passages which might be selected as specially characteristic of Alexandrian poetry. One would be the protest of Callimachus :[1] " *Great is the sweep of the river of Assyria ; but it bears many scourings of earth on the flood of it, and much driftwood to the sea. Apollo's bees draw not*

---

[1] Call. *Hymn Apollo,* 107 ff.

their water everywhere : a little dew from a holy fount, the
highest bloom of the flower."   The other would be Medea's
answer when Jason proposes to plead for mercy with her
father Aiêtes, and to make covenant for her hand, as
Theseus once sued for Ariadne from Minos :—

> " *Speak not of ruth nor pact.   They dwell not here.*
> *Aiêtes keeps no bond, nor knows no fear,*
> *Nor walks with men as Minos walked of old ;*
> *And I am no Greek princess gentle-souled.*
> *—One only thing : when thou art saved and free,*
> *Think of Medea, and I will think of thee*
> *Always, though all forbid.   And be there heard*
> *Some voice from far away, or some wild bird*
> *Come crying on the day I am forgot.*
> *Or may the storm-winds hear, and spurn me not,*
> *And lift me in their arms through wastes of sky*
> *To face thee in thy falseness, and once cry,*
> *' I saved thee.'   Yea, a-sudden at thy hall*
> *And hearthstone may I stand when those days fall.*

Apollonius is, of course, subject to the vices of his
age.   He has long picture-like descriptions, he has a
tiresome amount of pseudo - Homeric language, he
has passages about the toilette of Aphrodite and the
archery of Eros which might have been written by
Ovid or Cowley.   But there is a genuine originality
and power of personal observation and feeling in him ;
witness the similes about the Oriental child-wife whose
husband is killed, the wool-worker bending over the fire
for light as she labours before sunrise, the wild thoughts
that toss in Medea's heart like the reflected light dancing
from troubled water, the weird reaping of the Earth-
children in the fire of sunset—which force us to admit that
in him Greece found expression for things that had been
mute ever before.   And for romantic love on the higher
side he is without a peer even in the age of Theocritus.

THEOCRITUS is perhaps the most universally attractive of all Greek poets. It is common to find young students who prefer him to Homer, and most people are conscious of a certain delighted surprise when they first make his acquaintance. In his own sweet and lowly domain he is absolute monarch; one might almost say that there is hardly anything beautiful in the pastoral poetry of the world that does not come from Theocritus. His first idyll, the *Dirge on Daphnis*, has perhaps had a greater number of celebrated imitations than any poem of its length in existence—from Bion's *Adonis*, Moschus's *Bion*, Vergil's *Daphnis*, to our own *Lycidas*, *Adonais*, and *Thyrsis*.

That habit of retrospect, that yearning over the past, which pervades all the poetry, though not the scientific work, of Alexandria, is peculiarly marked in Theocritus. There are poems in plenty about the present; there are even poems about the future, and the hopes which the poet reposes in his patrons. But the present is rather ugly and the future unreal. The true beauty of Theocritus's world lies in the country life of the past. The Sicilian peasants of his own day, it has been well remarked, were already far on the road to becoming the agricultural slave population of the Roman Empire, "that most miserable of all proletariats." Yet even long afterwards, under the oppression of Verres, they were known for their cheerfulness and songfulness; and it is probable that the rustic bards whom we meet in Theocritus are not mere figments of the imagination. It was in the old Sicilian poetry of Stêsichorus that the type first appeared. The Sicilian villager, like the Provençal, the Roumanian, and the Highlander, seems to have taken verse-making and singing as part of the ordinary business of life.

There is such unity of style and atmosphere in Theocritus that one easily overlooks the great variety of his
subjects. We call his poems 'Idylls,' and expect them
to be 'idyllic.' But in origin the word εἰδύλλιον is merely
the diminutive of εἶδος, 'form' or 'style'; and our use of
the name appears to come from the practice of heading
these pastoral poems with the musical direction εἰδύλλιον
βουκολικὸν, or αἰπολικὸν, 'cow-herd style,' or 'goat-herd
style,' or whatever the case might require. Only ten of
the thirty-two Idylls of Theocritus which have come down
to us are strictly about pastoral life, real or idealised;
six are epic, two are written for 'occasions,' two are
addresses to patrons, six are definite love-poems, and four
are realistic studies of common life. The most famous
of these last is the *Adôniazûsæ* (Id. xv.), a mime describing the mild adventures of two middle-class Syracusan
women, Gorgo and Praxinoa, at the great feast of
Adonis celebrated at Alexandria by Ptolemy II. The
piece is sometimes acted in Paris, and has some real
beauty amid its humorous but almost unpleasant close-
ness to life. There is not so much beauty in the preceding mime (xiv.) with its brief sketch of the kind of
thing that drives young men to enlist for foreign service;
but there is perhaps even more depth and truth, and, we
must add, more closely-studied vulgarity. The second
Idyll, narrating the unhappy love of Simætha and her
heart-broken sorceries, is hard to classify: it is realistic,
beautiful, tragic, strangely humorous, and utterly unfor-
gettable. It does for the heart of life what the ordinary
mime does for the surface; and, in spite of several
conscious imitations, has remained a unique masterpiece
in literature. Three poems appear to express the poet's
personal feelings; they are addressed to his squire, and

represent, perhaps, in their serious and gentle idealism,
the highest level reached by that species of emotion. It
is one of these (Id. xxix.) that formulates the oft-repeated
sentiment about the place of love or deep friendship
in life :

> " *A single nest built in a single tree,*
> *Where no wild crawling thing shall ever climb.*"

The appeals to Hiero and Ptolemy are as good as such
appeals are entitled to be ; and the little epics, reminding
one in form of the expanded *Eoiai*, are never without
passages of exquisite charm and freshness in the midst of
a certain general frigidity. The two occasional poems,
one describing a country walk in Cos upon a day of
fruit-gathering, the other accompanying a present of a
distaff to the wife of the poet's friend, Nikias, are not only
gems in themselves, but leave the fragrance of a lovable
character behind them.

The other bucolic poets, BION and MOSCHUS, are
confessed imitators of Theocritus. Bion was a younger
contemporary of his model, and probably wrote his
Dirge of Adonis for the particular festival referred to in
the *Adôniazûsæ*. The *Dirge* is a magnificent piece of
work in its way ; florid, unreal, monotonous, almost
oriental in its passionate and extravagant imagery, it
exactly suits the subject for which it was composed.
There is very likely no genuine emotion whatever at the
back of it ; but it carries the imagination by storm, and
was calculated to leave such persons as Gorgo and
Praxithea in floods of tears. Moschus represents himself as a pupil of Bion ; and is said to have been a friend
of Aristarchus, though his style suggests the product of
a later time. It is as ornate as that of a Silver-Age

2 B

Roman, and as full of those little phrases that smack of the Gradus and suggest self-satisfaction—Bion is "*the Dorian Orpheus,*" Homer is "*that sweet mouth of Calliopê.*" Yet his bad manner cannot hide his inborn gifts. Among the innumerable echoes of the Greek pastoral which are still ringing in the ears of modern Europe, a good many come from Moschus's *Lament for Bion ;* for instance, Matthew Arnold's dream, to

> "*Make leap up with joy the beauteous head*
> *Of Proserpine, among whose crownèd hair*
> *Are flowers first opened on Sicilian air ;*
> *And flute his friend, like Orpheus, from the dead.*"

The other great mark of the Alexandrian epos and elegy, besides the love interest, was the learned interest. There were numerous archæological poems. RHIÂNUS wrote on the Messenian Wars, making a kind of Wallace out of Aristomenes. Callimachus wrote four elegiac books of *Aitia* or 'Origins,' and an antiquarian epos '*Hecalê,*' centring upon Theseus and the Bull of Marathon, but admitting many digressions. There were still more philosophical poems. ARÂTUS of Soli wrote on *Phænomena* or 'Things Seen in the Sky,' with an appendix on the signs of the weather ; Nicander, on natural history, and on poisons and antidotes, as well as on the origins and legends of various cities. Neither of these two poets appeals much to our own age, which prefers its science pure, untempered with make-believe. The extraordinary influence and reputation enjoyed by Arâtus in antiquity appear to be due to the fact that he succeeded in annexing, so to speak, as his private property, one of the great emotions of mankind. In the centuries following him it almost seems as if no cultured man was capable of looking long at the stars without

murmuring a line from the *Phænomena*. The greatest
man of learning of the whole Ptolemaic age, ERATOS-
THENES, kept his geography and chronology, and his
works on the Old Comedy, to a prose form. His
little epos about the death and avenging of Hesiod, and
his elegy *Erigonê*, are on legendary and what we should
call ' poetical 'subjects.

In Prose, learning and research set the prevailing tone.
The marches of Alexander had thrown open an immense
stretch of the world to Greek science, and the voyages
of his admiral Nearchus, and of men like Polemon and
Pytheas, completely altered ancient geography. Our
chief handbooks are a *Tour of the World* and a *Periplûs*
or 'Voyage-round' various coasts, current under the
names of SKYMNUS and SKYLAX respectively. The scientific organisation of geography was carried out by men
like Eratosthenes and Hipparchus, involving the invention of systems for calculating latitude and longitude, and
the use of trigonometry. Mathematics, pure and applied,
were developed by a great number of distinguished men,
including EUCLID, in the time of Ptolemy I., and ARCHI-
MÊDES, who died in 212. Mechanics — the machines
being largely of wood, and the motive power generally
water or mere gravitation, though in some cases steam—
flourished both for military purposes and for ordinary
uses of life. There is a curious passage in the extant
works of HÊRO, describing a marionette-machine, which
only required setting at the beginning to perform unaided a four-act tragedy, including a shipwreck and a
conflagration.

Learning was very especially applied to literature.
There were two great libraries in Alexandria—the first
by the museum and the palace ; the second, both in age

and importance, near the temple of Serâpis.   They were projected by the first Ptolemy with the help of Dêmê-trius of Phalêrum, actually organised by the second (Philadelphus); and they formed the centre of culture for the next centuries.   Zenodotus, Callimachus, Eratos-thenes, Aristophanes of Byzantium, and Aristarchus were the first five librarians ; what institution has ever had such a row of giants at its head ?   The most immediate work of these libraries was to collect and preserve books ; every ship visiting Alexandria was searched for them, and neither money nor intrigue was spared in acquiring them.   The next task was to form a *catalogue raisonné*— the work mainly of Callimachus, in 120 volumes ;[1] the next, to separate the genuine works from the spurious, and to explain the difficult and obsolete writers.   The other kings of the time formed libraries too, that of the Attalids at Pergamus being the most famous.   Pergamus was a greater centre of art than even Alexandria, but in literature proper it was at a disadvantage.   It had started too late, when Alexandria had snapped up most of the unique books.   It had no papyrus.   The plant only grew in Egypt, and the Ptolemies forbade the export of it ; so that Pergamus was reduced to using the costly material which bears its name, 'parch-ment.'   In criticism generally Pergamus was allied with the Stoic schools ; and devoted itself to inter-preting, often fancifully enough, the spirit rather than the letter of its ancient writers, and protesting against the dictatorship of Aristarchus and the worship of exact knowledge.

One of the first fields for the spirit of research and

---

[1] Πίνακες τῶν ἐν πάσῃ παιδείᾳ διαλαμψάντων καὶ ὧν συνέγραψαν.

learning was naturally the record of the past. Soon after the death of Thucydides, and before that of Xenophon, the Greek physician CTÊSIAS, who was attached to Artaxerxes, wrote Persian and Indian history and a 'Periplûs,' with a view, partly of correcting the errors of Herodotus, partly, it is to be feared, of improving upon his stories. He was more important as a source of romance than as a historian. The Sicilian general PHILISTUS wrote in banishment a history of his own times; he made Thucydides his model, but is said to have flattered Dionysius II. in the hope of being restored. He was killed in Dion's rising in 357.

The characteristic of the historians of the later fourth century is that they are not practical statesmen and soldiers, but professional students. Two disciples of Isocrates stand at the head of the list. EPHORUS of Kymê wrote a universal history reaching from the Dorian Migration to the year 340. He was a collector and a critic, not a researcher; he used previous writers freely and sometimes verbally; but he rejected the earliest periods as mythical, and corrected his sources by comparing them. Being an Isocratean, he laid great stress both on style and on edification. Polybius says his descriptions of battles are 'simply ridiculous'; but Polybius says much the same of all civilians. A large part of Ephorus has been more or less transcribed in the extant history of Diodôrus Siculus.

The other Isocratean who wrote history was a more interesting man, THEOPOMPUS (born 380). He was a Chian, and had the islander's prejudice against the Athenian Empire, while other circumstances prejudiced

him still more against the military despots.   His two
great works were *Hellenica,* in twelve, and *Philippica,* in
fifty-eight books.   Like other verbose men, he liked to
preach silence and simplicity.   He was possibly a professed member of the Cynic sect; at any rate, he was
a hater of the world, and a despiser of the great.   He
believed that all the evils of Greece were due to her
'*three heads,*' Athens, Sparta, and Thebes, and that kings
and statesmen and 'leaders of the people' were generally the scum of society.   He is praised for his skill
in seeing secret causes and motives—chiefly bad ones
—behind the veils of diplomacy, and his style is almost
universally admired.   The so-called Longînus, *On the
Sublime,* quotes his description of the entry of the Great
King into Egypt, beginning with magnificent tents and
chariots, ending with bundles of shoe-leather and pickled
meats.   The critic complains of bathos; but the passage
reads like the intentional bathos of satire.   His military
descriptions fail to please Polybius, and it is hard to
excuse the long speeches he puts into the mouth of
generals in action.

The Sicilian TIMÆUS was a historian of the same
tendency, a pure student, ignorant of real warfare, who
wrote the history of his own island in thirty-eight books.
He, too, took a severe view, not only of kings and
diplomats, but also of other historians;[1] but he possessed the peculiar merit of having thoroughly mastered
his sources, including inscriptions and monuments, and
even Carthaginian and Phœnician archives.   Polybius
also praises the accuracy of his chronology.

Turning aside from special histories like the *Atthis*
of Philochorus and the *Samian Chronicle* of Dûris, we

[1] Hence his nickname 'Επιτίμαιος, Diod. Sic. 5. 1, and Ath. 272.

find the old rationalism of Herodôrus revived in a quasi-historical shape by EUHÊMERUS and his follower PALÆPHATUS. They reduced myth and religion to common-sense by the principle that the so-called gods were all mortal men who had been worshipped after death by the superstition or gratitude of their fellow-creatures. Euhêmerus had the great triumph of finding in Crete what he believed to be a tomb with the inscription, Ζὰν Κρόνου (' Zeus, son of Cronos'). And we find an interesting product of the international spirit of the time— the spirit which was to produce the Septuagint and the works of Philo—in the histories of Bêrôsus, priest of Bel in Babylon, and Manetho, priest of Serâpis in Alexandria.

But the greatest of the later Greek historians is, without question, POLYBIUS of Megalopolis (about 205– 123 B.C.). His father, Lycortas, was general of the Achæans, and the first forty years of the historian's life were spent in military and diplomatic work for the league, especially in its resistance to Rome. In 166 he was sent to Rome as a hostage, and for sixteen years he was kept there, becoming a close friend of the Scipios. He followed the younger Africanus on most of his expeditions, and saw the fall of Numantia and of Carthage. In his last years he was the principal mediator between Rome and Greece, possessing the confidence of both sides, and combining in a singular degree the patriotism of the old Achæan cavalryman with a disinterested and thorough-going admiration for Rome. His history started from 264 B.C., where Timæus ended, and led up to his own days in the first two books; then it expanded into a universal history, giving the rise of Rome, step by step, down

to the destruction of Carthage and the final loss of
Greek independence. As a philosophic historian, a
student of causes and principles, of natural and geographical conditions, of customs and prices, above all
of political constitutions, he is not equalled even by
Thucydides. He combines the care and broadness of
view of a philosophic modern writer with the practical
experience of an ancient historian. Only the first five
books of his history are extant in a complete form ; the
next thirteen, in extracts. As for the style of Polybius,
Dionysius classes him among the writers "whom no
human being can expect to finish." That is natural
in the professional Atticist, who could not forgive
Polybius for writing the current common Greek of
his time. But it is odd that modern scholars, especially if they have read the Atticist historians and Polybius close together, should echo the rhetor's protest
against the strong living speech of the man of affairs.
Polybius does not leave the same impression of personal genius as Thucydides ; but he is always interesting, accurate, deep - thinking, and clear - sighted. He
has one or two prejudices, no doubt — against Cleomenes for instance, and against the Ætolians. But
how he sees into the minds and feels the aims of
almost all the great men he mentions ! His Arâtus
and his Scipio are among the most living characters
of history ; and his Hannibal is not Livy's theatrical
villain, but a Semite of genius, seen straight and
humanly. Polybius was prosaic in temperament ; he
was harsh in criticising other historians. But, apart from
his mere scientific achievement, he has that combination of moral and intellectual nobleness which enables
a consistent patriot to do justice to his country's

enemies, a beaten soldier to think more of the truth than of his own hindered glory. How different from the splendid but jaundiced genius of Tacitus, or the mere *belles lettres* of the Isocratean Livy !

II

THE ROMAN AND BYZANTINE PERIODS

The establishment of the Roman Empire shifted the centre of gravity in Europe, and threw upon the Greek intellect a subordinate and somewhat narrowing task. Greece became essentially the paid teacher of the Roman world. In the East, indeed, the great Hellenistic civilisation founded by Alexander remained to some extent self-sufficing and independent of Rome; and in the East, Greek literature retained much creative power and original impulse. But our remains of the first two centuries A.D. consist chiefly of the books that were read in Rome; and for the most part the Western world was calling so loud for the Greeks to come and educate her that they forgot everything else in this mission. The original poets almost cease. BABRIUS, the fabulist, is no poet ; OPPIAN'S poem on fish is seldom very interesting. Only the sentimental elegy, now contracted into epigrams about eight lines long, really flourishes. MELEÂGER of Gadara wrote spontaneously; he was scholar and educator enough to form the collection from which our Palatine Anthology has been gradually built up ; but he was also a real and exquisite poet in a somewhat limited domain. His numerous little love-poems are full of sweetness, and there is great tenderness in his elegies on death. Yet even in Meleâger signs cf the age are not wanting.

There is something faint in his emotion, something contracted and over-refined in his range of interests.   And
a certain lack of spring and nimbleness amid all his
grace of diction and versification seems sometimes to
betray the foreigner.   One suspects that, at home in
Gadara, Greek was only his second language, and that
he had talked Aramaic out of school.   Perhaps his most
ingenious work is the Proem to the Anthology, describing
that metaphorical Garland :

> *"Whereunto many blooms brought Anytê,*
> *Wild flags ; and Mœro many,—lilies white ;*
> *And Sappho few, but roses."*

ANTIPATER of Sidon was nearly equal to him ; CRINA-
GORAS is always good to read.   And, as a matter of
fact, there was work of this kind produced, much of it
beautiful, much of it offensively corrupt, right on to the
days of PALLADAS in the fifth century, of AGATHIAS and
PAUL the Silentiary in the sixth.

One cardinal obstacle to poetry in imperial times was
the non-correspondence between metrical rules and real
pronunciation.   Æschylus and Sophocles had based their
poetry on metre, on long and short syllables, because that
was what they heard in the words they spoke.   Aristophanes of Byzantium (257–180 B.C.) noticed, besides the
divisions of long and short, a certain musical pitch in the
words of an Attic sentence, and invented the system of
accents for the instruction of foreigners in pronunciation.
It is hard to realise the exact phonetic value of this 'pitch-
accent' ; but it is certain that it did not affect poetry
or even attract the notice of the ear in classical times,
and that as late as the second century B.C. it was something quite different from what we call accent, to wit,

stress-accent.   But in the fourth century after Christ
the poet NONNUS, an Egyptian Greek from Panopolis,
in his *Dionysiaca*, begins suddenly to reckon with accent.
Dividing his hexameters into halves at the cæsura, he
insists that in the second half the accent *shall not* fall on
the ante-penultimate syllable ; while in the first half
before the cæsura he mostly insists that it *shall* fall
on the ante-penultimate.   The accent must by his time
have become a stress-accent, and the ingenious man is
attempting to serve two masters.   A verse like

οὐρανὸν ὑψιμέδοντος
ἀιστῶσαι Διὸς ἕδρην

is in metre a good hexameter ; by accent it is next
door to

" A captain bold of Hálifax,
Who lived in country quárters"—

that is to say, to the so-called 'politic' verses scanned by
accent, which were normal in Byzantine times, and were
used by the vulgar even in the fourth century.   Quintus
of Smyrna, an epic poet preceding Nonnus, does not
observe these rules about accent ; but Coluthus, Try-
phiodorus, and Musæus do.   The *Dionysiaca* made an
epoch.

In prose there is much history and geography and
sophistic literature from the age of Augustus on.   Diodôrus Siculus, Dionysius of Halicarnassus, Josephus the
Jew are followed by the Xenophon of the deçadence,
Arrian ; by Appian, Dion Cassius, and Herodian.   ARRIAN
wrote an Anabasis of Alexander, like Xenophon's Anabasis
of Cyrus, and devoted himself to expounding Epictêtus
a great deal better than Xenophon expounded Socrates ;
this besides tactics and geography.   Above all, PLUTARCH

(46–120 A.D.) wrote his immortal *Lives*, perhaps the most widely and permanently attractive work by one author known to the world, and the scarcely less interesting mass of treatises which are quoted under the general name of *Moralia*. He was no scientific historian, and the value of his statements depends entirely on the authorities he chances to follow ; but he had a gift of sympathy, and a power of seeing what was interesting. As a thinker he is perhaps over-anxious to edify, and has his obvious limitations ; but he is one of the most tactful and charming writers, and one of the most lovable characters, in antiquity.

In pure literature or 'sophistic' we have many names. Dion Chrysostomus, Herôdes Atticus, and Aristîdes are mere stylists, and that only in the sense that they can write very fair stuff in a language remarkably resembling that of Demosthenes or Plato. The Philostrati are more interesting, both as a peculiarly gifted family, and for the subjects of their work. There were four of them. Of the first we have only a dialogue about Nero and the Corinthian Canal. Of the second we have the admirable Life of Apollonius of Tyana, the Neo-Pythagorean saint and philosopher who maintained a short-lived concur-rence with the founder of Christianity; also a treatise on *Gymnastic*, and some love-letters. Of the third and fourth we have a peculiar series of '*Eikones*' (Pictures), descriptions of works of art in elaborate poetical prose. They are curious and very skilful as literature, and are valued by archæologists as giving evidence about real paintings. The description of pictures was a recognised form of sophistic, which flourished especially at the revival of art under the Antonines, and lasted on to the days of Longus and Achilles Tatius.

Among the Sophists we must class the oft-quoted ATHENÆUS, a native of Naucratis, in Egypt, who wrote his *Banquet-Philosophers*, in fifteen books, about the end of the second century. The guests are all learned men of the time of Marcus Aurelius, and the book gives their conversation. An extraordinary conversation it is. They discuss every dish and every accessory of banqueting in a spirit compounded of 'Notes and Queries' and an antiquarian encyclopædia. All that there is to know about wine vessels, dances, cooking utensils, eels, the weaknesses of philosophers, and the witticisms of notorious 'hetairai,' is collected and tabulated with due care. Whatever sources Athenæus used, he must have been a man of enormous reading and a certain sense of humour ; and the book, misleading as its devotion to convivial subjects makes it, forms a valuable instrument for the study of antiquities.

The greatest of the second-century Sophists was LUCIAN. He and Plutarch are the only writers of the period who possess a real importance to the world, who talk as no one else can talk, and who continue to attract readers on their own merits. Lucian has been compared to Erasmus in general cast of mind. He is learned, keen-eyed, before all things humorous ; too anxious for honesty, too critical, and too little inspired, to be carried into the main currents of his time. He lived through the great reformation and literary revival of Marcus, but he seems not to have shared in it. He read philosophy deeply and widely, but always as an outsider and with an amused interest in its eccentricities. To judge from the amount of personal apologia in his writings, he seems to have suffered much from personal attacks, especially on the part of the Cynics, whose combination of dirt,

ignorance, and saintliness especially offended him. He
was intended by his father for a sculptor, but broke away
into literature. He began as a rhetorical sophist of the
ordinary sort, then found his real vocation in satirical
dialogues, modelled on Plato in point of style, but with
the comic element outweighing the philosophical. In
the last years of his life he accepted a government office
in Egypt, and resumed his rhetorical efforts. He is an
important figure, both as representing a view of life which
has a certain permanent value for all ages, and also as
a sign of the independent vigour of Eastern Hellenism
when it escaped from its state patronage or rebelled against
its educational duties.

In philosophy, which is apt to be allied with education, and which consequently flourished under the early
Empire, there is a large and valuable literature extant.
There are two great philosophic doctors. GALEN was
a learned and bright, though painfully voluminous,
writer, as well as a physician, in the time of M. Aurelius.
SEXTUS EMPIRICUS, a contemporary of Caligula, was a
member of the Sceptic school ; his two sets of books
Against the Mathematici, or professors of general learning, and *Against the Dogmatici*, or sectarian philosophers, are full of strong thought and interesting
material. There are two philosophical geographers—
STRABO in the Augustan age, PTOLEMY in the time of
Marcus. The former was strongest on the practical and
historical side, while Ptolemy's works on geography
and on astronomy are the most capable and scientific
that have come down to us from ancient times. Another 'geographus,' PAUSANIAS, who wrote his *Tour
of Greece* (Περιήγησις Ἑλλάδος), in ten books, under the

Antonines, seems to have travelled for pleasure, and
then, after he had come home, compiled an account
of what he had seen, or ought to have seen, out of some
book or books at least three hundred years old ! That
is the only way to explain his odd habit of not mention-
ing even the most conspicuous monuments erected after
150 B.C. Nay, his modern critics assure us that sometimes when he says '*I was told*' or '*I myself saw*,' he
is only quoting his old traveller without changing the
person of the verb. This is damaging to Pausanias personally, but it increases the value of his guide-book ;
which, if often inaccurate and unsystematic, is a most
rich and ancient source of information, quite unique in
value both to archæologists and to students of custom
and religion. It was Pausanias, for instance, who
directed Schliemann to Mycenæ.

In philosophy proper, the professional Stoic is best
represented to us in the *Lectures* and the *Handbook* of
EPICTÊTUS, a Phrygian slave by origin, and a cripple,
who obtained his freedom and became a lecturer at
Rome. Expelled thence, in 94 A.D., by Domitian's
notorious edict against the philosophers, he settled at
Nicopolis, in Epirus, where he lived to enjoy the
friendship of Trajan, and, it is said, also of Hadrian
(117–138 A.D.). Epictêtus illustrates the difference of
this age from that of Plato or even of Chrysippus,
in that he practically abandons all speculation, and
confines himself to dogmatic practical ethics. He
accepts, indeed, and hands on the speculative basis
of morality as laid down by the earlier Stoics, but his
real strength is in preaching and edification. He
called his school a "*healing-place for diseased souls.*"
Such a profession is slightly repellent ; but the breadth

and concreteness of the teacher's conceptions, his sublimity of thought, and his humour, win the affection of
most readers. Yet picturesque as the external circumstances of Epictêtus are, they are dimmed by comparison
with those which make the figure of MARCUS AURELIUS
so uniquely fascinating. And the clear, strong style of
the professional lecturer does not attain that extraordinary power of appeal which underlies the emperor's
awkward *Communings with Himself.* With Marcus,
as with so many great souls, everything depends on
whether you love him or not. If the first three chapters
win you, every word he writes seems precious ; but
many people, not necessarily narrow-minded or vicious
in taste, will find the whole book dreary and unmeaning. It would be hard to deny, however, that
the ethical teaching of the old Stoa, as expounded by
these two men, is one of the very highest, the most
spiritual, and the most rational ever reached by the
human intellect. Marcus died in 180; the great philosopher of the next century was born in 204, PLOTÎNUS,
the chief of the Neo-Platonists. Though he professes
for the most part merely to interpret Plato, he is
probably the boldest thinker, and his philosophy the
most complete and comprehensive system, of Roman
times. His doctrine is an uncompromising idealism :
the world all comes from one Original Force, which
first differentiates itself into Mind, *i.e.* into the duality
of Thought and Being. Nature is the result of Thoughts
contemplating themselves, and the facts of nature, again,
are her self-contemplations. There is a religious element in this system which was developed, first by the
master's biographer and editor, Porphyry, and then by
Iamblichus, into what ultimately became a reasoned

system of paganism intended to stand against the polemics of the Christians.

It is usual to leave these last out of the accounts of Greek literature. Their intimate dependence, indeed, on ancient Greek speculation and habits of thought is obvious upon the most casual reading. But the connection, if treated at all, needs to be traced in detail ; and there is a certain sense in which the death and failure of the Emperor JULIAN marks an epoch, amounting almost to the final extinction of ancient culture and untheological ideals. The career of that extraordinary man was well matched with a character which would appear theatrical but for its almost excessive frankness and sincerity, and which seems to typify the ancient heroic spirit struggling helplessly in the toils of the decadence. He seeks to be a philosopher, and ends in mysticism. He champions enlightenment, and becomes almost more superstitious than the fanatics with whom he wars. He fires his soldiers and dependents with the love of justice and temperance and strict discipline, and then debauches them by continual sacrifices to the gods. He preaches toleration on the house-tops, and men answer him by a new persecution. The prince of saintly life, who spends his nights in prayer and meditation, who lives like a pauper because he has given up all his privy purse to the relief of distress in the provinces, and who seems to find his only real consolation in blindly following always the very highest and noblest course abstractly possible, regardless of practical considerations, is curiously near to some of those wild Christian anchorites to whom he so strongly objected. There was something very great and true

2 C

which Julian was striving towards and imperfectly grasping all through his life, which he might, in a sense, have attained permanently in happier ages. He was a great and humane general, an able and unselfish statesman. But there is fever in his ideals; there is a horror of conscious weakness in his great attempts. It is the feeling that besets all the Greek mind in its decadence. Roman decadence tends to exaggeration, vainglory, excess of ornament; Greek decadence is humble and weary. "*I pray that I may fulfil your hopes,*" writes Julian to Themistius, "*but I fear I shall fail. The promise you make about me to yourself and others is too large. Long ago I had fancies of emulating Alexander and Marcus and other great and good men; and a shrinking used to come over me and a strange dread of knowing that I was utterly lacking in the courage of the one, and could never even approach the perfect virtue of the other. That was what induced me to be a student. I thought with relief of the 'Attic Essays,' and thought it right to go on repeating them to you my friends, as a man with a heavy burden lightens his trouble by singing. And now your letter has increased the old fear, and shown the struggle to be much, much harder, when you talk to me of the post to which God has called me.*"

One form of literature, indeed, contemporary with Julian, and equally condemned by him and by his chief opponents, shows a curious combination of decay and new life, the Romance. The two earliest traces of prose romance extant are epitomes. There is perhaps no spontaneous fiction in the Love Stories of PARTHENIUS, an Alexandrian who taught Vergil, and collected these myths for the use of Roman poets who liked to introduce mythical names without reading the original authorities.

But the work may have looked different before it was epitomised. There is real invention in the work of one ANTONIUS DIOGENES about *The Incredible Wonders beyond Thule.* He lived before Lucian, who parodies him. The book was full of adventures, and included a visit to the moon; but, to judge from the epitome, it repeated itself badly, and the characters seem to have been mere puppets. One particular effect, the hero or heroine or both being taken for ghosts, seems especially to have fascinated the author. There is some skill in the elaborate and indirect massing of the imaginary sources from which the story is derived. Romance was popular in the third century, which has left us the complete story of *Habrocomês and Antheia* by XENOPHON of Ephesus. The two best Greek novelists are with little doubt LONGUS and HELIODÔRUS: the former for mere literary and poetic quality; the latter for plot and grouping and effective power of narrative. Heliodôrus writes like the opener of a new movement. He is healthy, exuberant, full of zest and self-confidence. His novel is good reading even in our own age, which has reached such exceptional skill in the technique of novel-writing. You feel that he may well be, what as a matter of fact he was, the forerunner of a long array of notable writers, and one of the founders of an exceptionally prolific and durable form of literature. It is said that Heliodôrus was a Christian and bishop of Salonîca, and that the synod of his province called upon him either to burn his book or to resign his bishopric, whereupon the good man did the latter. The story rests on weak evidence, but it would be like the Heliodôrus that we know. Longus is very different—an unsanguine man and a pagan. Not that his morals are low: it needs an unintelligent reader or a morbid translator to find harm in his *History of Daphnis and Chloe*. But a feeling of discouragement pervades all his work, a wish to shut out the world, to shrink from ambitions and problems, to live for innocent and unstrenuous things. He reminds one of a tired Theocritus writing in prose. Some of the later novelists, like Achilles Tatius and Chariton, wrote romances which, judged by vulgar standards, will rank above that of Longus. They are stronger, better constructed, more exciting ; some of them are immoral. But there is no such poet as Longus among them.

He is the last man, unless the present writer's knowledge is at fault, who lives for mere Beauty with the old whole-hearted devotion, as Plotînus lived for speculative Truth, as Julian for the "great city of gods and men." Of these three ideals, to which, beyond all others, Greece had opened the eyes of mankind, that of Political Freedom and Justice had long been relegated from practical life to the realm of thought, and those who had power paid no heed to it. The search for Truth was finally made hopeless when the world, mistrusting Reason, weary of argument and wonder, flung itself passionately under the spell of a system of authoritative Revelation, which claimed a censorship over all Truth, and stamped free questioning as sin. And who was to preach the old Beauty, earnest and frank and innocent, to generations which had long ceased to see it or to care for it ? The intellect of Greece died ultimately of that long discouragement which works upon nations like slow poison. She ceased to do her mission because her mission had ceased to bear fruit. And the last great pagans, men like Plotînus, Longus, and Julian, pronounce their own doom and plead for their own pardon, when they refuse to strike new notes or to try the ring of their own voices, content to rouse mere echoes of that old call to Truth, to Beauty, to Political Freedom and Justice, with which Greece had awakened the world long ago, when the morning was before her, and her wings were strong.

CHRONOLOGICAL TABLE

CHRONOLOGICAL TABLE

I.—BEFORE THE SEVENTH CENTURY ALL THE DATES ARE MERELY LEGENDARY, AND THE POETS MAINLY FABULOUS.

II.—BEFORE MARATHON.

Each author is placed according to his traditional *floruit* or ἀκμή, which is fixed either at the man's fortieth year, or, when the date of birth is unknown, at some year in which he distinguished himself. The geographical name appended denotes the writer's place of activity; where the birth-place is different, it is added in brackets.

680?	'Tyrtæus,' Elegiacus . . .	Lacedæmon	Second Messenian War (685–668).
?	'Terpander,' Lyricus . . .	Lesbos . .	Victor in Carnea, 676.
660	Callinus, Elegiacus	Ephesus.	
650	Alcman, Choricus.	Lacedæmon.	
	Archilochus, Iambicus . .	Paros.	
	Pisander, Epicus	Camirus . .	But see p. 69.
630	Mimnermus, Elegiacus . .	Colophon.	
	Semonides, Iambicus. . .	Amorgos.	
620	Arion, Choricus	Lesbos	
600	Alcæus, Lyricus	Lesbos . .	But both perhaps fifty years later.
	Sappho, Lyrica	Lesbos . .	
	Solon, Poeta Politicus . .	Athens.	
	Stesichorus, Choricus. . .	Himera.	
590	Thales, Philosophus . . .	Miletus . .	Observed eclipse of sun in 585.
570	Anaximander, Philosophus . .	Miletus.	
560	Bion, Historicus	Proconnesus.	
	Xanthus, Historicus . . .	Lydia.	
550	Anaximenes, Philosophus . .	Miletus.	
540	Anacreon, Lyricus . . .	Teos	Went to Abdera, 545.
	Ibycus, Choricus	Rhegium.	
	Demodocus, Gnomicus . . .	Leros.	

	Phocylides, Gnomicus . . .	Miletus.	
	Hipponax, Iambicus	Ephesus.	
	Xenophanes, Poeta Philosophicus	} Colophon.	
	Thespis, Tragicus	Attica.	
530	Pythagoras, Philosophus .	} Croton (Samos).	
	Theagenes, Historicus . .	Rhegium.	
520	Theognis, Elegiacus	Megara.	
	Simonides, Choricus	Ceos.	
	Lasus, Choricus	Hermione.	
	Hecatæus, Historicus . .	Miletus.	
	Dionysius, Historicus . .	Miletus.	
	Alcmæon, Philosophus . .	Croton.	
510	Onomacritus, Poeta Orphicus .	Athens . .	} Court of Hippias.
	Zopyrus, Poeta Orphicus . .	Heraclea .	
	Charon, Historicus	Lampsacus.	
	Eugæon, Historicus	Samos.	
500	Pratinas, Tragicus. . . .	} Athens . . (Phlius) .	} Competed against Æschylus, 499.
	Choirilus, Tragicus	Athens.	
	Heraclitus, Philosophus . . .	Ephesus.	
	Herodorus, Historicus . .	Heraclea.	
494	Phrynichus, Tragicus. . . .	Athens . . .	First tragic victory, 511.

III.—The Attic Period.

490	Battle of Marathon.
	Pindar, *Pyth.* 7.
489	PANYASIS, Epicus, Halicarnassus.
486	Pindar, *Pyth.* 3.
485	HIPPYS, Historicus, Rhegium (fabulous ?).
484	EPICHARMUS, Comicus, Syracuse (Cos).
	ÆSCHYLUS, Tragicus, Athens ; b. 525, d. 456. First victory.
	Pindar, *Olym.* 10 and 11.
480	PINDAR, Choricus, Thebes ; b. 522, d. 448.
	Pindar, *Isthm.* 7.
477	Formation of Delian Confederacy.
476	Phrynichus, *Phœnissæ.*
475	PARMENIDES, Poeta Philosophicus, Elea.
472	Pindar, *Olym.* 1 and 12 ; Æschylus, *Persæ.*
470	BACCHYLIDES, Choricus, Sicily.

468 Pindar, *Olym.* 6. The first victory of Sophocles.
466 Pindar, *Pyth.* 4 and 5.
CORAX, Rhetor, Sicily.
464 Pindar, *Olym.* 7 and 13.
460 CHIONIDES, Comicus, Athens.
MAGNES   ,,   ,,
ECPHANTIDES ,,   ,,
ANAXAGORAS, Philosophus, Athens (Clazomenæ).
BRYSON, Sophistes, Heraclea.
458 Æschylus, *Oresteia.*
456 Pindar, *Olym.* 9.
SOPHOCLES, Tragicus, Athens ; b. 496, d. 406.
455 Euripides, *Peliades.*
452 Pindar, *Olym.* 4 and 5.
451 ION, Tragicus, Chios.
450 GORGIAS, Sophistes, Leontini.
STESIMBROTUS, Sophistes, Thasos.
CRATES, Comicus, Athens.
ZENO, Philosophus, Elea.
    Anaxagoras leaves Athens.
448 CRATINUS, Comicus, Athens.
445 HERMIPPUS, Comicus, Athens.
EMPEDOCLES, Poeta Philosophicus, Agrigentum.
444 HERODOTUS, Historicus, Halicarnassus ; b. 484, d. 425 (?).
443   Herodotus goes to Thurii.
442 PROTAGORAS, Sophistes, Abdera ; b. 482 (?), d. 411.
440 Sophocles, *Antigone* (or 442 ?).
ANTIPHON, Orator, Athens.
ARCHELAUS, Philosophus, Athens.
EURIPIDES, Tragicus, Athens ; b. 480, d. 406.
MELISSUS, Philosophus, Samos.
SOPHRON, Mimographus, Syracuse.
438   Parthenon dedicated.
Euripides, *Alcestis* (with *Cressæ, Alcmæon, Telephus*).
435 LEUKIPPUS, Philosophus, Miletus or Abdera.
432   Corinthians defeat Corcyreans, supported by Athenians, in a sea-
        fight.
Pheidias and Aspasia prosecuted for impiety.   Also Anaxagoras.
431   Peloponnesian War.
Euripides, *Medea* (with *Dictys, Philoctetes*).
430 Herodotus publishes last part of his history.
HIPPIAS, Sophistes, Elis.
HELLANICUS, Historicus, Lesbos.
PHERECRATES, Comicus, Athens.

THUCYDIDES, Historicus, Athens.
HIPPOCRATES, Medicus, Cos.
429 PHRYNICHUS, Comicus, Athens.
SOCRATES, Philosophus, Athens ; b. 468, d. 399.
428 Euripides, *Hippolytus.*
427 Gorgias comes to Athens as chief envoy of Leontini.
Aristophanes, *Daitales.*
426 Aristophanes, *Babylonians.*
425 DIOGENES, Philosophus, Apollonia in Crete.
Aristophanes, *Acharnians.*
Capture of Sphacteria.
424 DIAGORAS, Philosophus, Melos.
Aristophanes, *Knights.*
423 ANTIOCHUS, Historicus, Syracuse.
Thucydides leaves Athens.
Aristophanes, *Clouds* (1st edit.).
422 Aristophanes, *Wasps.*
421 Peace of Nikias.
Eupolis, *Flatterers.*
420 DAMASTES, Historicus, Sigeum.
THRASYMACHUS, Rhetor, Chalcedon.
DEMOCRITUS, Philosophus, Abdera.
GLAUCUS, Historicus, Rhegium.
419 PRODICUS, Sophistes, Ceos.
417 Old Oligarch on *Constitution of Athens.*
Antiphon, Or. 5, *On the Murder of Herodes.*
416 AGATHON, Tragicus, Athens ; b. 447, d. 400.
415 Mutilation of the Hermæ. Expedition to Sicily.
Euripides, *Troades.*
EUPOLIS, Comicus, Athens.
HEGEMON, Comicus, Athens (Thasos).
ALKIDAMAS, Rhetor, Elea.
CRITIAS, Politicus, Athens.
414 ARISTOPHANES, Comicus, Athens ; b. 450, d. 385 ; *Birds.*
413 Athenian fleet destroyed at Syracuse.
Euripides, *Electra.*
412 Lysias comes to Athens.
Euripides, *Helene, Andromeda.*
411 Aristophanes, *Lysistrata, Thesmophoriazusæ.*
Government of the Four Hundred.
410 Lysias 20, *For Polystratus.*
409 Sophocles, *Philoctetes.*
408 Euripides, *Orestes.*
Aristophanes, *Plutus* (1st edit.).

406 TIMOTHEUS, Dithyrambicus, Athens (Miletus).
405 PLATO, Comicus, Athens.
    Aristophanes, *Frogs.* Euripides, *Bacchæ* (?).
404   Tyranny of the Thirty.
    AMEIPSIAS, Comicus, Athens.
    ANTIMACHUS, Epicus, Colophon.
    CHOIRILUS, Epicus, Samos.
403   Democracy restored.
    Lysias, Or. 12, *Against Eratosthenes*; Or. 34, *For the Constitution.*
402 Lysias, Or. 21, *Defence on a Charge of Taking Bribes.*
401   Expedition of Cyrus the younger.
    Lysias, Or, 25, *Defence on a Charge of Seeking to Abolish the Democracy.*
    Sophocles, *Œdipus at Colonus* (produced by the poet's grandson).
    Thucydides's History published.
    SOPHAINETUS, Historicus, Stymphalus.
400 ÆSCHINES, Philosophus, Sphettus in Attica.
    CTESIAS, Historicus, Cnidus.
    STRATTIS, Comicus, Athens.
399 Andocides, *On the Mysteries.*
        Death of Socrates.
    EUCLEIDES, Philosophus, Megara.
395 ISOCRATES, Orator, Athens; b. 436, d. 338.
    PHILISTUS, Historicus, Syracuse.
    PHILOXENUS, Dithyrambicus, Athens (Cythera); b. 435, d. 380.
    POLYCRATES, Sophistes, Athens.
    XENARCHUS, Mimographus, Sicily.
394 XENOPHON, Historicus, Attica; b. 434, d. 354.
    Isocrates, Or. 20, *Against Lochites*; Or. 19, *Ægineticus*; Or. 17, *Trapeziticus.*
393   Long Walls of Athens restored by Conon.
392 Aristophanes, *Ecclesiazusæ.*
391 Isocrates, Or. 13, *Against the Sophists.*
390 Isæus, Or. 5, *On the Estate of Dicæogenes.*
    PHÆDO, Philosophus, Athens.
388 Lysias, Or. 33, *Olympiacus.*
    Aristophanes, *Plutus.*
387 PLATO, Philosophus, Athens; b. 427, d. 347.
380 EUBULUS, Comicus, Attica.
    Isocrates, *Panegyricus.*
378   Athens head of a new Naval Confederacy.
374 Isocrates, Or. 2, *Ep. to Nicocles.*
373 Isocrates, Or. 14, *Plataicus.*
371   Battle of Leuctra.

370 ISÆUS, Orator, Athens.
ANAXANDRIDES, Comicus, Athens (Camirus).
ÆNEAS, Tacticus, Stymphalus.
369 Isæus, Or. 9, *On the Estate of Astyphilus.*
367 Aristotle comes to Athens.
366 ANTISTHENES, Philosophus, Athens.
ARISTIPPUS, Philosophus, Cyrene.
Isocrates, Or. 6, *Archidamus.*
365 ANTIPHANES, Comicus, Athens (a foreigner); b. 404, d. 330.
364 Isæus, Or. 6, *On the Estate of Philoctemon.*
363 Demosthenes, Or. 27 and 28, *Against Aphobus.*
362 Battle of Mantinea. Death of Epaminondas.
Demosthenes, Or. 30 and 31, *Against Onetor I and II.*
360 LYCURGUS, Orator, Athens; b. 396 (?), d. 323.
Hyperides, *Against Autocles.*
359 Isocrates, Letter VI., *To the Children of Jason.*
357 Social War begins.
355 End of Second Athenian Empire.
Isocrates, Or. 8, *On the Peace;* Or. 7, *Areopagiticus.*
354 Eubulus in power at Athens.
Demosthenes, Or. 14, *On the Navy Boards;* Or. 20, *Against Leptines.*
ALEXIS, Comicus, Athens (Thurii); b. 394, d. 288.
353 Isocrates, Or. 15, *On the Antidosis.*
352 Demosthenes, Or. 16, *On behalf of the Megalopolitans.*
THEODECTES, Tragicus, Athens (Phaselis).
THEOPOMPUS, Historicus, Chios.
351 Demosthenes, Or. 4, *Against Philip I.*
349 Demosthenes, Or. 1 and 2, *Olynthiacs* I. and II.
347 Death of Plato. Speusippus at the Academy.
346 Peace of Philocrates.
345 ÆSCHINES, Orator, Athens; b. 389, d. 314.
Æschines, *Against Timarchus.*
344 DEMOSTHENES, Orator, Athens; b. 383, d. 322.
EPHORUS, Historicus, Kyme.
ARISTOTLE, Philosophus, Stagirus.
343 Demosthenes, Or. 19. Æschines, Or. 2 (*Falsa Legatio*).
342 Hegesippus (?), *About Halonnesus.*
341 Demosthenes, Or. 8, *On the Chersonnese;* Or. 9, *Against Philip III.*
340 War with Philip.
ANAXIMENES, Rhetor, Athens.
DEMADES, Orator, Athens.
HYPERIDES, Orator, Athens; d. 322.
339 Isocrates, Or. 12, *Panathenaicus.*
Xenocrates at the Academy.

338   Battle of Chæronea.

336   Philip assassinated.   Alexander the Great succeeds.

334   Aristotle teaches at the Lyceum in Athens.

         Alexander sets out for Persia.

330 Demosthenes, Or. 18, *On the Crown.*

     Æschines, Or. 3, *Against Ctesiphon.*

     Lycurgus, *Against Leocrates.*

324 DEINARCHUS, Orator, Athens (Corinth) ; b. 361 ; Or. 1, *Against Demosthenes ;* Or. 2, *Against Aristogeiton.*

323   Epicurus comes to Athens.

         Death of Alexander.   Lamian War.

322 Hyperides, *Epitaphius.*

         Death of Demosthenes, Hyperides, and Aristotle.

321   Alexander's Empire divided among his Generals.

INDEX

PHOENIX BOOKS *Titles in print*

THE UNIVERSITY OF CHICAGO PRESS